Volume 2
Created by
Yuna Kagesaki

TOKYOPOP®

HAMBURG // LONDON // LOS ANGELES // TOKYO

AiON Volume 2
Created by Yuna Kagesaki

Translation and English Adaptation - Katherine Schilling
Retouch and Lettering - Star Print Brokers
Production Artist - Rui Kyo
Graphic Designer - Marguerite DuLac

Editor - Asako Suzuki
Print Production Manager - Lucas Rivera
Managing Editor - Vy Nguyen
Senior Designer - Louis Csontos
Art Director - Al-Insan Lashley
Director of Sales and Manufacturing - Allyson De Simone
Associate Publisher - Marco F. Pavia
President and C.O.O. - John Parker
C.E.O. and Chief Creative Officer - Stu Levy

A  Manga

TOKYOPOP and  are trademarks or registered trademarks of TOKYOPOP Inc.

TOKYOPOP Inc.
5900 Wilshire Blvd. Suite 2000
Los Angeles, CA 90036

E-mail: info@TOKYOPOP.com
Come visit us online at www.TOKYOPOP.com

ISBN: 978-1-4278-3188-0

First TOKYOPOP printing: February 2011
10 9 8 7 6 5 4 3 2 1
Printed in the USA

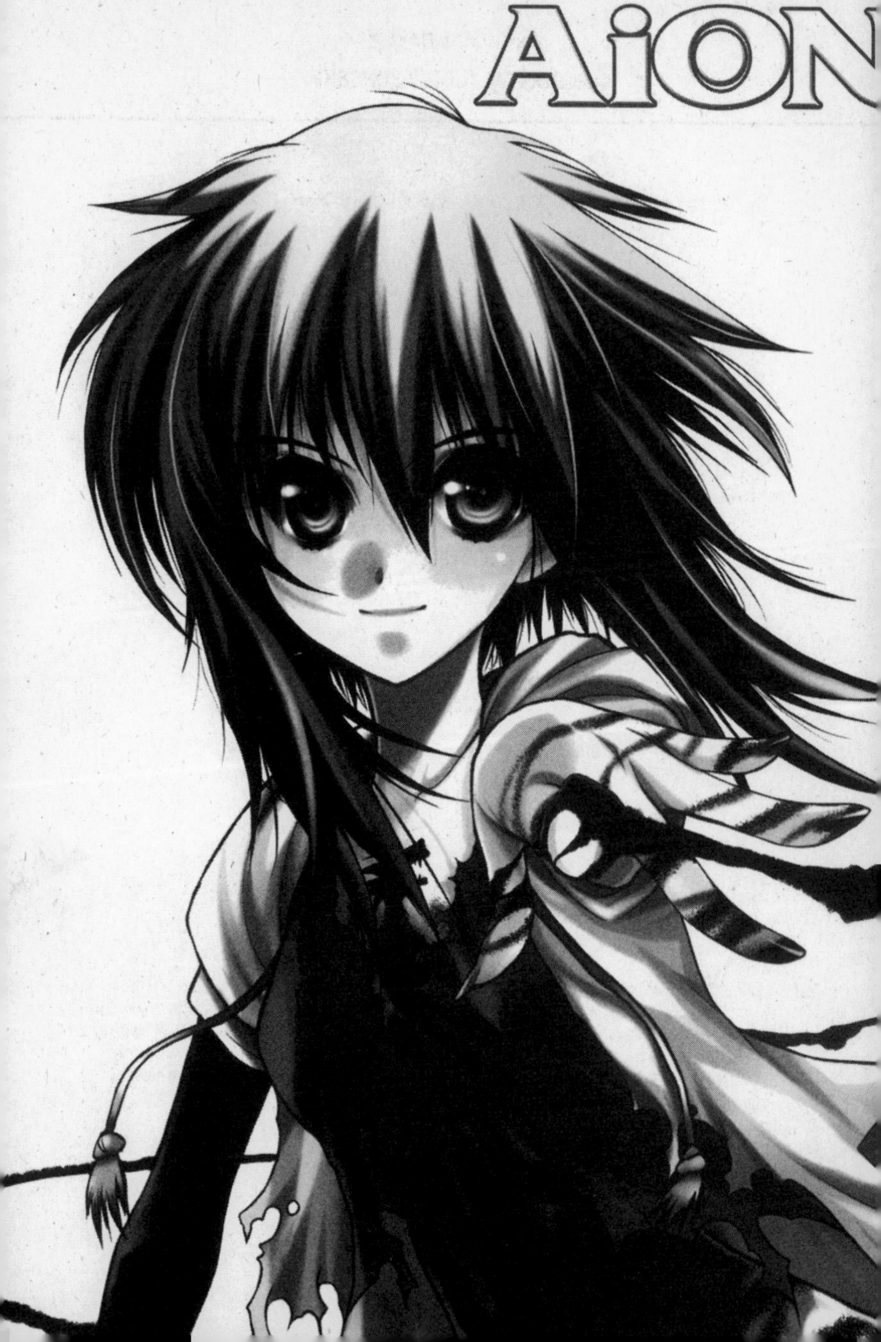
AiON

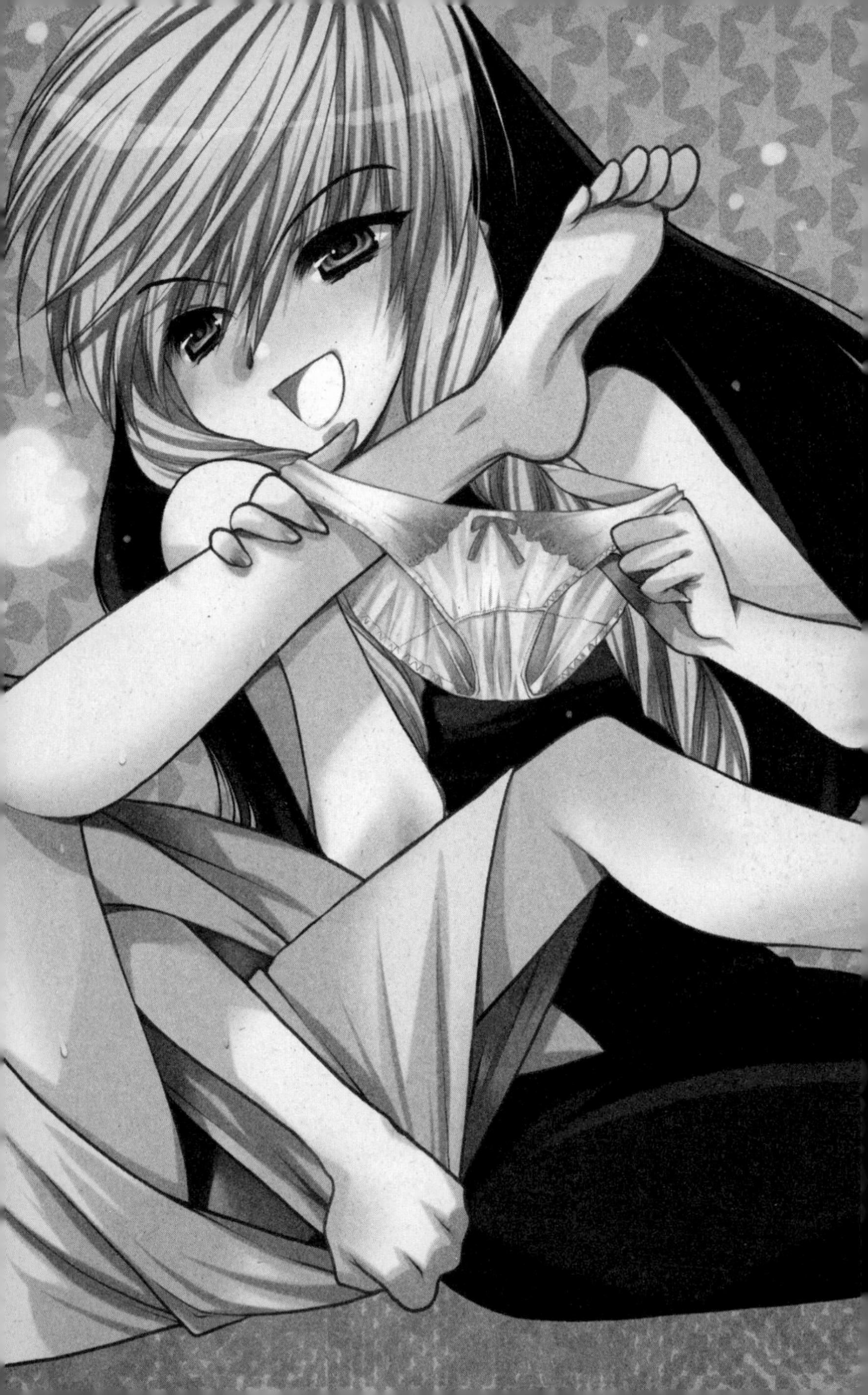

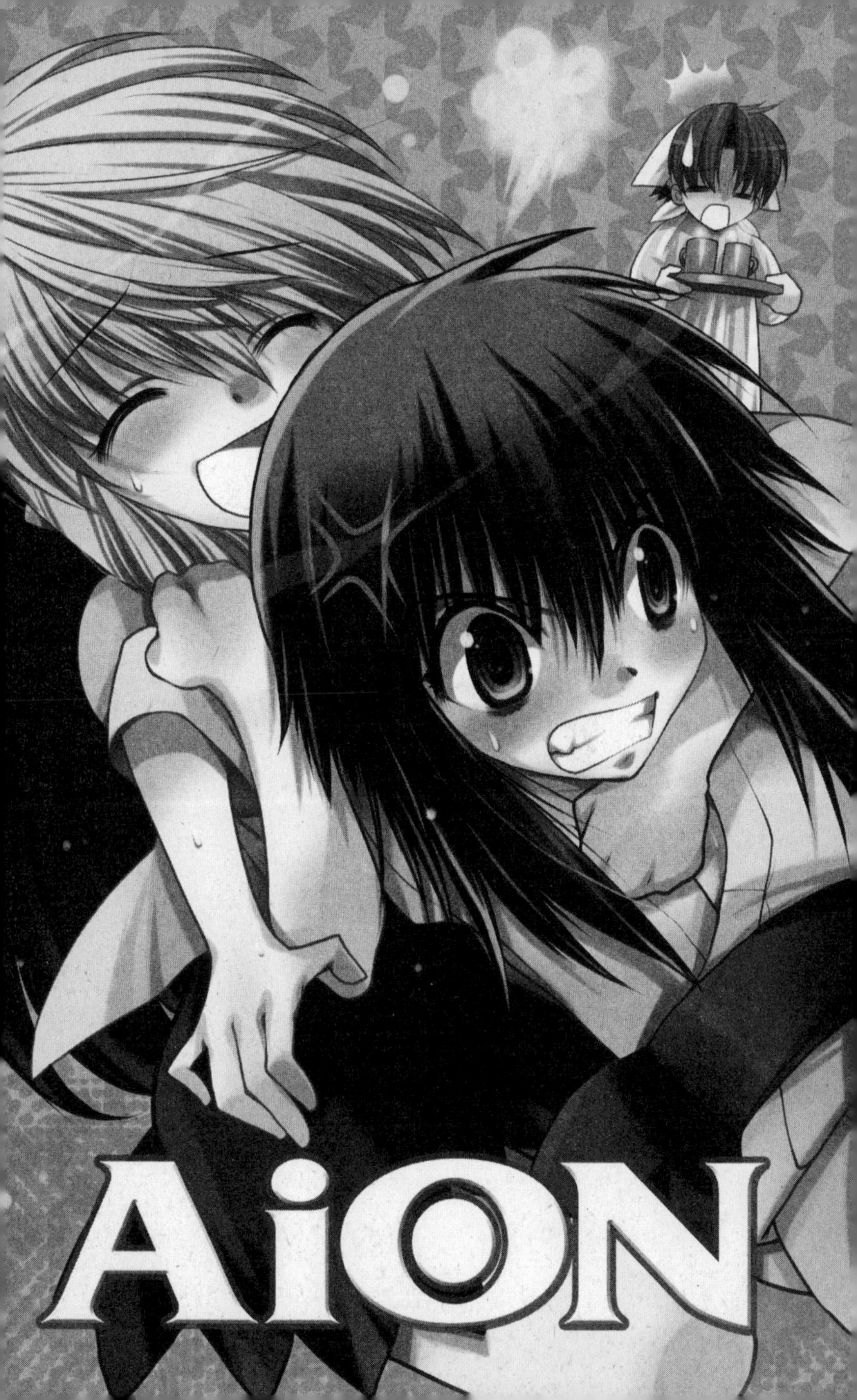
AiON

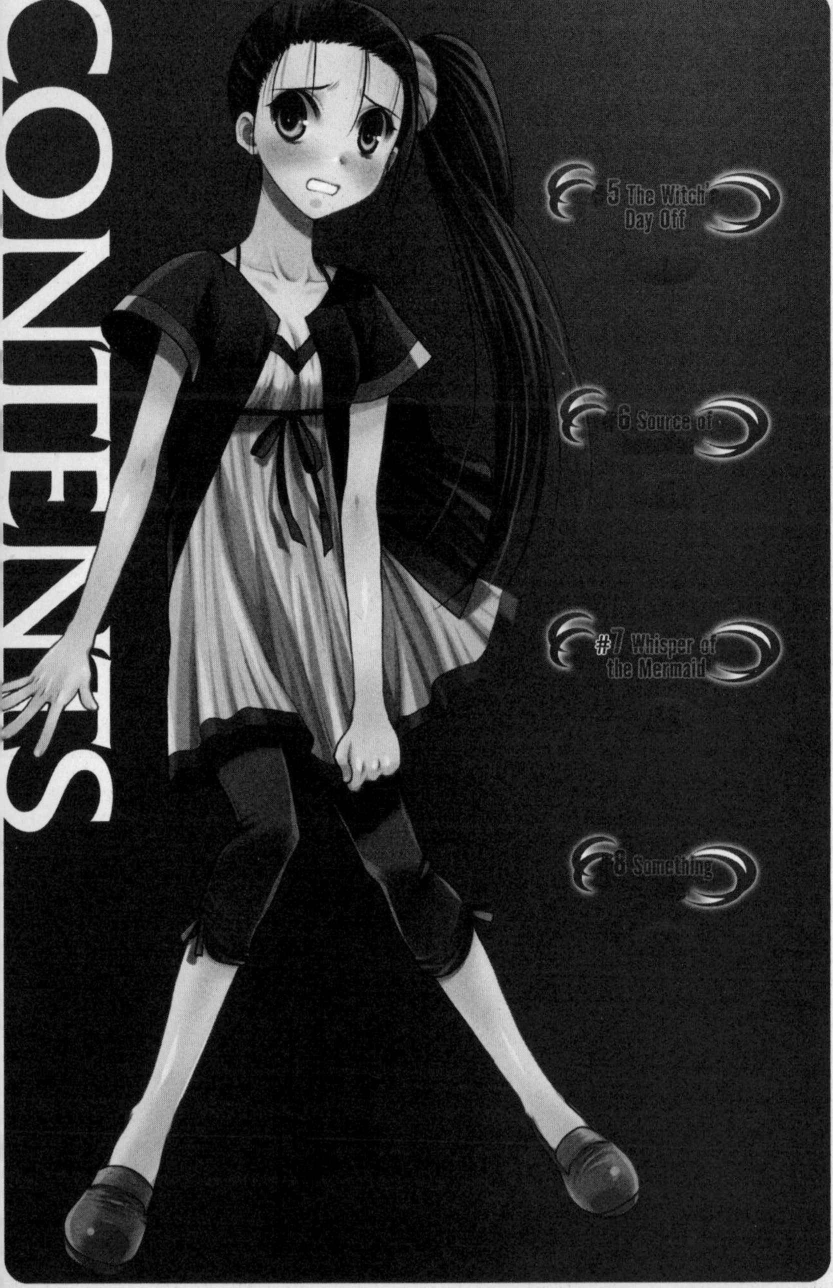
CONTENTS
5 The Witch'
Day Off
6 Source of
#7 Whisper of
the Mermaid
8 Something

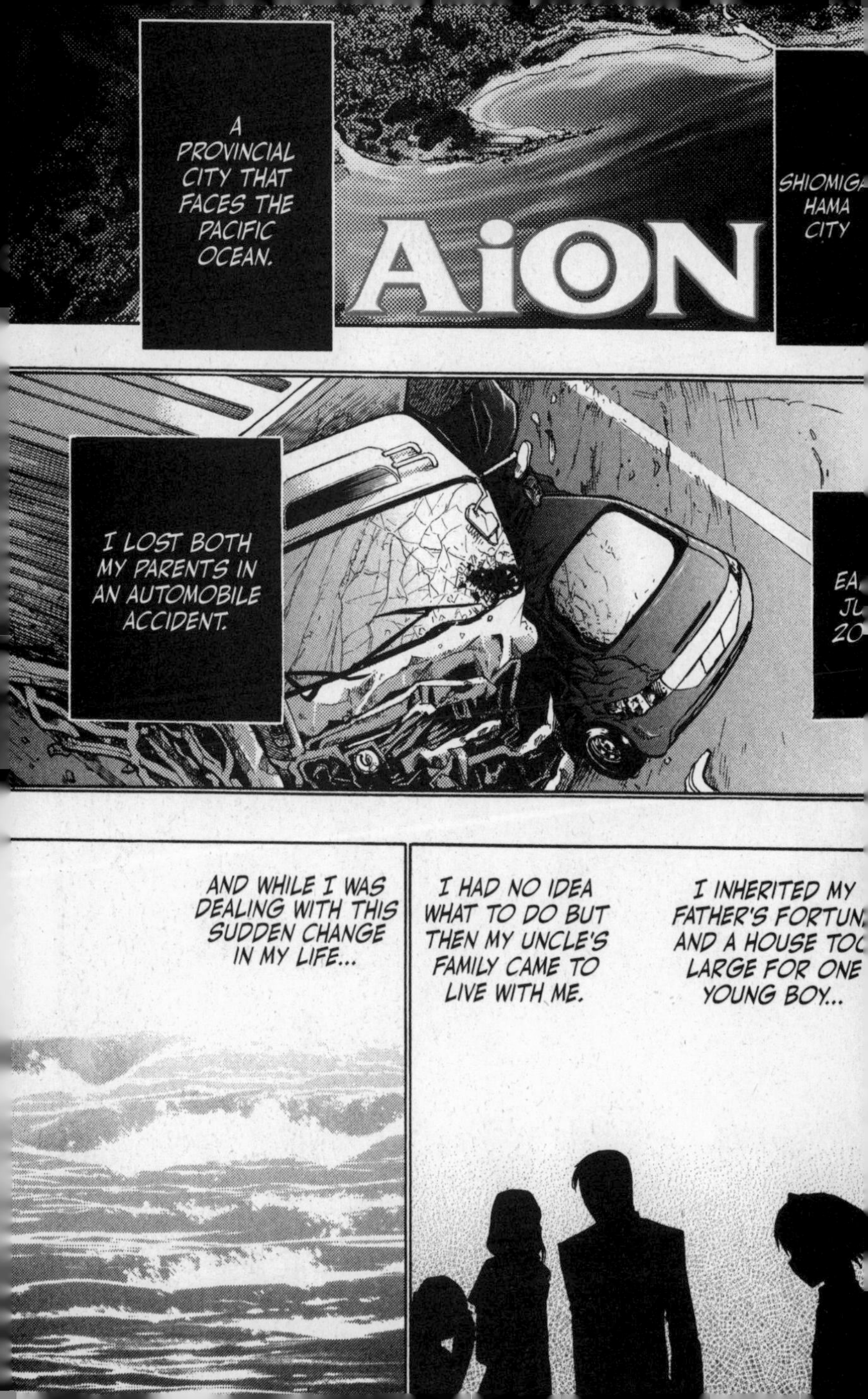
SHIOMIG HAMA CITY
AiON
A PROVINCIAL CITY THAT FACES THE PACIFIC OCEAN.
I LOST BOTH MY PARENTS IN AN AUTOMOBILE ACCIDENT.
I INHERITED MY FATHER'S FORTUN AND A HOUSE TO LARGE FOR ONE YOUNG BOY...
I HAD NO IDEA WHAT TO DO BUT THEN MY UNCLE'S FAMILY CAME TO LIVE WITH ME.
AND WHILE I WAS DEALING WITH THIS SUDDEN CHANGE IN MY LIFE...

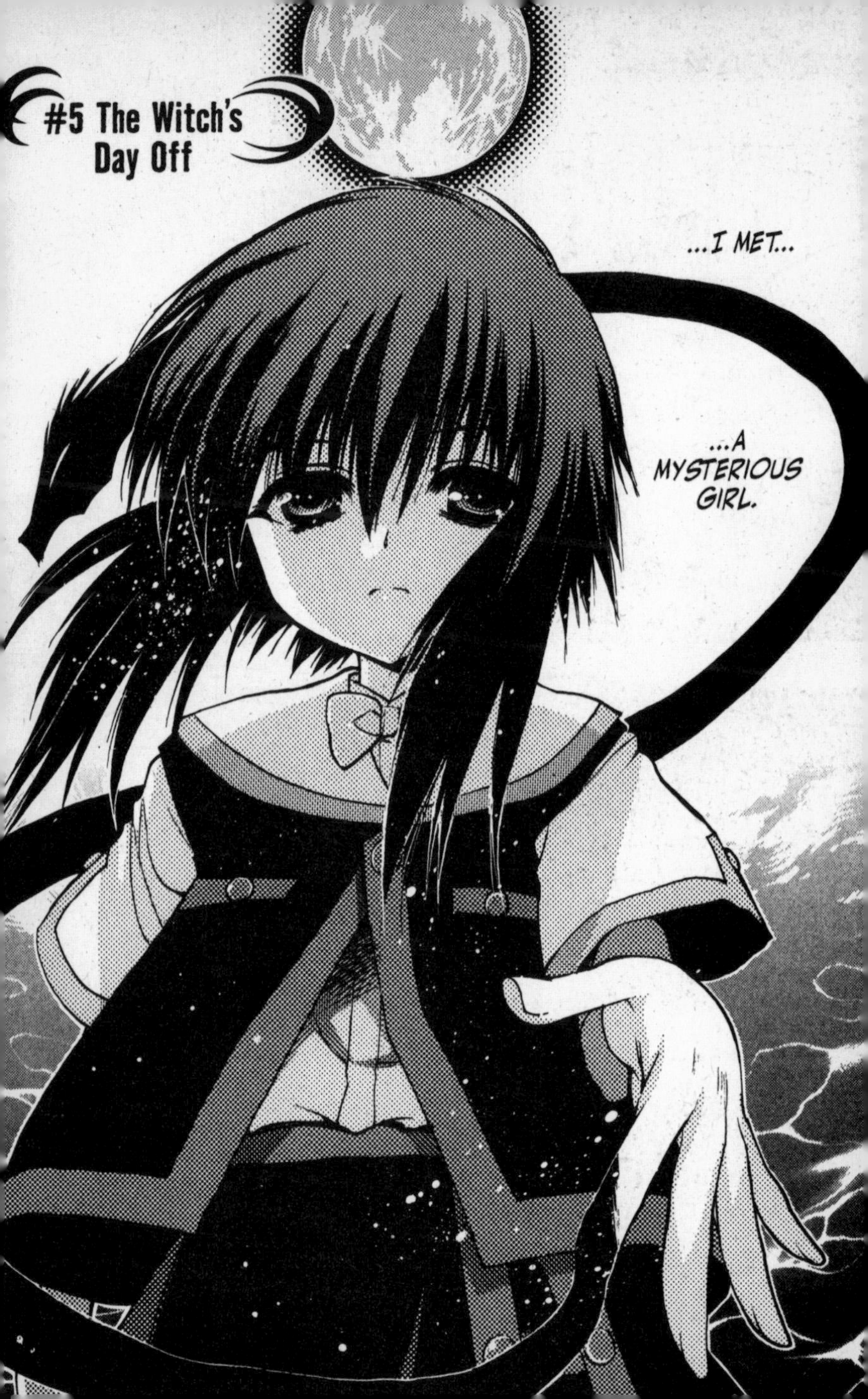
#5 The Witch's Day Off
...I MET...
...A MYSTERIOUS GIRL.

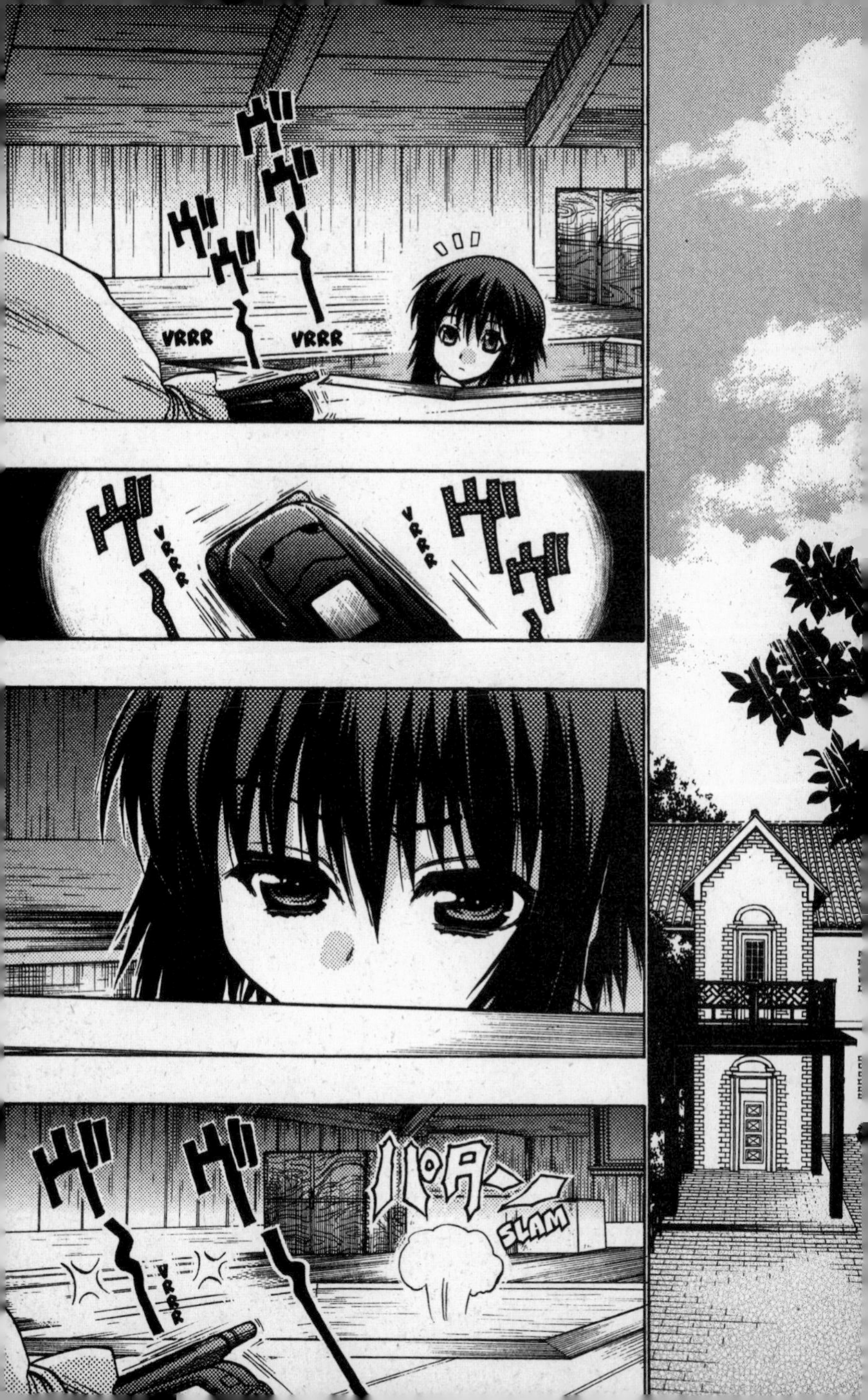
VRRR
VRRR
VRRR
VRRR
VRRR
SLAM

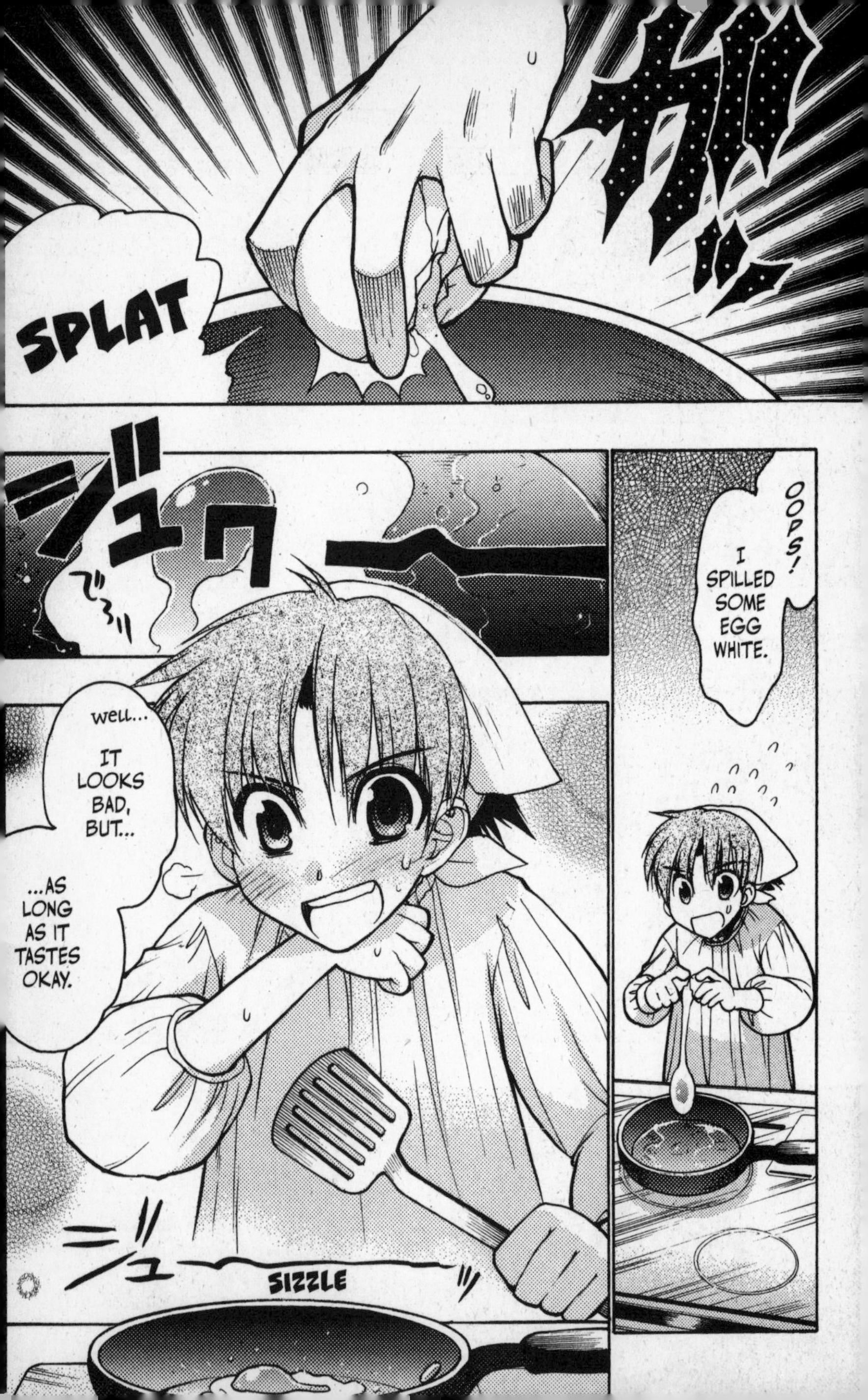
SPLAT
OOPS! I SPILLED SOME EGG WHITE.
WELL... IT LOOKS BAD, BUT...
...AS LONG AS IT TASTES OKAY.
SIZZLE

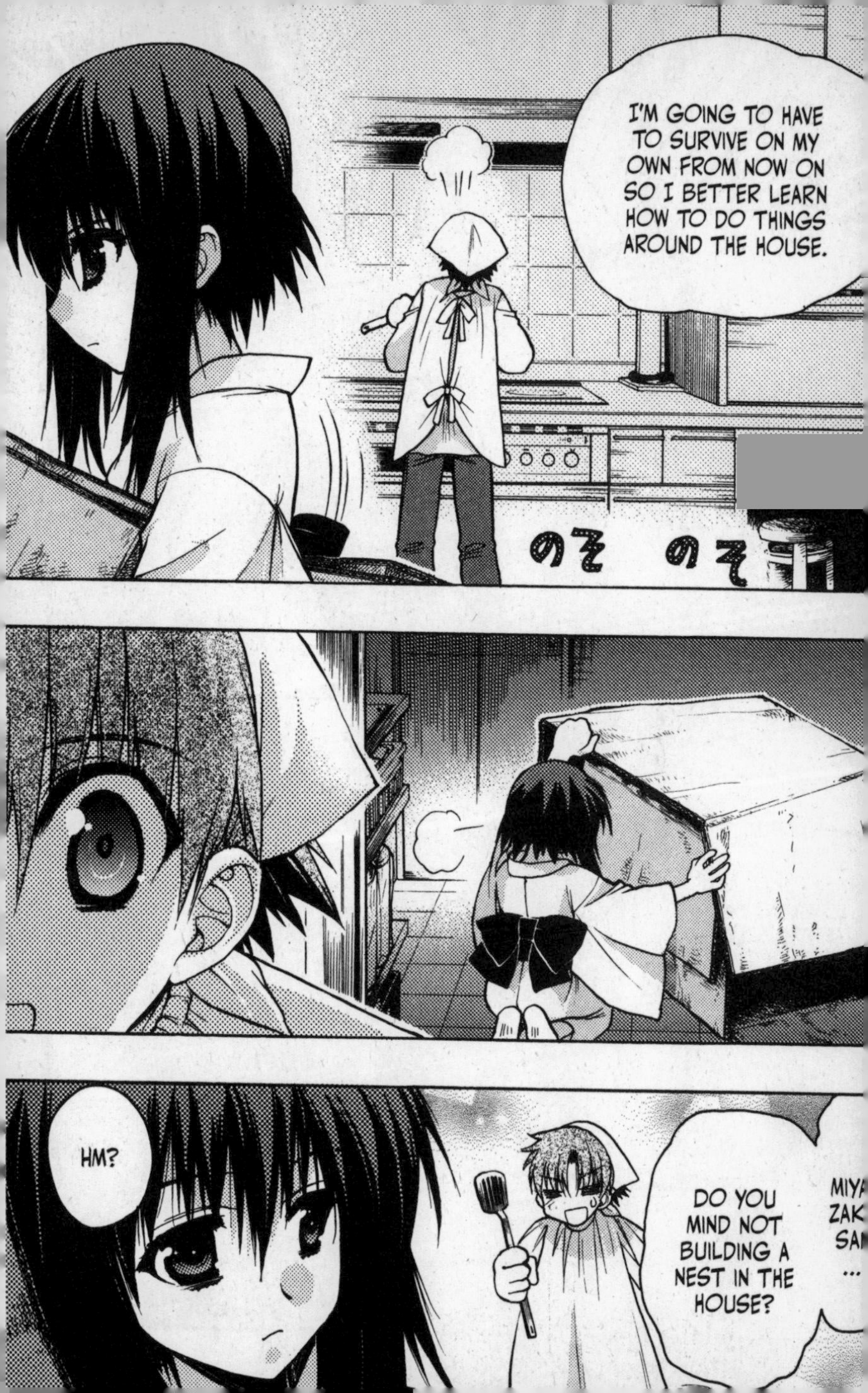
I'M GOING TO HAVE TO SURVIVE ON MY OWN FROM NOW ON SO I BETTER LEARN HOW TO DO THINGS AROUND THE HOUSE.
のぞ のぞ
MIYA ZAK SA …
DO YOU MIND NOT BUILDING A NEST IN THE HOUSE?
HM?

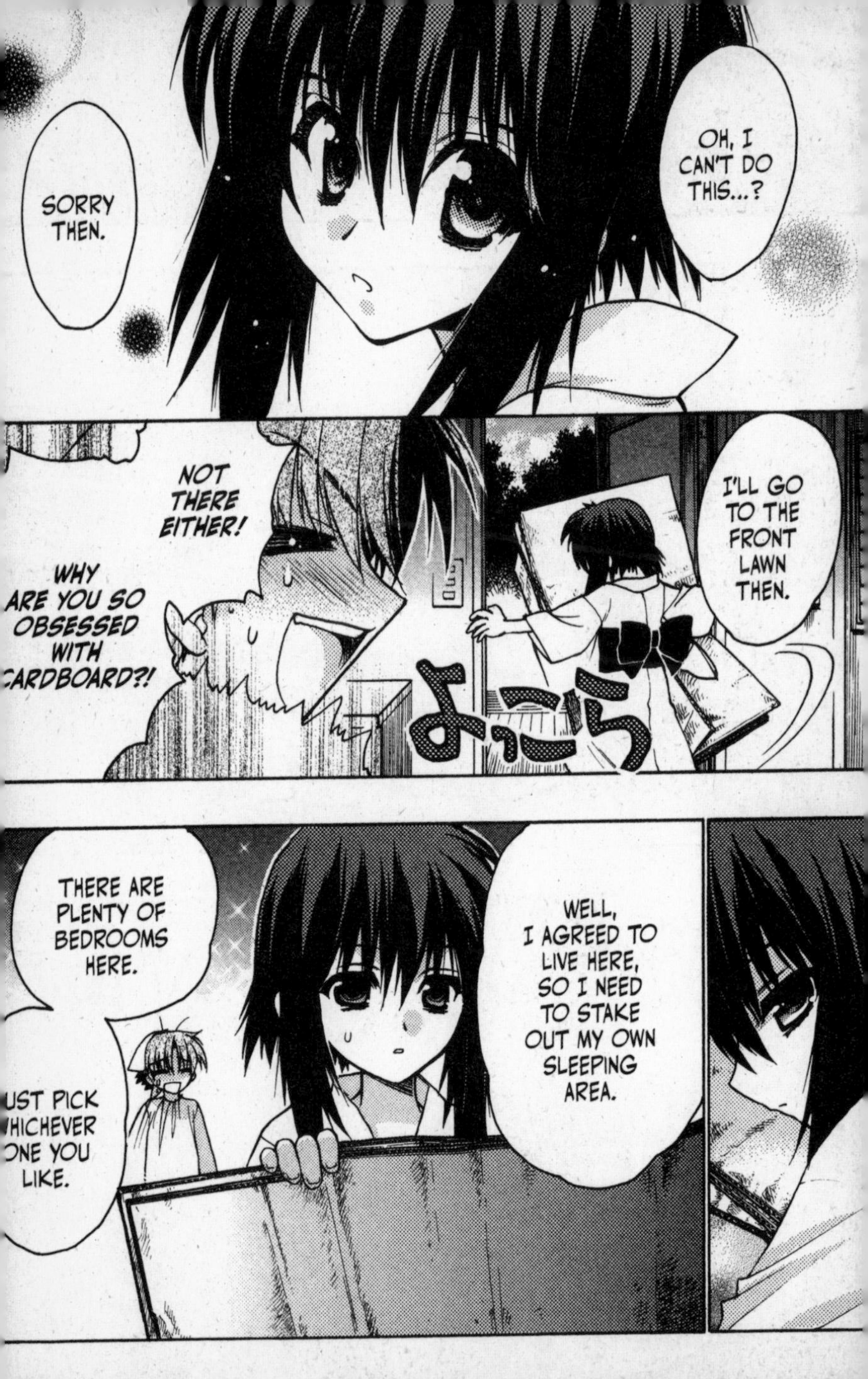
OH, I CAN'T DO THIS...?
SORRY THEN.
I'LL GO TO THE FRONT LAWN THEN.
よっこら
NOT THERE EITHER!
WHY ARE YOU SO OBSESSED WITH CARDBOARD?!
WELL, I AGREED TO LIVE HERE, SO I NEED TO STAKE OUT MY OWN SLEEPING AREA.
THERE ARE PLENTY OF BEDROOMS HERE.
UST PICK HICHEVER ONE YOU LIKE.

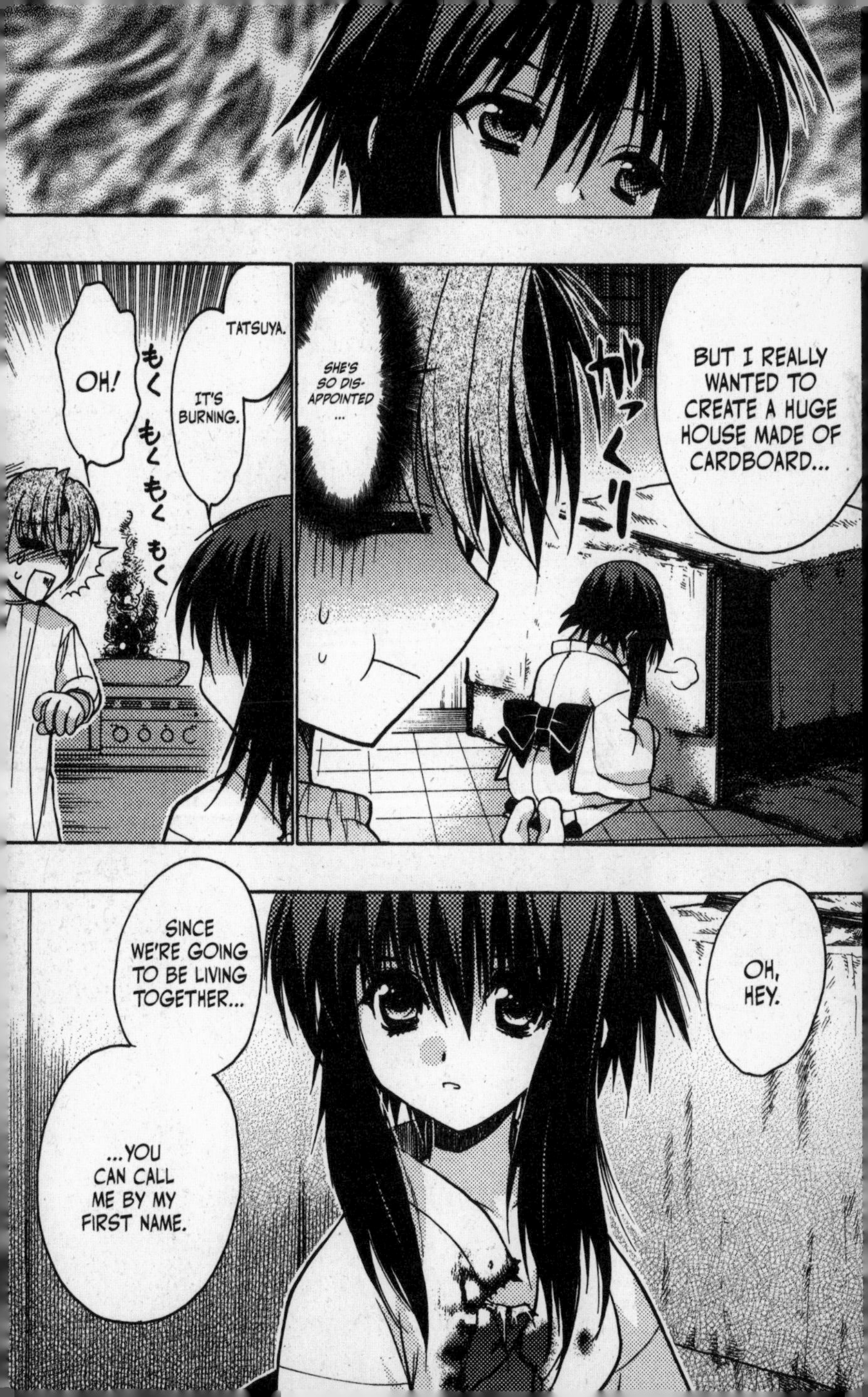

BUT I REALLY WANTED TO CREATE A HUGE HOUSE MADE OF CARDBOARD...
がっくり
SHE'S SO DIS-APPOINTED ...
TATSUYA.
IT'S BURNING.
もく もく もく もく もく
OH!
OH, HEY.
SINCE WE'RE GOING TO BE LIVING TOGETHER...
...YOU CAN CALL ME BY MY FIRST NAME.

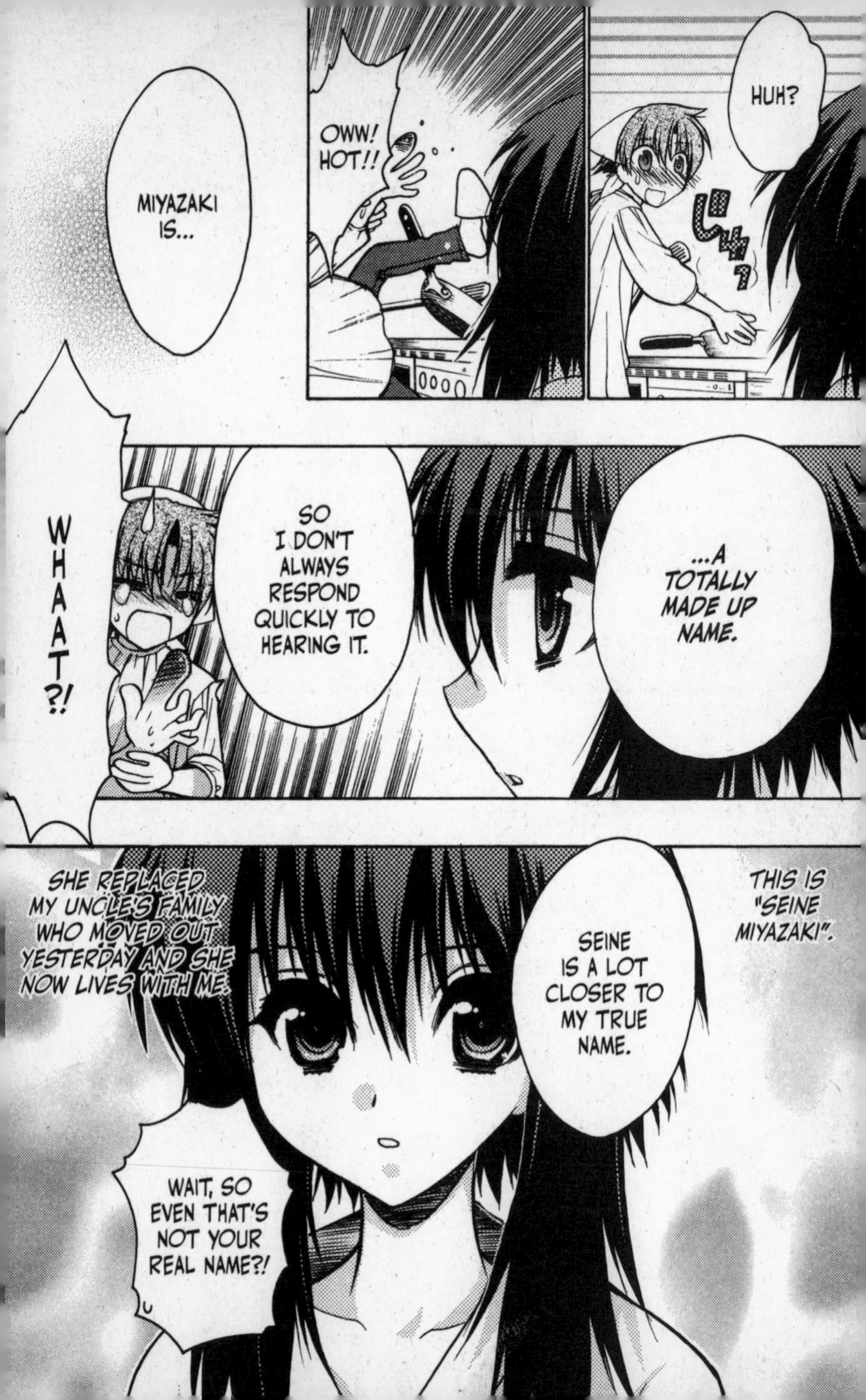
HUH?
OWW! HOT!!
MIYAZAKI IS...
...A TOTALLY MADE UP NAME.
SO I DON'T ALWAYS RESPOND QUICKLY TO HEARING IT.
WHAAT?!
THIS IS "SEINE MIYAZAKI".
SEINE IS A LOT CLOSER TO MY TRUE NAME.
SHE REPLACED MY UNCLE'S FAMILY WHO MOVED OUT YESTERDAY AND SHE NOW LIVES WITH ME.
WAIT, SO EVEN THAT'S NOT YOUR REAL NAME?!

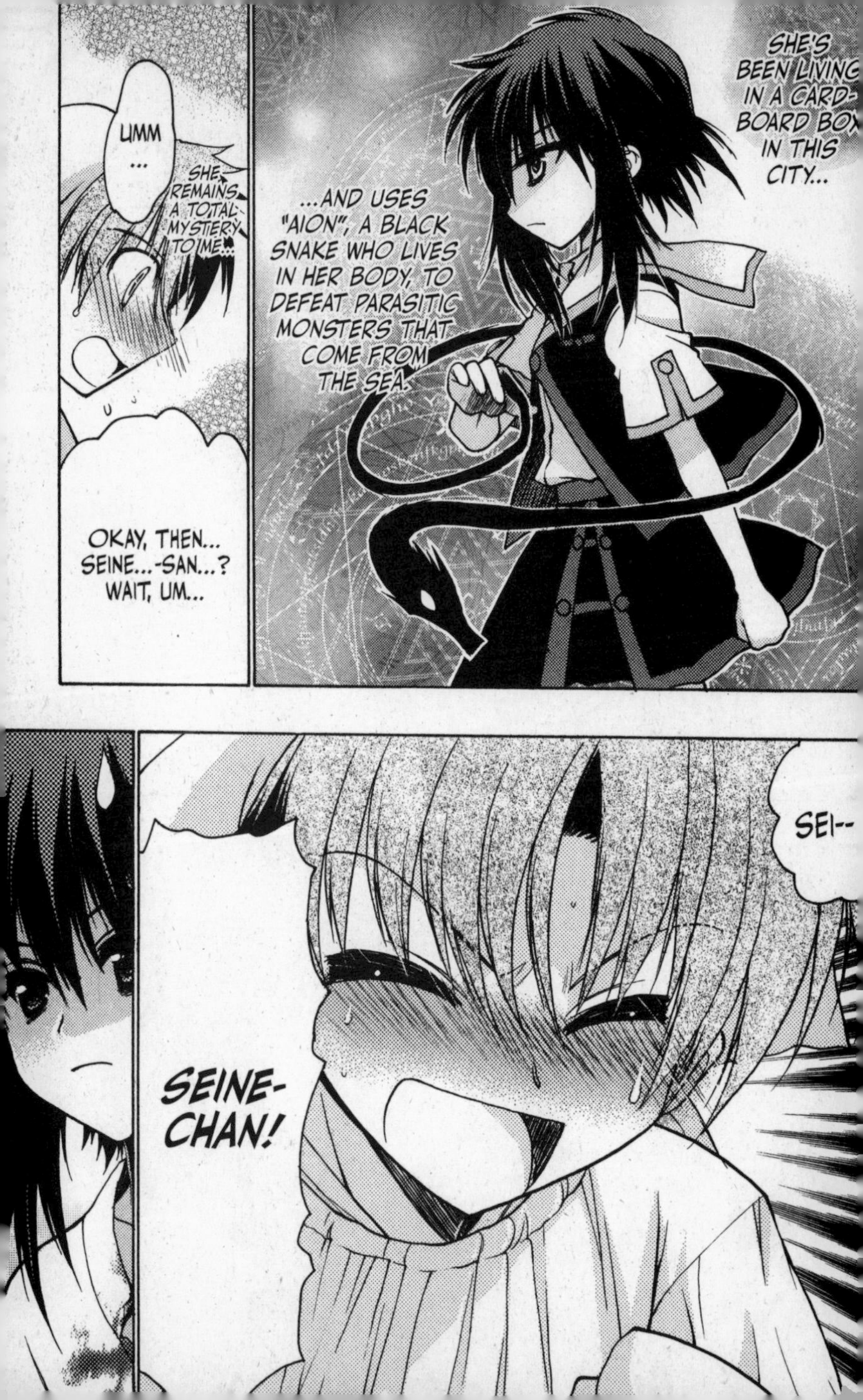
SHE'S BEEN LIVING IN A CARD-BOARD BOX IN THIS CITY...
...AND USES "AION", A BLACK SNAKE WHO LIVES IN HER BODY, TO DEFEAT PARASITIC MONSTERS THAT COME FROM THE SEA.
UMM ...
SHE REMAINS A TOTAL MYSTERY TO ME...
OKAY, THEN... SEINE...-SAN...? WAIT, UM...
SEI--
SEINE-CHAN!

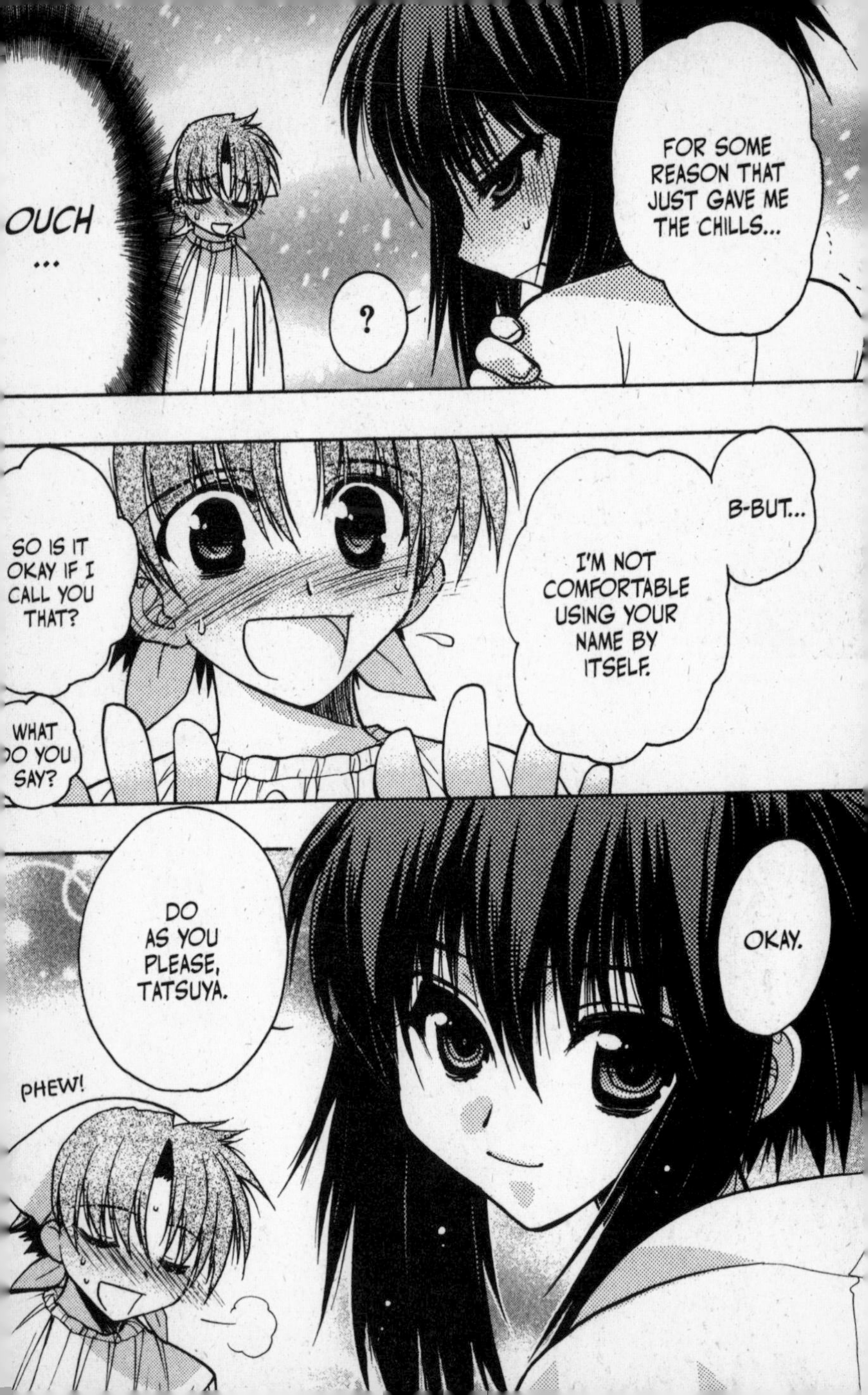
FOR SOME REASON THAT JUST GAVE ME THE CHILLS...
?
OUCH ...
B-BUT...
I'M NOT COMFORTABLE USING YOUR NAME BY ITSELF.
SO IS IT OKAY IF I CALL YOU THAT?
WHAT DO YOU SAY?
OKAY.
DO AS YOU PLEASE, TATSUYA.
PHEW!

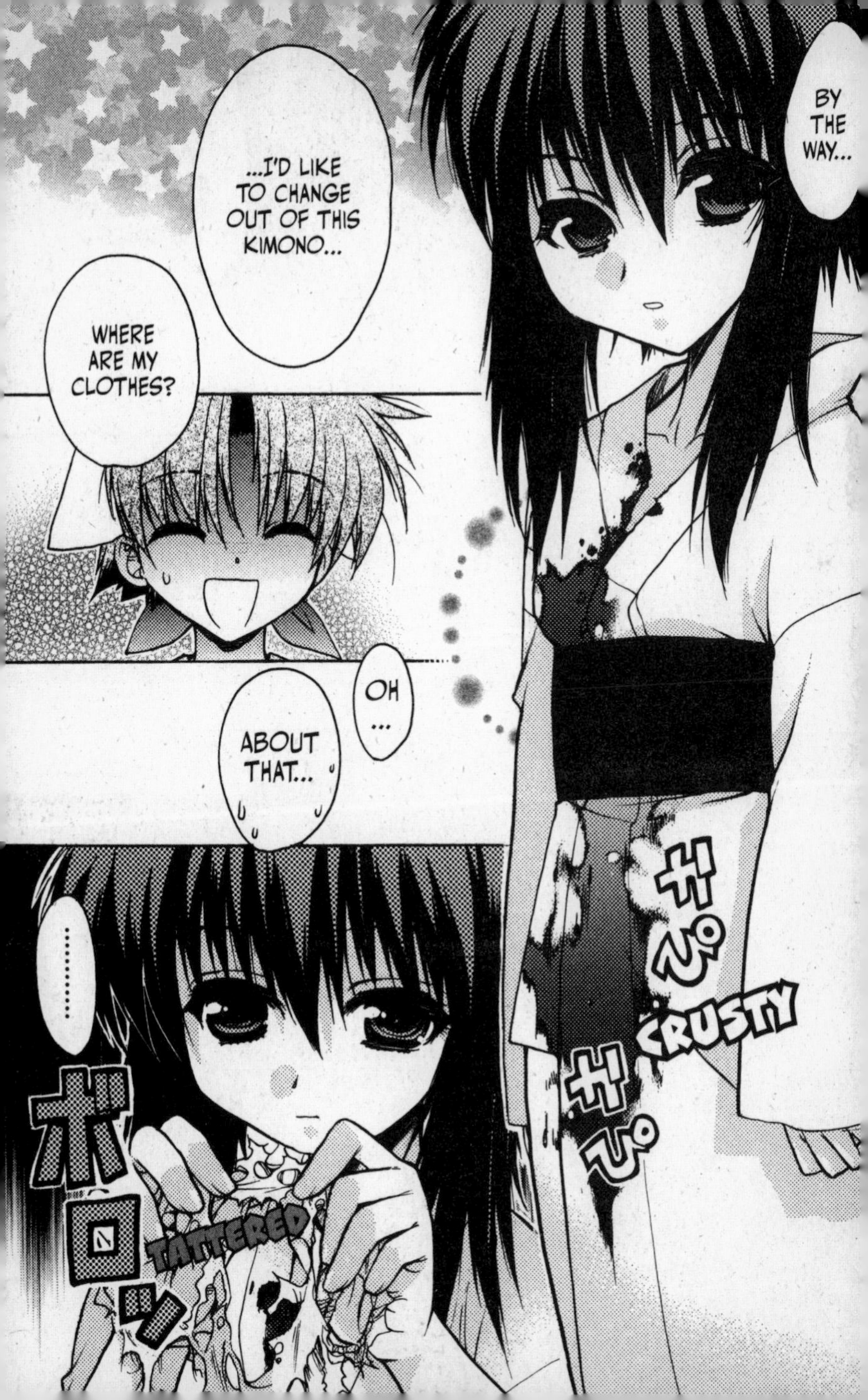
BY THE WAY...
CRUSTY
...I'D LIKE TO CHANGE OUT OF THIS KIMONO...
WHERE ARE MY CLOTHES?
OH ...
ABOUT THAT...
....
ボロッ
TATTERED

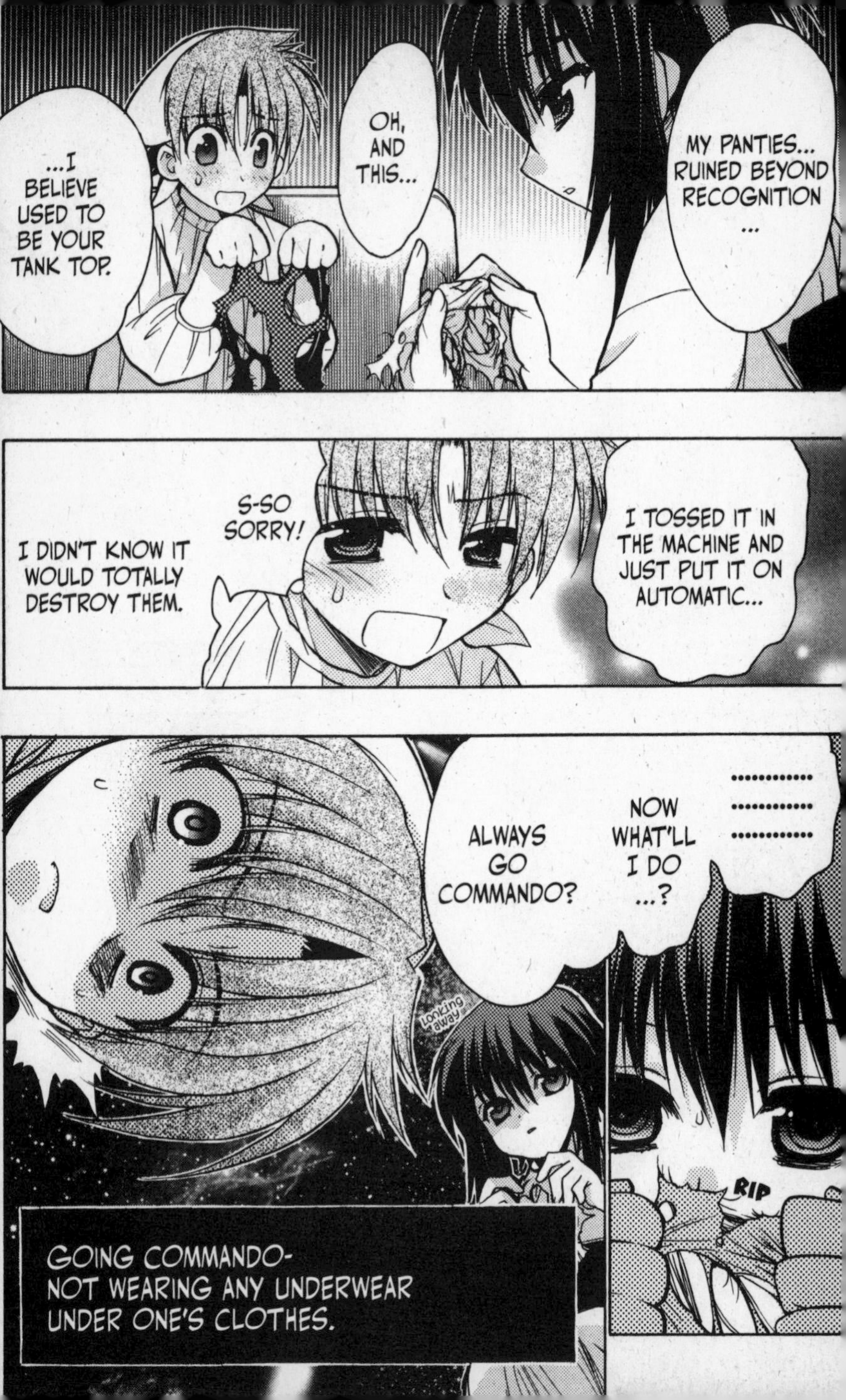
MY PANTIES... RUINED BEYOND RECOGNITION ...
OH, AND THIS...
...I BELIEVE USED TO BE YOUR TANK TOP.
I TOSSED IT IN THE MACHINE AND JUST PUT IT ON AUTOMATIC...
S-SO SORRY!
I DIDN'T KNOW IT WOULD TOTALLY DESTROY THEM.
....
NOW WHAT'LL I DO ...?
ALWAYS GO COMMANDO?
RIP
Looking away
GOING COMMANDO- NOT WEARING ANY UNDERWEAR UNDER ONE'S CLOTHES.

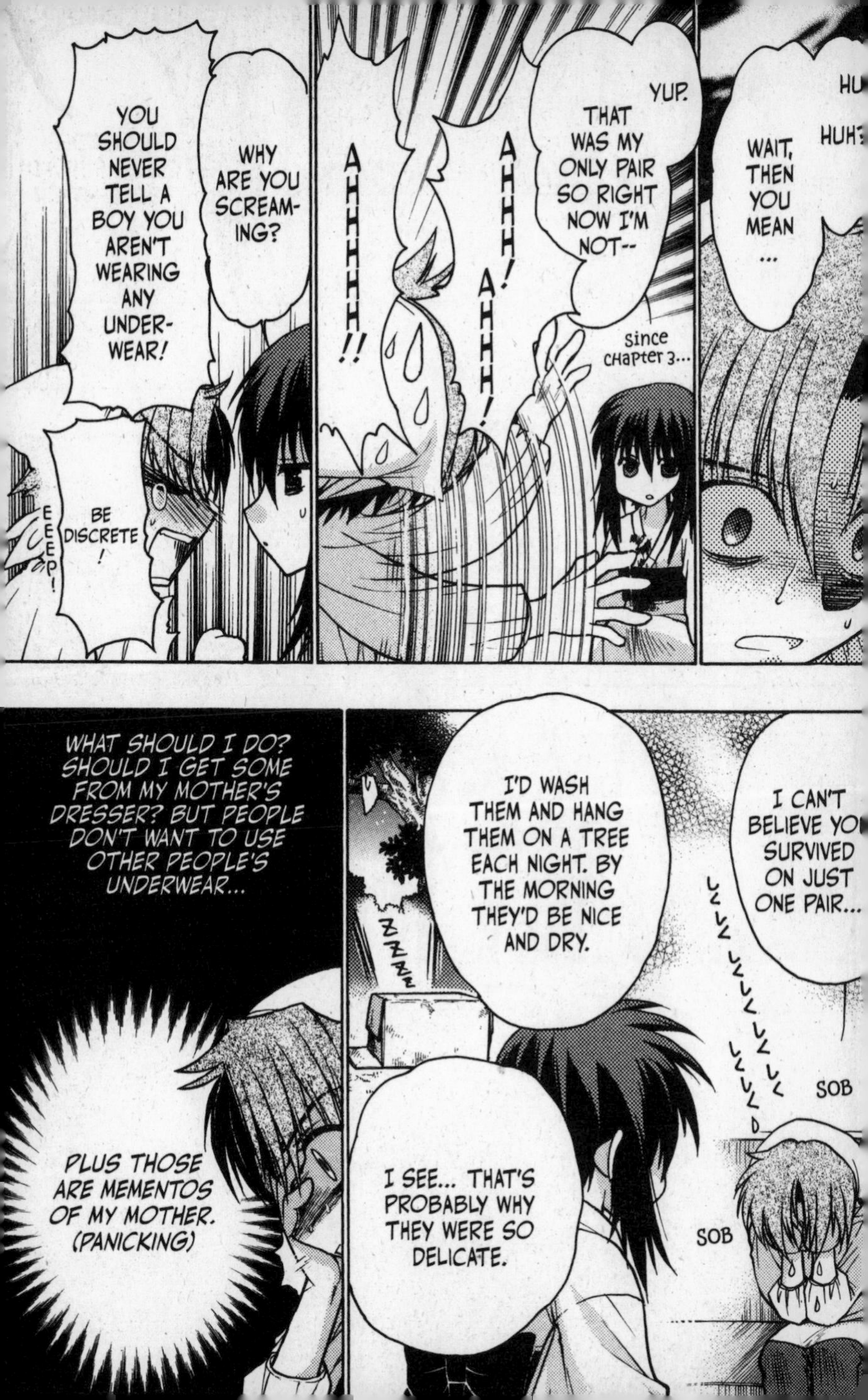
HU
HUH
WAIT, THEN YOU MEAN ...
YUP. THAT WAS MY ONLY PAIR SO RIGHT NOW I'M NOT--
AHHH! AHHH!
AHHHHHH!!
Since Chapter 3...
WHY ARE YOU SCREAMING?
YOU SHOULD NEVER TELL A BOY YOU AREN'T WEARING ANY UNDERWEAR!
BE DISCRETE!
EEEP!
I CAN'T BELIEVE YO SURVIVED ON JUST ONE PAIR...
SOB
SOB
I'D WASH THEM AND HANG THEM ON A TREE EACH NIGHT. BY THE MORNING THEY'D BE NICE AND DRY.
ZZZ
I SEE... THAT'S PROBABLY WHY THEY WERE SO DELICATE.
WHAT SHOULD I DO? SHOULD I GET SOME FROM MY MOTHER'S DRESSER? BUT PEOPLE DON'T WANT TO USE OTHER PEOPLE'S UNDERWEAR...
PLUS THOSE ARE MEMENTOS OF MY MOTHER. (PANICKING)

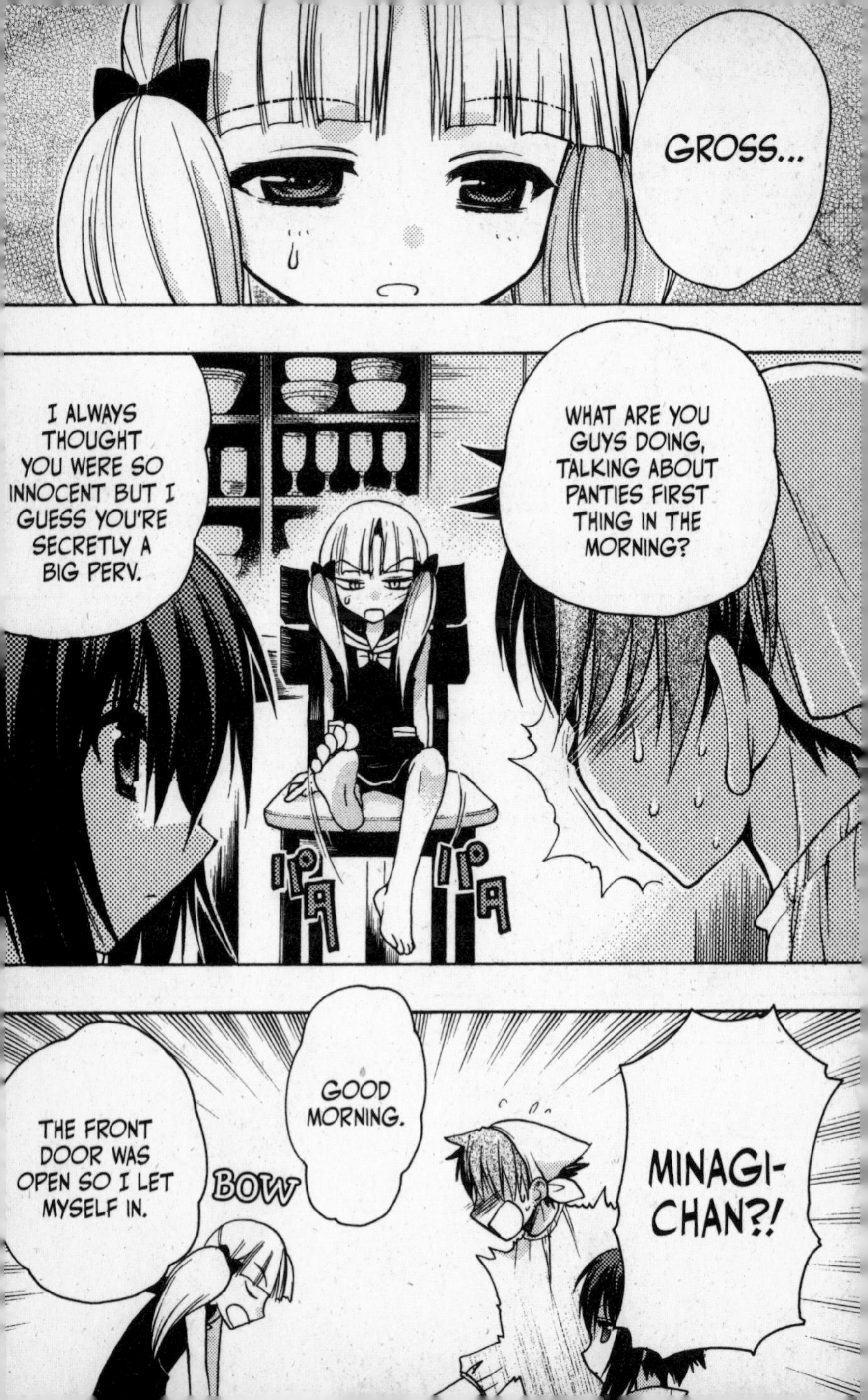
GROSS...
WHAT ARE YOU GUYS DOING, TALKING ABOUT PANTIES FIRST THING IN THE MORNING?
I ALWAYS THOUGHT YOU WERE SO INNOCENT BUT I GUESS YOU'RE SECRETLY A BIG PERV.
MINAGI-CHAN?!
GOOD MORNING.
BOW
THE FRONT DOOR WAS OPEN SO I LET MYSELF IN.

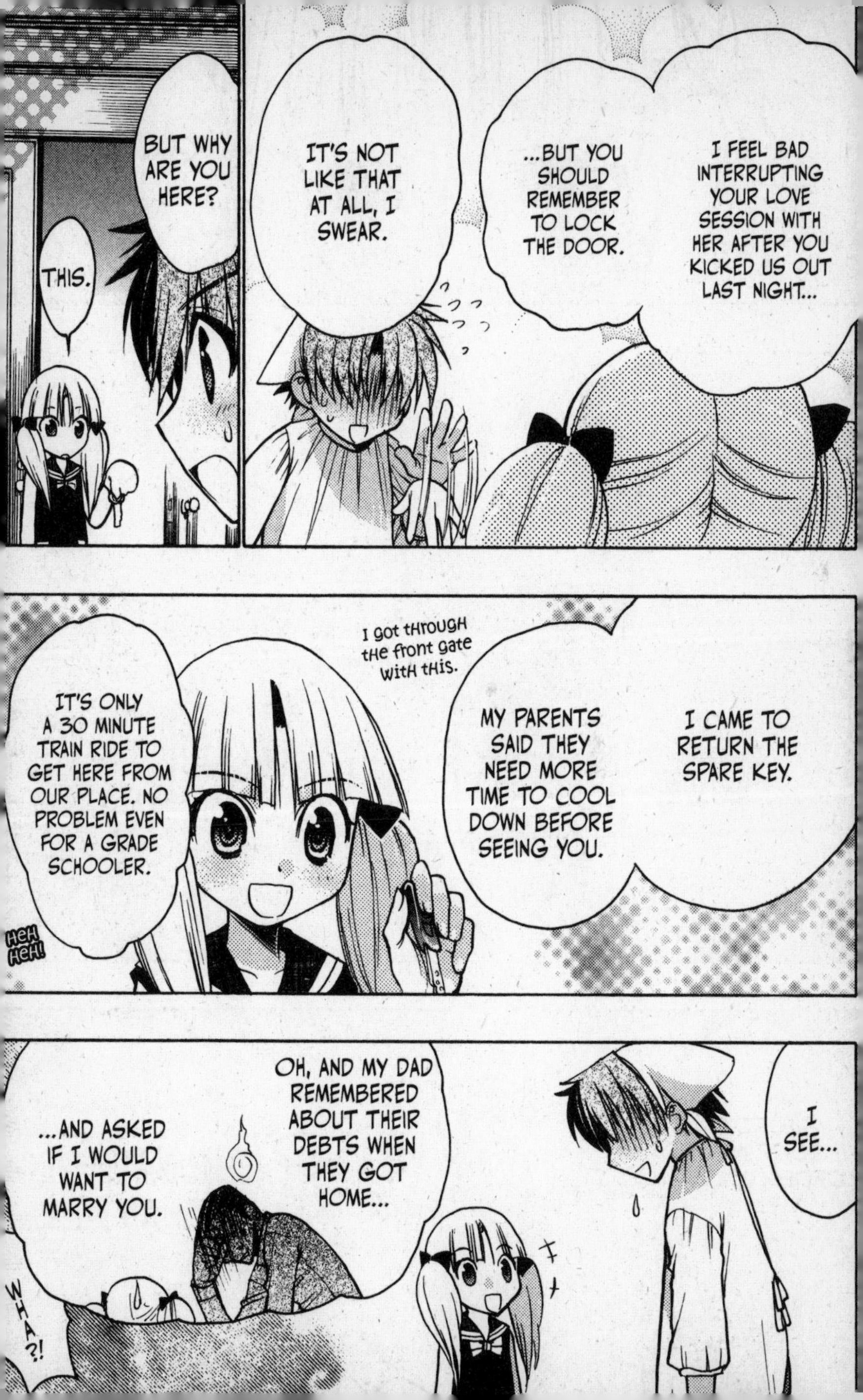
I FEEL BAD INTERRUPTING YOUR LOVE SESSION WITH HER AFTER YOU KICKED US OUT LAST NIGHT...
...BUT YOU SHOULD REMEMBER TO LOCK THE DOOR.
IT'S NOT LIKE THAT AT ALL, I SWEAR.
BUT WHY ARE YOU HERE?
THIS.
I CAME TO RETURN THE SPARE KEY.
MY PARENTS SAID THEY NEED MORE TIME TO COOL DOWN BEFORE SEEING YOU.
I got through the front gate with this.
IT'S ONLY A 30 MINUTE TRAIN RIDE TO GET HERE FROM OUR PLACE. NO PROBLEM EVEN FOR A GRADE SCHOOLER.
HEH HEH!
I SEE...
OH, AND MY DAD REMEMBERED ABOUT THEIR DEBTS WHEN THEY GOT HOME...
...AND ASKED IF I WOULD WANT TO MARRY YOU.
WHA?!

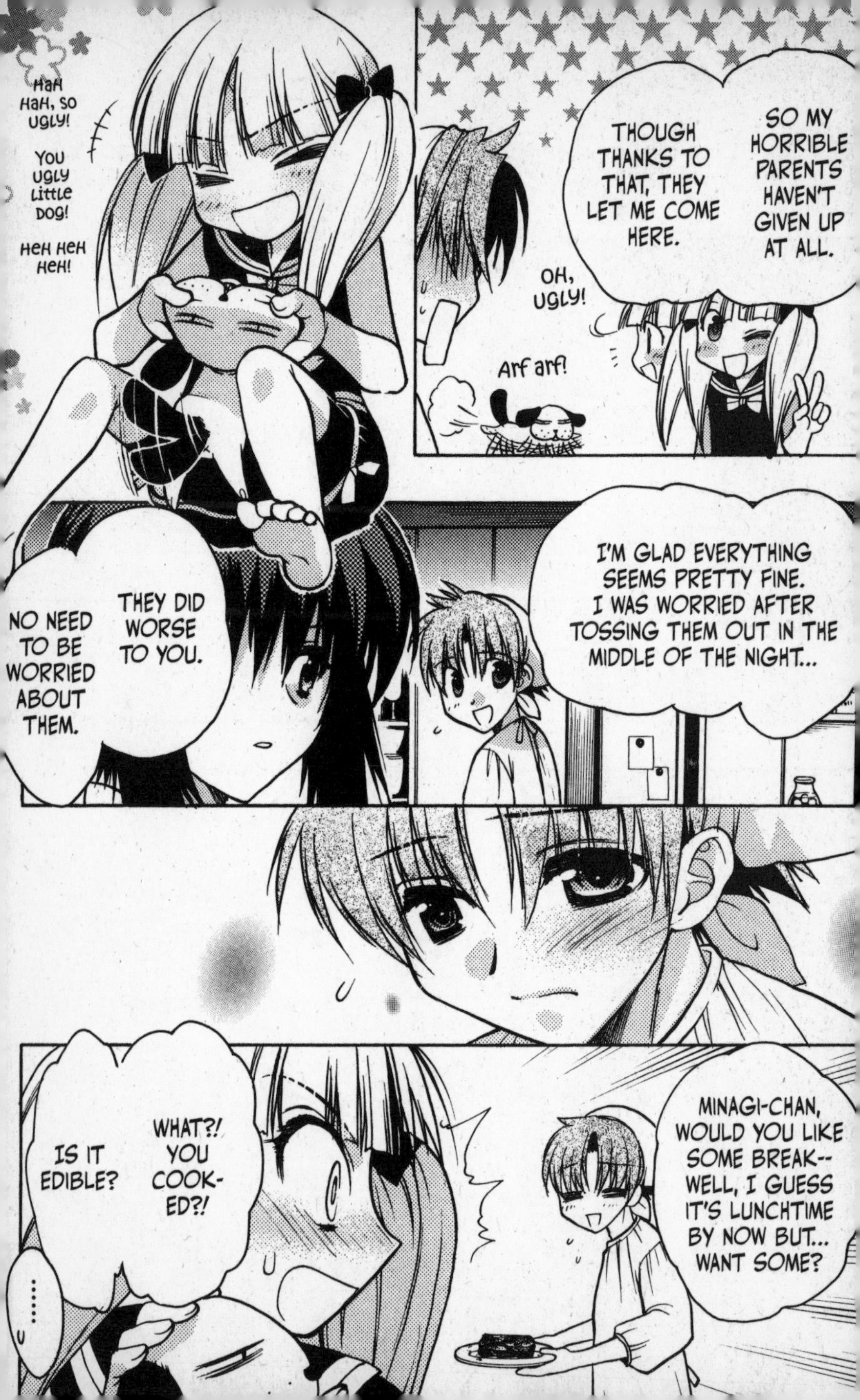
SO MY HORRIBLE PARENTS HAVEN'T GIVEN UP AT ALL.
THOUGH THANKS TO THAT, THEY LET ME COME HERE.
OH, UGLY!
Arf arf!
Hah hah, so ugly!
You ugly little dog!
Heh heh heh!
I'M GLAD EVERYTHING SEEMS PRETTY FINE. I WAS WORRIED AFTER TOSSING THEM OUT IN THE MIDDLE OF THE NIGHT...
THEY DID WORSE TO YOU.
NO NEED TO BE WORRIED ABOUT THEM.
MINAGI-CHAN, WOULD YOU LIKE SOME BREAK-- WELL, I GUESS IT'S LUNCHTIME BY NOW BUT... WANT SOME?
WHAT?! YOU COOK-ED?!
IS IT EDIBLE?
......

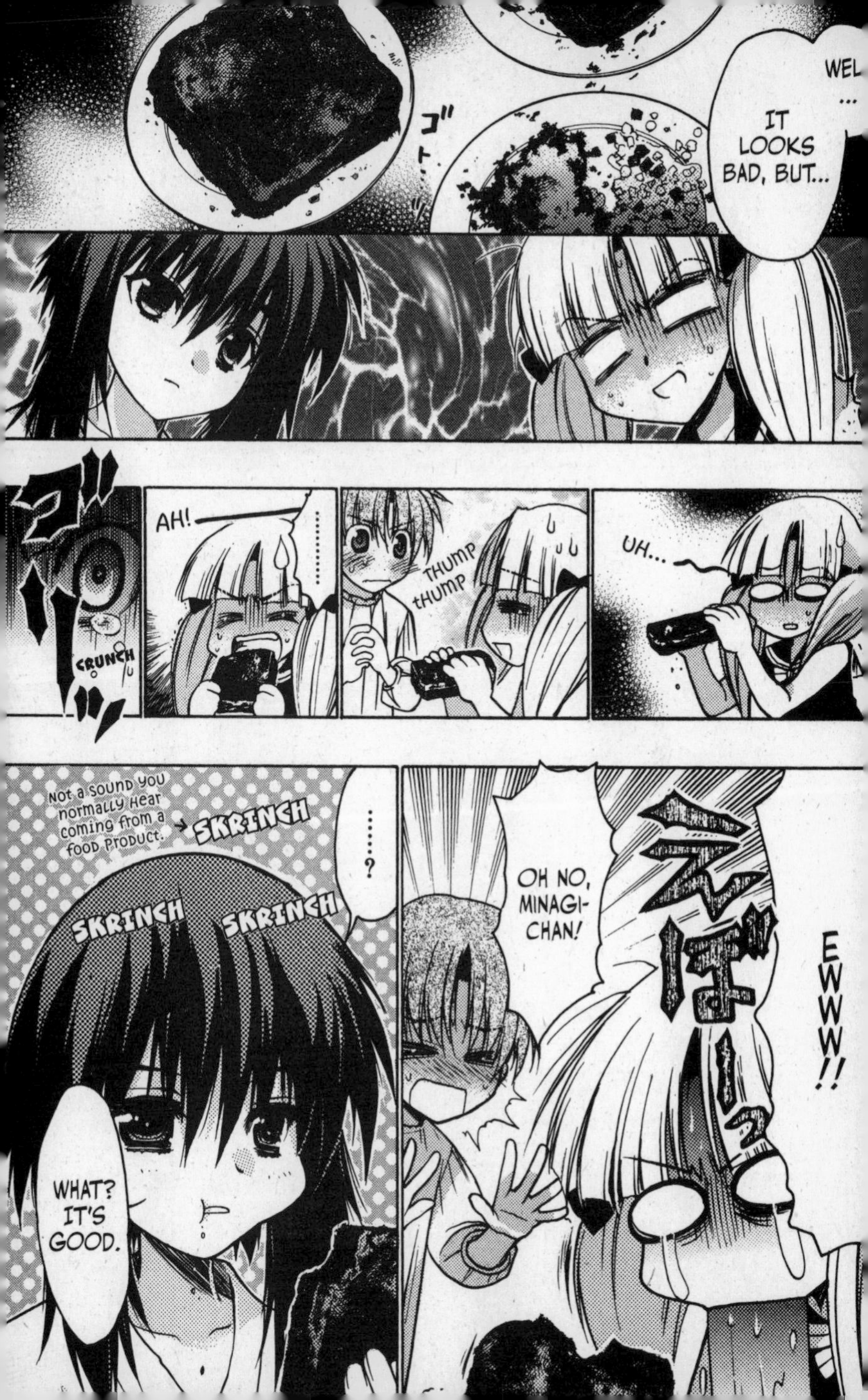

WEL... IT LOOKS BAD, BUT...
UH...
THUMP THUMP
......
AH!
CRUNCH
EWWW!!
OH NO, MINAGI-CHAN!
......?
Not a sound you normally hear coming from a food product. → SKRINCH
SKRINCH SKRINCH
WHAT? IT'S GOOD.

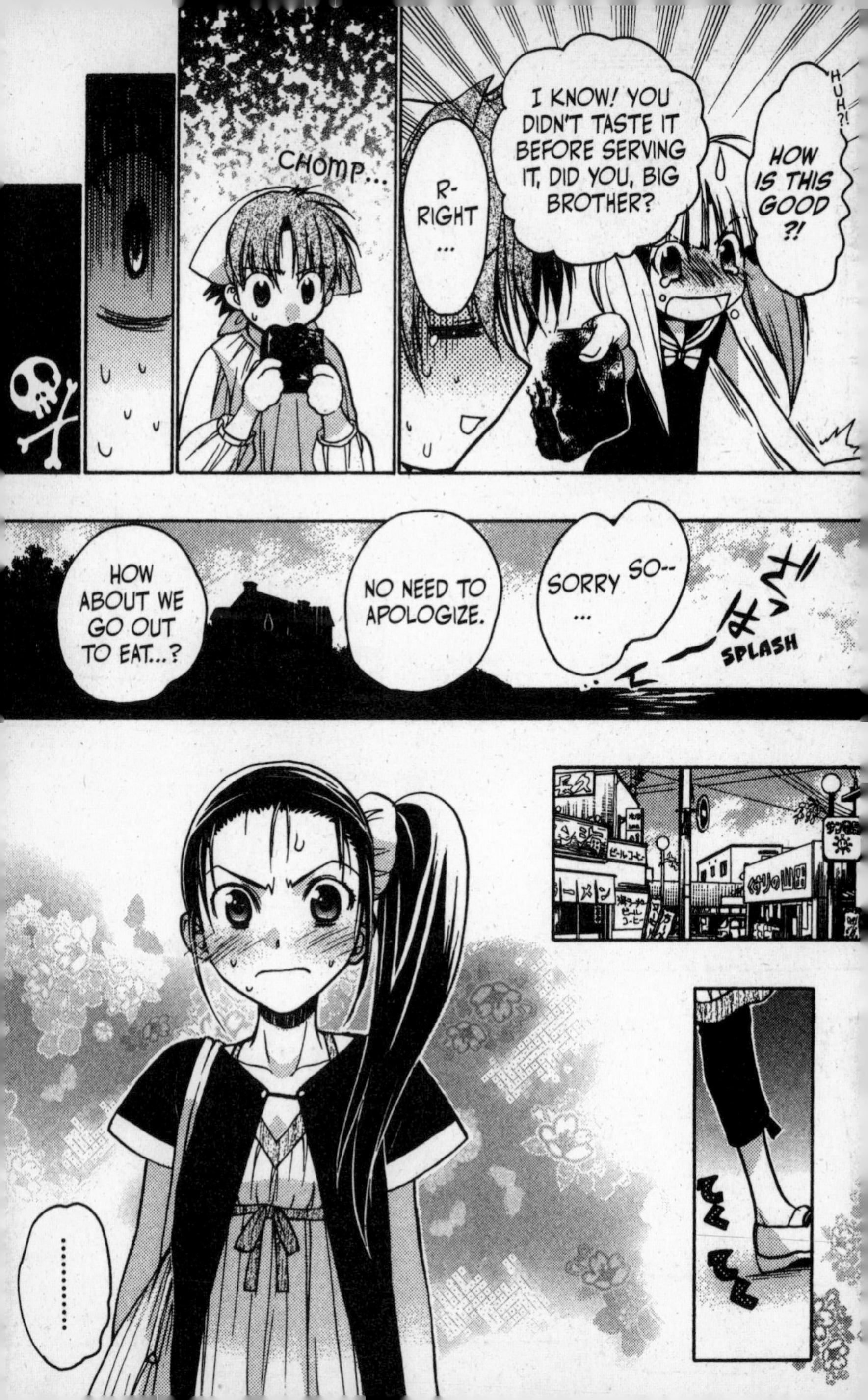

HUH?!
HOW IS THIS GOOD?!
I KNOW! YOU DIDN'T TASTE IT BEFORE SERVING IT, DID YOU, BIG BROTHER?
R-RIGHT...
CHOMP...
SPLASH
SO-- SORRY...
NO NEED TO APOLOGIZE.
HOW ABOUT WE GO OUT TO EAT...?
......

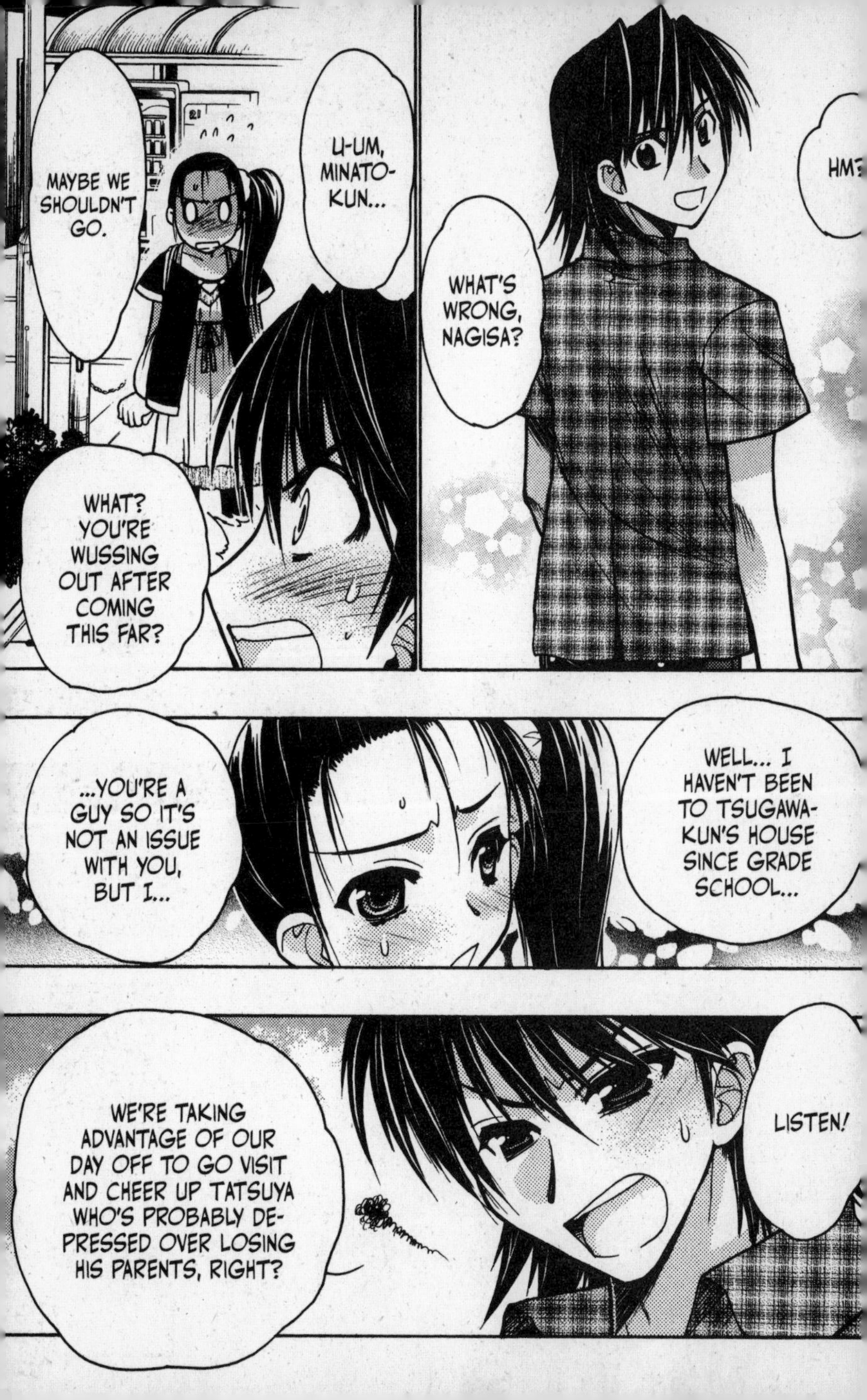
HM?
WHAT'S WRONG, NAGISA?
U-UM, MINATO-KUN...
MAYBE WE SHOULDN'T GO.
WHAT? YOU'RE WUSSING OUT AFTER COMING THIS FAR?
WELL... I HAVEN'T BEEN TO TSUGAWA-KUN'S HOUSE SINCE GRADE SCHOOL...
...YOU'RE A GUY SO IT'S NOT AN ISSUE WITH YOU, BUT I...
LISTEN!
WE'RE TAKING ADVANTAGE OF OUR DAY OFF TO GO VISIT AND CHEER UP TATSUYA WHO'S PROBABLY DE-PRESSED OVER LOSING HIS PARENTS, RIGHT?

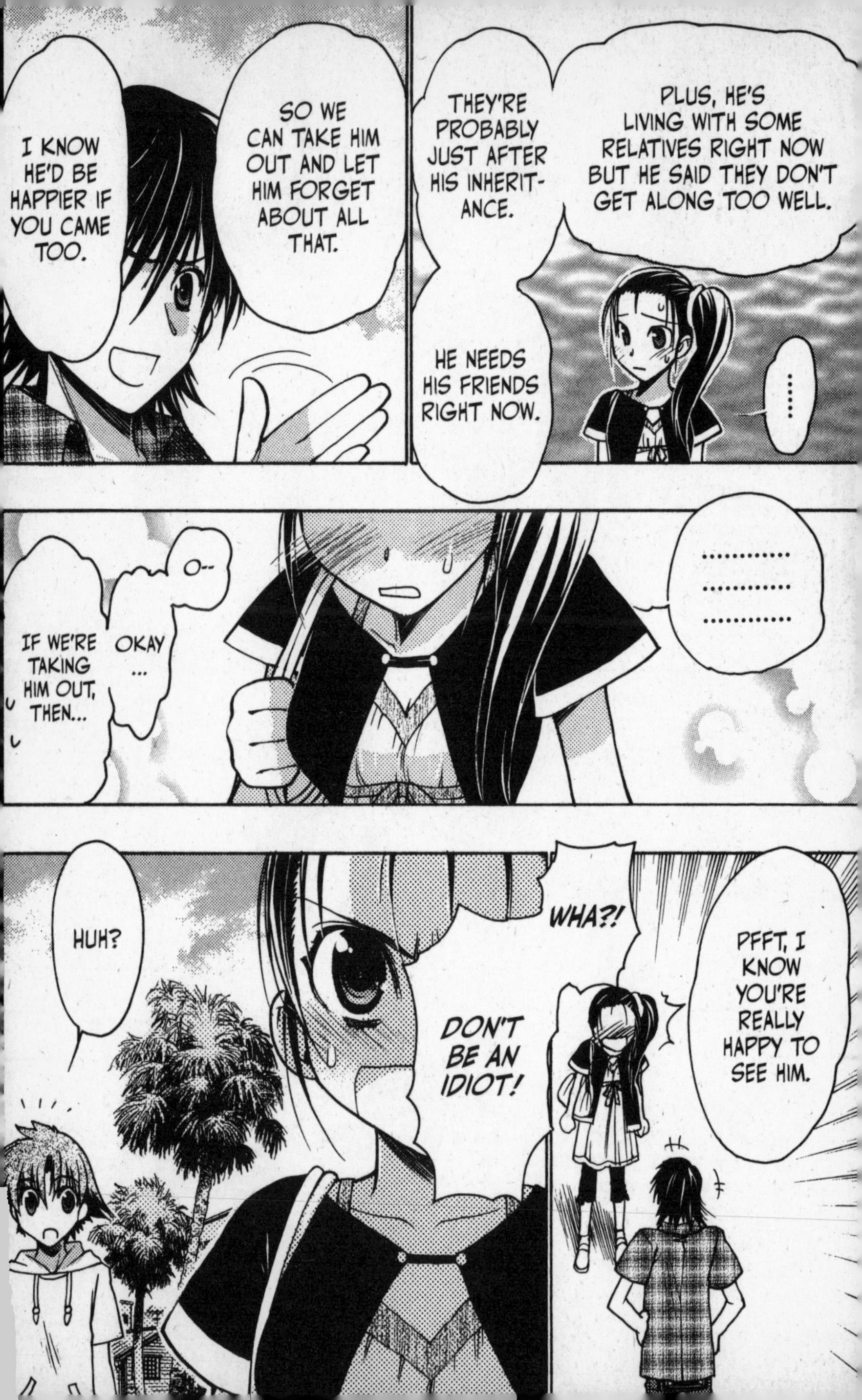
PLUS, HE'S LIVING WITH SOME RELATIVES RIGHT NOW BUT HE SAID THEY DON'T GET ALONG TOO WELL.
THEY'RE PROBABLY JUST AFTER HIS INHERIT-ANCE.
......
HE NEEDS HIS FRIENDS RIGHT NOW.
SO WE CAN TAKE HIM OUT AND LET HIM FORGET ABOUT ALL THAT.
I KNOW HE'D BE HAPPIER IF YOU CAME TOO.
....
O--
OKAY ...
IF WE'RE TAKING HIM OUT, THEN...
PFFT, I KNOW YOU'RE REALLY HAPPY TO SEE HIM.
WHA?!
DON'T BE AN IDIOT!
HUH?

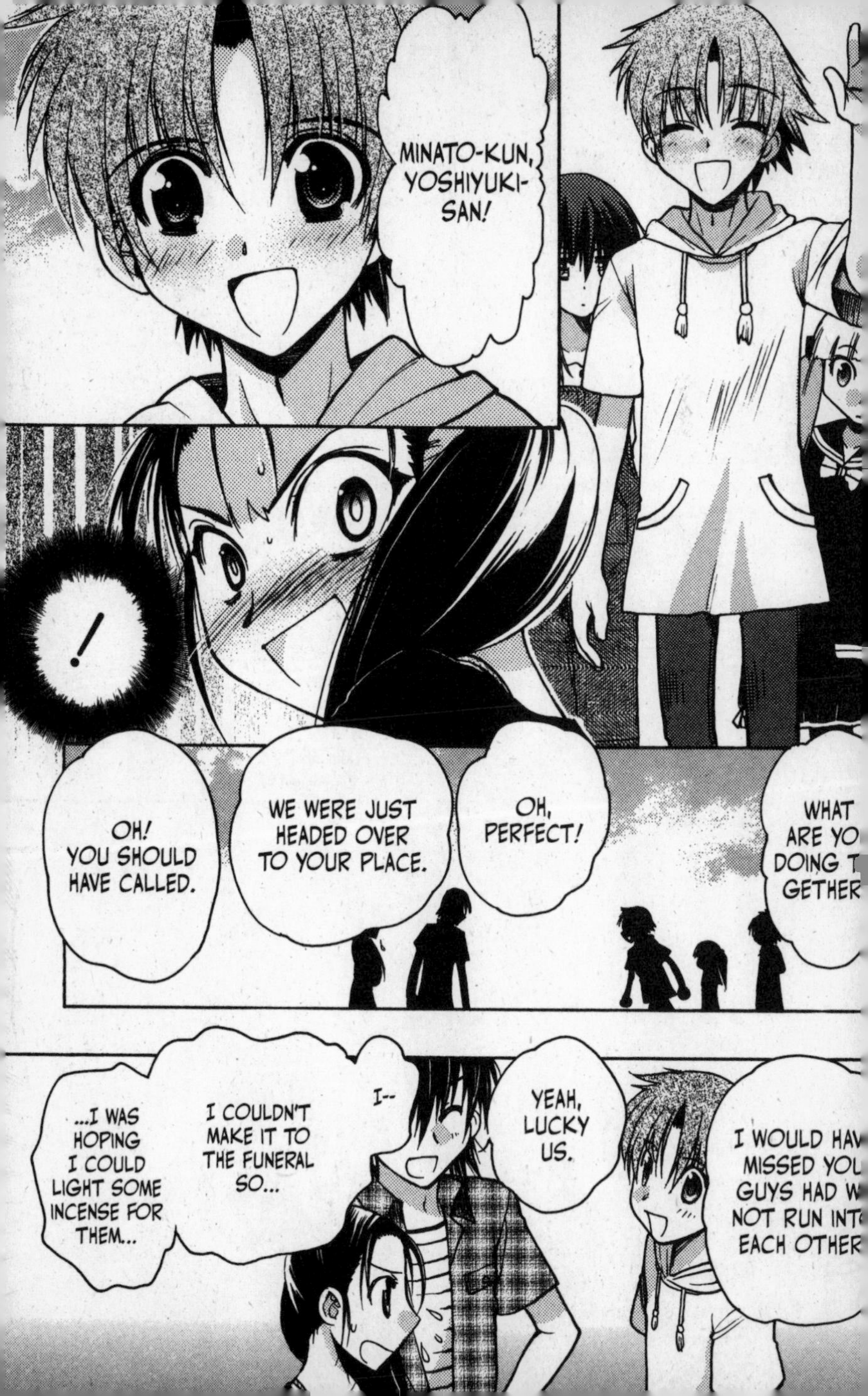
MINATO-KUN, YOSHIYUKI-SAN!
!
WHAT ARE YO DOING T GETHER
OH, PERFECT!
WE WERE JUST HEADED OVER TO YOUR PLACE.
OH! YOU SHOULD HAVE CALLED.
I WOULD HAV MISSED YOU GUYS HAD W NOT RUN INT EACH OTHER
YEAH, LUCKY US.
I--
I COULDN'T MAKE IT TO THE FUNERAL SO...
...I WAS HOPING I COULD LIGHT SOME INCENSE FOR THEM...

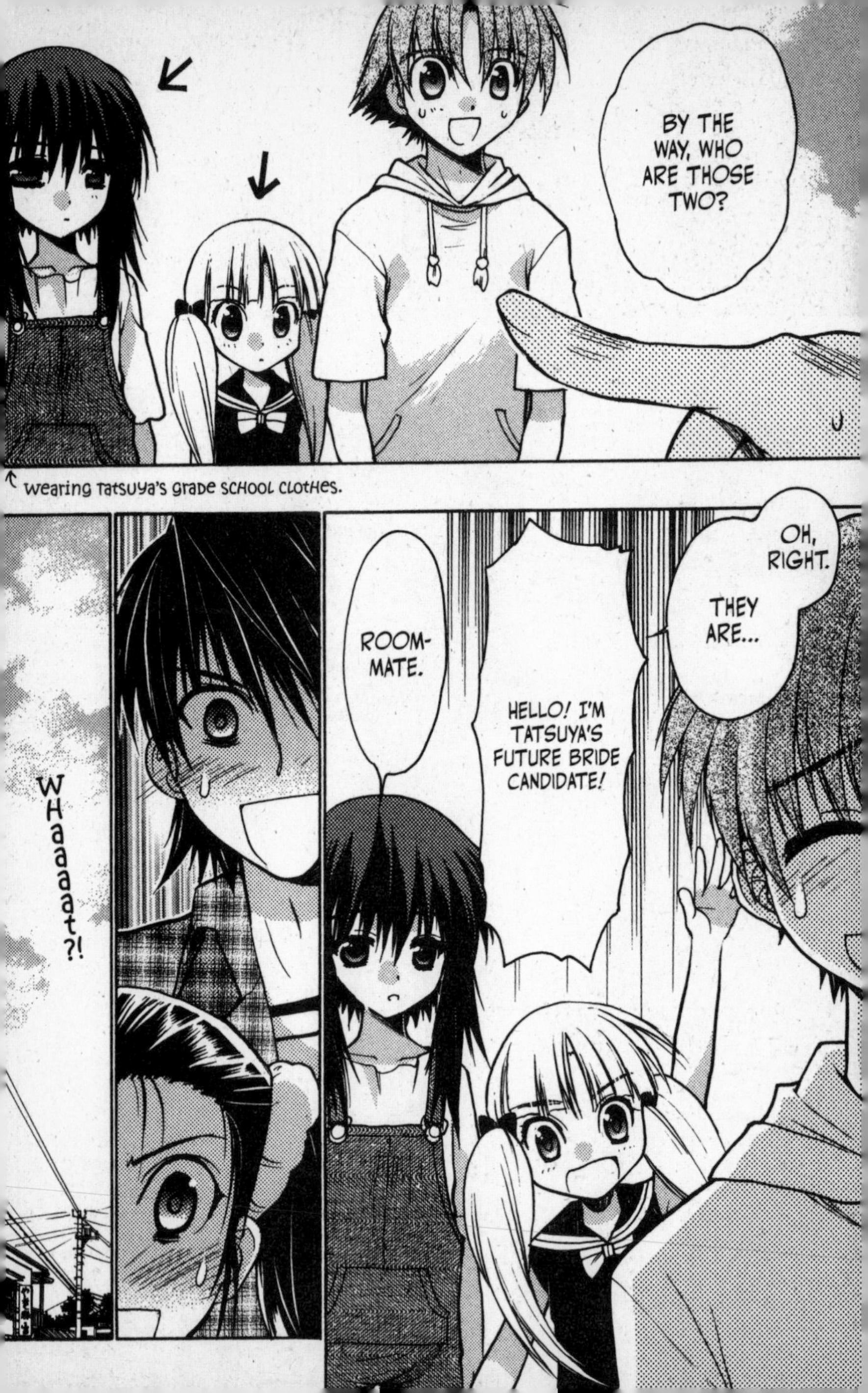
BY THE WAY, WHO ARE THOSE TWO?
wearing Tatsuya's grade school clothes.
OH, RIGHT.
THEY ARE...
HELLO! I'M TATSUYA'S FUTURE BRIDE CANDIDATE!
ROOM-MATE.
WHaaaaat?!

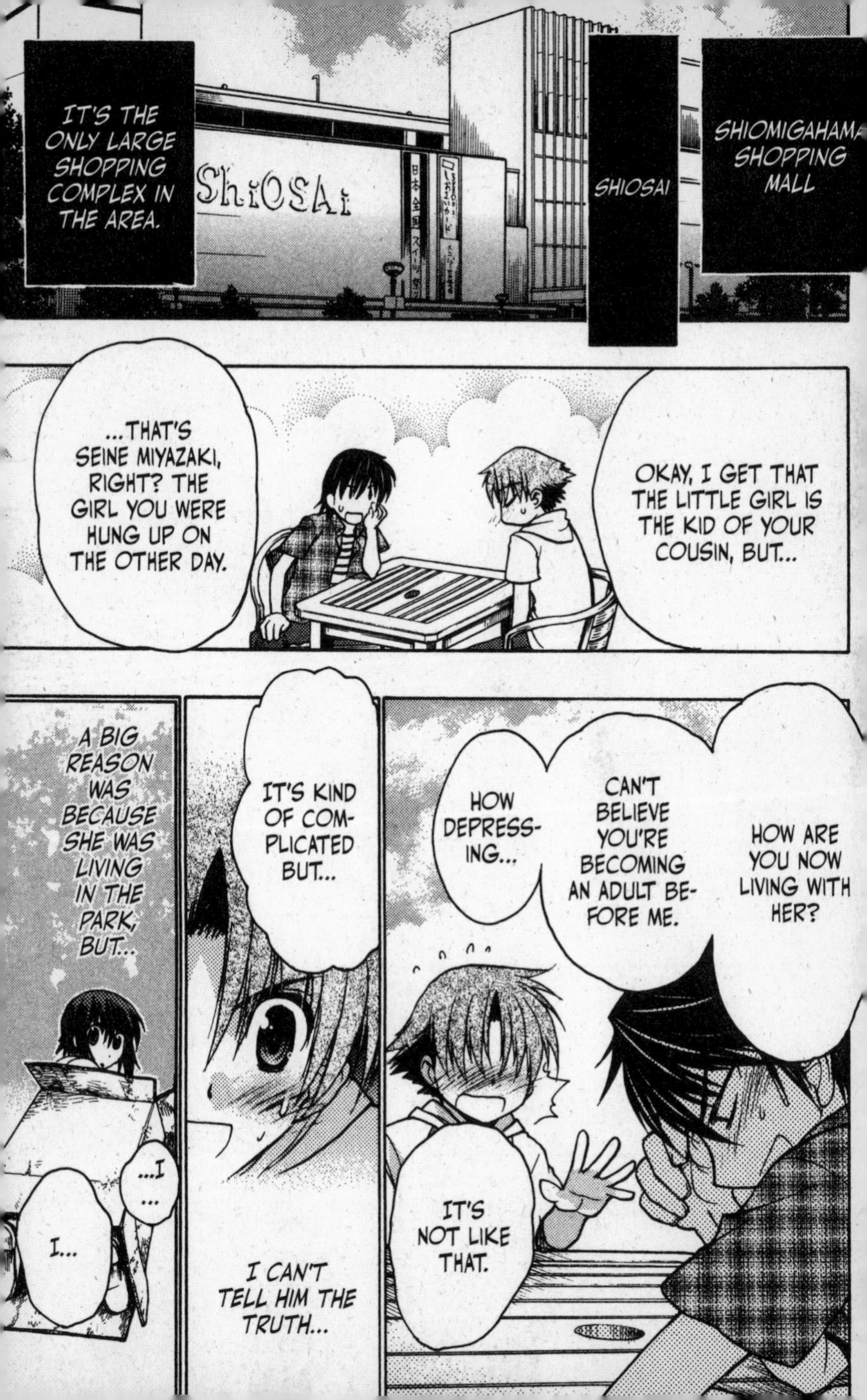
SHIOMIGAHAMA SHOPPING MALL
SHIOSAI
IT'S THE ONLY LARGE SHOPPING COMPLEX IN THE AREA.
ShiOSAi
OKAY, I GET THAT THE LITTLE GIRL IS THE KID OF YOUR COUSIN, BUT...
...THAT'S SEINE MIYAZAKI, RIGHT? THE GIRL YOU WERE HUNG UP ON THE OTHER DAY.
HOW ARE YOU NOW LIVING WITH HER?
CAN'T BELIEVE YOU'RE BECOMING AN ADULT BEFORE ME.
HOW DEPRESSING...
IT'S NOT LIKE THAT.
IT'S KIND OF COMPLICATED BUT...
I CAN'T TELL HIM THE TRUTH...
A BIG REASON WAS BECAUSE SHE WAS LIVING IN THE PARK, BUT...
...I ...
I...

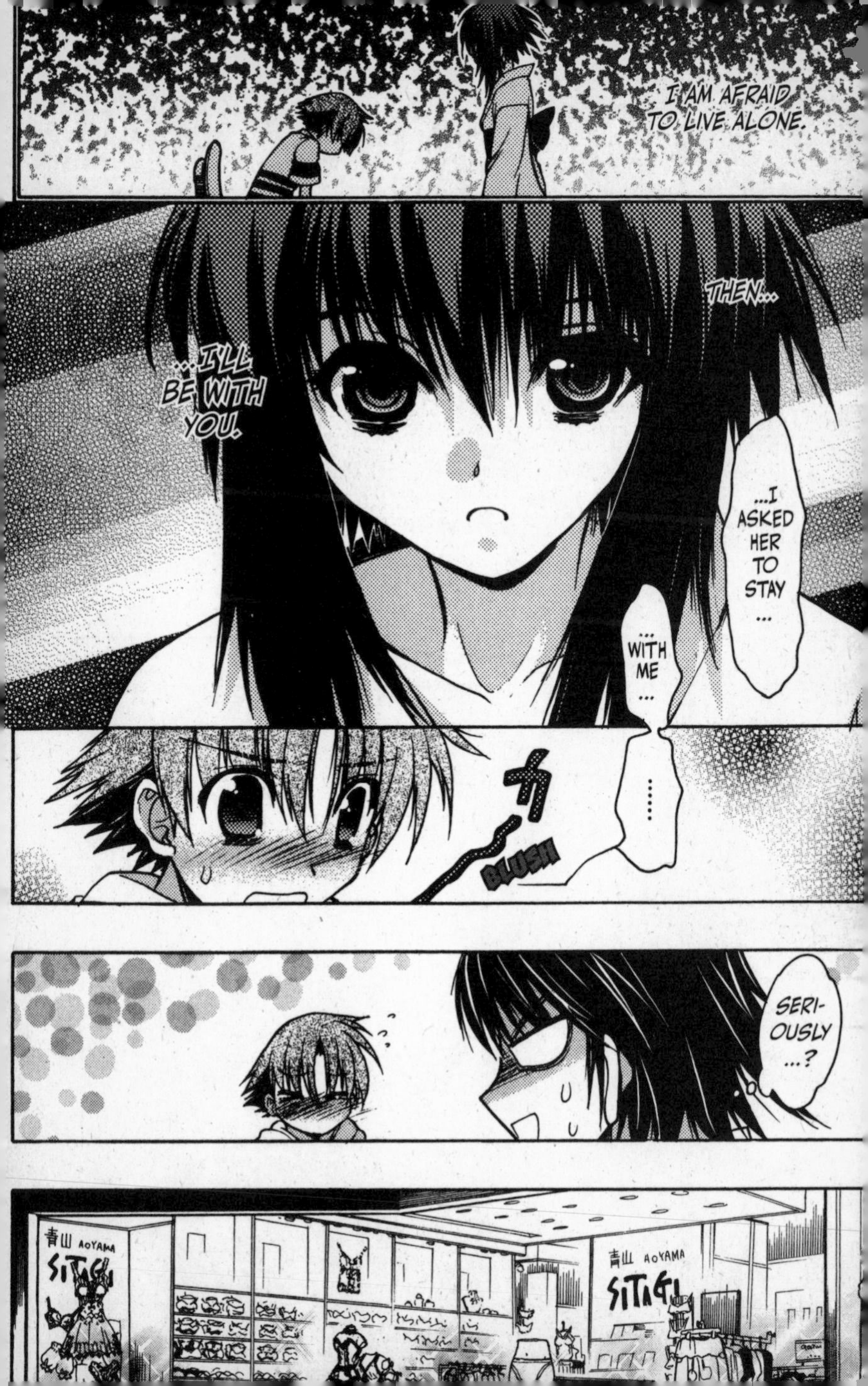
I AM AFRAID TO LIVE ALONE.
THEN...
...I'LL BE WITH YOU.
...I ASKED HER TO STAY ...
... WITH ME ...
......
BLUSH
SERI-OUSLY ...?
青山 AOYAMA SITAGI
青山 AOYAMA SITAGI

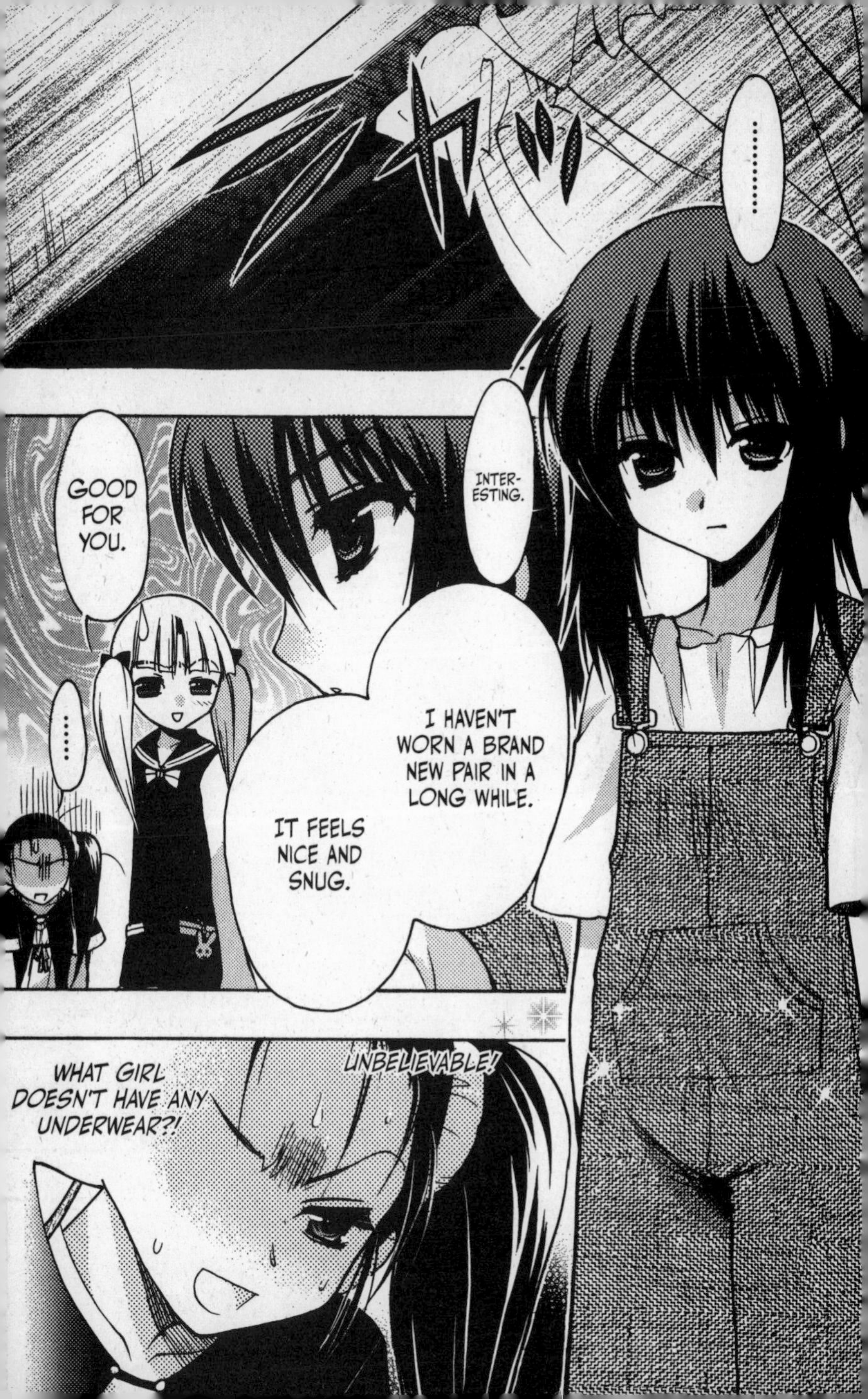
......
INTER-ESTING.
I HAVEN'T WORN A BRAND NEW PAIR IN A LONG WHILE.
IT FEELS NICE AND SNUG.
GOOD FOR YOU.
......
UNBELIEVABLE!
WHAT GIRL DOESN'T HAVE ANY UNDERWEAR?!

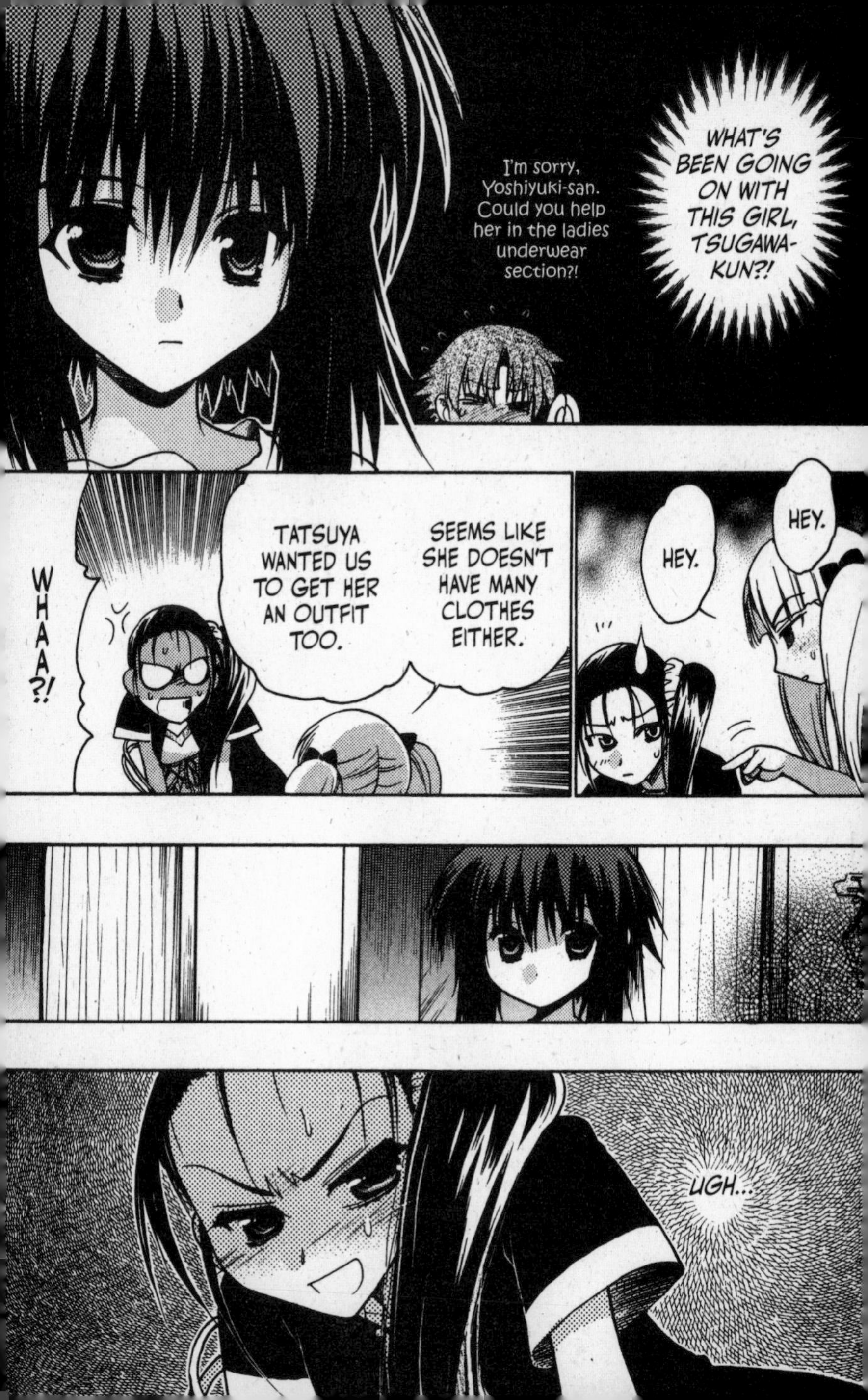
WHAT'S BEEN GOING ON WITH THIS GIRL, TSUGAWA-KUN?!
I'm sorry, Yoshiyuki-san. Could you help her in the ladies underwear section?!
HEY.
HEY.
SEEMS LIKE SHE DOESN'T HAVE MANY CLOTHES EITHER.
TATSUYA WANTED US TO GET HER AN OUTFIT TOO.
WHAAA?!
UGH...

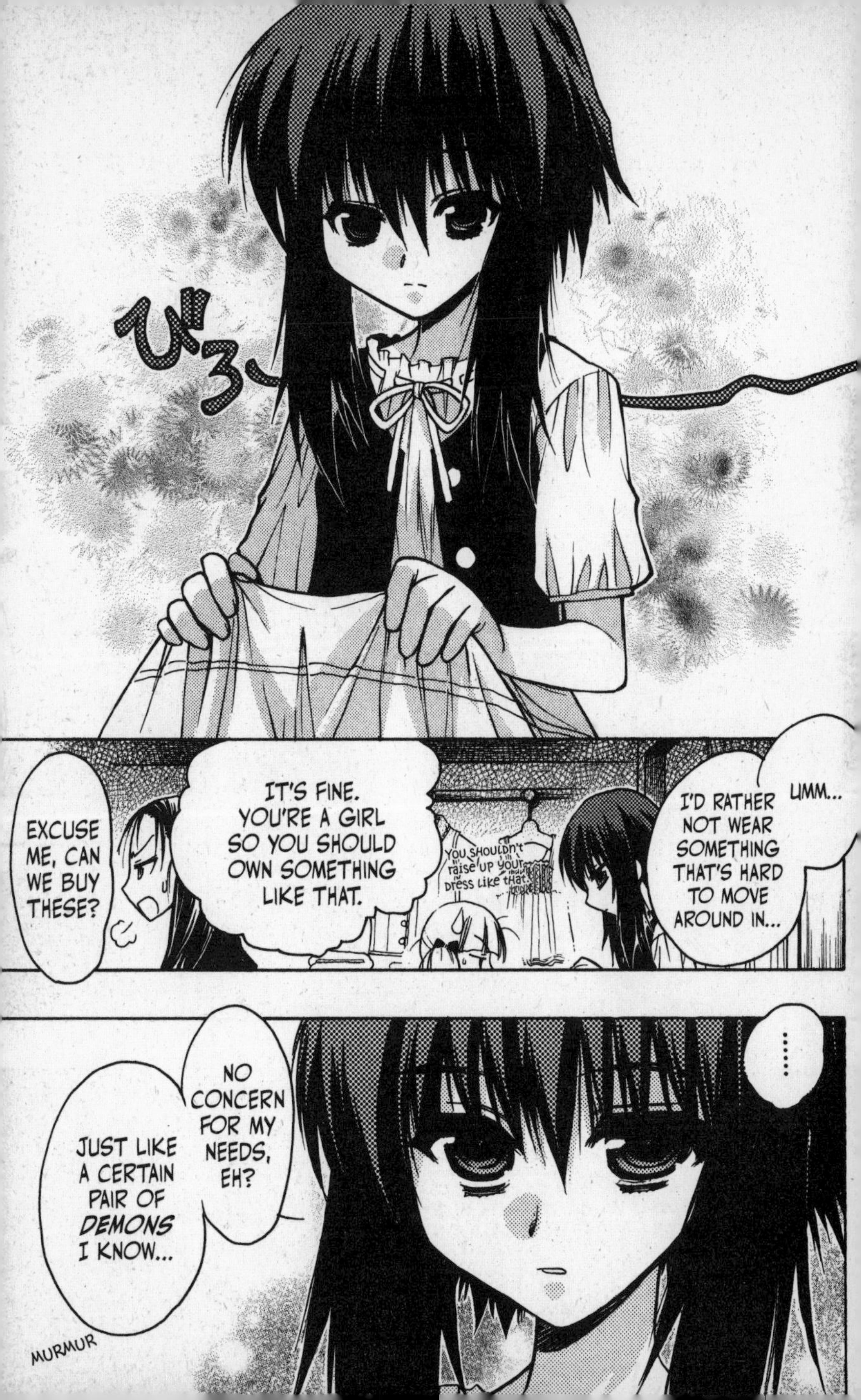
びろ〜
UMM...
I'D RATHER NOT WEAR SOMETHING THAT'S HARD TO MOVE AROUND IN...
You shouldn't raise up your dress like that
IT'S FINE. YOU'RE A GIRL SO YOU SHOULD OWN SOMETHING LIKE THAT.
EXCUSE ME, CAN WE BUY THESE?
......
NO CONCERN FOR MY NEEDS, EH?
JUST LIKE A CERTAIN PAIR OF *DEMONS* I KNOW...
MURMUR

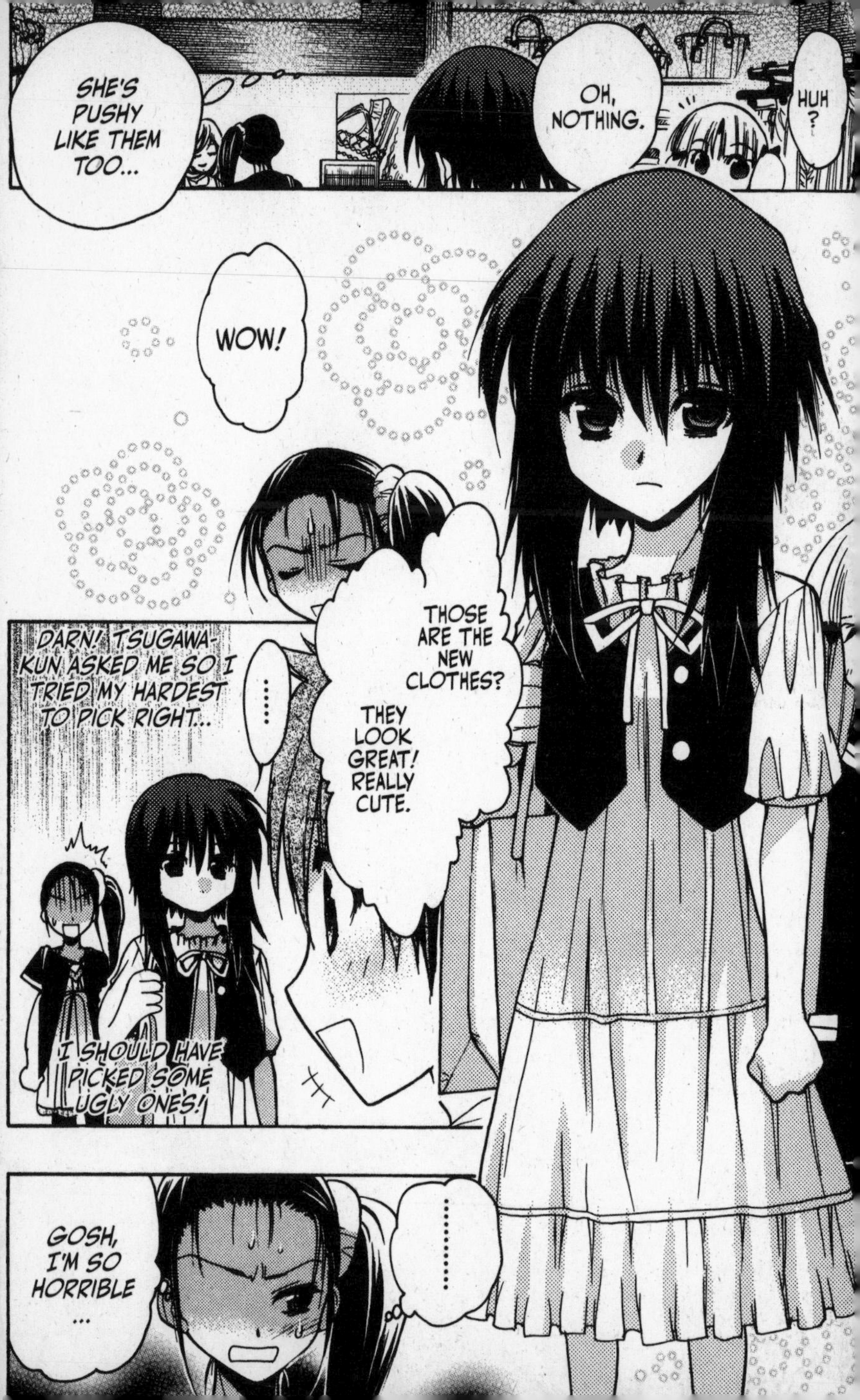
HUH ?
OH, NOTHING.
SHE'S PUSHY LIKE THEM TOO...
WOW!
THOSE ARE THE NEW CLOTHES?
THEY LOOK GREAT! REALLY CUTE.
......
DARN! TSUGAWA-KUN ASKED ME SO I TRIED MY HARDEST TO PICK RIGHT...
I SHOULD HAVE PICKED SOME UGLY ONES!
....
GOSH, I'M SO HORRIBLE ...

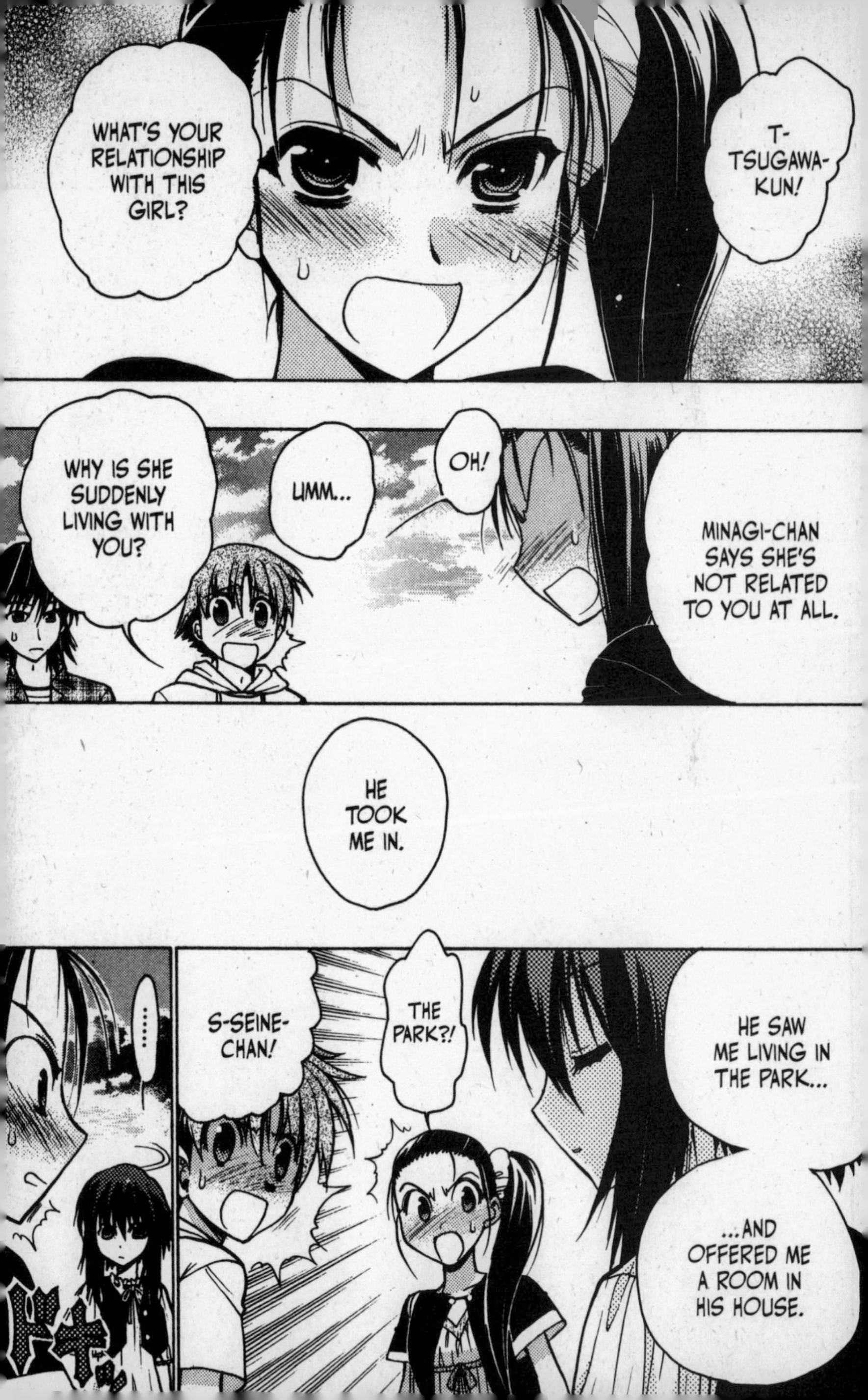
T-TSUGAWA-KUN!
WHAT'S YOUR RELATIONSHIP WITH THIS GIRL?
MINAGI-CHAN SAYS SHE'S NOT RELATED TO YOU AT ALL.
WHY IS SHE SUDDENLY LIVING WITH YOU?
OH!
UMM...
HE TOOK ME IN.
HE SAW ME LIVING IN THE PARK...
...AND OFFERED ME A ROOM IN HIS HOUSE.
THE PARK?!
S-SEINE-CHAN!
......
ドキ

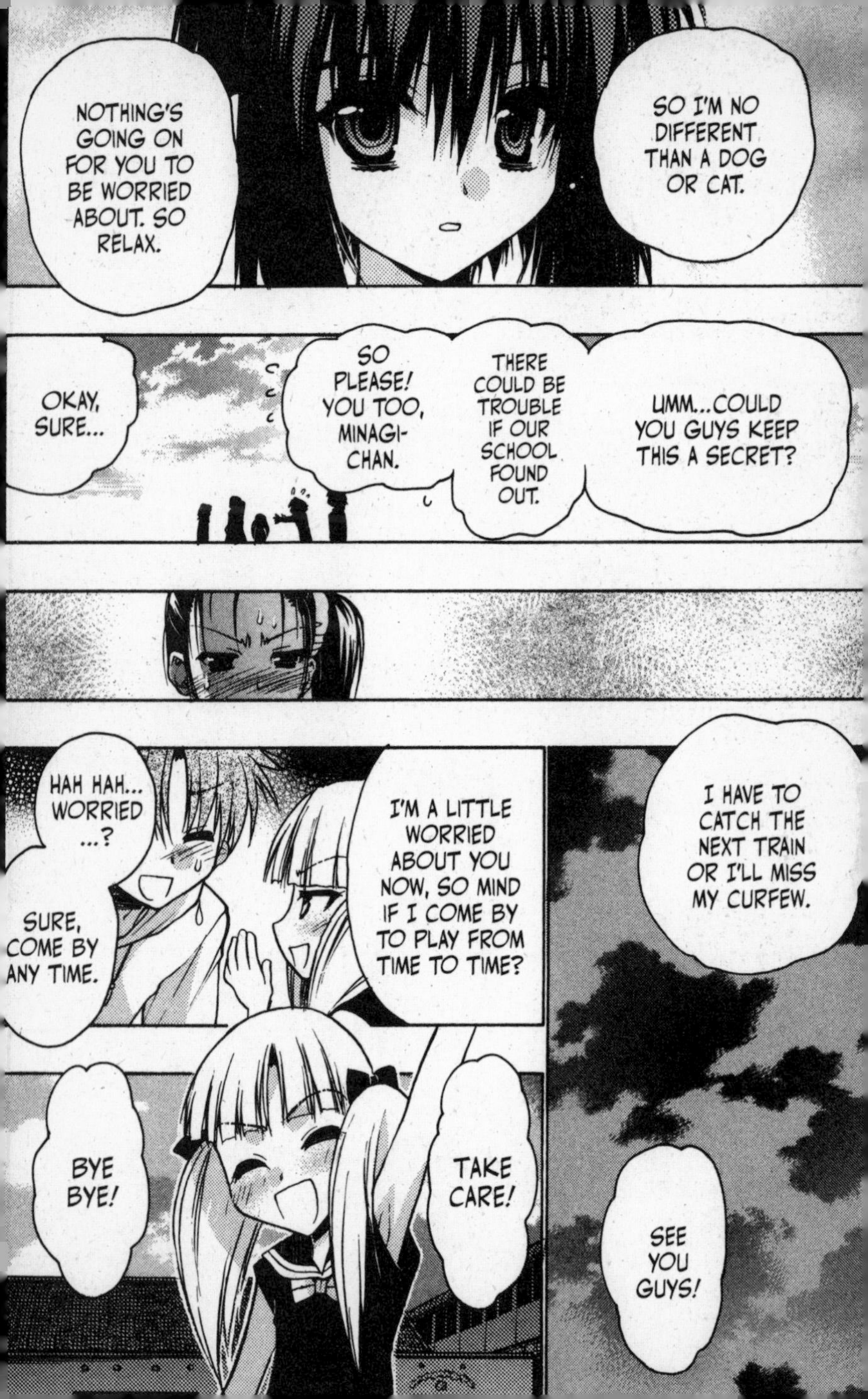
SO I'M NO DIFFERENT THAN A DOG OR CAT.
NOTHING'S GOING ON FOR YOU TO BE WORRIED ABOUT. SO RELAX.
UMM...COULD YOU GUYS KEEP THIS A SECRET?
THERE COULD BE TROUBLE IF OUR SCHOOL FOUND OUT.
SO PLEASE! YOU TOO, MINAGI-CHAN.
OKAY, SURE...
I HAVE TO CATCH THE NEXT TRAIN OR I'LL MISS MY CURFEW.
SEE YOU GUYS!
I'M A LITTLE WORRIED ABOUT YOU NOW, SO MIND IF I COME BY TO PLAY FROM TIME TO TIME?
HAH HAH... WORRIED ...?
SURE, COME BY ANY TIME.
TAKE CARE!
BYE BYE!

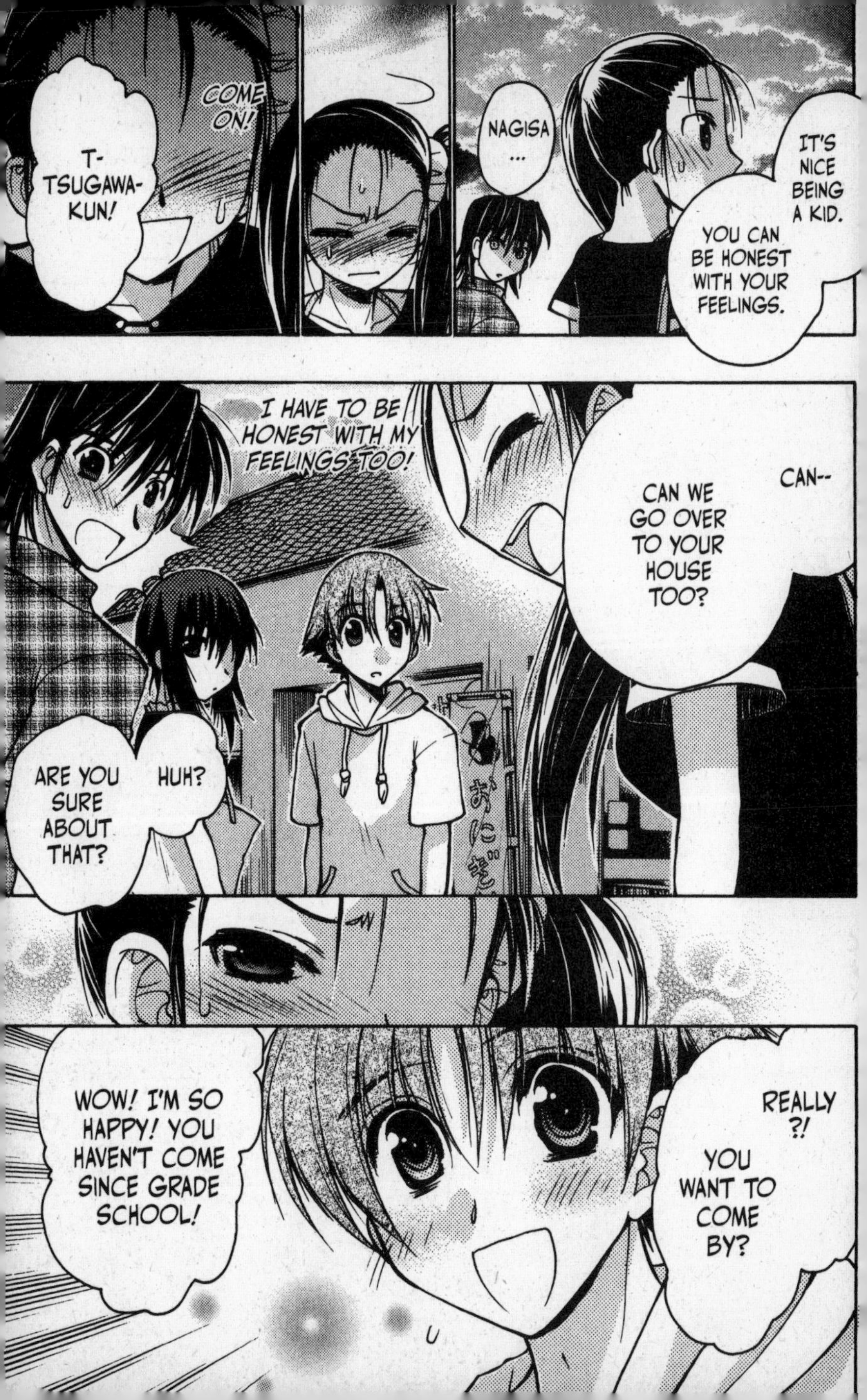
IT'S NICE BEING A KID.
YOU CAN BE HONEST WITH YOUR FEELINGS.
NAGISA ...
COME ON!
T-TSUGAWA-KUN!
CAN--
CAN WE GO OVER TO YOUR HOUSE TOO?
I HAVE TO BE HONEST WITH MY FEELINGS TOO!
HUH?
ARE YOU SURE ABOUT THAT?
REALLY?!
YOU WANT TO COME BY?
WOW! I'M SO HAPPY! YOU HAVEN'T COME SINCE GRADE SCHOOL!

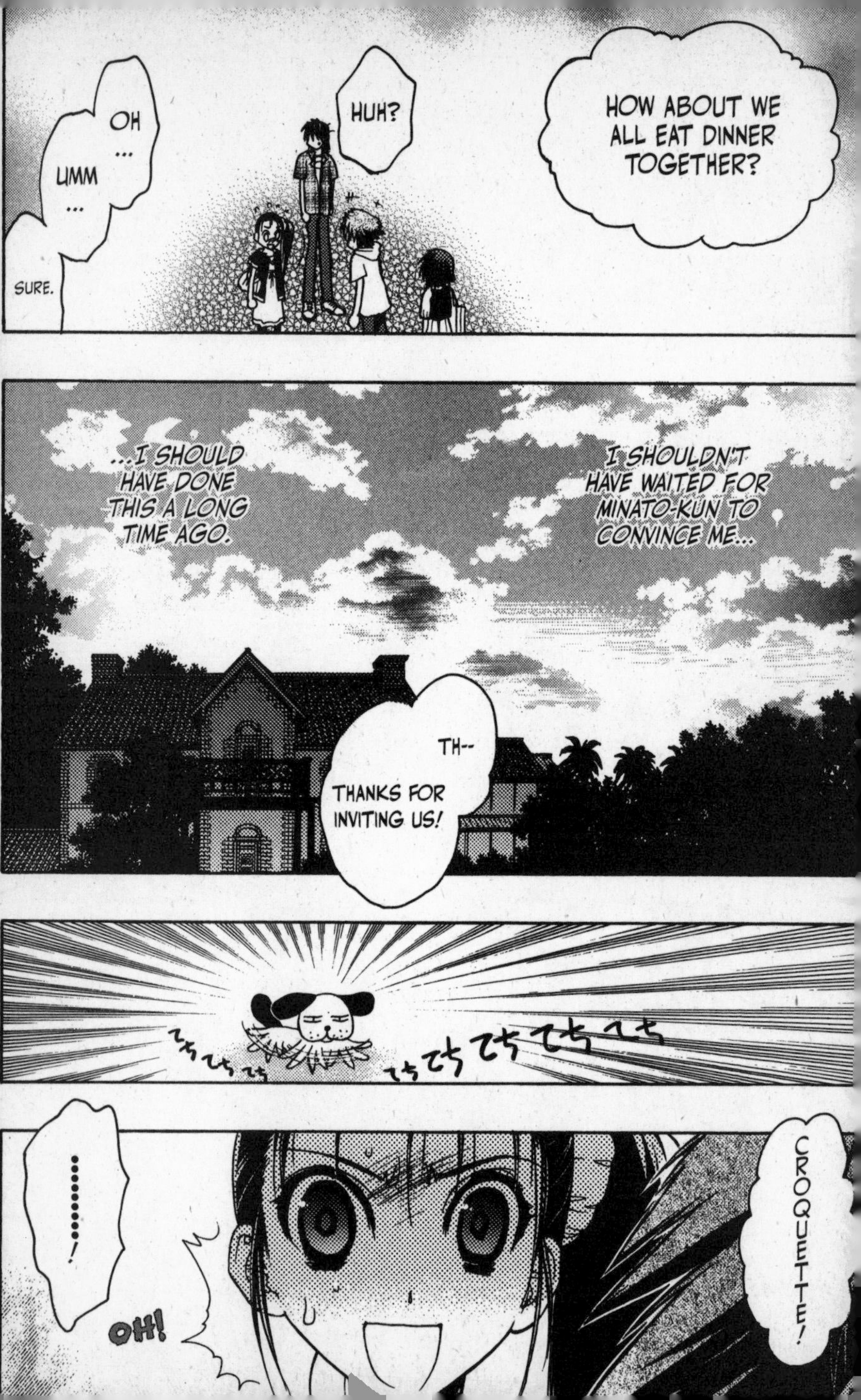
HOW ABOUT WE ALL EAT DINNER TOGETHER?
HUH?
OH ... UMM ... SURE.
I SHOULDN'T HAVE WAITED FOR MINATO-KUN TO CONVINCE ME...
...I SHOULD HAVE DONE THIS A LONG TIME AGO.
TH-- THANKS FOR INVITING US!
CROQUETTE!
OH!
.........!

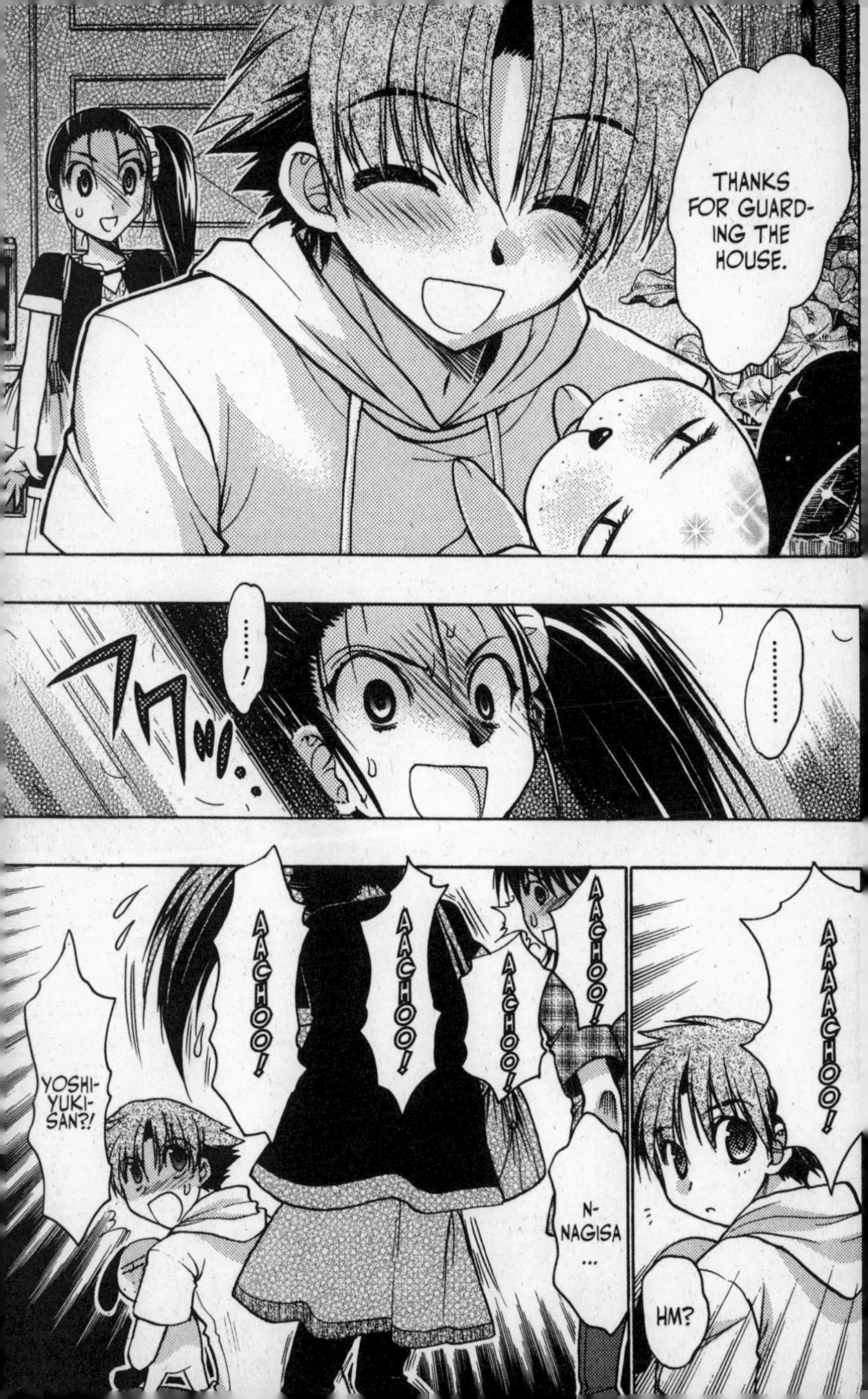
THANKS FOR GUARD-ING THE HOUSE.
....
......!
ヘクッ!!..
AAAACHOO!
HM?
AACHOO!
AACHOO!
AACHOO!
AACHOO!
N-NAGISA...
YOSHI-YUKI-SAN?!

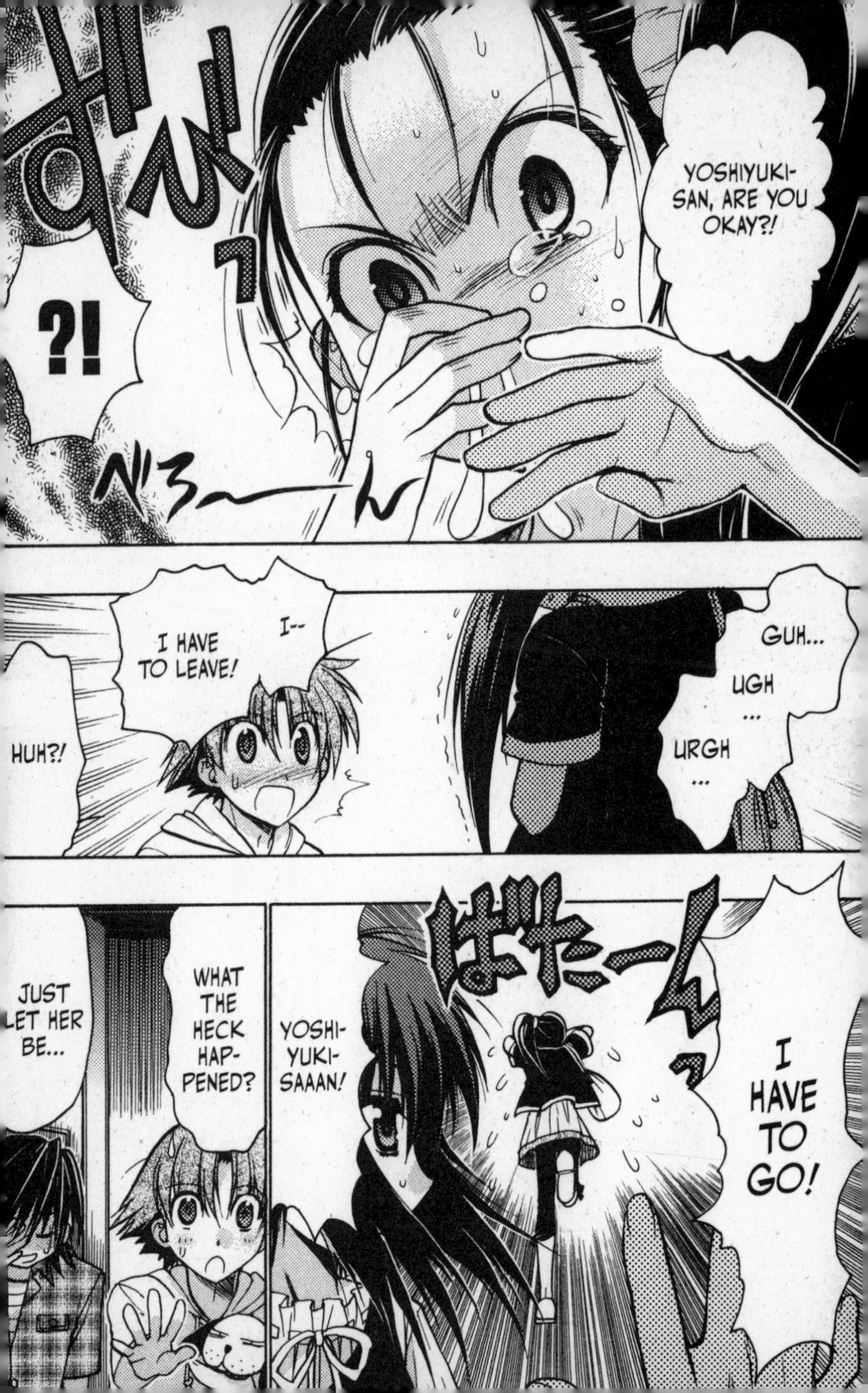
YOSHIYUKI-SAN, ARE YOU OKAY?!
ずびっ
?!
べろ〜〜ん
GUH... UGH... URGH...
I--
I HAVE TO LEAVE!
HUH?!
I HAVE TO GO!
ばたーん
YOSHI-YUKI-SAAAN!
WHAT THE HECK HAPPENED?
JUST LET HER BE...

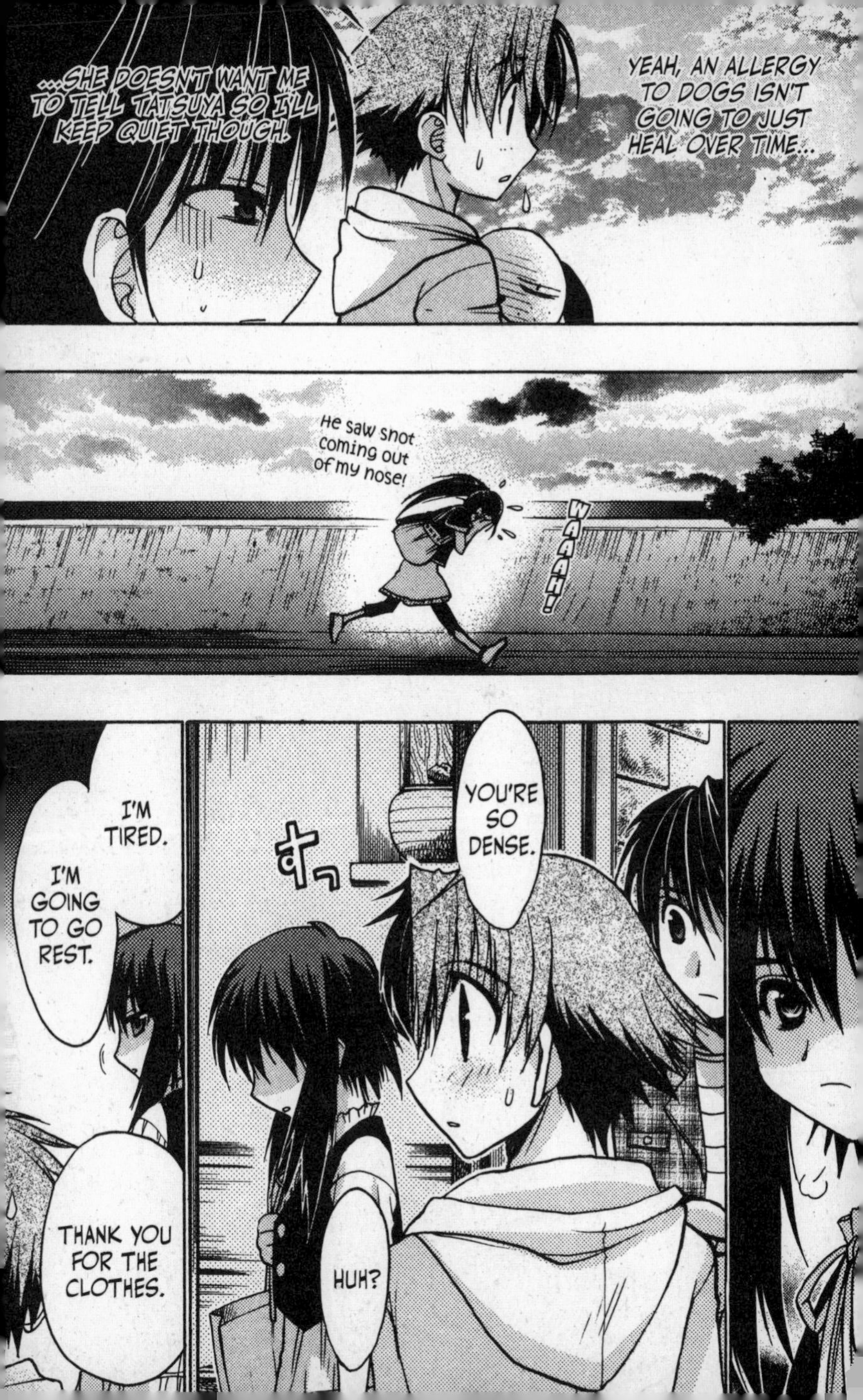
YEAH, AN ALLERGY TO DOGS ISN'T GOING TO JUST HEAL OVER TIME...
...SHE DOESN'T WANT ME TO TELL TATSUYA SO I'LL KEEP QUIET THOUGH.
He saw snot coming out of my nose!
WAAAAH!
YOU'RE SO DENSE.
すっ
HUH?
I'M TIRED. I'M GOING TO GO REST.
THANK YOU FOR THE CLOTHES.

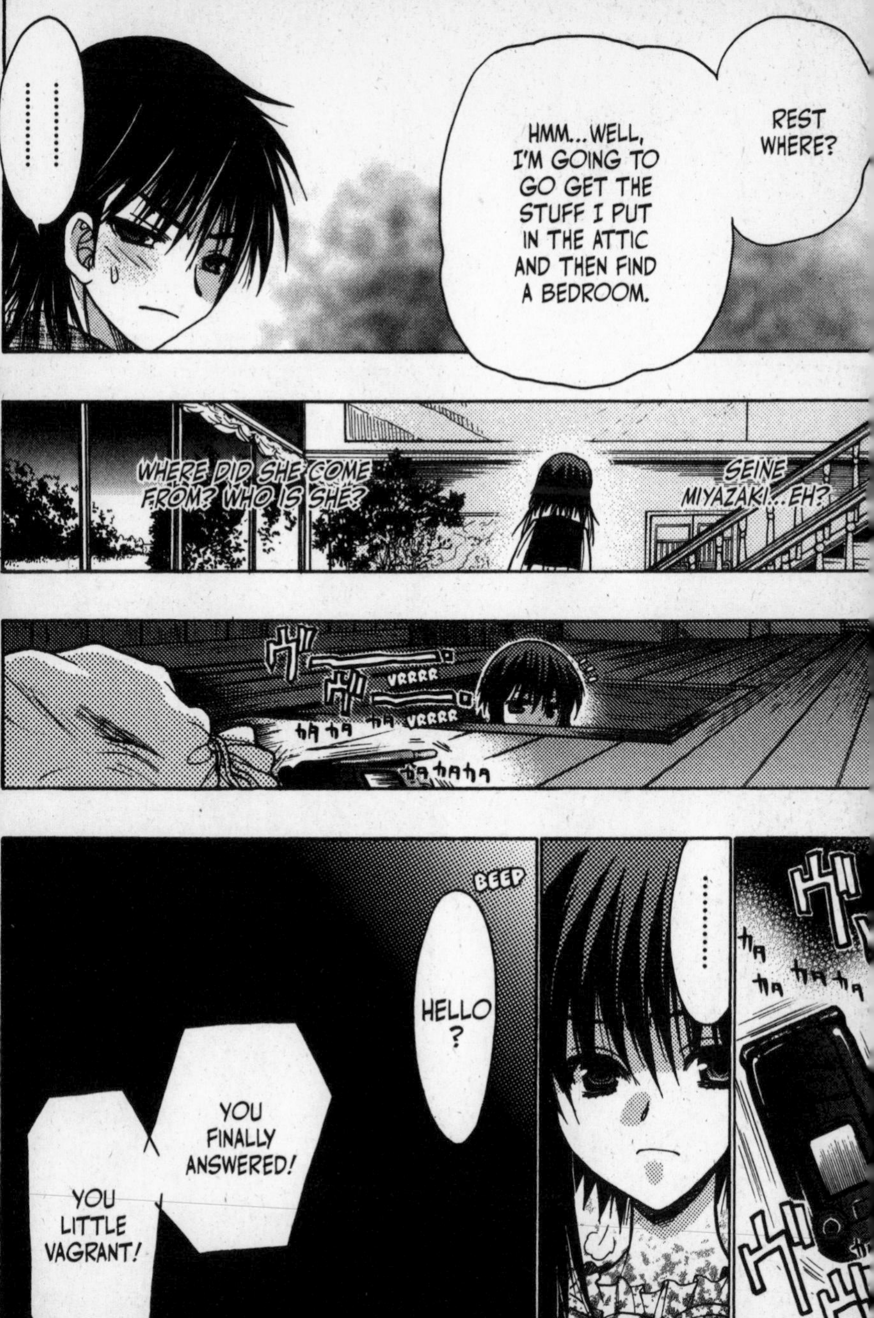
REST WHERE?
HMM...WELL, I'M GOING TO GO GET THE STUFF I PUT IN THE ATTIC AND THEN FIND A BEDROOM.
......
SEINE MIYAZAKI...EH?
WHERE DID SHE COME FROM? WHO IS SHE?
VRRRR
VRRRR
......
BEEP
HELLO?
YOU FINALLY ANSWERED!
YOU LITTLE VAGRANT!

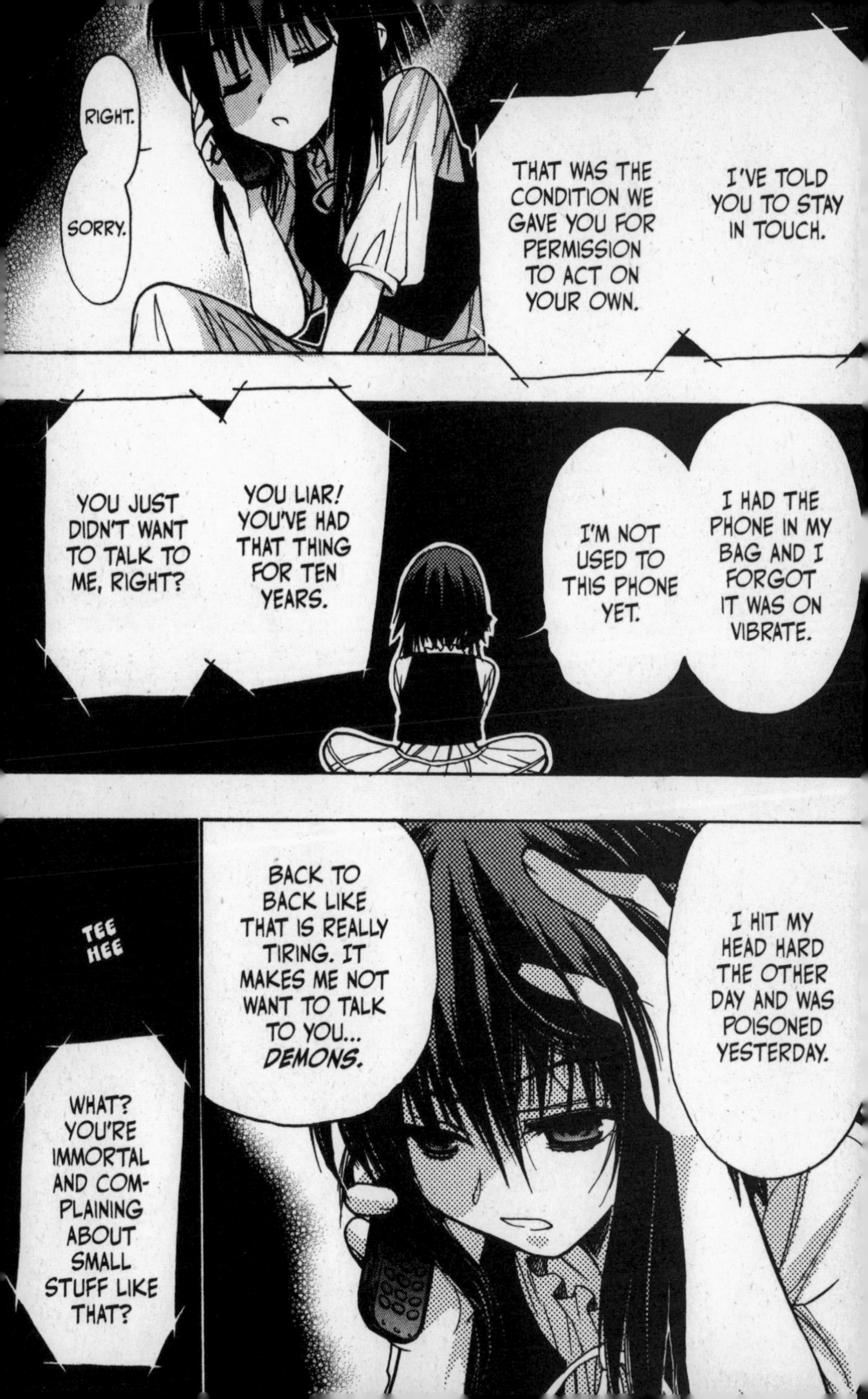
I'VE TOLD YOU TO STAY IN TOUCH.
THAT WAS THE CONDITION WE GAVE YOU FOR PERMISSION TO ACT ON YOUR OWN.
RIGHT.
SORRY.
I HAD THE PHONE IN MY BAG AND I FORGOT IT WAS ON VIBRATE.
I'M NOT USED TO THIS PHONE YET.
YOU LIAR! YOU'VE HAD THAT THING FOR TEN YEARS.
YOU JUST DIDN'T WANT TO TALK TO ME, RIGHT?
I HIT MY HEAD HARD THE OTHER DAY AND WAS POISONED YESTERDAY.
BACK TO BACK LIKE THAT IS REALLY TIRING. IT MAKES ME NOT WANT TO TALK TO YOU... *DEMONS.*
TEE HEE
WHAT? YOU'RE IMMORTAL AND COM-PLAINING ABOUT SMALL STUFF LIKE THAT?

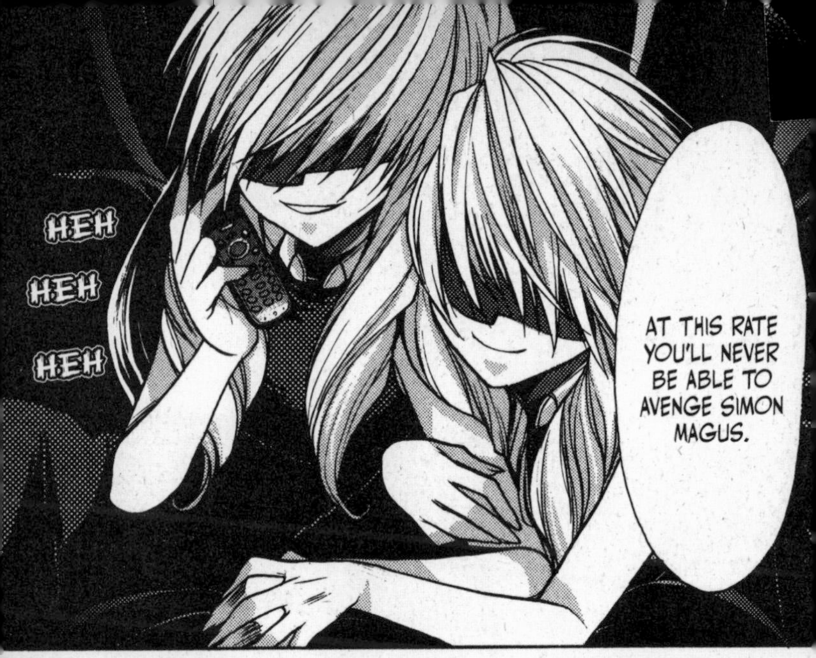
AT THIS RATE YOU'LL NEVER BE ABLE TO AVENGE SIMON MAGUS.
HEH
HEH
HEH

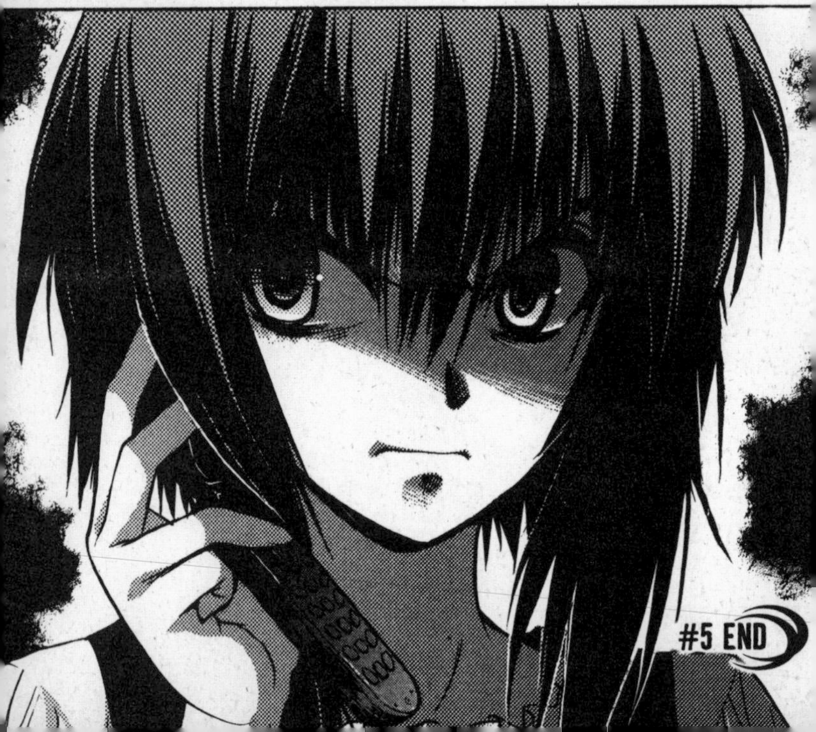
#5 END

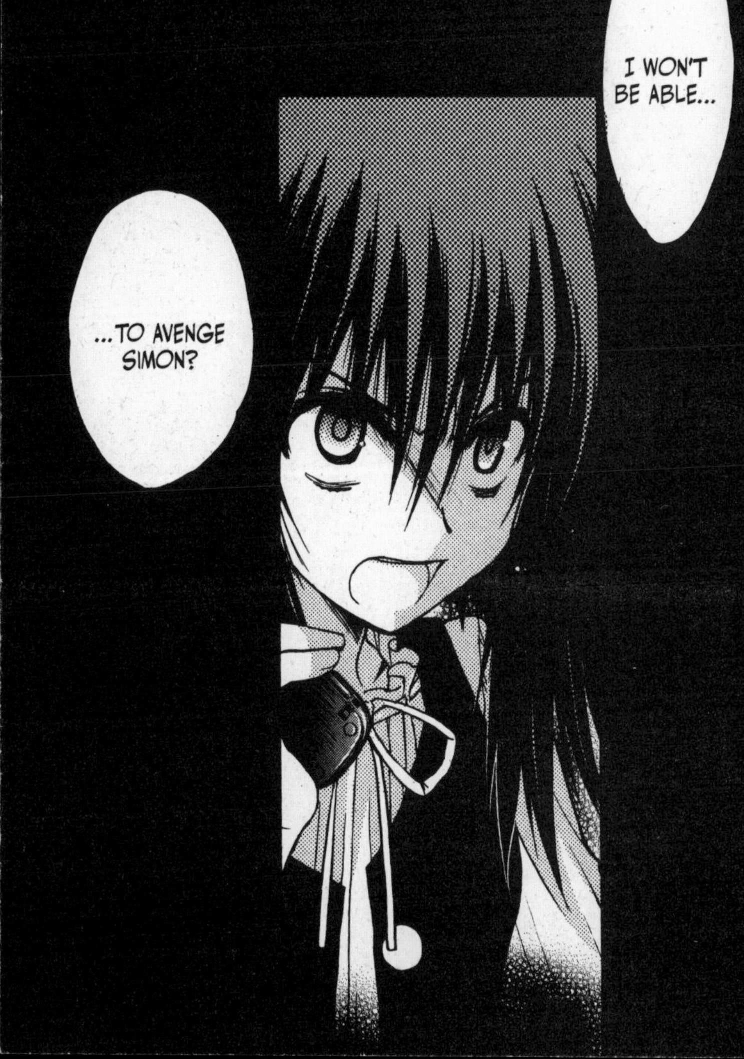
I WON'T BE ABLE...
...TO AVENGE SIMON?

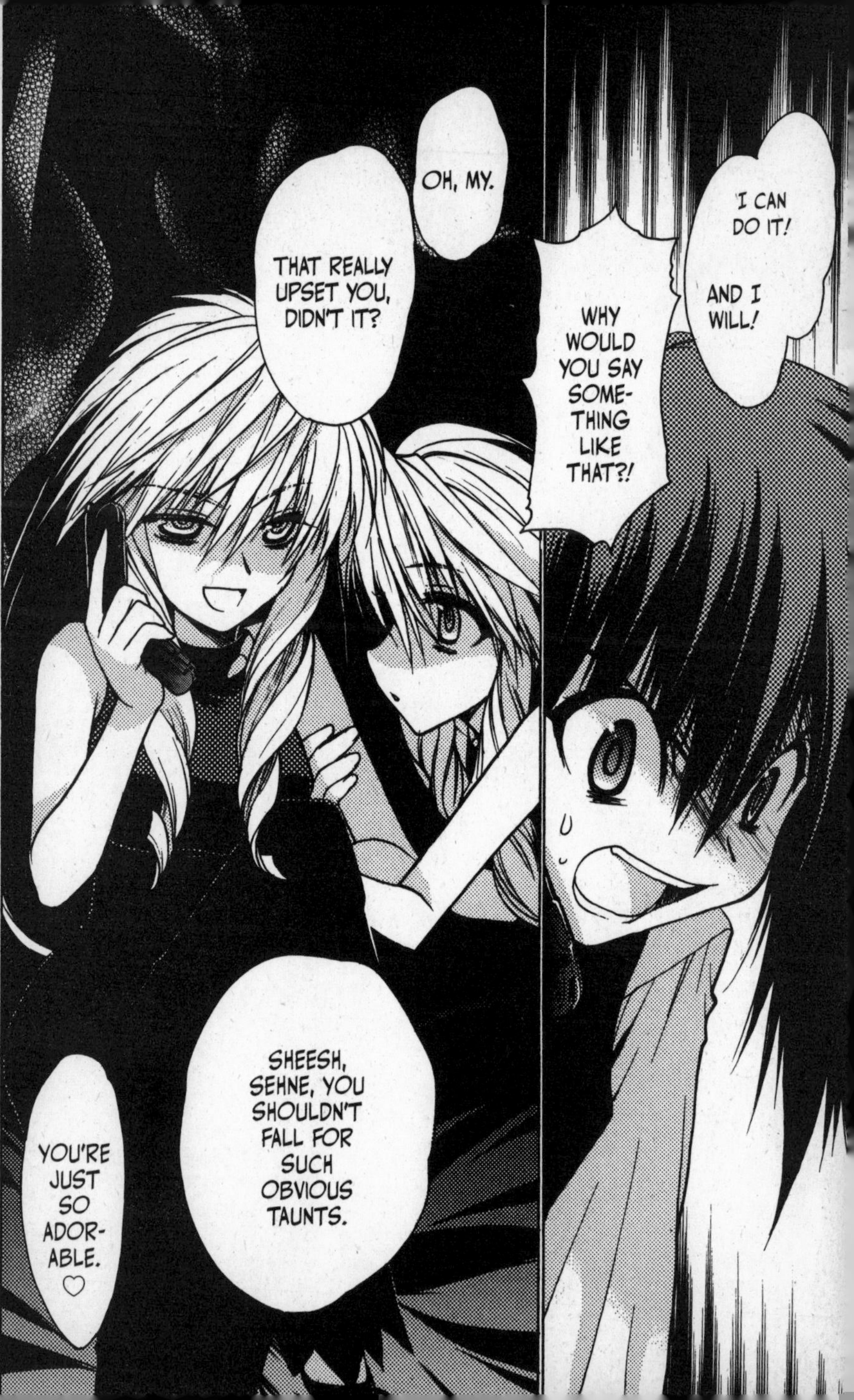
I CAN DO IT! AND I WILL!
WHY WOULD YOU SAY SOME-THING LIKE THAT?!
OH, MY.
THAT REALLY UPSET YOU, DIDN'T IT?
SHEESH, SEHNE, YOU SHOULDN'T FALL FOR SUCH OBVIOUS TAUNTS.
YOU'RE JUST SO ADOR-ABLE. ♡

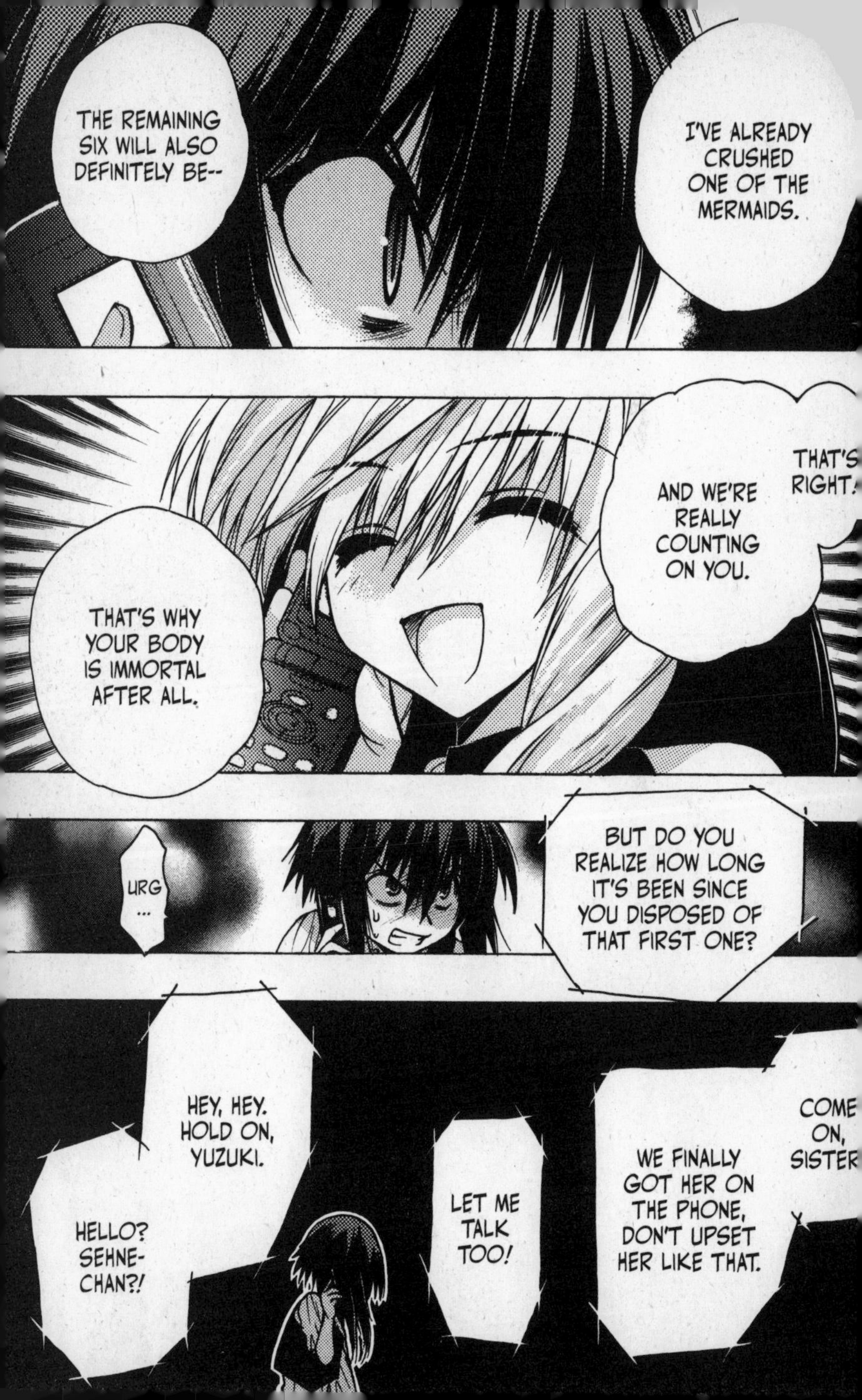
I'VE ALREADY CRUSHED ONE OF THE MERMAIDS.
THE REMAINING SIX WILL ALSO DEFINITELY BE--
THAT'S RIGHT
AND WE'RE REALLY COUNTING ON YOU.
THAT'S WHY YOUR BODY IS IMMORTAL AFTER ALL.
BUT DO YOU REALIZE HOW LONG IT'S BEEN SINCE YOU DISPOSED OF THAT FIRST ONE?
URG ...
COME ON, SISTER
WE FINALLY GOT HER ON THE PHONE, DON'T UPSET HER LIKE THAT.
LET ME TALK TOO!
HEY, HEY. HOLD ON, YUZUKI.
HELLO? SEHNE-CHAN?!

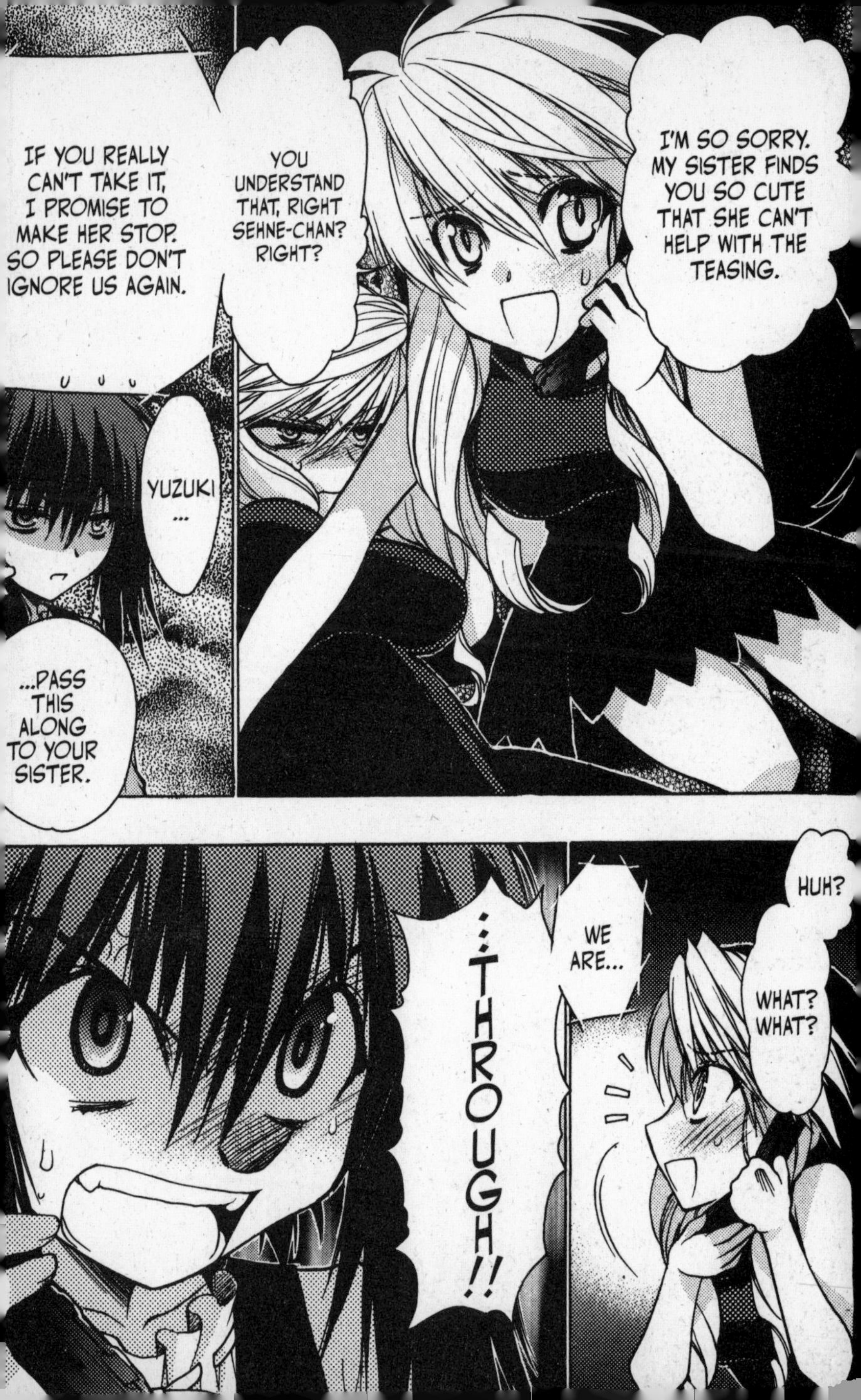
I'M SO SORRY. MY SISTER FINDS YOU SO CUTE THAT SHE CAN'T HELP WITH THE TEASING.
YOU UNDERSTAND THAT, RIGHT SEHNE-CHAN? RIGHT?
IF YOU REALLY CAN'T TAKE IT, I PROMISE TO MAKE HER STOP. SO PLEASE DON'T IGNORE US AGAIN.
YUZUKI ...
...PASS THIS ALONG TO YOUR SISTER.
HUH?
WHAT? WHAT?
WE ARE...
...THROUGH!!

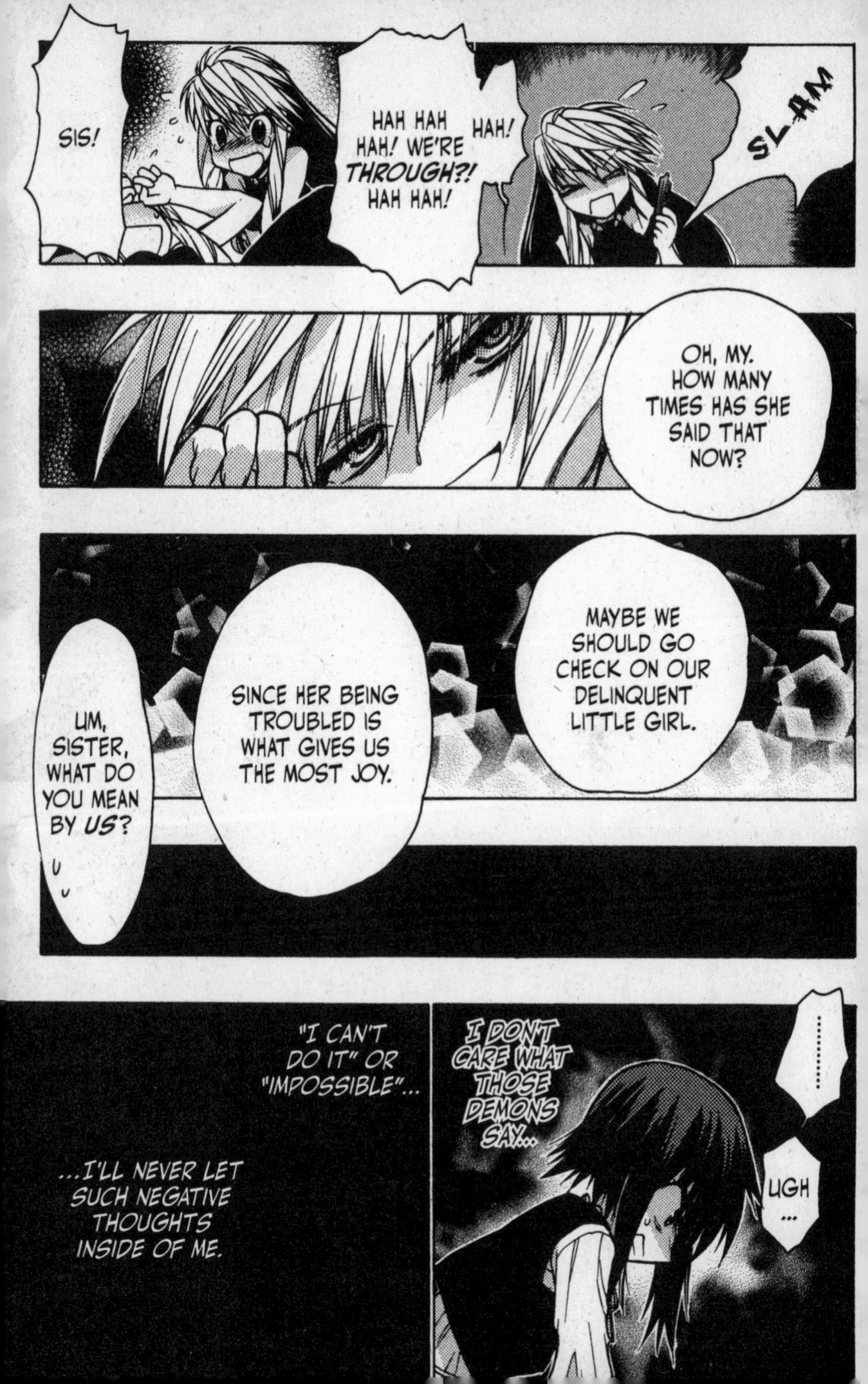
SLAM
HAH HAH HAH! WE'RE THROUGH?! HAH HAH!
SIS!
OH, MY. HOW MANY TIMES HAS SHE SAID THAT NOW?
MAYBE WE SHOULD GO CHECK ON OUR DELINQUENT LITTLE GIRL.
SINCE HER BEING TROUBLED IS WHAT GIVES US THE MOST JOY.
UM, SISTER, WHAT DO YOU MEAN BY US?
......
I DON'T CARE WHAT THOSE DEMONS SAY...
UGH ...
"I CAN'T DO IT" OR "IMPOSSIBLE"...
...I'LL NEVER LET SUCH NEGATIVE THOUGHTS INSIDE OF ME.

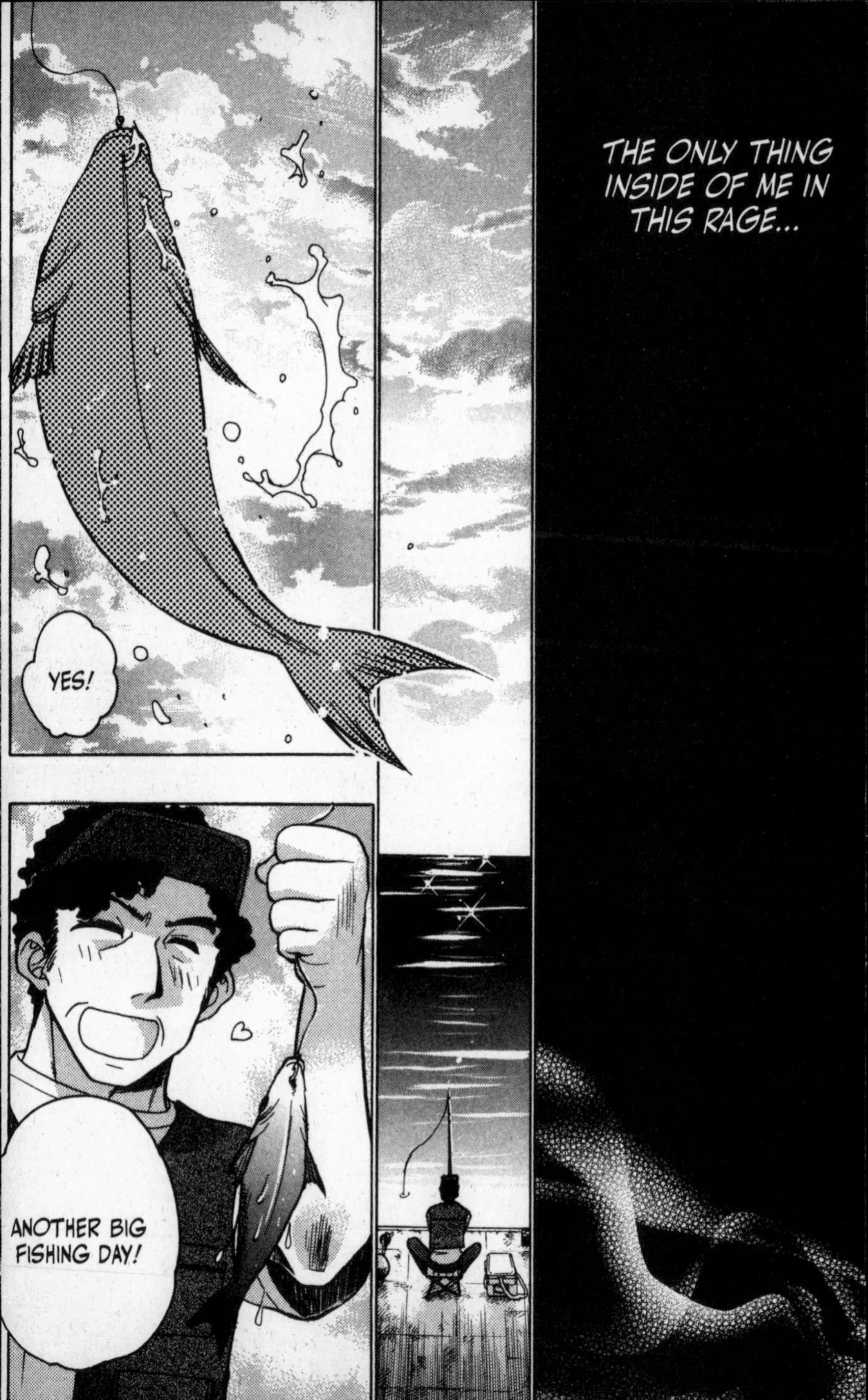
THE ONLY THING INSIDE OF ME IN THIS RAGE...
YES!
ANOTHER BIG FISHING DAY!

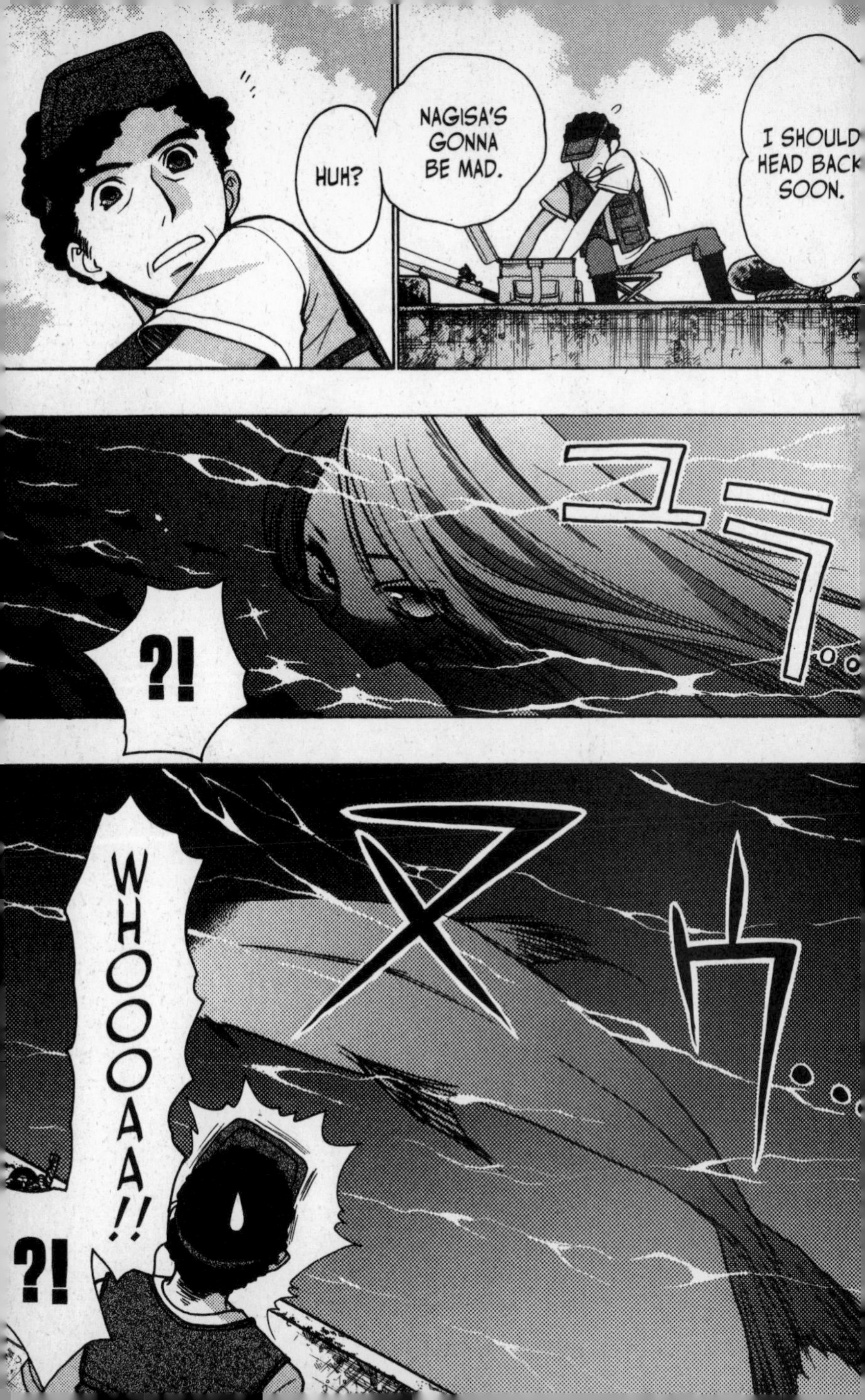
I SHOULD HEAD BACK SOON.
NAGISA'S GONNA BE MAD.
HUH?
ユラ…
?!
ヌウ…
WHOOOAA!!
?!

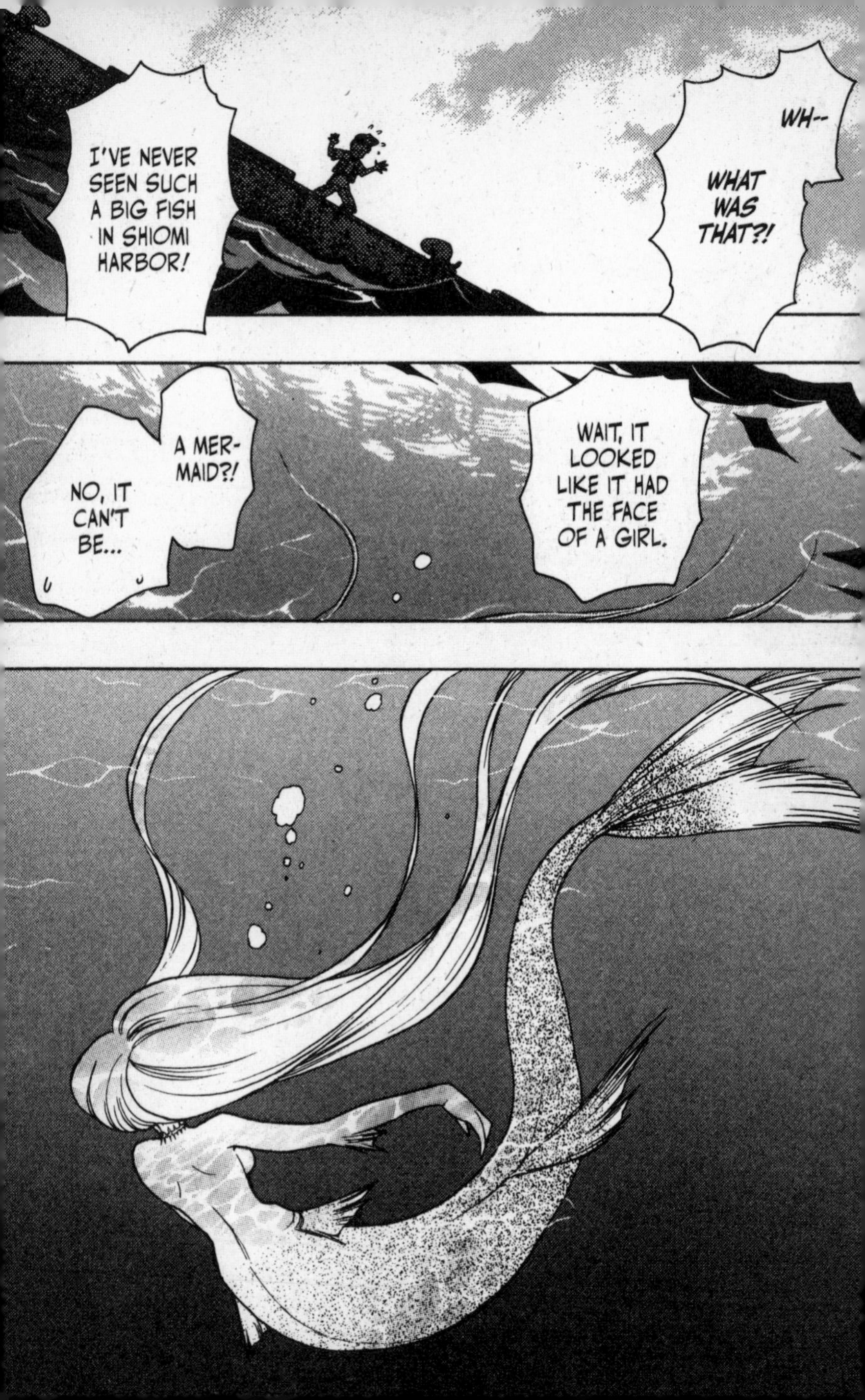
WH-- WHAT WAS THAT?!
I'VE NEVER SEEN SUCH A BIG FISH IN SHIOMI HARBOR!
WAIT, IT LOOKED LIKE IT HAD THE FACE OF A GIRL.
A MER-MAID?!
NO, IT CAN'T BE...

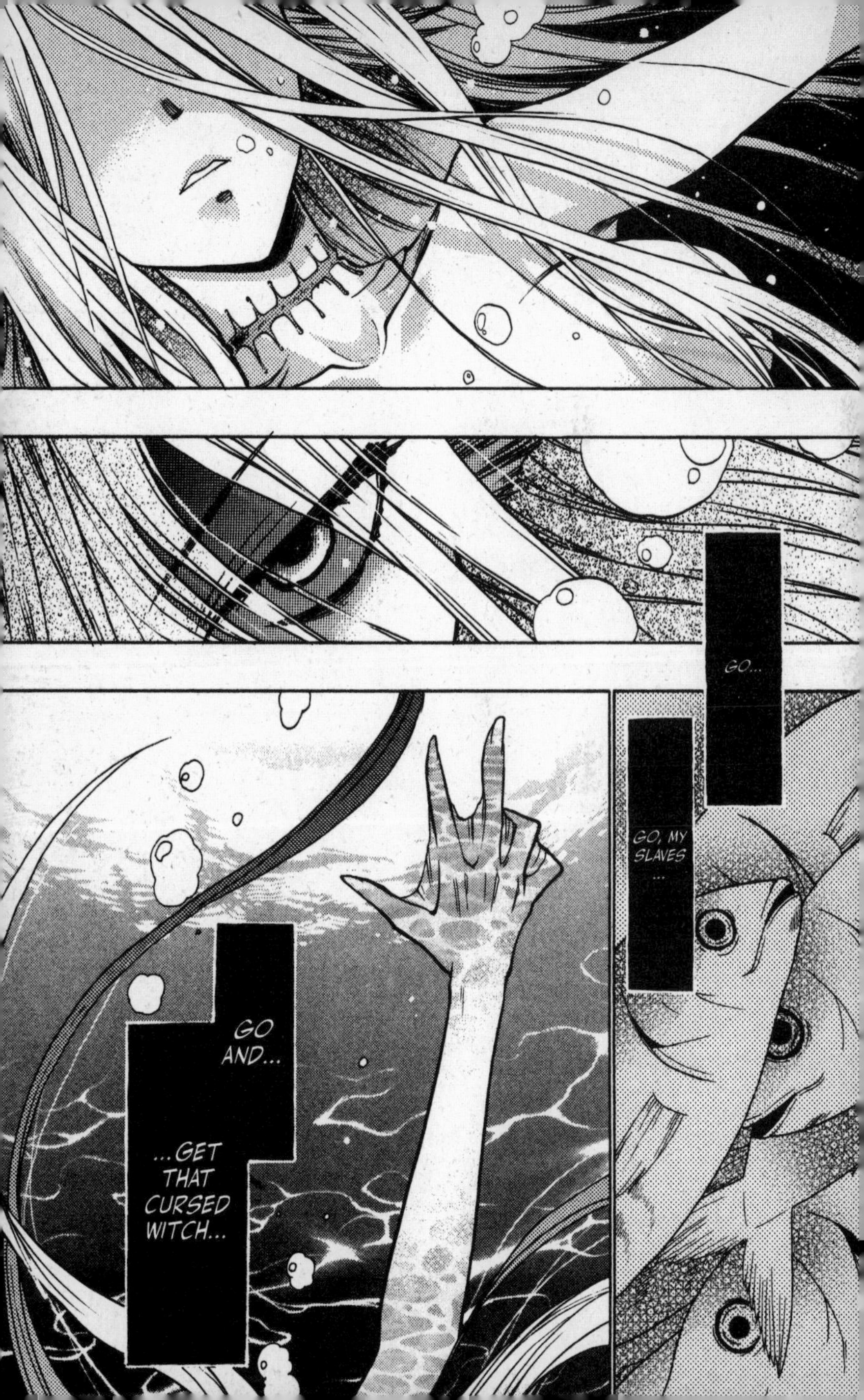
GO...
GO, MY SLAVES ...
GO AND...
...GET THAT CURSED WITCH...

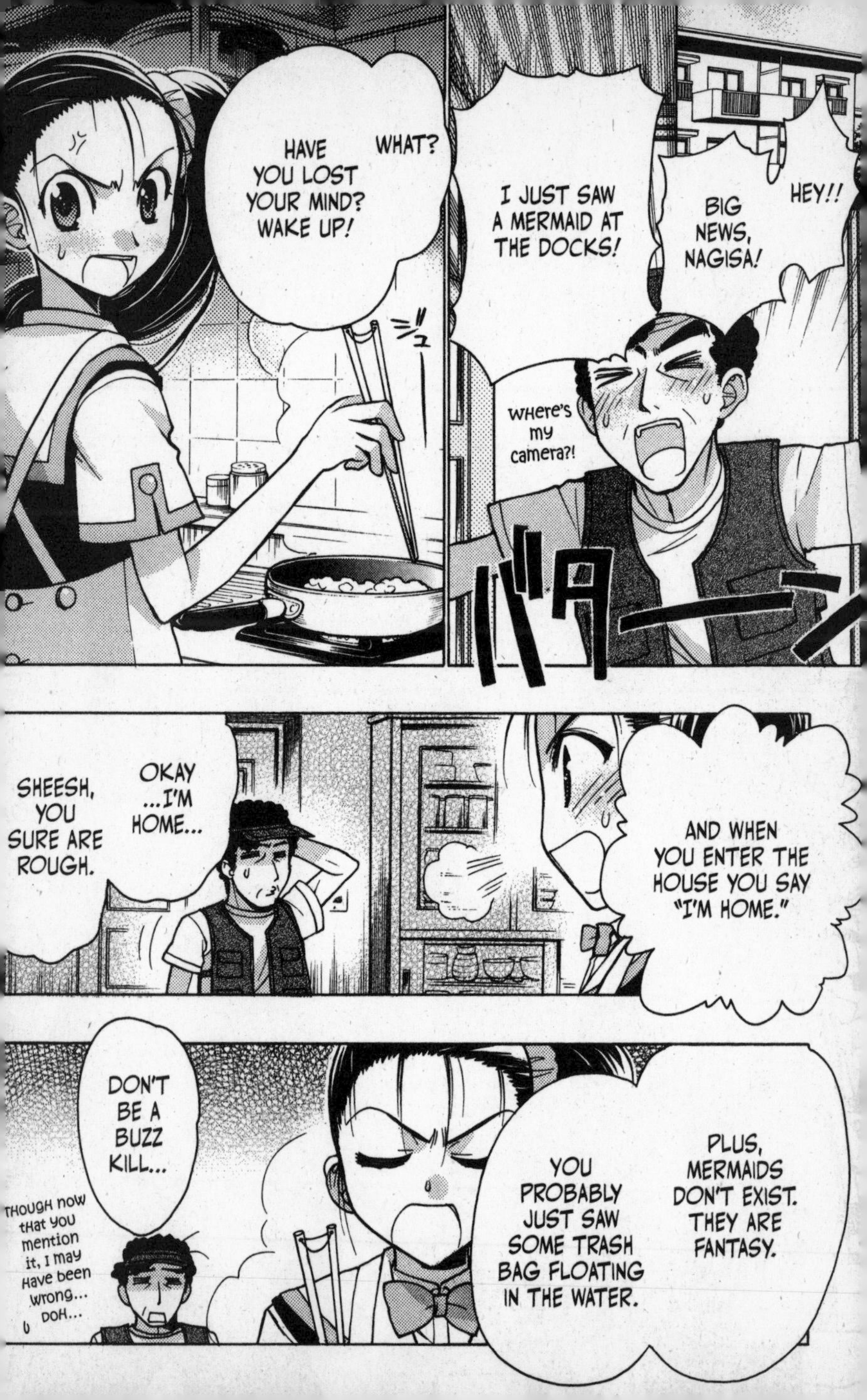
HEY!!
BIG NEWS, NAGISA!
I JUST SAW A MERMAID AT THE DOCKS!
Where's my camera?!
バターン
WHAT?
HAVE YOU LOST YOUR MIND? WAKE UP!
ジュ
AND WHEN YOU ENTER THE HOUSE YOU SAY "I'M HOME."
OKAY ...I'M HOME...
SHEESH, YOU SURE ARE ROUGH.
PLUS, MERMAIDS DON'T EXIST. THEY ARE FANTASY.
YOU PROBABLY JUST SAW SOME TRASH BAG FLOATING IN THE WATER.
DON'T BE A BUZZ KILL...
Though now that you mention it, I may have been wrong... DOH...

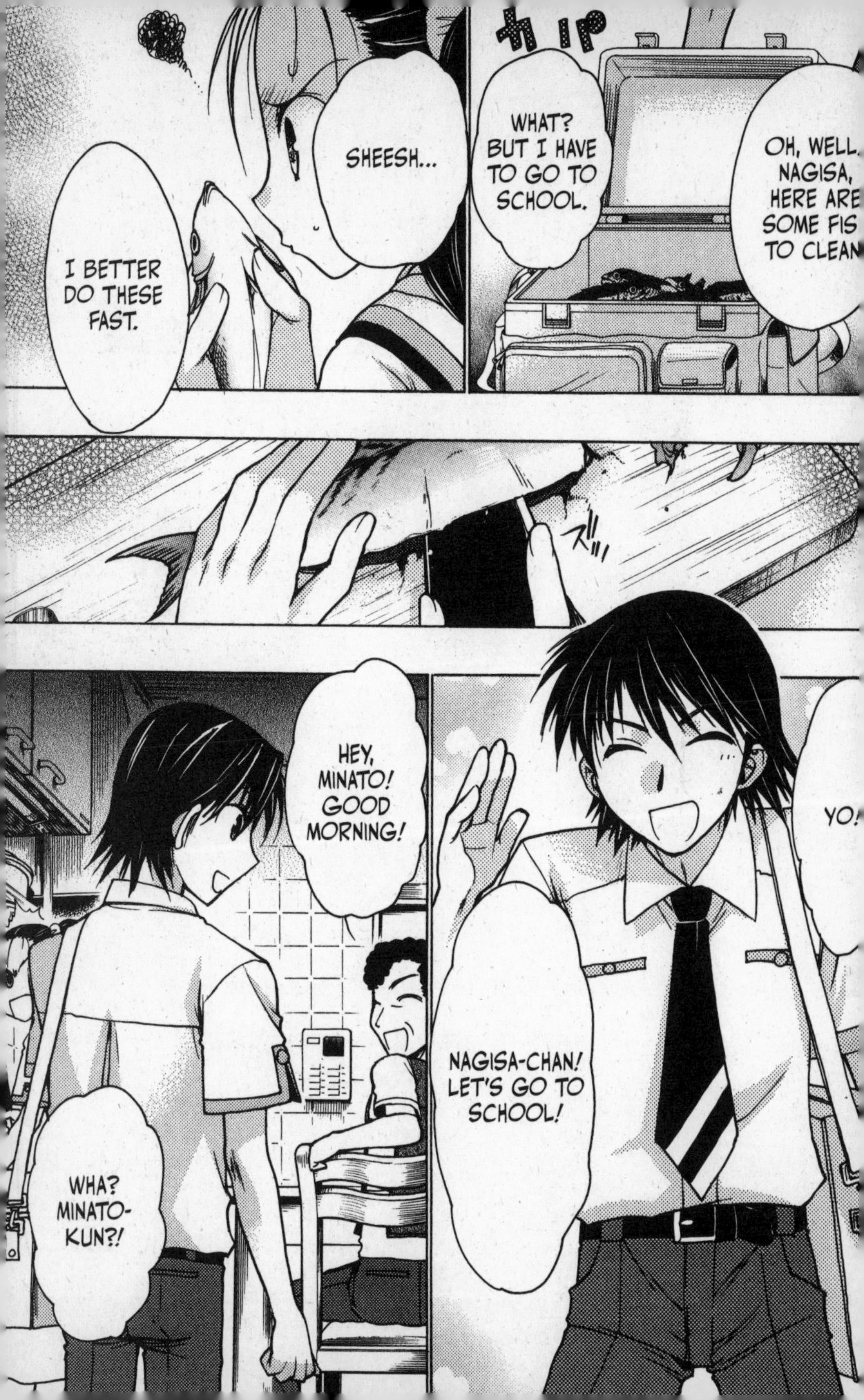
カパ
OH, WELL. NAGISA, HERE ARE SOME FIS TO CLEAN
WHAT? BUT I HAVE TO GO TO SCHOOL.
SHEESH...
I BETTER DO THESE FAST.
YO!
NAGISA-CHAN! LET'S GO TO SCHOOL!
HEY, MINATO! GOOD MORNING!
WHA? MINATO-KUN?!

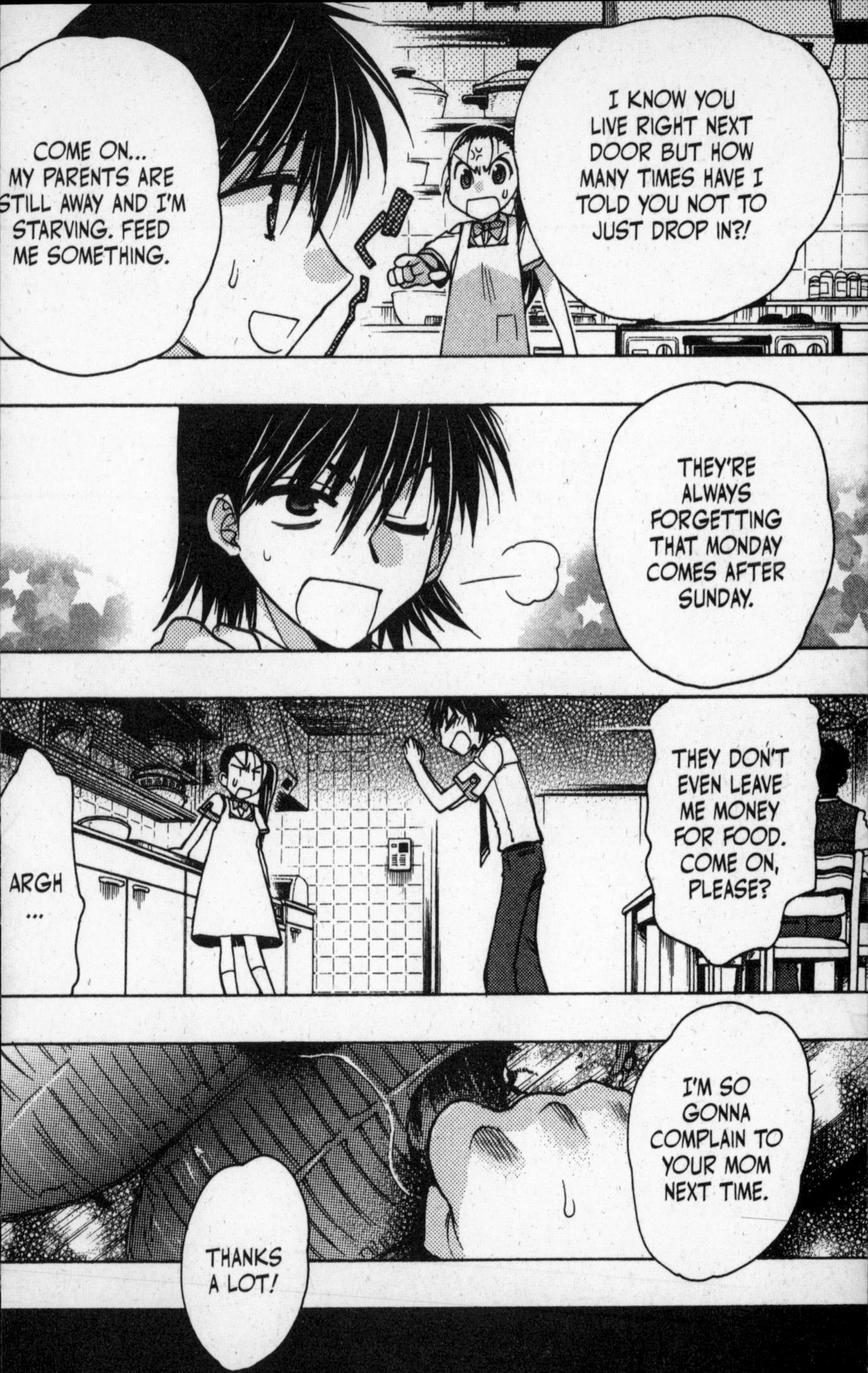

I KNOW YOU LIVE RIGHT NEXT DOOR BUT HOW MANY TIMES HAVE I TOLD YOU NOT TO JUST DROP IN?!
COME ON... MY PARENTS ARE STILL AWAY AND I'M STARVING. FEED ME SOMETHING.
THEY'RE ALWAYS FORGETTING THAT MONDAY COMES AFTER SUNDAY.
THEY DON'T EVEN LEAVE ME MONEY FOR FOOD. COME ON, PLEASE?
ARGH ...
I'M SO GONNA COMPLAIN TO YOUR MOM NEXT TIME.
THANKS A LOT!

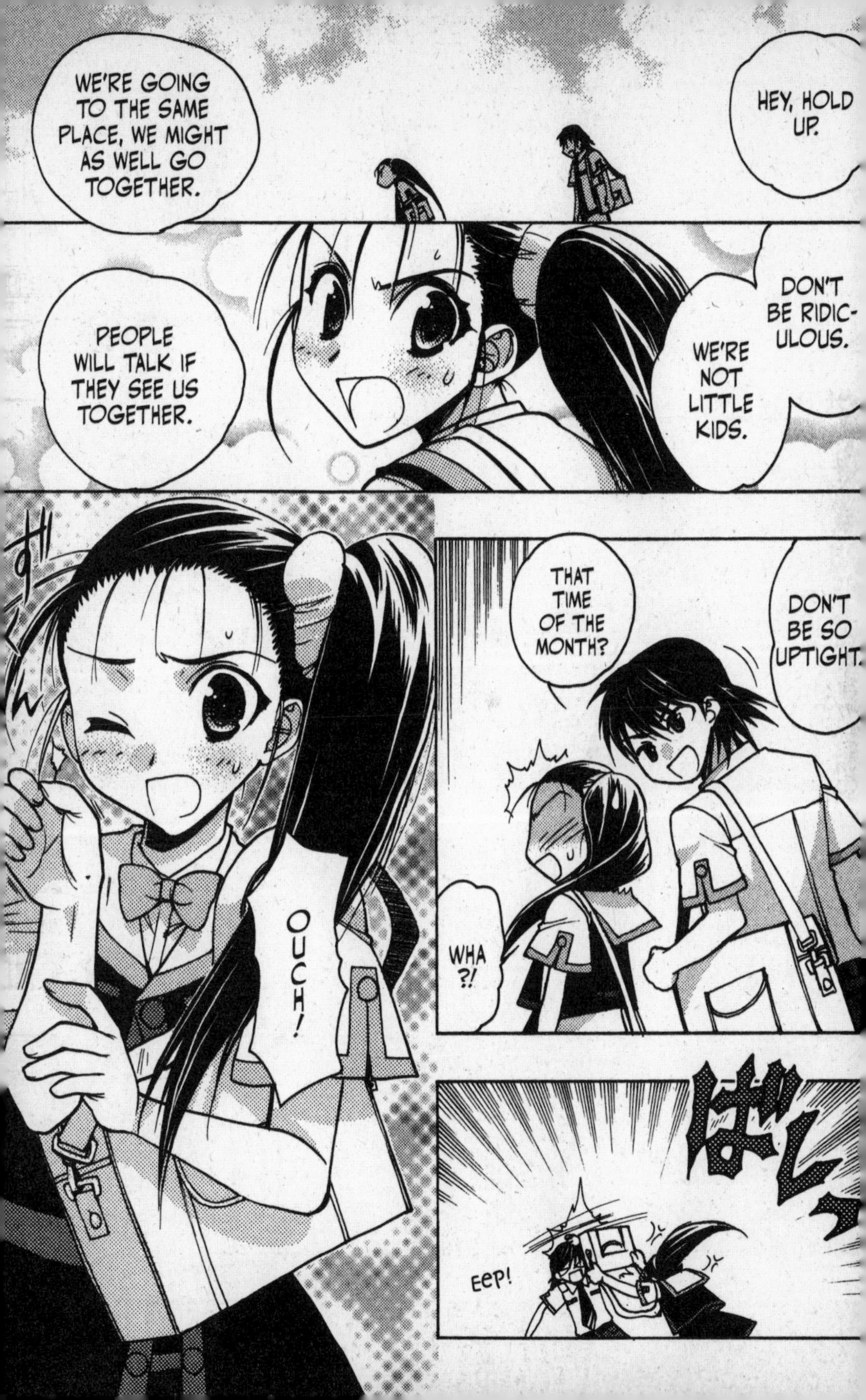
HEY, HOLD UP.
WE'RE GOING TO THE SAME PLACE, WE MIGHT AS WELL GO TOGETHER.
DON'T BE RIDICULOUS.
WE'RE NOT LITTLE KIDS.
PEOPLE WILL TALK IF THEY SEE US TOGETHER.
DON'T BE SO UPTIGHT.
THAT TIME OF THE MONTH?
WHA?!
ばしっ
EEP!
OUCH!

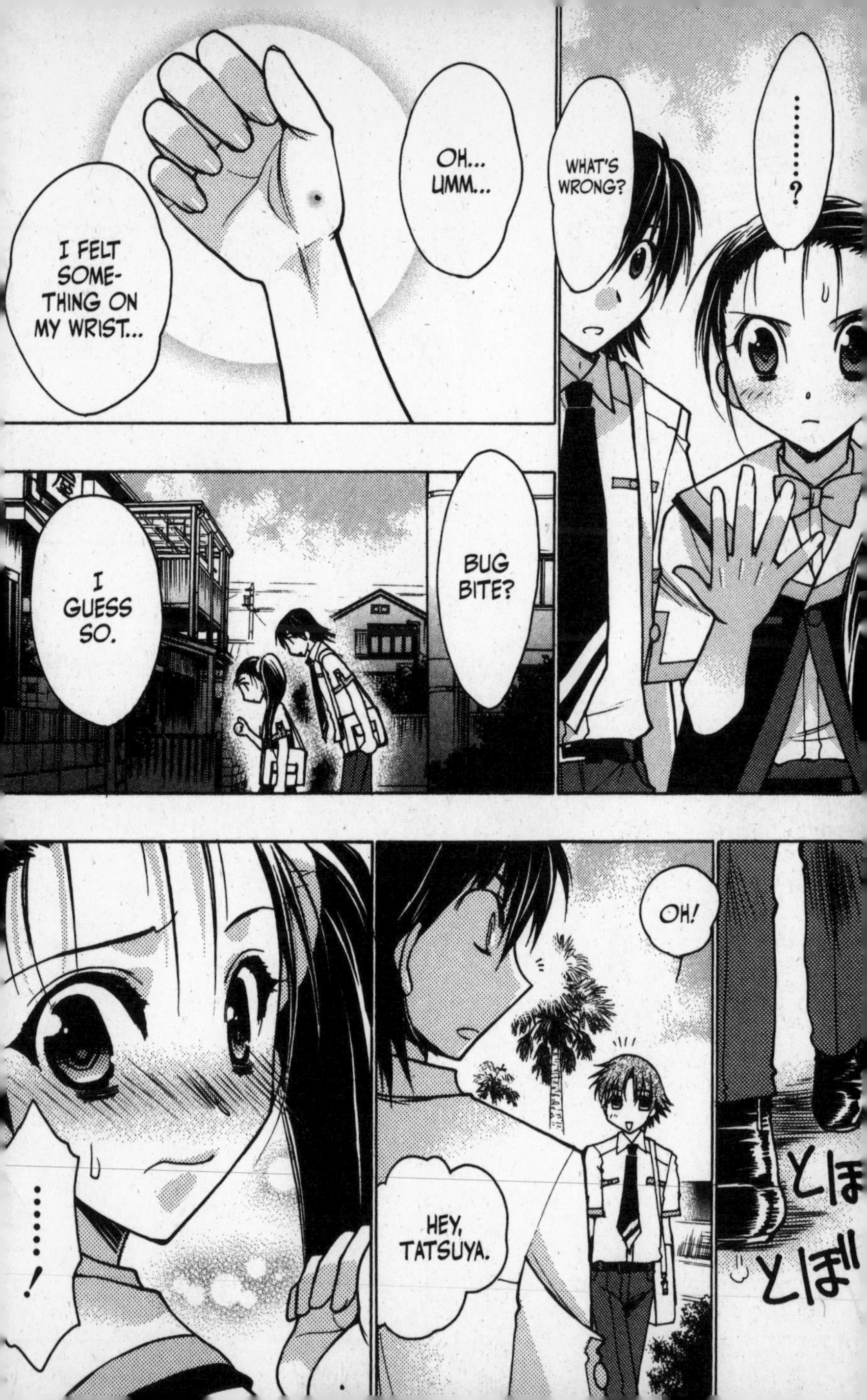
......?
WHAT'S WRONG?
OH... UMM...
I FELT SOME-THING ON MY WRIST...
BUG BITE?
I GUESS SO.
とぼ とぼ
OH!
HEY, TATSUYA.
......!

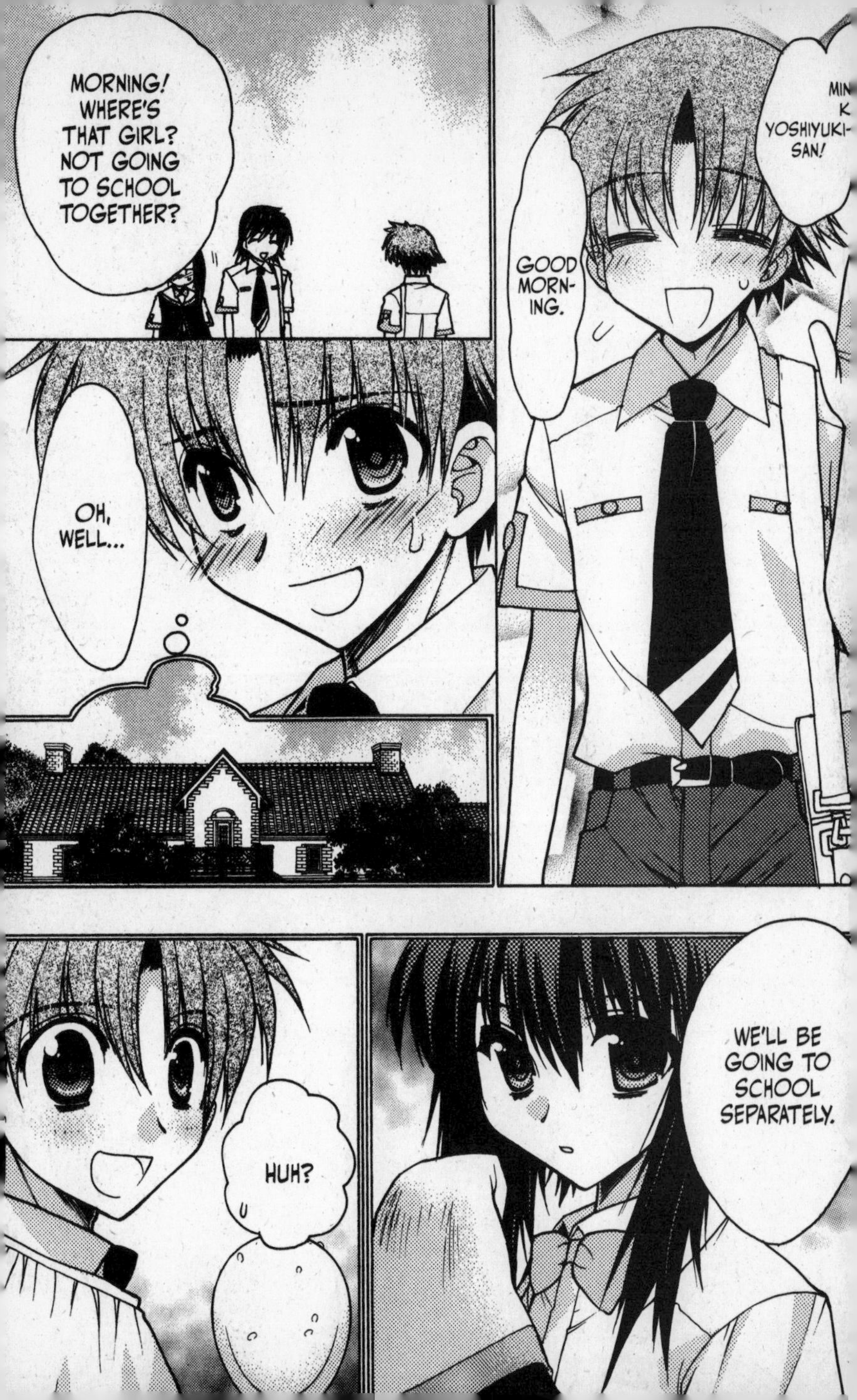
MIN
K
YOSHIYUKI-SAN!
GOOD MORNING.
MORNING! WHERE'S THAT GIRL? NOT GOING TO SCHOOL TOGETHER?
OH, WELL...
WE'LL BE GOING TO SCHOOL SEPARATELY.
HUH?

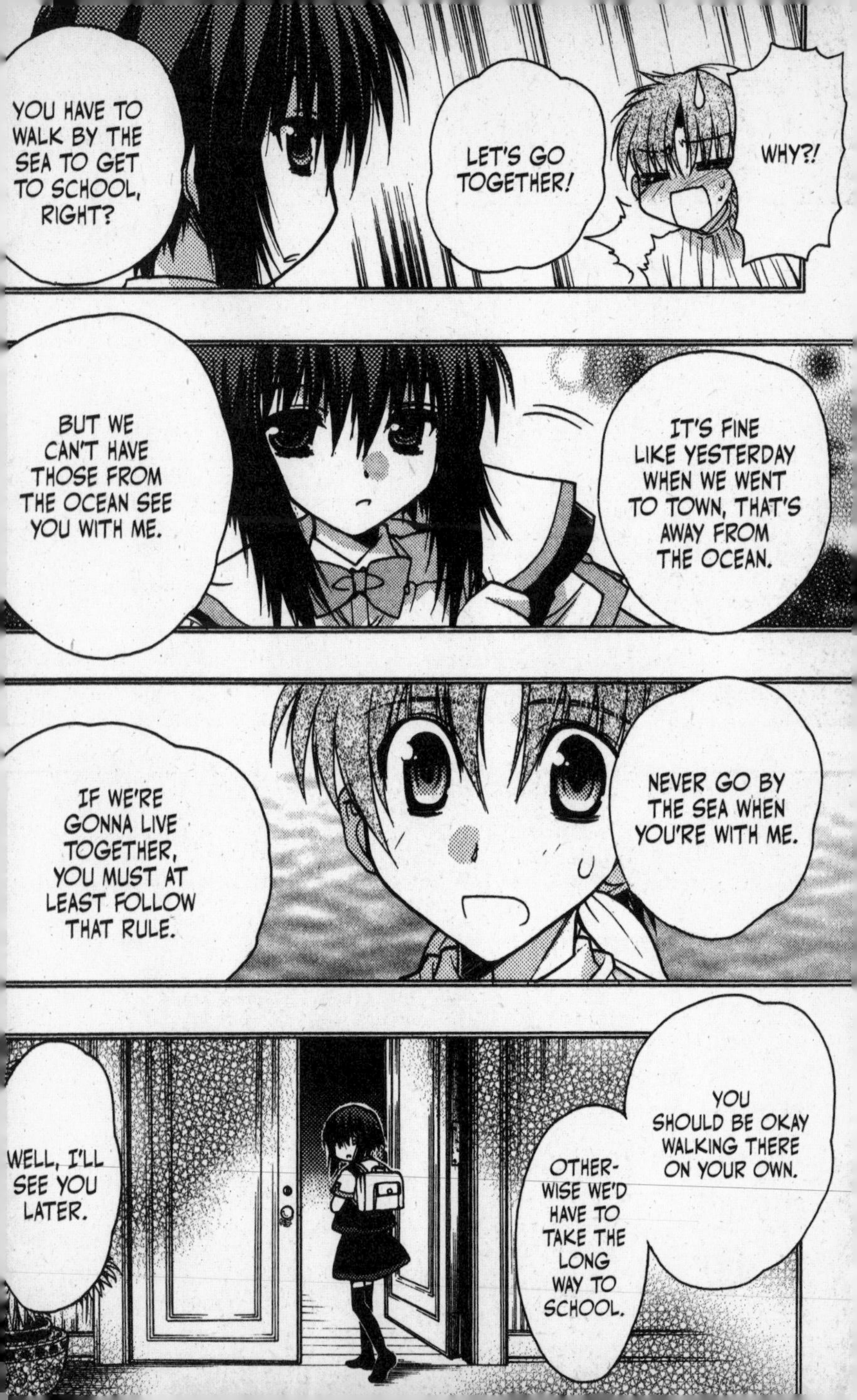
WHY?!
LET'S GO TOGETHER!
YOU HAVE TO WALK BY THE SEA TO GET TO SCHOOL, RIGHT?
IT'S FINE LIKE YESTERDAY WHEN WE WENT TO TOWN, THAT'S AWAY FROM THE OCEAN.
BUT WE CAN'T HAVE THOSE FROM THE OCEAN SEE YOU WITH ME.
NEVER GO BY THE SEA WHEN YOU'RE WITH ME.
IF WE'RE GONNA LIVE TOGETHER, YOU MUST AT LEAST FOLLOW THAT RULE.
YOU SHOULD BE OKAY WALKING THERE ON YOUR OWN.
OTHER-WISE WE'D HAVE TO TAKE THE LONG WAY TO SCHOOL.
WELL, I'LL SEE YOU LATER.

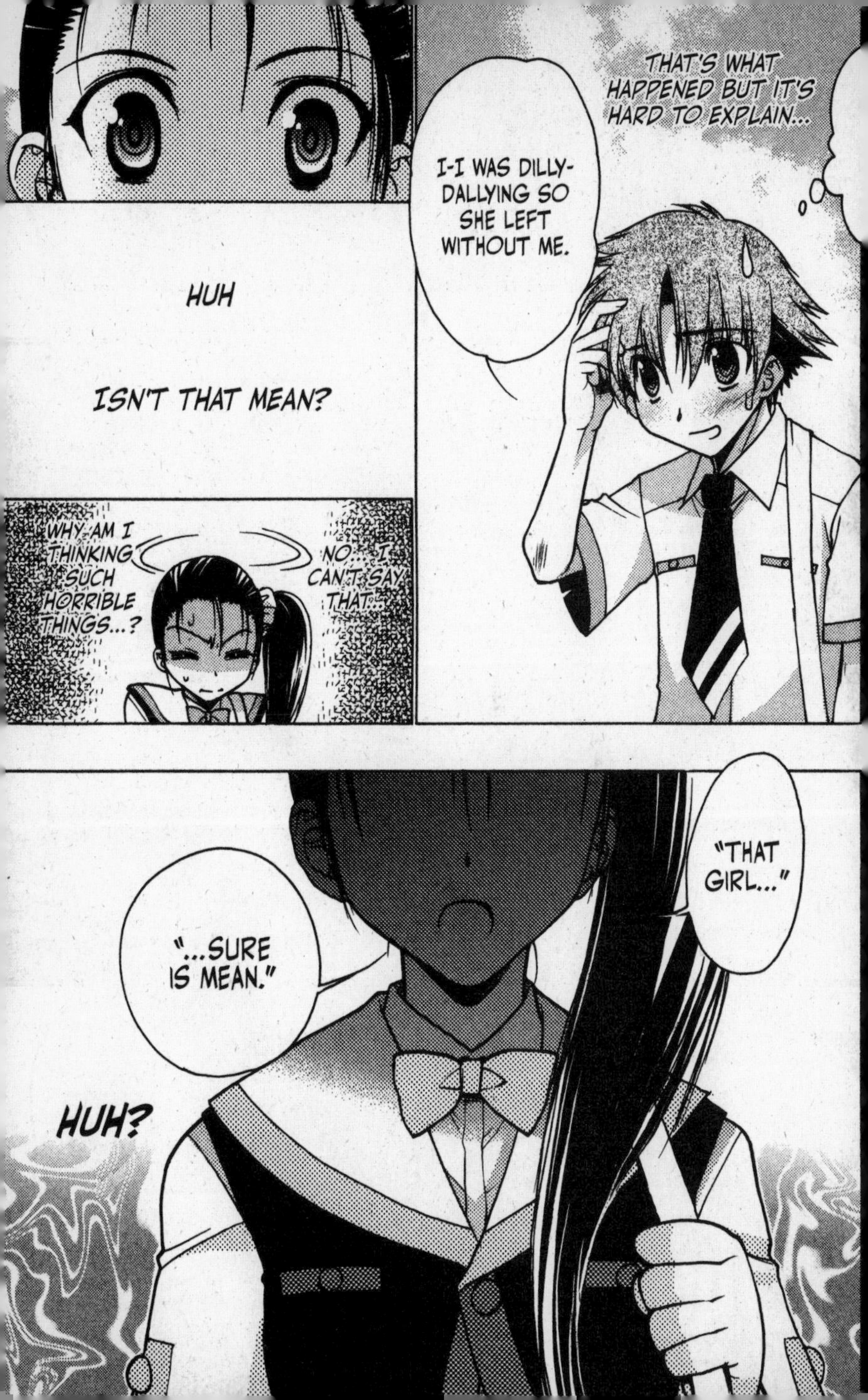
THAT'S WHAT HAPPENED BUT IT'S HARD TO EXPLAIN...
I-I WAS DILLY-DALLYING SO SHE LEFT WITHOUT ME.
HUH
ISN'T THAT MEAN?
NO... I CAN'T SAY THAT..
WHY AM I THINKING SUCH HORRIBLE THINGS...?
"THAT GIRL..."
"...SURE IS MEAN."
HUH?

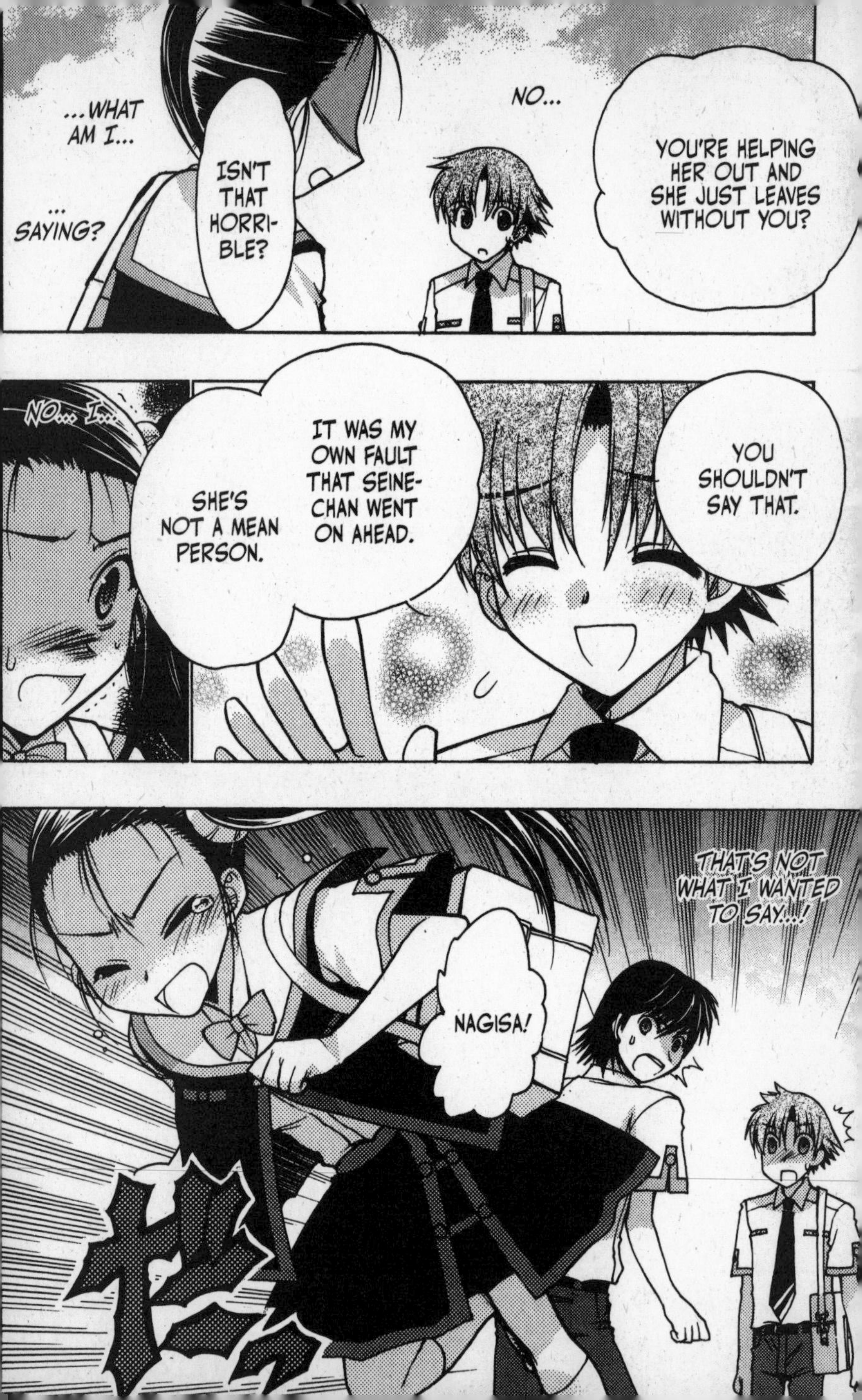
YOU'RE HELPING HER OUT AND SHE JUST LEAVES WITHOUT YOU?
NO...
ISN'T THAT HORRI-BLE?
...WHAT AM I...
...SAYING?
YOU SHOULDN'T SAY THAT.
IT WAS MY OWN FAULT THAT SEINE-CHAN WENT ON AHEAD.
SHE'S NOT A MEAN PERSON.
NO... I...
THAT'S NOT WHAT I WANTED TO SAY...!
NAGISA!

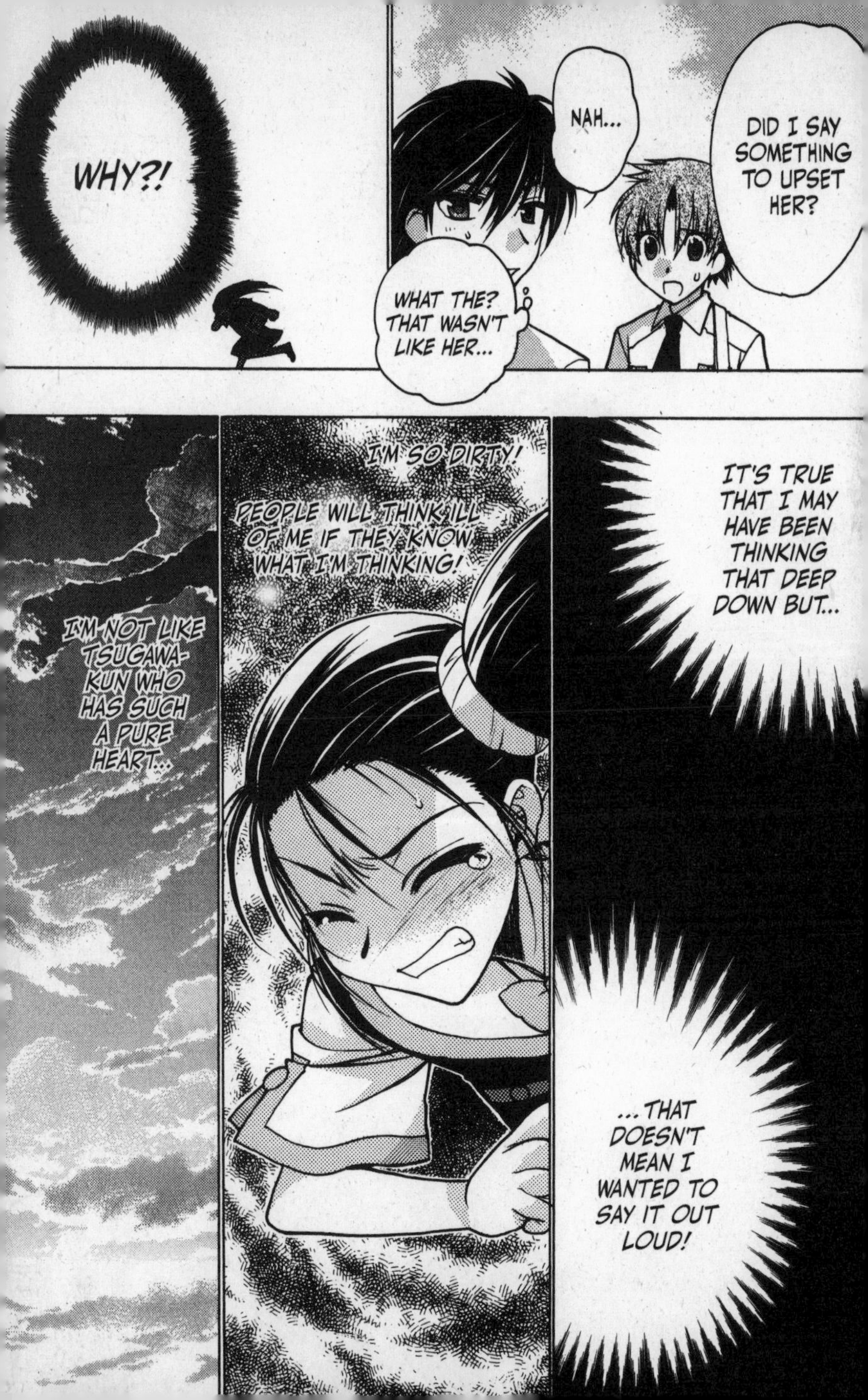
DID I SAY SOMETHING TO UPSET HER?
NAH...
WHAT THE? THAT WASN'T LIKE HER...
WHY?!
IT'S TRUE THAT I MAY HAVE BEEN THINKING THAT DEEP DOWN BUT...
...THAT DOESN'T MEAN I WANTED TO SAY IT OUT LOUD!
I'M SO DIRTY!
PEOPLE WILL THINK ILL OF ME IF THEY KNOW WHAT I'M THINKING!
I'M NOT LIKE TSUGAWA-KUN WHO HAS SUCH A PURE HEART...

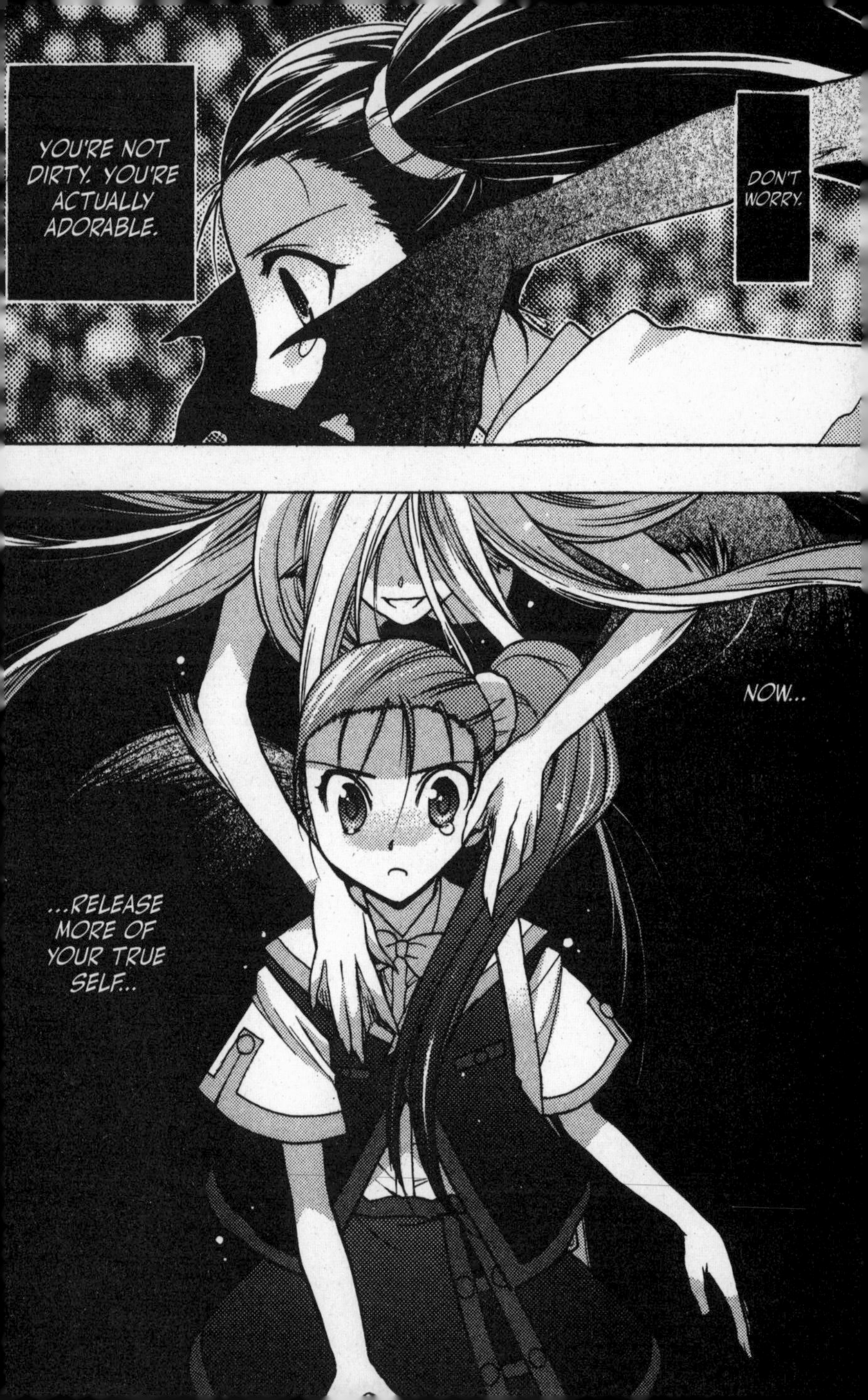
DON'T WORRY.
YOU'RE NOT DIRTY. YOU'RE ACTUALLY ADORABLE.
NOW...
...RELEASE MORE OF YOUR TRUE SELF...

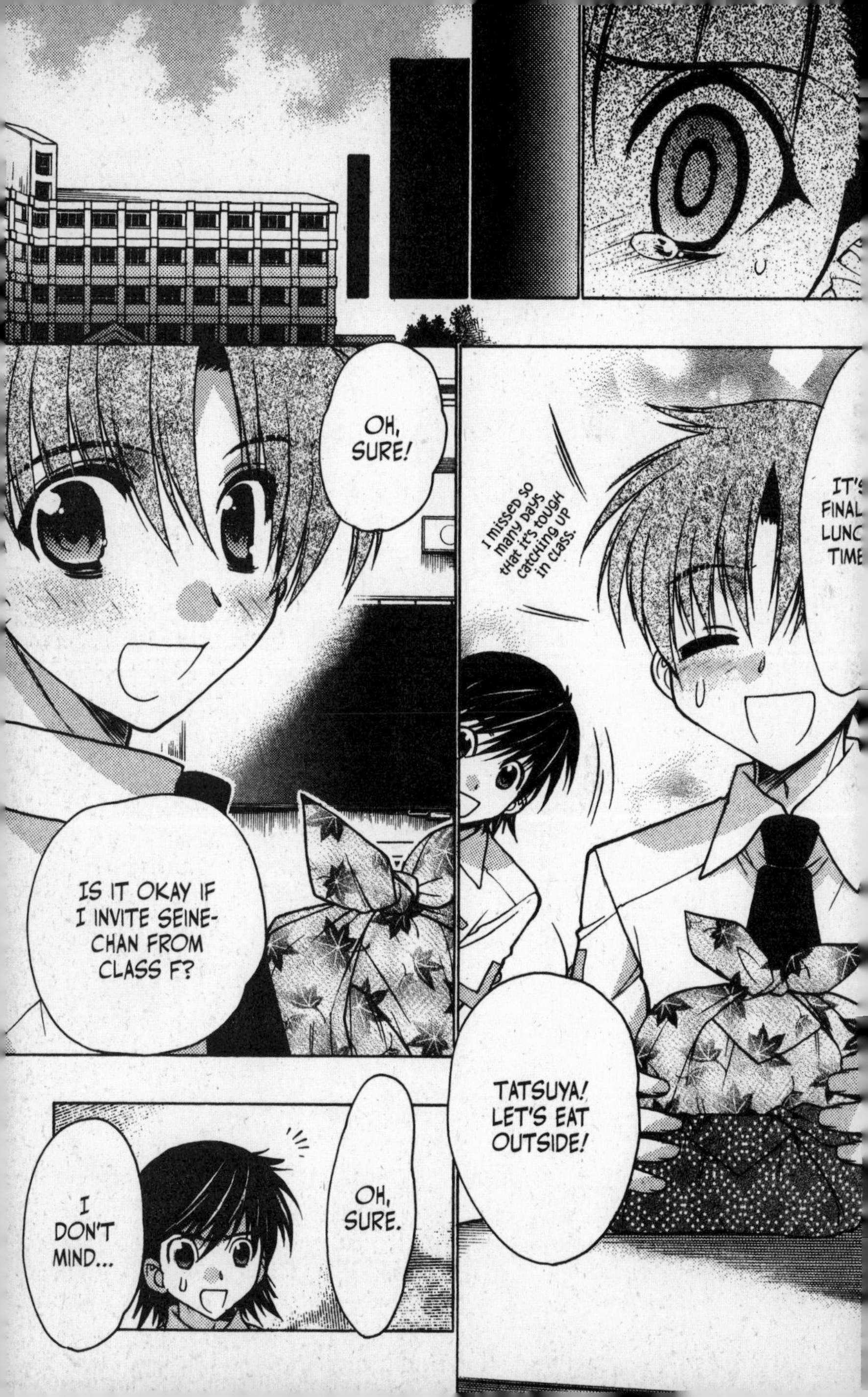
IT'S FINAL LUNC TIME
I missed so many days that it's tough catching up in class.
TATSUYA! LET'S EAT OUTSIDE!
OH, SURE!
IS IT OKAY IF I INVITE SEINE-CHAN FROM CLASS F?
OH, SURE.
I DON'T MIND...

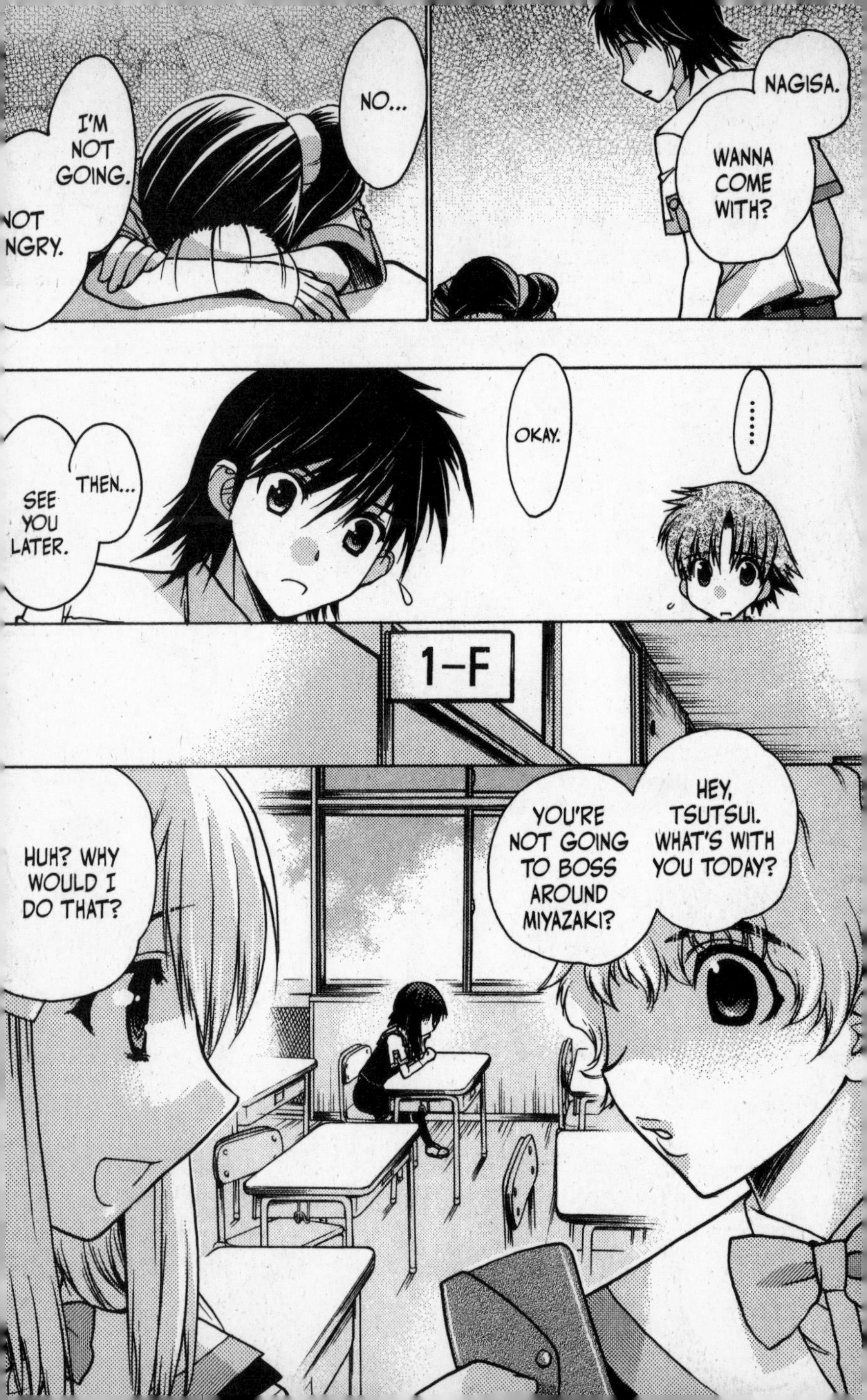
NAGISA.
WANNA COME WITH?
NO...
I'M NOT GOING.
NOT NGRY.
......
OKAY.
THEN...
SEE YOU LATER.
1-F
HEY, TSUTSUI. WHAT'S WITH YOU TODAY?
YOU'RE NOT GOING TO BOSS AROUND MIYAZAKI?
HUH? WHY WOULD I DO THAT?

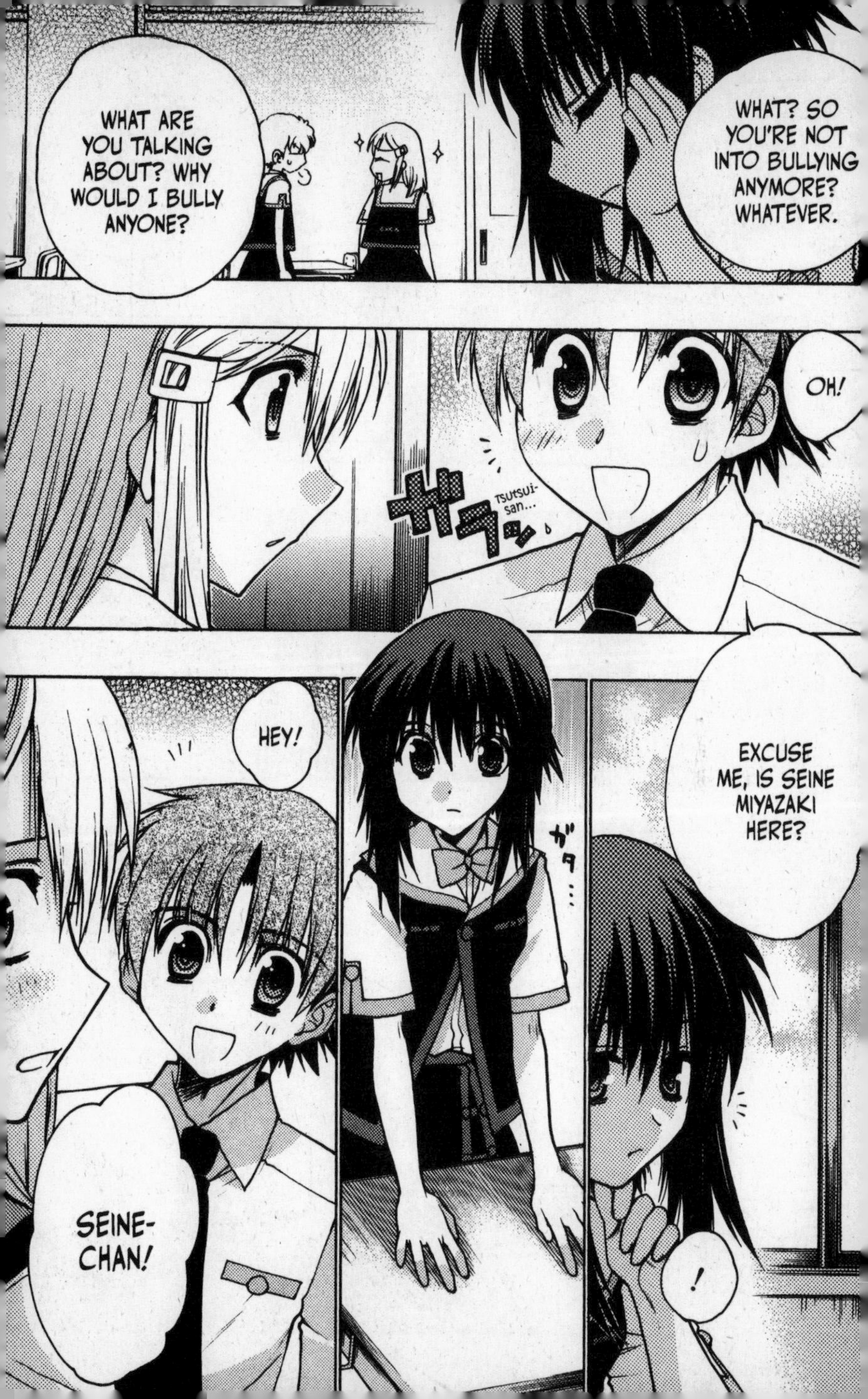
WHAT? SO YOU'RE NOT INTO BULLYING ANYMORE? WHATEVER.
WHAT ARE YOU TALKING ABOUT? WHY WOULD I BULLY ANYONE?
OH!
ガラッ
TSUTSUI-SAN...
EXCUSE ME, IS SEINE MIYAZAKI HERE?
!
ガタ…
HEY!
SEINE-CHAN!

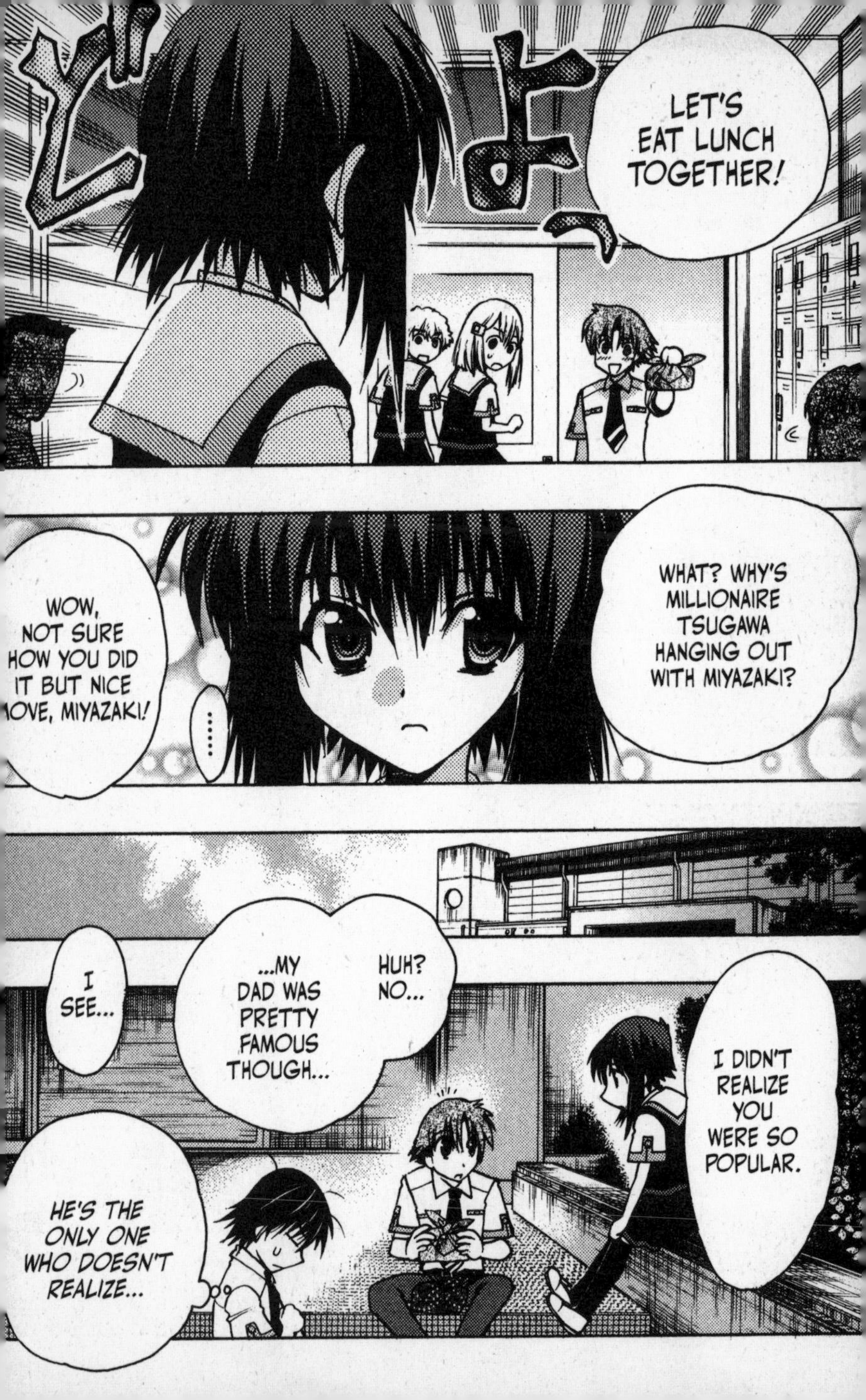
LET'S EAT LUNCH TOGETHER!
どよっ
WHAT? WHY'S MILLIONAIRE TSUGAWA HANGING OUT WITH MIYAZAKI?
......
WOW, NOT SURE HOW YOU DID IT BUT NICE OVE, MIYAZAKI!
I DIDN'T REALIZE YOU WERE SO POPULAR.
HUH? NO...
...MY DAD WAS PRETTY FAMOUS THOUGH...
I SEE...
HE'S THE ONLY ONE WHO DOESN'T REALIZE...

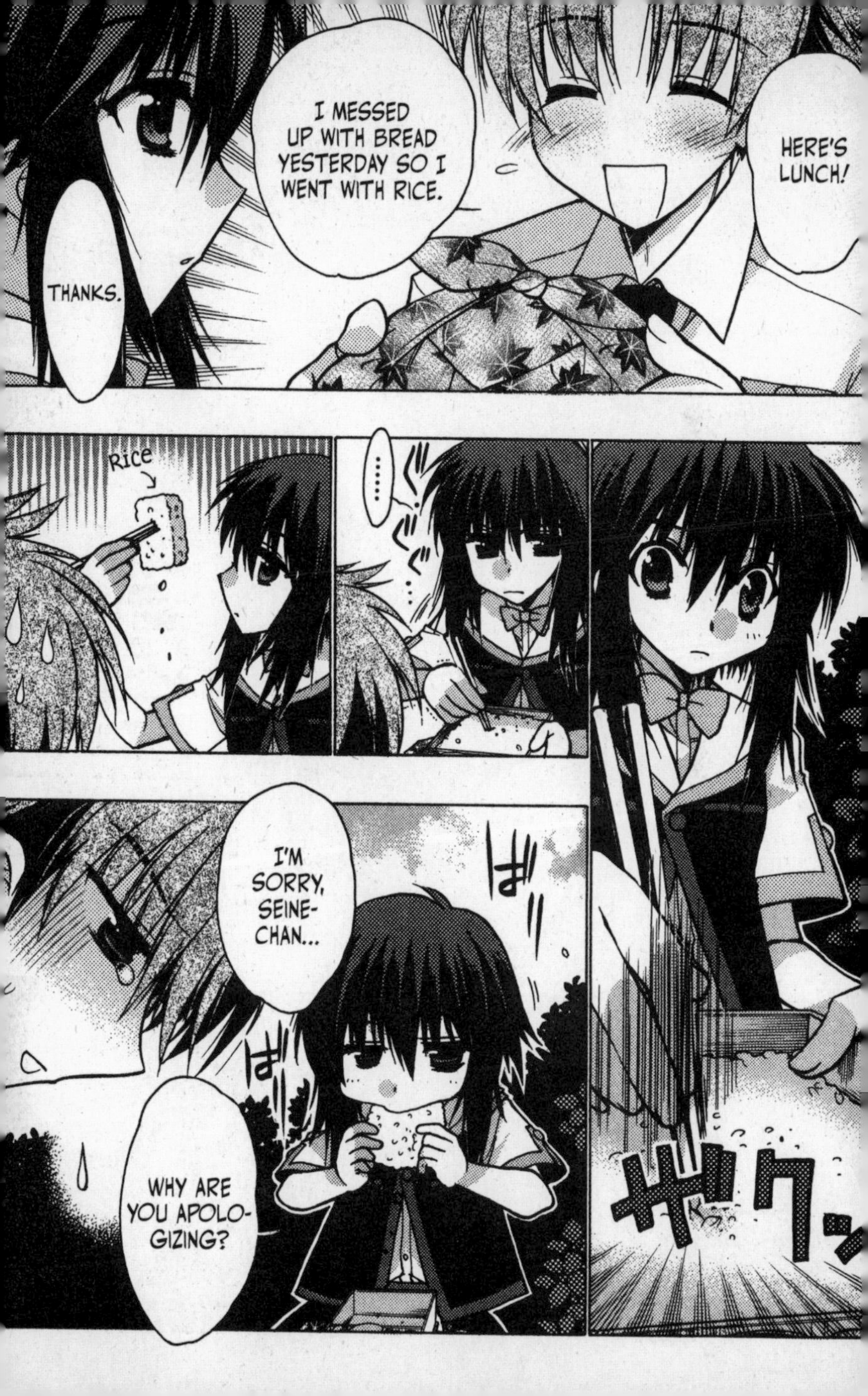
HERE'S LUNCH!
I MESSED UP WITH BREAD YESTERDAY SO I WENT WITH RICE.
THANKS.
ザクッ
......
Rice
I'M SORRY, SEINE-CHAN...
WHY ARE YOU APOLOGIZING?

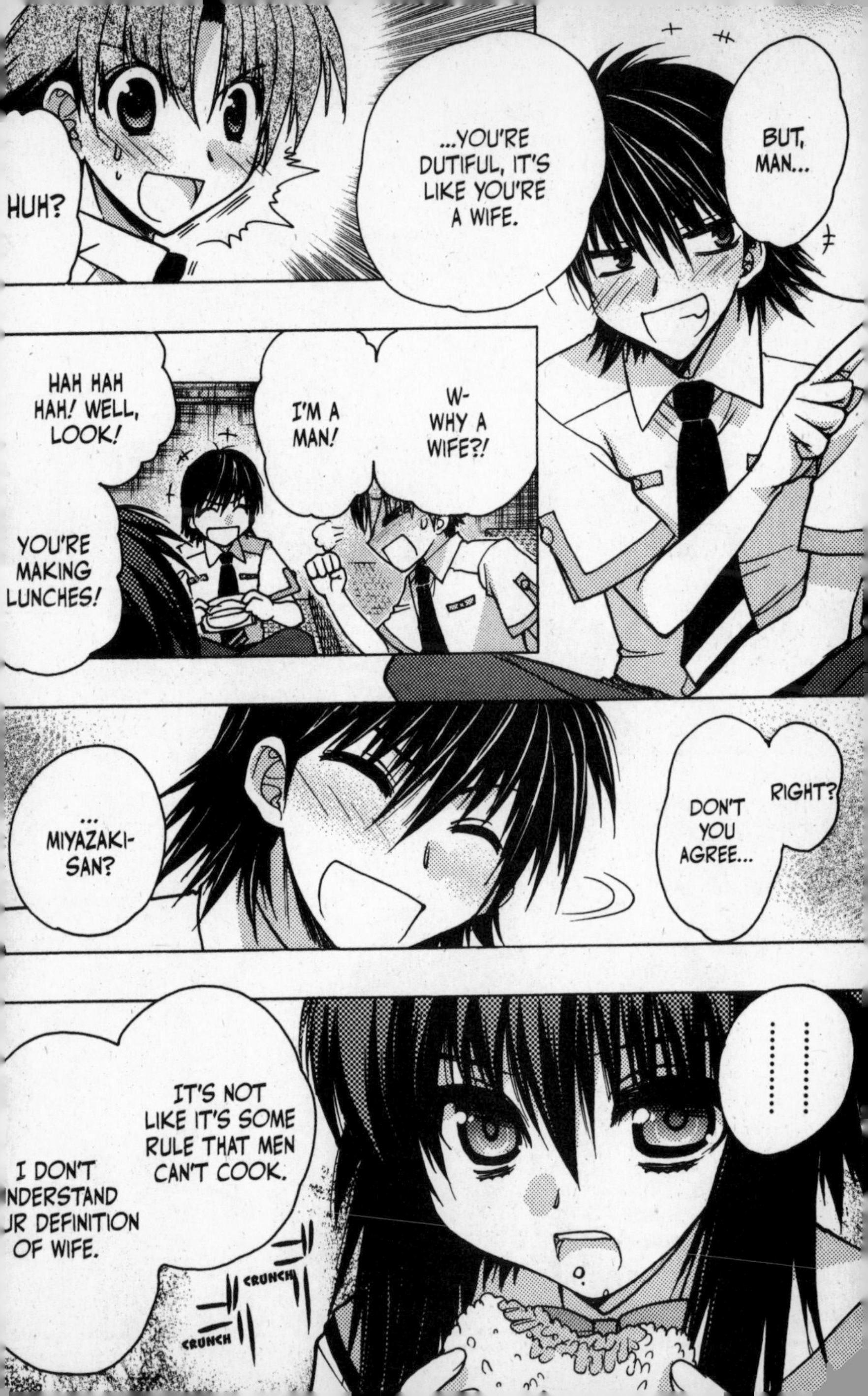

BUT, MAN...
...YOU'RE DUTIFUL, IT'S LIKE YOU'RE A WIFE.
HUH?
W- WHY A WIFE?!
I'M A MAN!
HAH HAH HAH! WELL, LOOK!
YOU'RE MAKING LUNCHES!
RIGHT?
DON'T YOU AGREE...
... MIYAZAKI-SAN?
......
IT'S NOT LIKE IT'S SOME RULE THAT MEN CAN'T COOK.
I DON'T NDERSTAND UR DEFINITION OF WIFE.
CRUNCH
CRUNCH

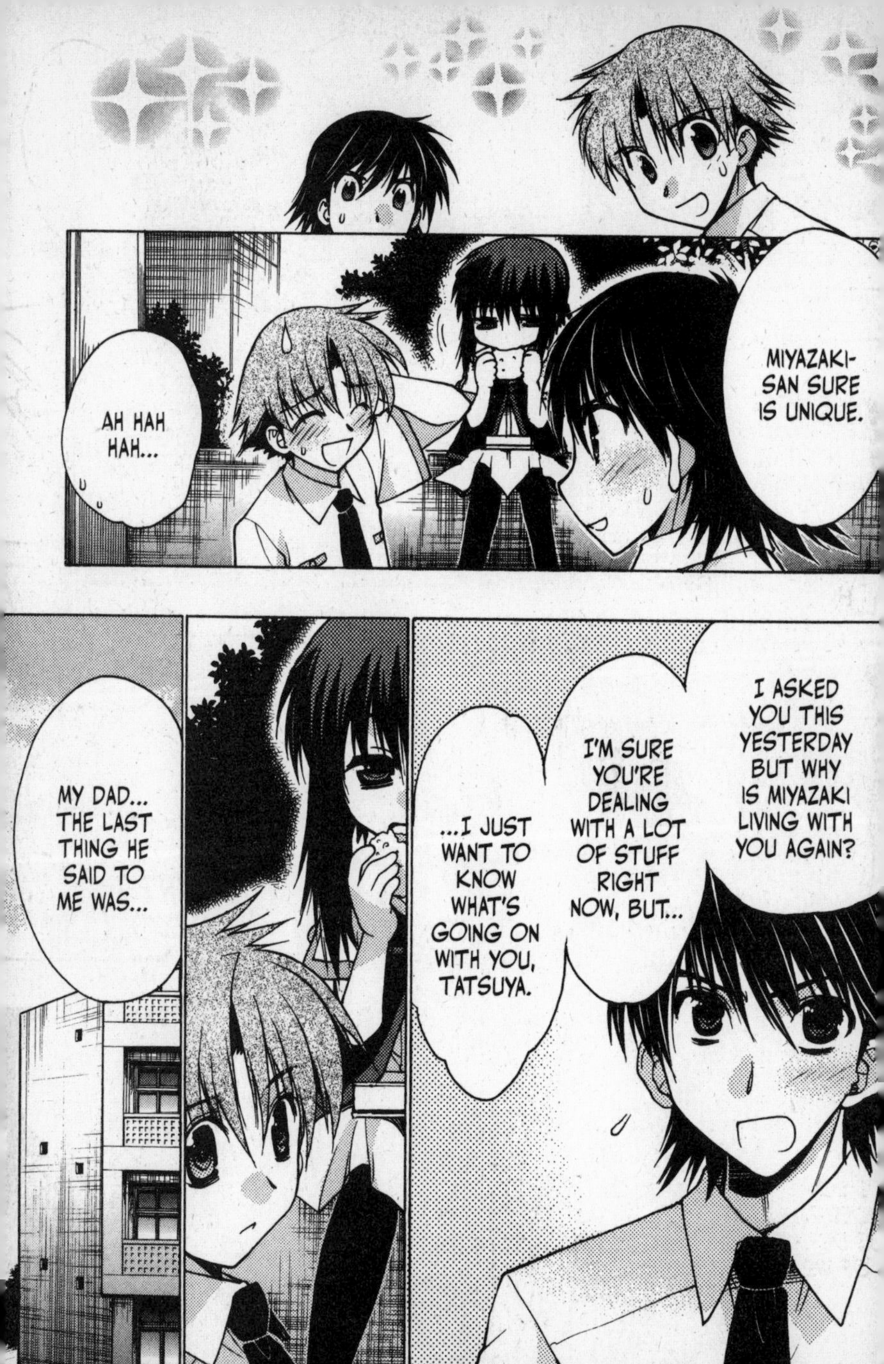
MIYAZAKI-SAN SURE IS UNIQUE.
AH HAH HAH...
I ASKED YOU THIS YESTERDAY BUT WHY IS MIYAZAKI LIVING WITH YOU AGAIN?
I'M SURE YOU'RE DEALING WITH A LOT OF STUFF RIGHT NOW, BUT...
...I JUST WANT TO KNOW WHAT'S GOING ON WITH YOU, TATSUYA.
MY DAD... THE LAST THING HE SAID TO ME WAS...

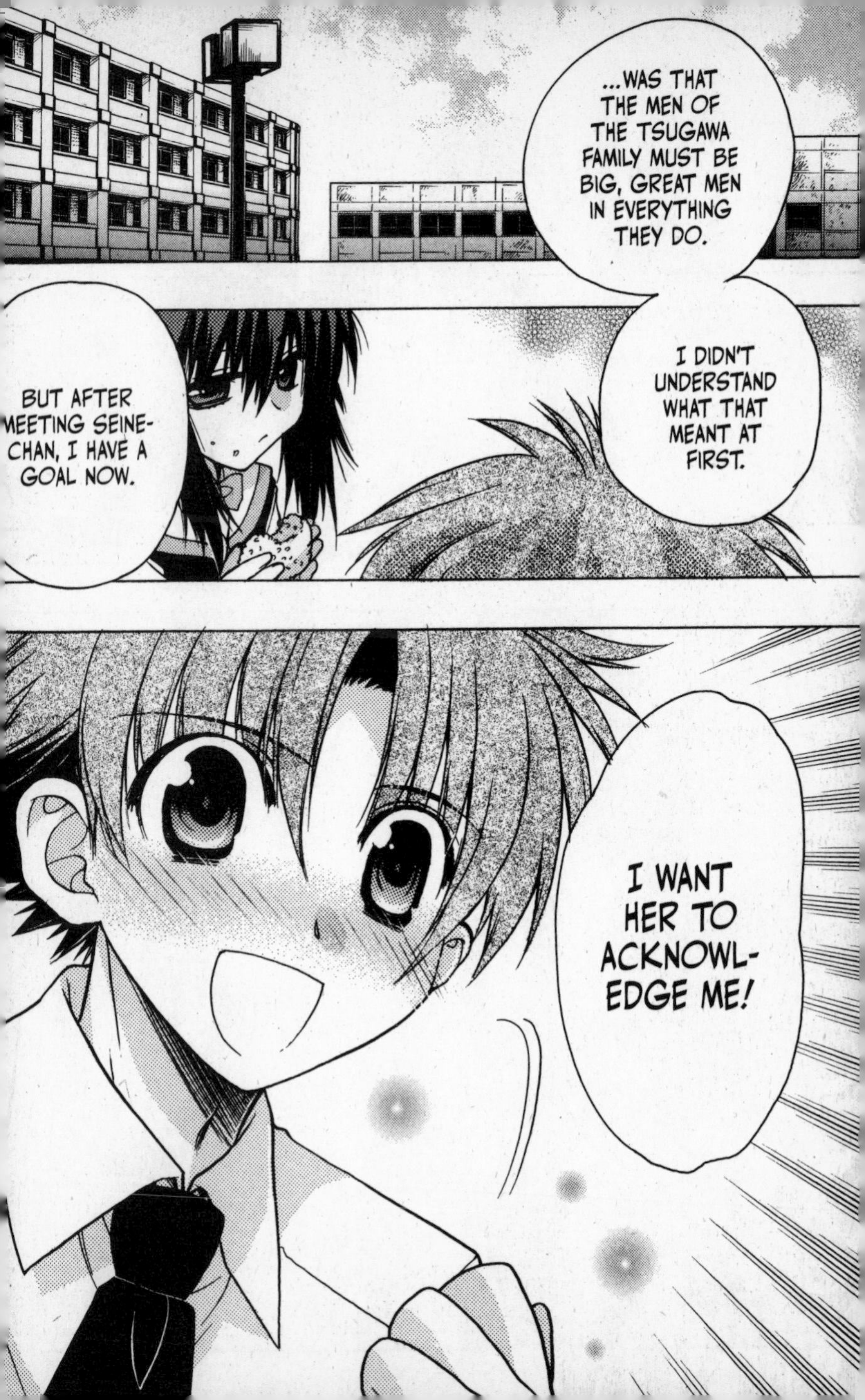
...WAS THAT THE MEN OF THE TSUGAWA FAMILY MUST BE BIG, GREAT MEN IN EVERYTHING THEY DO.
I DIDN'T UNDERSTAND WHAT THAT MEANT AT FIRST.
BUT AFTER MEETING SEINE-CHAN, I HAVE A GOAL NOW.
I WANT HER TO ACKNOWL-EDGE ME!

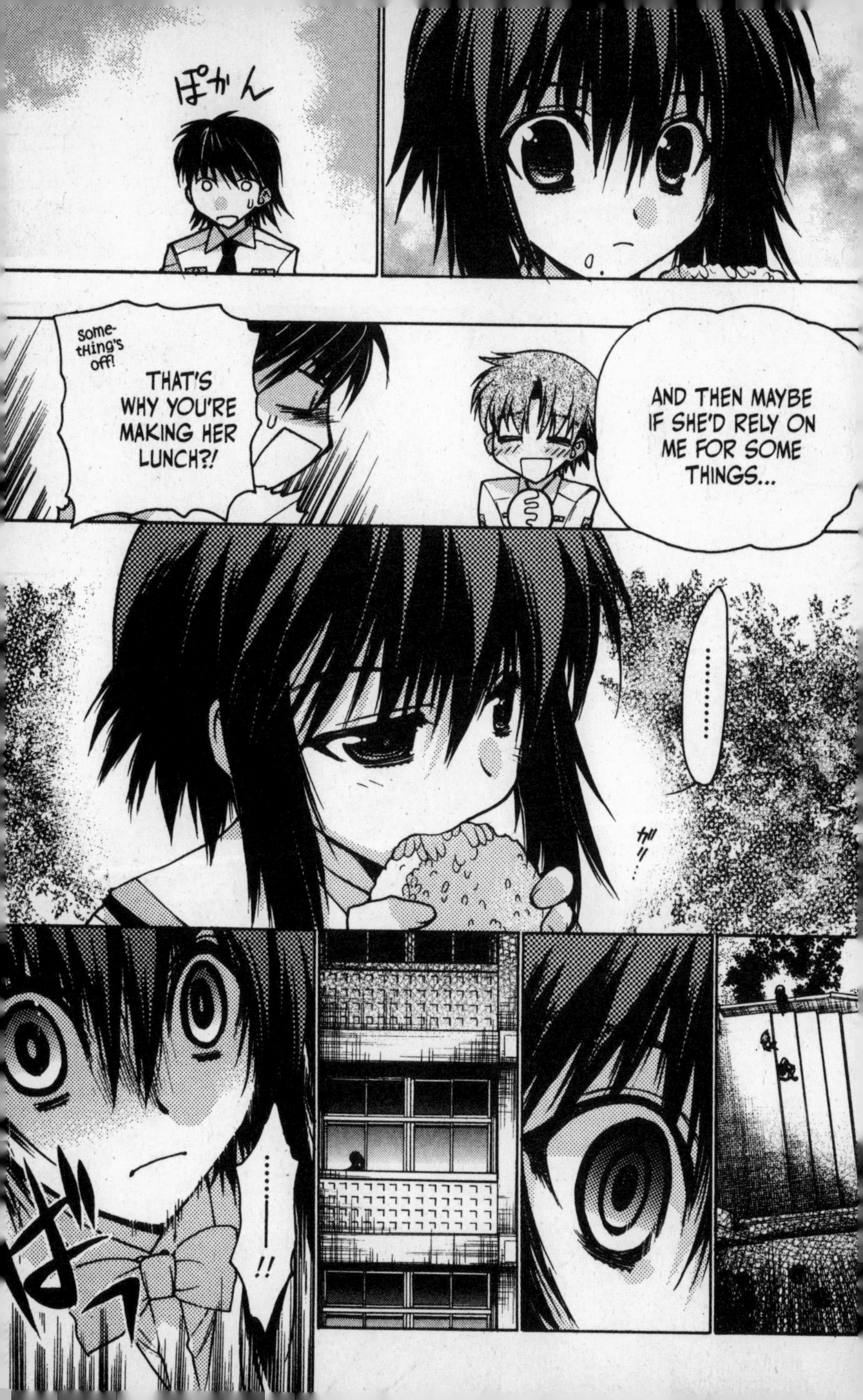
ぽかん
AND THEN MAYBE IF SHE'D RELY ON ME FOR SOME THINGS...
THAT'S WHY YOU'RE MAKING HER LUNCH?!
some-thing's off!
......
......!!

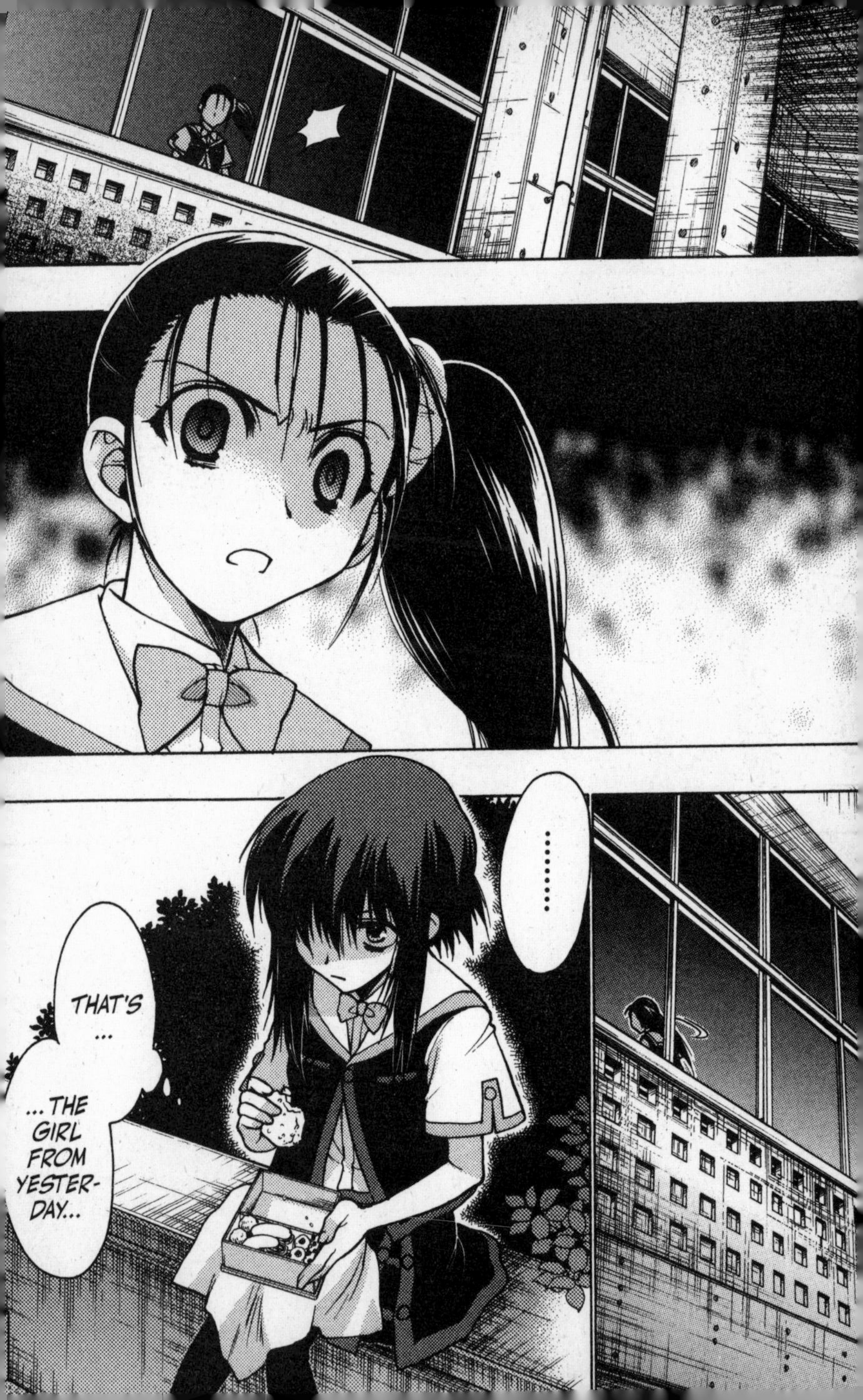

....
THAT'S ...
... THE GIRL FROM YESTER-DAY...

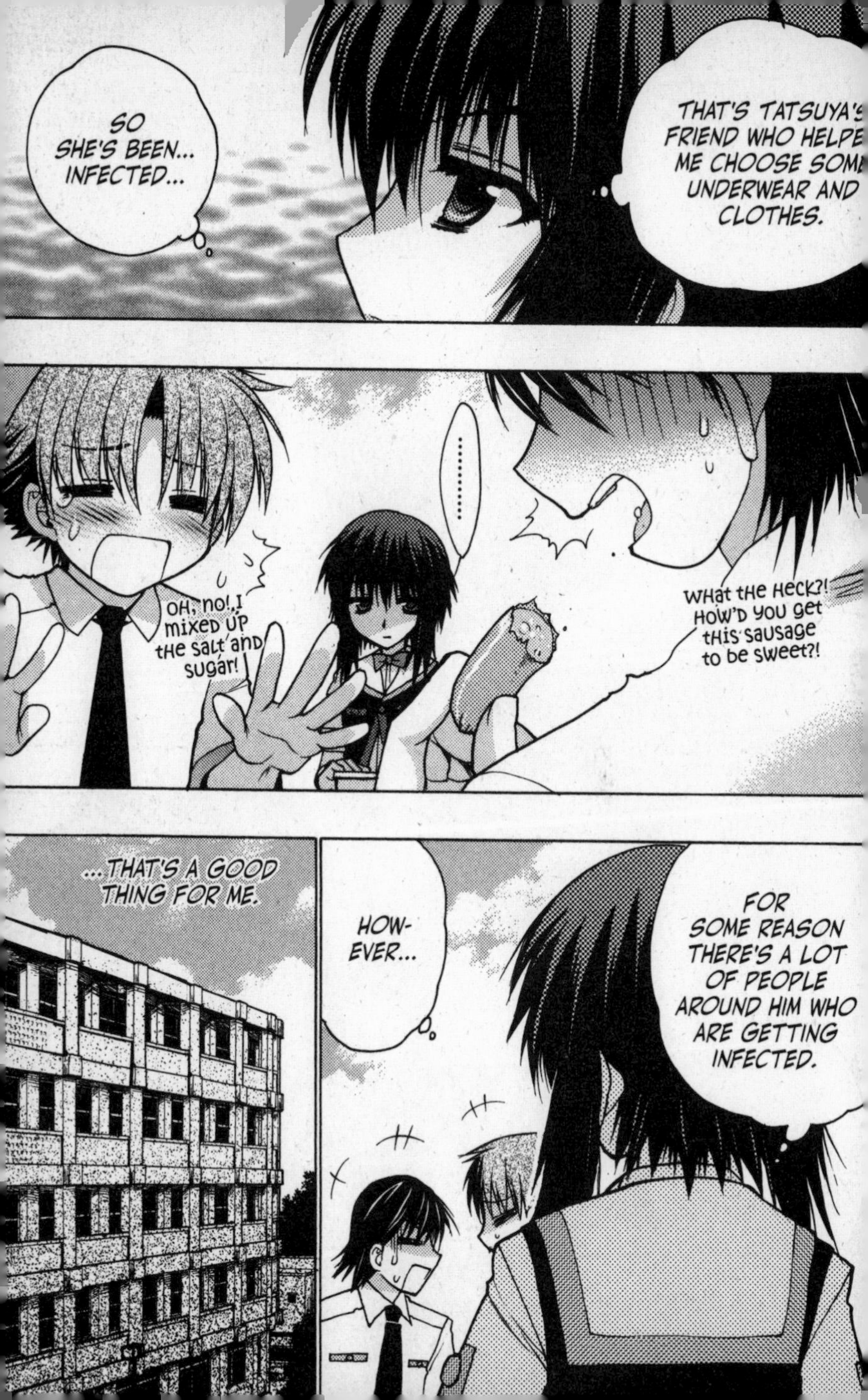
THAT'S TATSUYA'S FRIEND WHO HELPE ME CHOOSE SOM UNDERWEAR AND CLOTHES.
SO SHE'S BEEN... INFECTED...
......
WHAT THE HECK?! HOW'D YOU GET THIS SAUSAGE TO BE SWEET?!
OH, NO! I MIXED UP THE SALT AND SUGAR!
FOR SOME REASON THERE'S A LOT OF PEOPLE AROUND HIM WHO ARE GETTING INFECTED.
HOW-EVER...
...THAT'S A GOOD THING FOR ME.

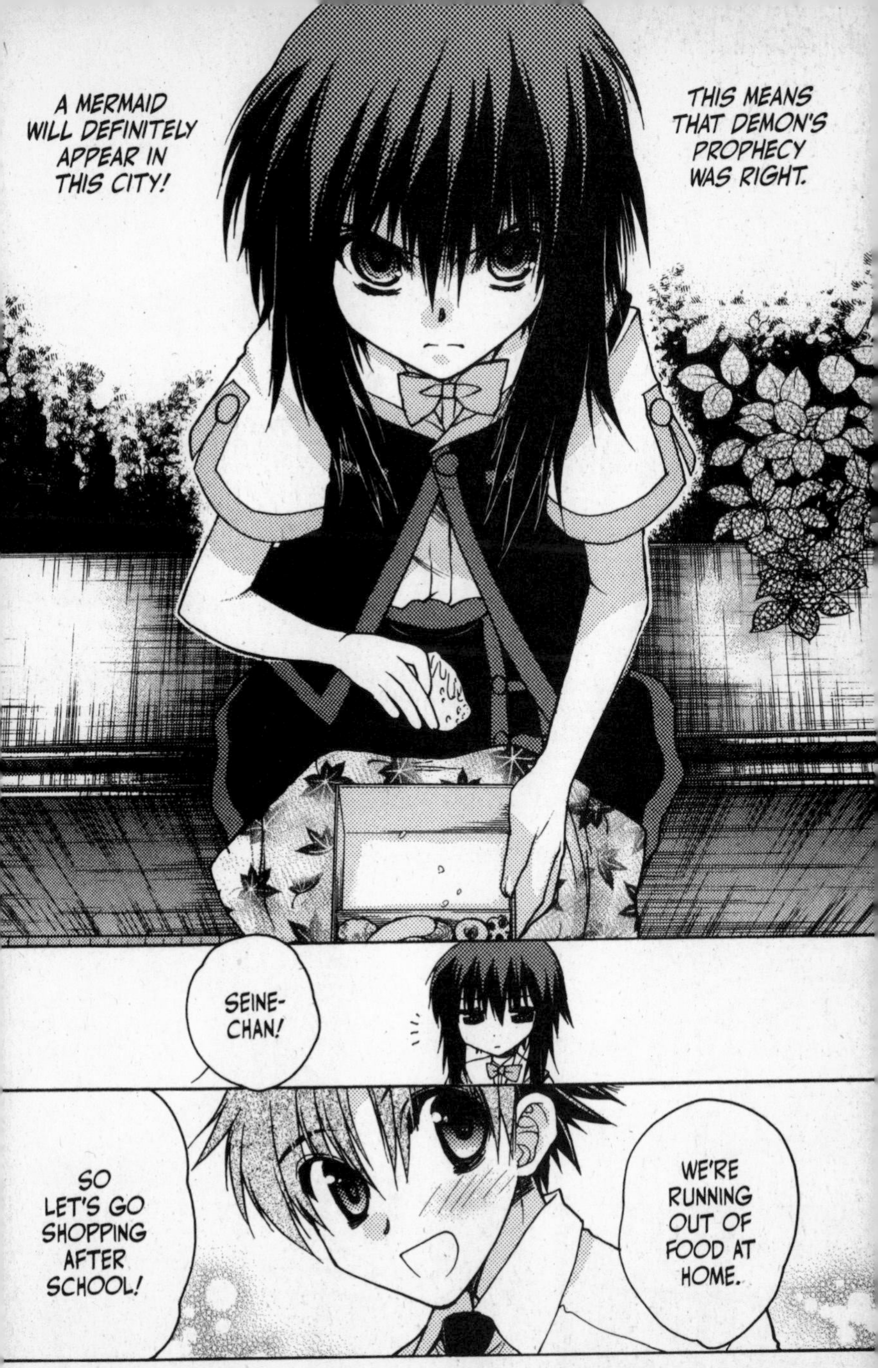
THIS MEANS THAT DEMON'S PROPHECY WAS RIGHT.
A MERMAID WILL DEFINITELY APPEAR IN THIS CITY!
SEINE-CHAN!
WE'RE RUNNING OUT OF FOOD AT HOME.
SO LET'S GO SHOPPING AFTER SCHOOL!

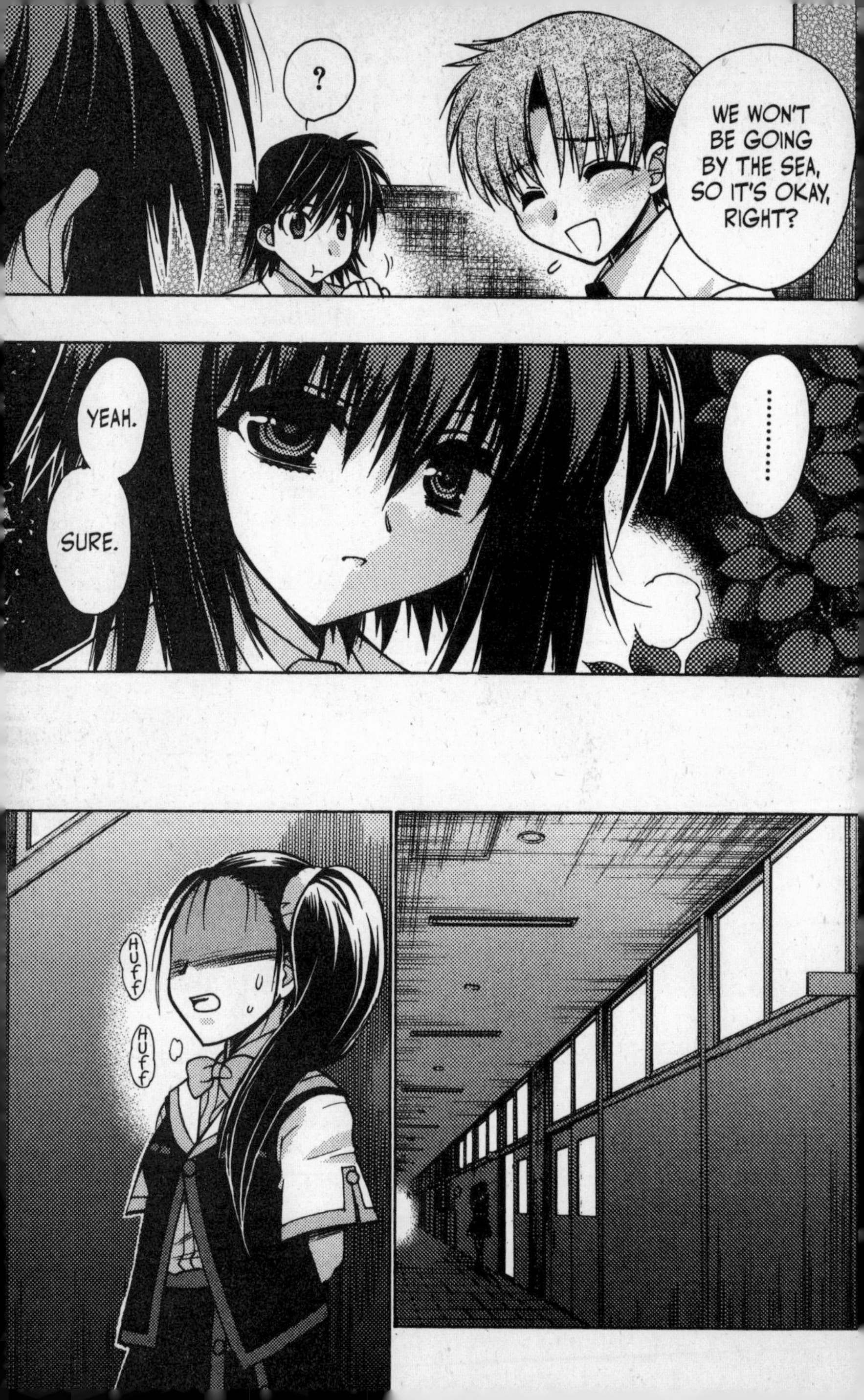
WE WON'T BE GOING BY THE SEA, SO IT'S OKAY, RIGHT?
?
....
YEAH.
SURE.
Huff
Huff

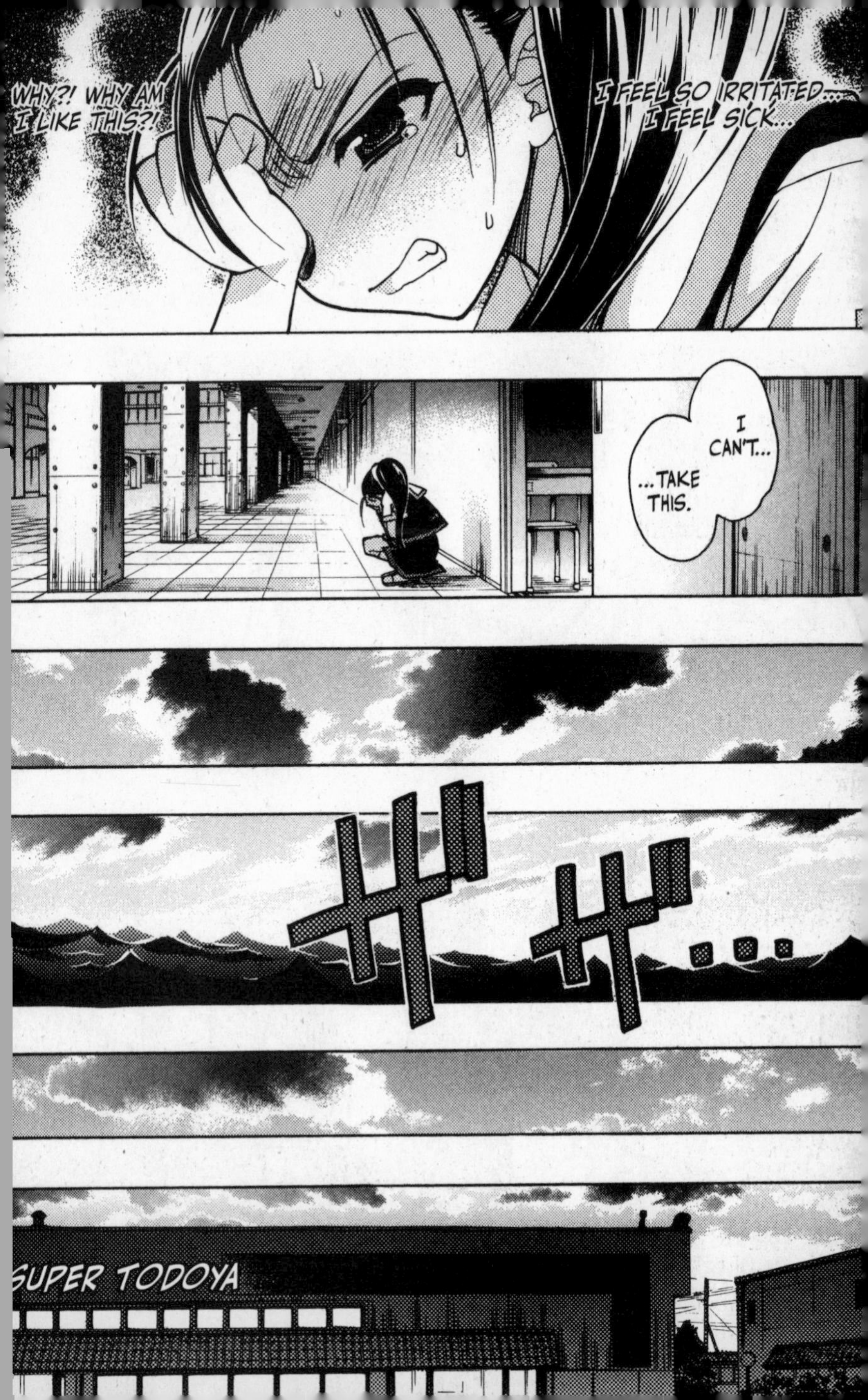
I FEEL SO IRRITATED... I FEEL SICK...
WHY?! WHY AM I LIKE THIS?!
I CAN'T...
...TAKE THIS.
ザザ...
SUPER TODOYA

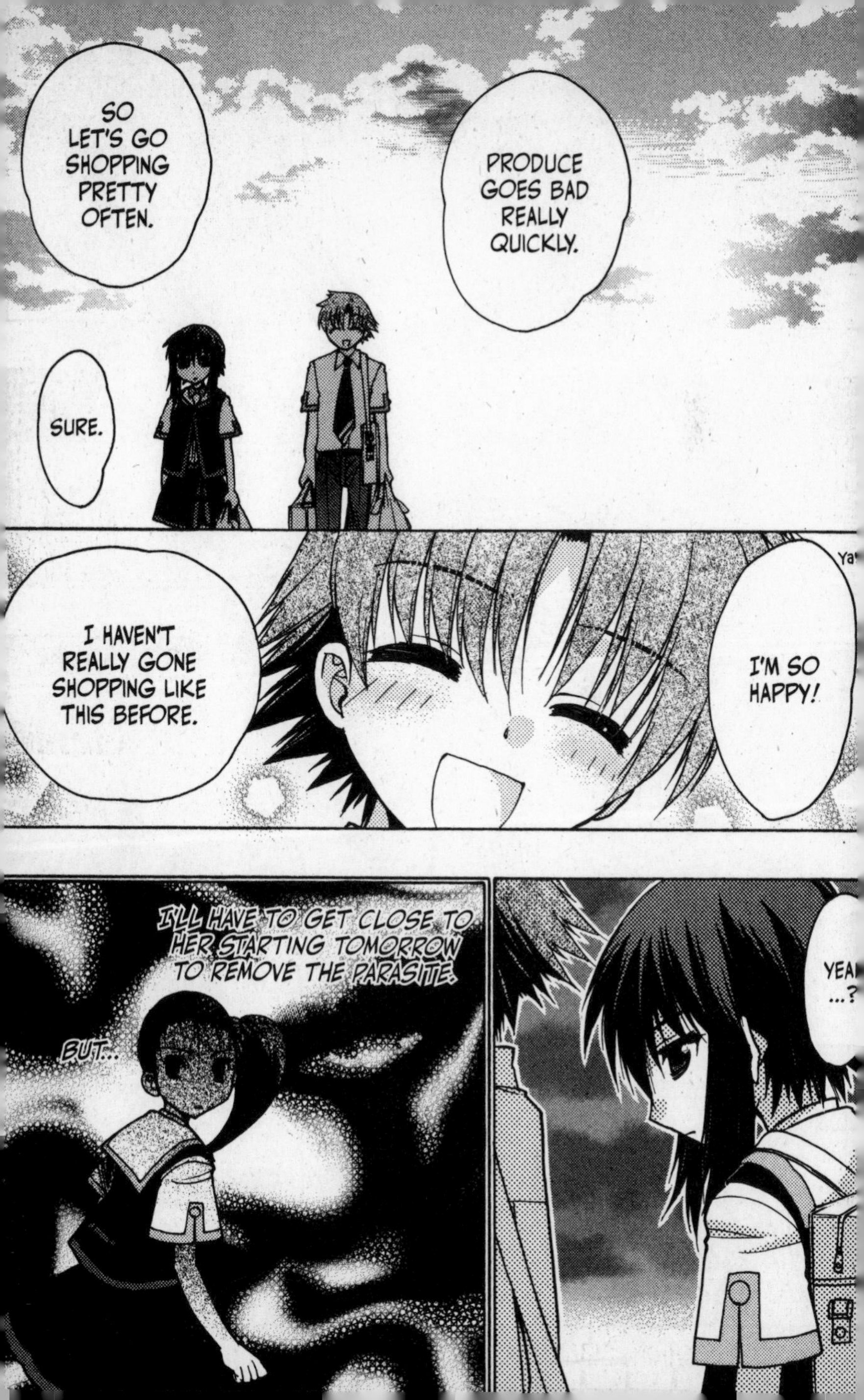
PRODUCE GOES BAD REALLY QUICKLY.
SO LET'S GO SHOPPING PRETTY OFTEN.
SURE.
Ya
I'M SO HAPPY!
I HAVEN'T REALLY GONE SHOPPING LIKE THIS BEFORE.
YEA ...?
I'LL HAVE TO GET CLOSE TO HER STARTING TOMORROW TO REMOVE THE PARASITE.
BUT...

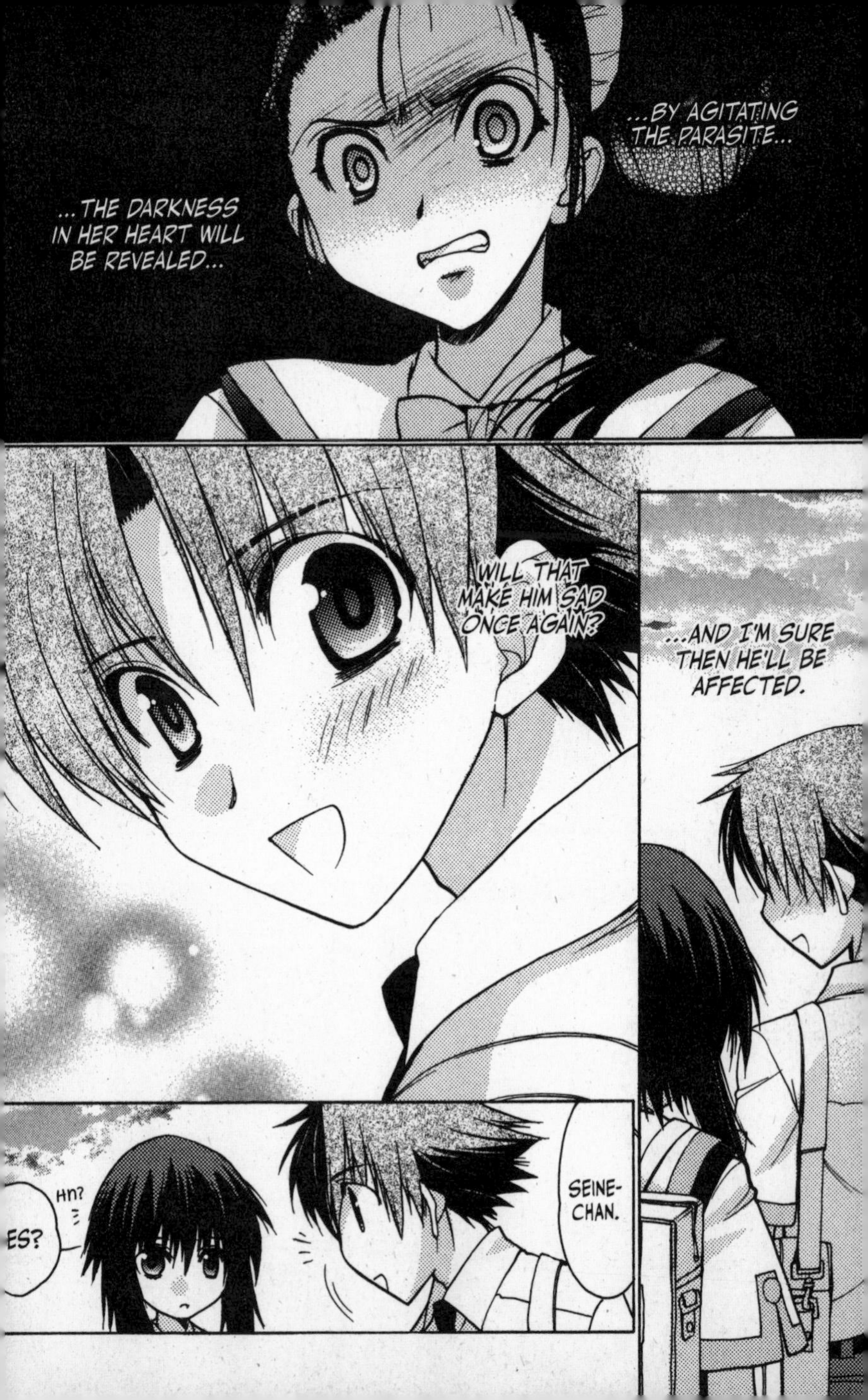
...BY AGITATING THE PARASITE...
...THE DARKNESS IN HER HEART WILL BE REVEALED...
...AND I'M SURE THEN HE'LL BE AFFECTED.
WILL THAT MAKE HIM SAD ONCE AGAIN?
SEINE-CHAN.
Hn?
ES?

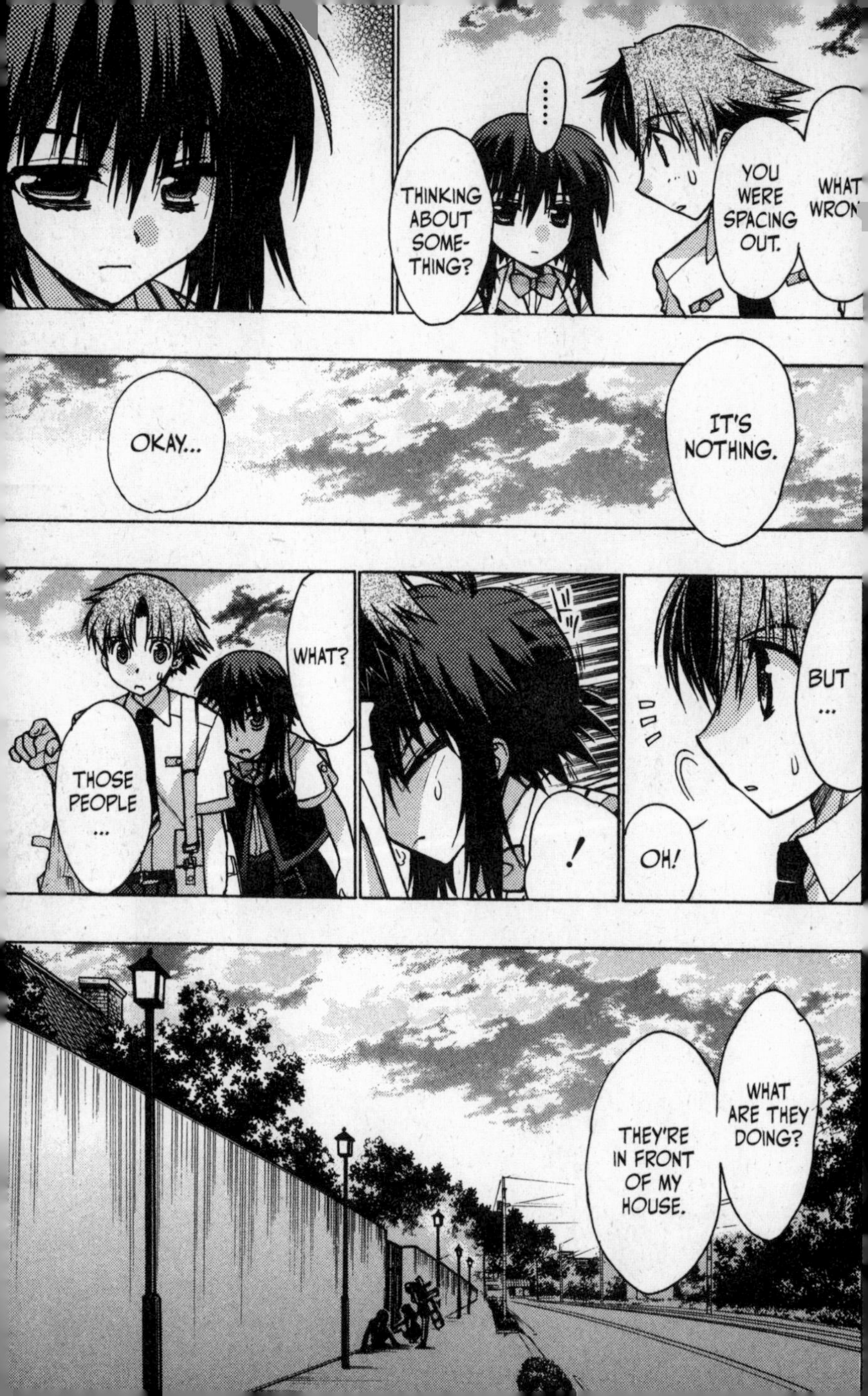
WHAT WRON
YOU WERE SPACING OUT.
……
THINKING ABOUT SOME-THING?
IT'S NOTHING.
OKAY...
BUT ...
OH!
!
WHAT?
THOSE PEOPLE ...
WHAT ARE THEY DOING?
THEY'RE IN FRONT OF MY HOUSE.

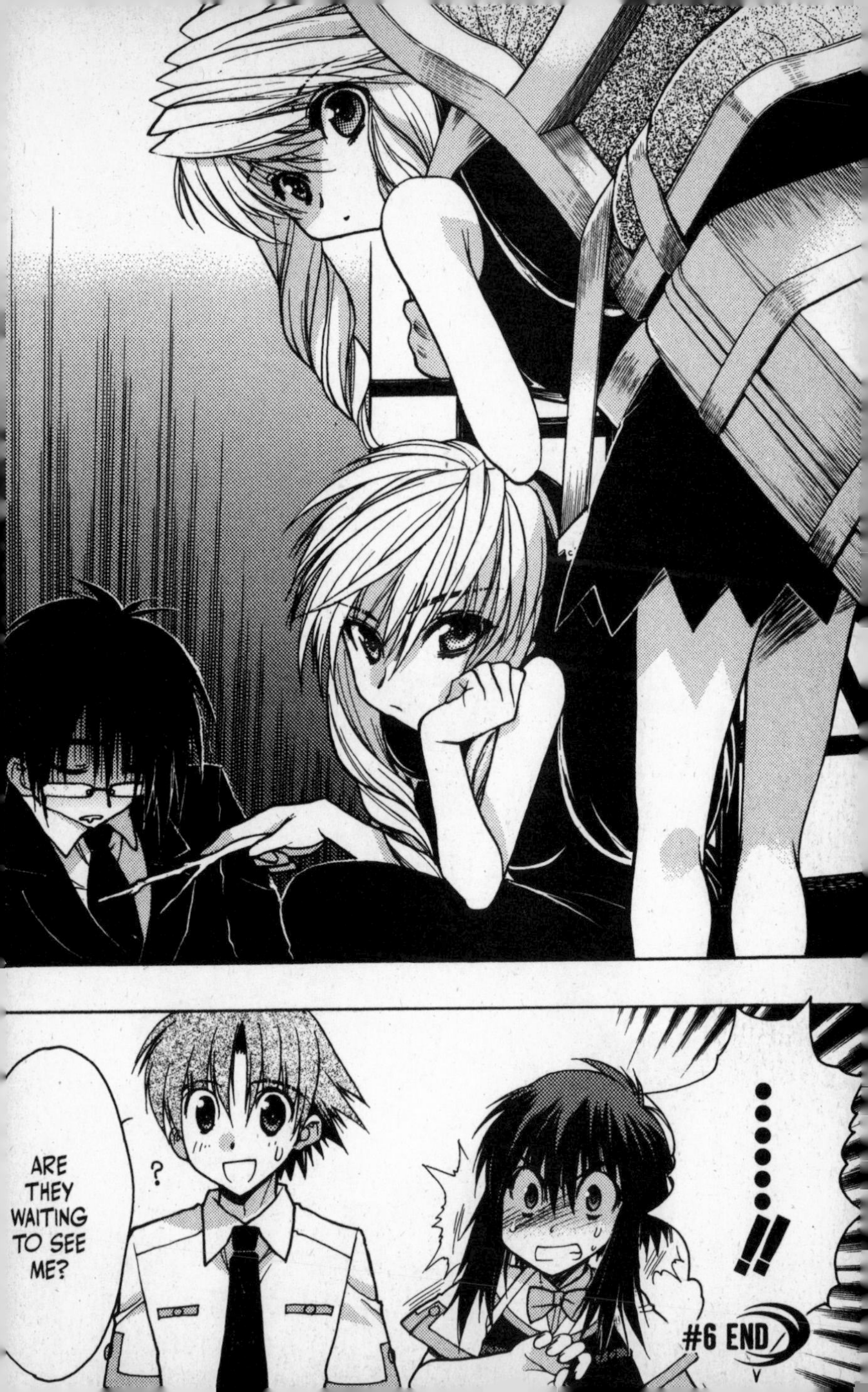

……!!
?
ARE THEY WAITING TO SEE ME?
#6 END

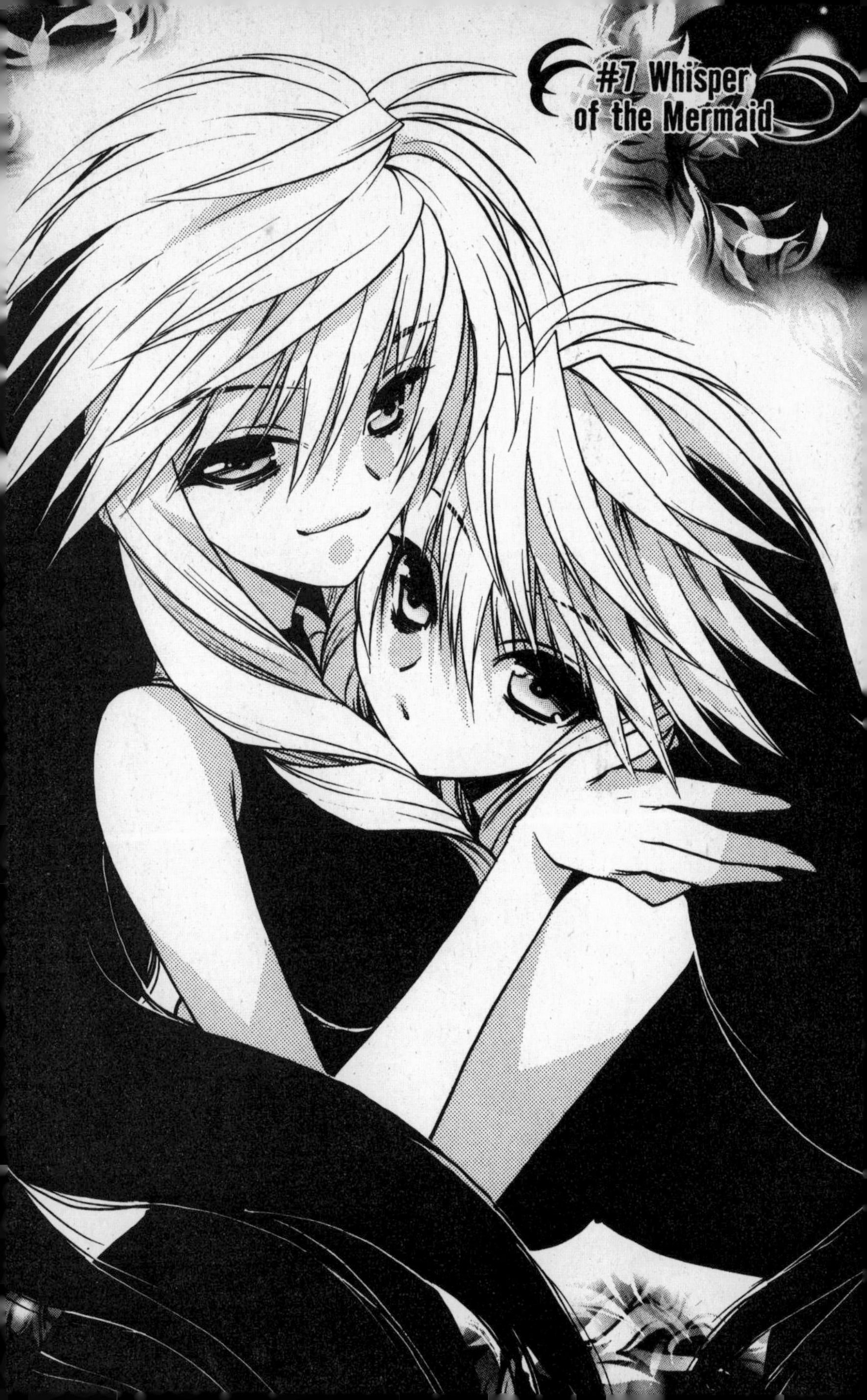
#7 Whisper
of the Mermaid

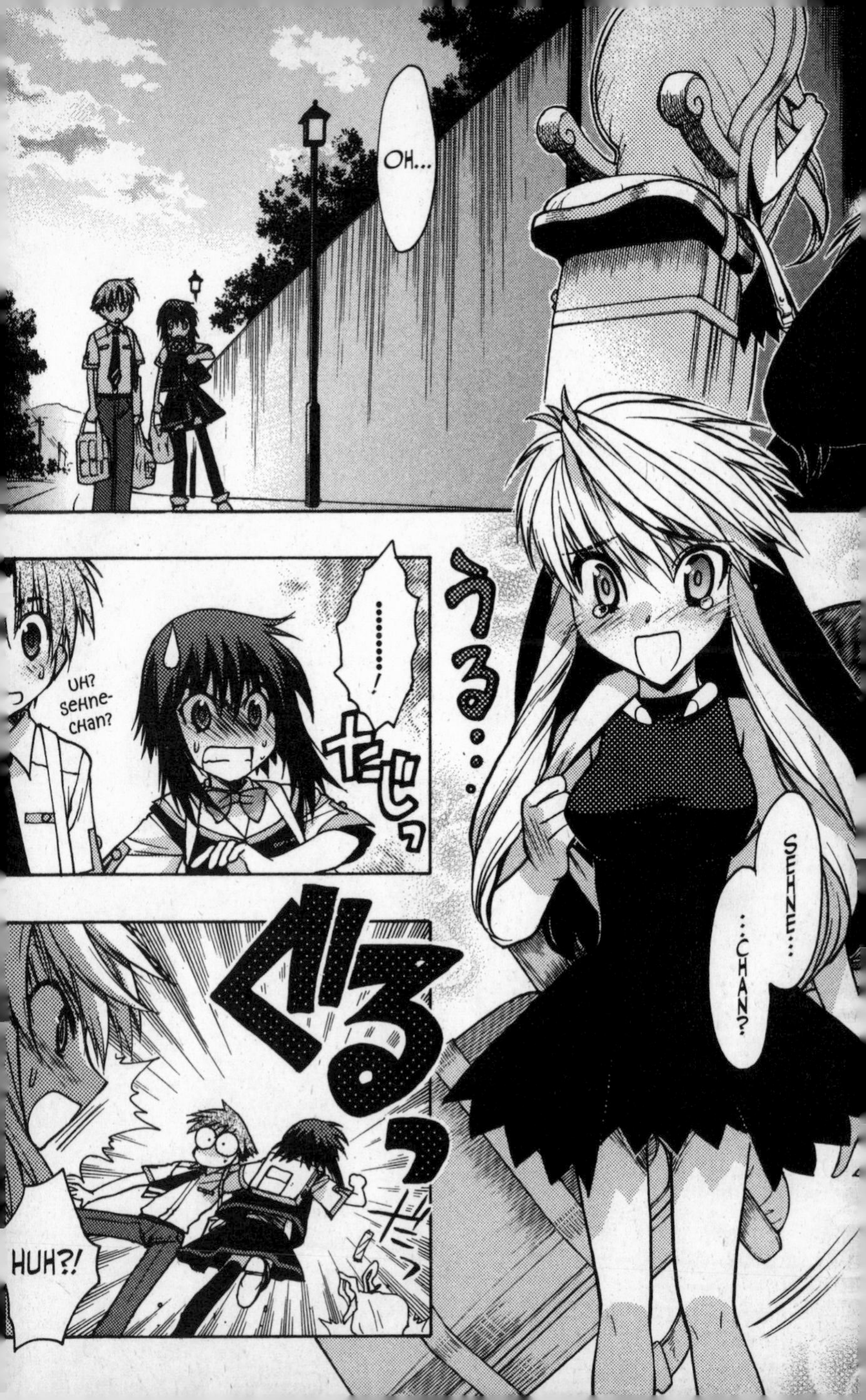
うる…
SEHNE… …CHAN?
OH…
…!
たじっ
UH? SEHNE-CHAN?
ぐるっ
HUH?!

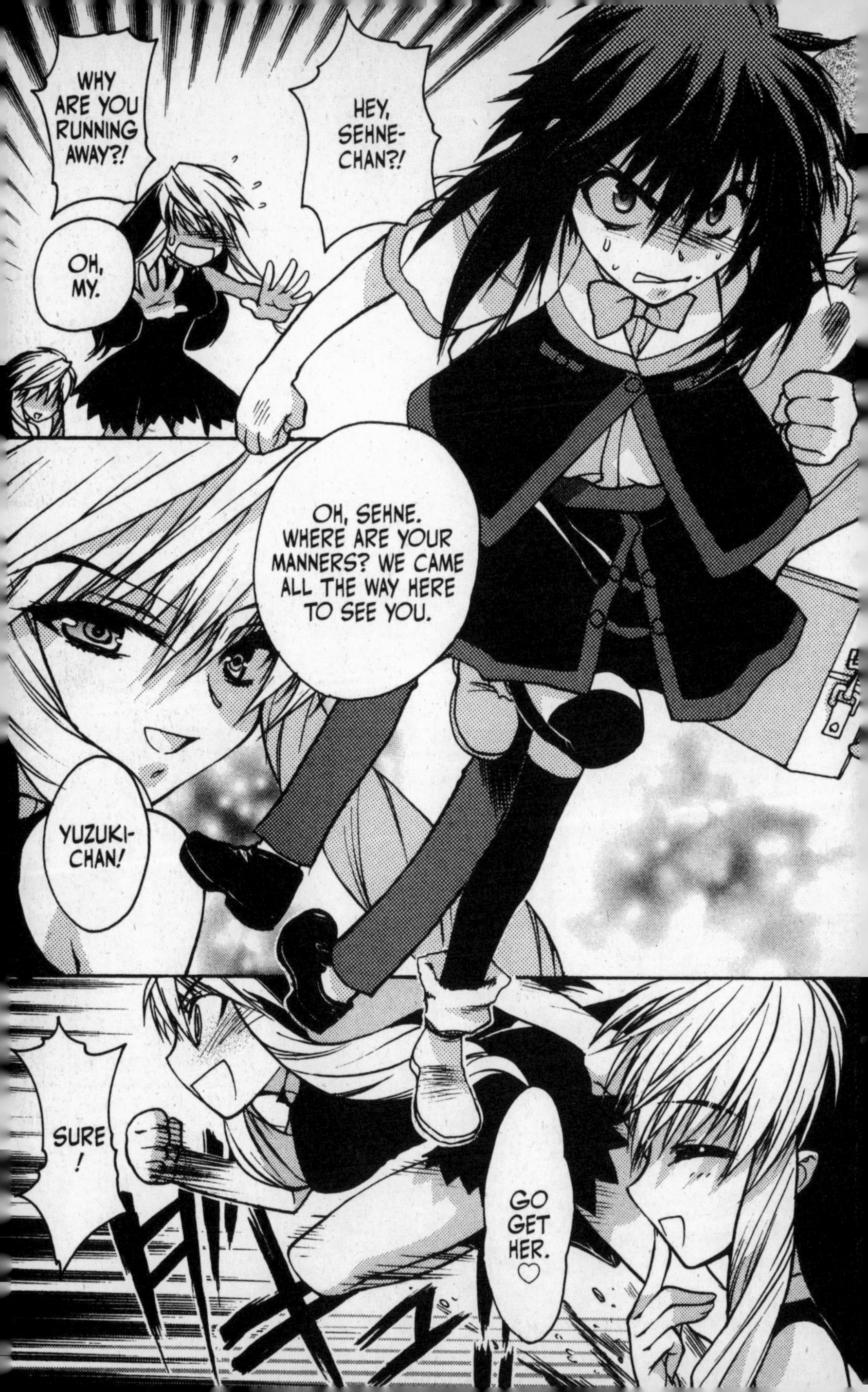
HEY, SEHNE-CHAN?!
WHY ARE YOU RUNNING AWAY?!
OH, MY.
OH, SEHNE. WHERE ARE YOUR MANNERS? WE CAME ALL THE WAY HERE TO SEE YOU.
YUZUKI-CHAN!
GO GET HER. ♡
SURE!

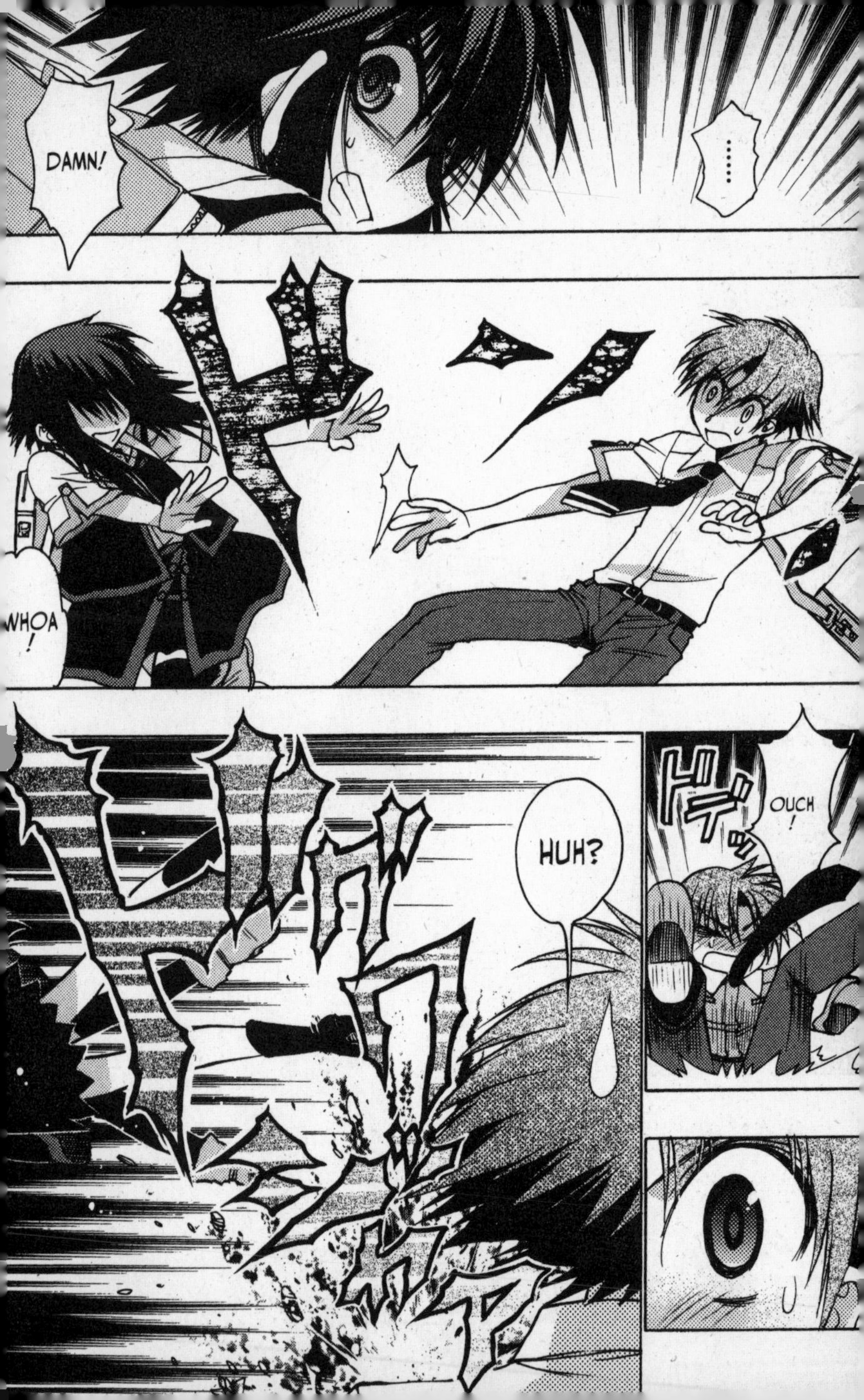
......
DAMN!
WHOA!
OUCH!
HUH?

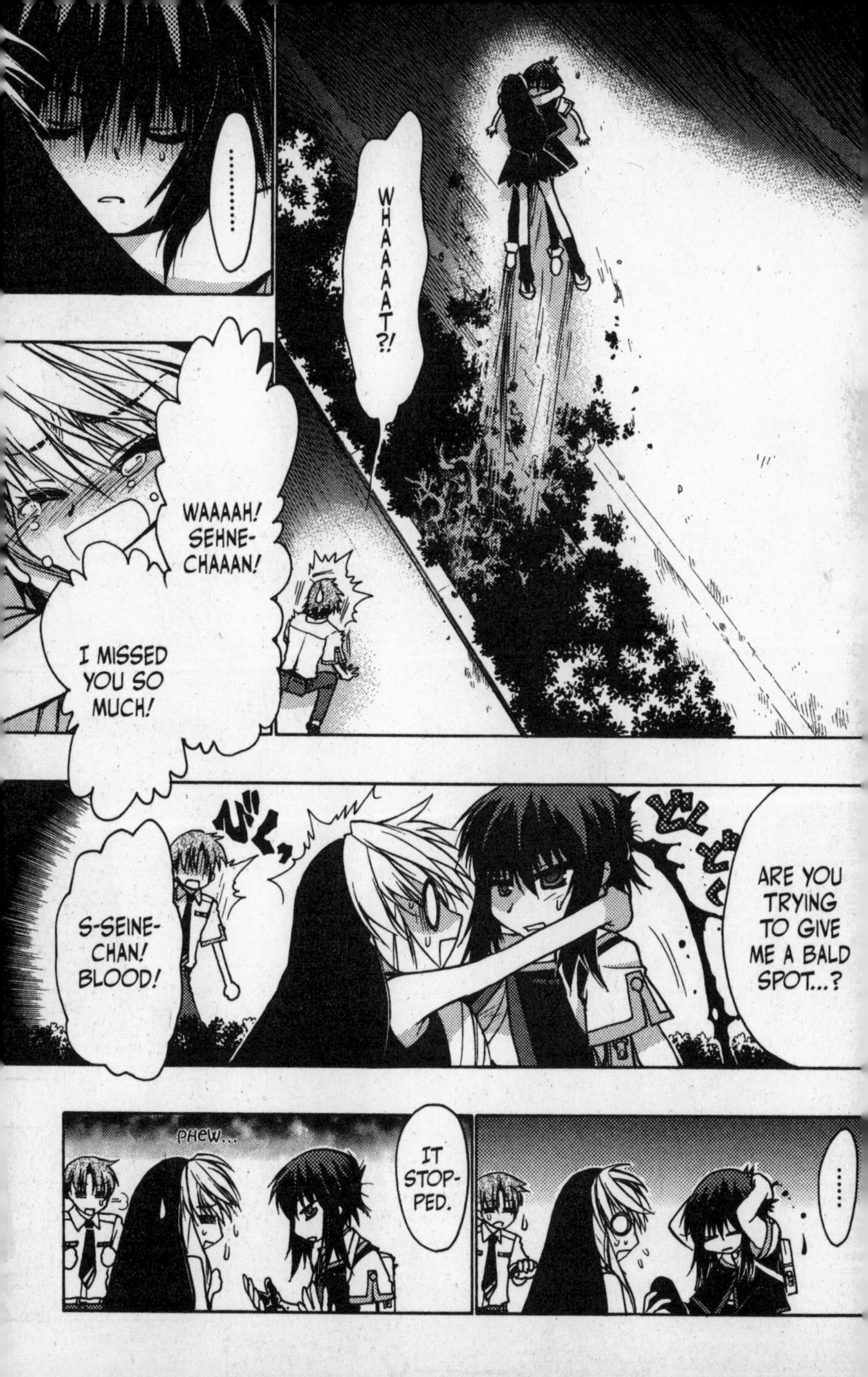
WHAAAAAT?!
......
WAAAAH! SEHNE-CHAAAN!
I MISSED YOU SO MUCH!
ARE YOU TRYING TO GIVE ME A BALD SPOT...?
S-SEINE-CHAN! BLOOD!
......
IT STOP-PED.
PHEW...

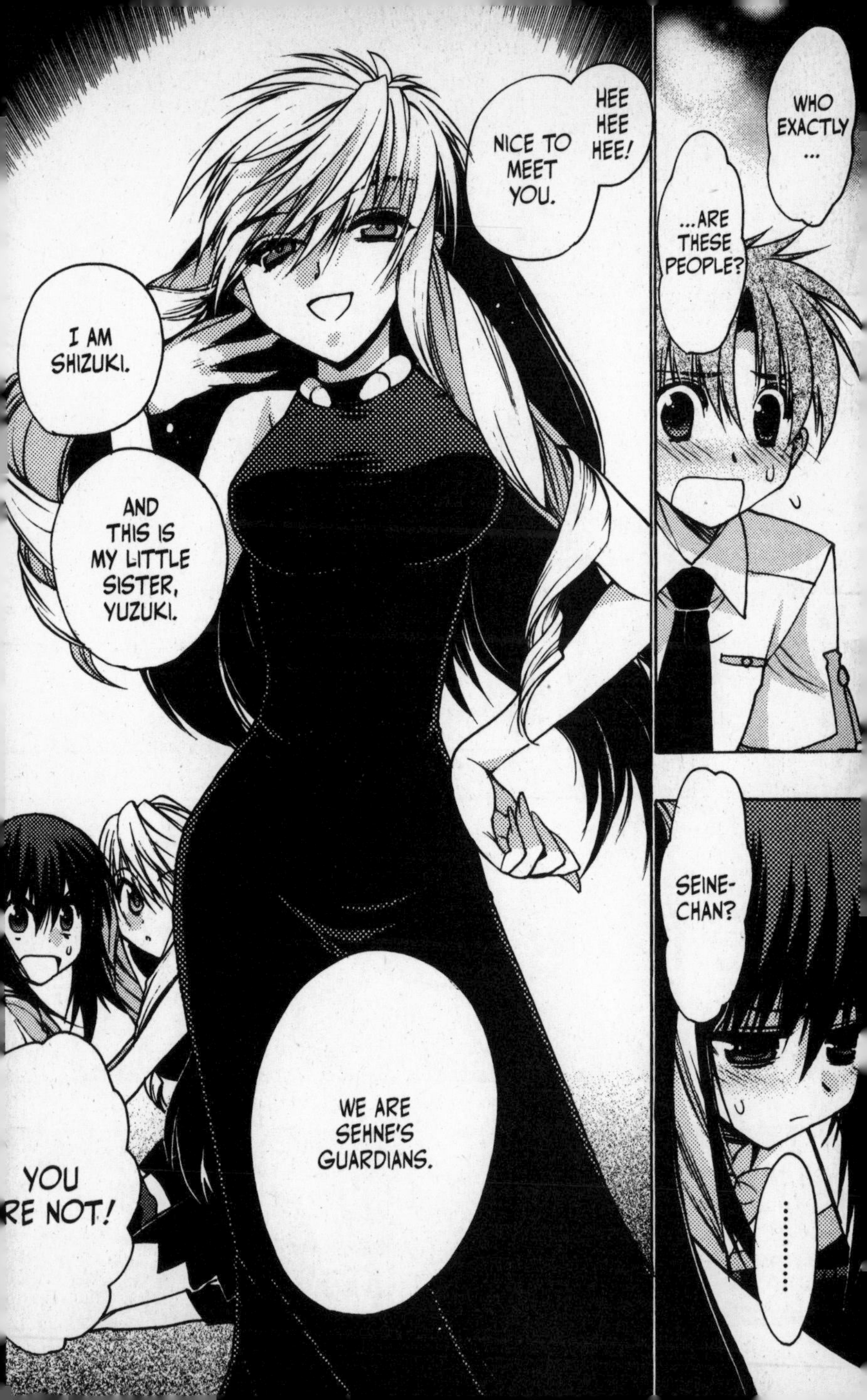
WHO EXACTLY ...
...ARE THESE PEOPLE?
SEINE-CHAN?
......
HEE HEE HEE!
NICE TO MEET YOU.
I AM SHIZUKI.
AND THIS IS MY LITTLE SISTER, YUZUKI.
WE ARE SEHNE'S GUARDIANS.
YOU RE NOT!

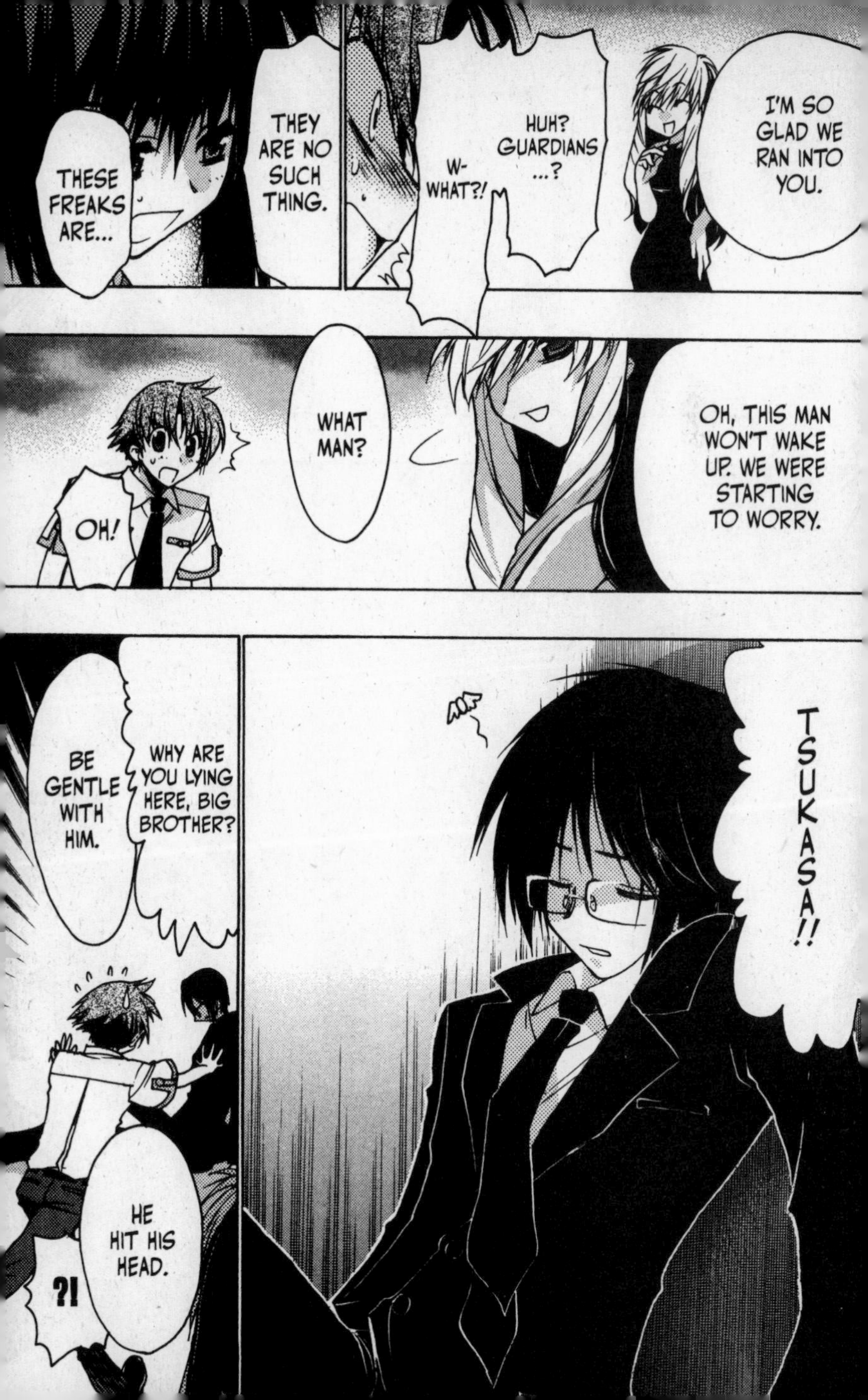
I'M SO GLAD WE RAN INTO YOU.
HUH? GUARDIANS ...?
W-WHAT?!
THEY ARE NO SUCH THING.
THESE FREAKS ARE...
OH, THIS MAN WON'T WAKE UP. WE WERE STARTING TO WORRY.
WHAT MAN?
OH!
TSUKASA!!
WHY ARE YOU LYING HERE, BIG BROTHER?
BE GENTLE WITH HIM.
HE HIT HIS HEAD.
?!

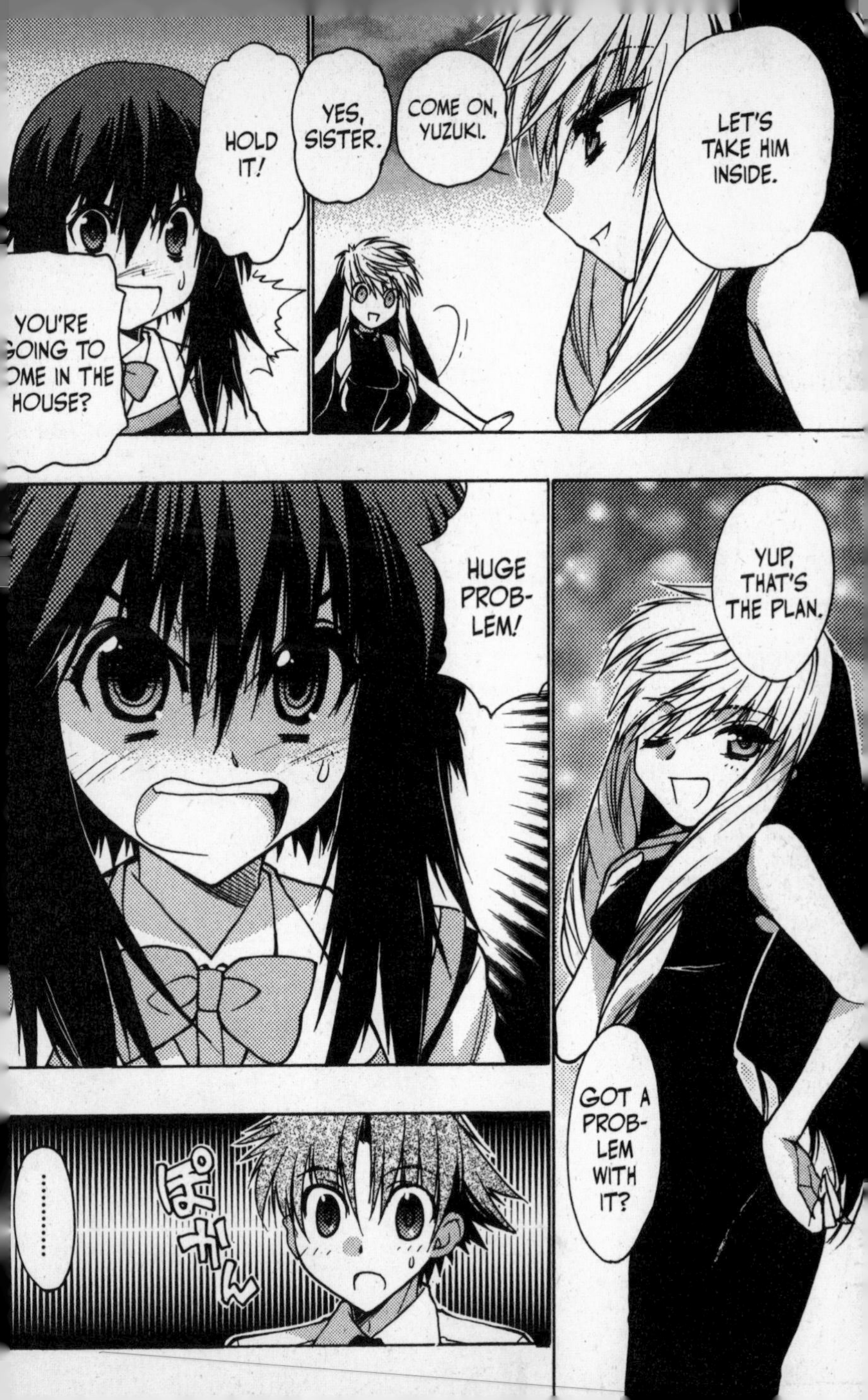
LET'S TAKE HIM INSIDE.
COME ON, YUZUKI.
YES, SISTER.
HOLD IT!
YOU'RE GOING TO OME IN THE HOUSE?
YUP, THAT'S THE PLAN.
GOT A PROB-LEM WITH IT?
HUGE PROB-LEM!
ぽかん
……

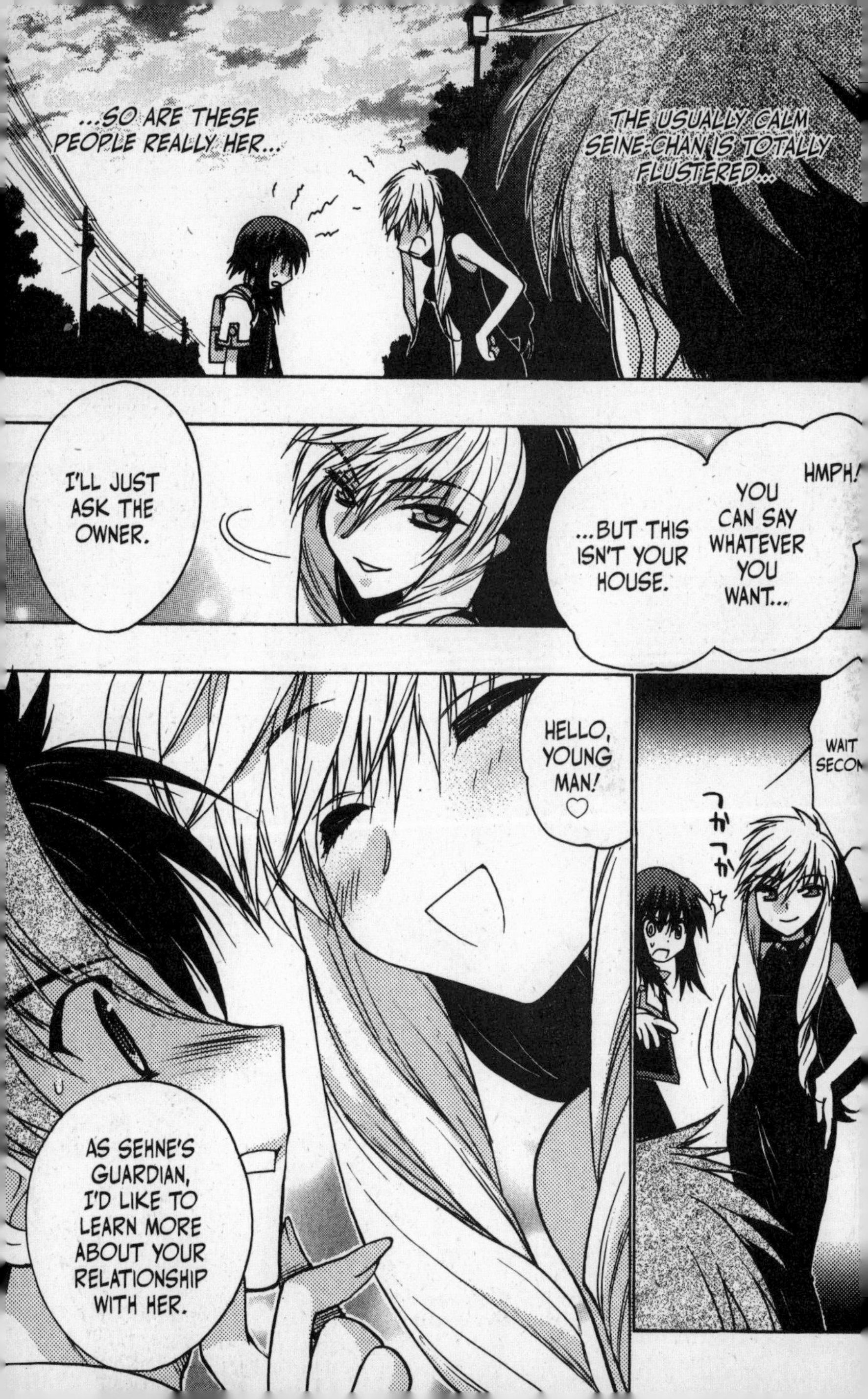
THE USUALLY CALM SEINE-CHAN IS TOTALLY FLUSTERED...
...SO ARE THESE PEOPLE REALLY HER...
HMPH! YOU CAN SAY WHATEVER YOU WANT...
...BUT THIS ISN'T YOUR HOUSE.
I'LL JUST ASK THE OWNER.
WAIT SECON
つかつか
HELLO, YOUNG MAN! ♡
AS SEHNE'S GUARDIAN, I'D LIKE TO LEARN MORE ABOUT YOUR RELATIONSHIP WITH HER.

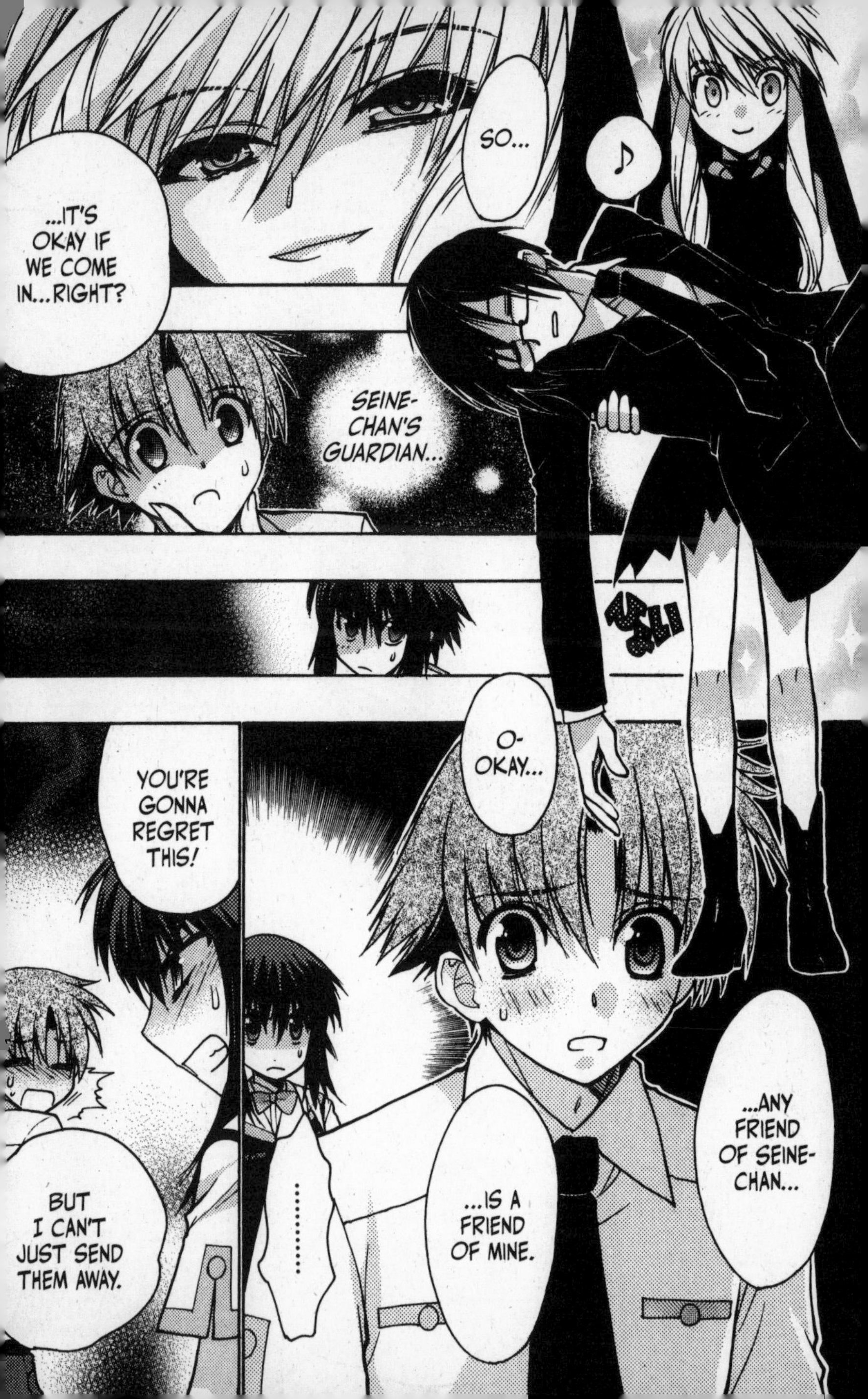
♪
SO...
...IT'S OKAY IF WE COME IN...RIGHT?
SEINE-CHAN'S GUARDIAN...
O-OKAY...
...ANY FRIEND OF SEINE-CHAN...
...IS A FRIEND OF MINE.
......
YOU'RE GONNA REGRET THIS!
BUT I CAN'T JUST SEND THEM AWAY.

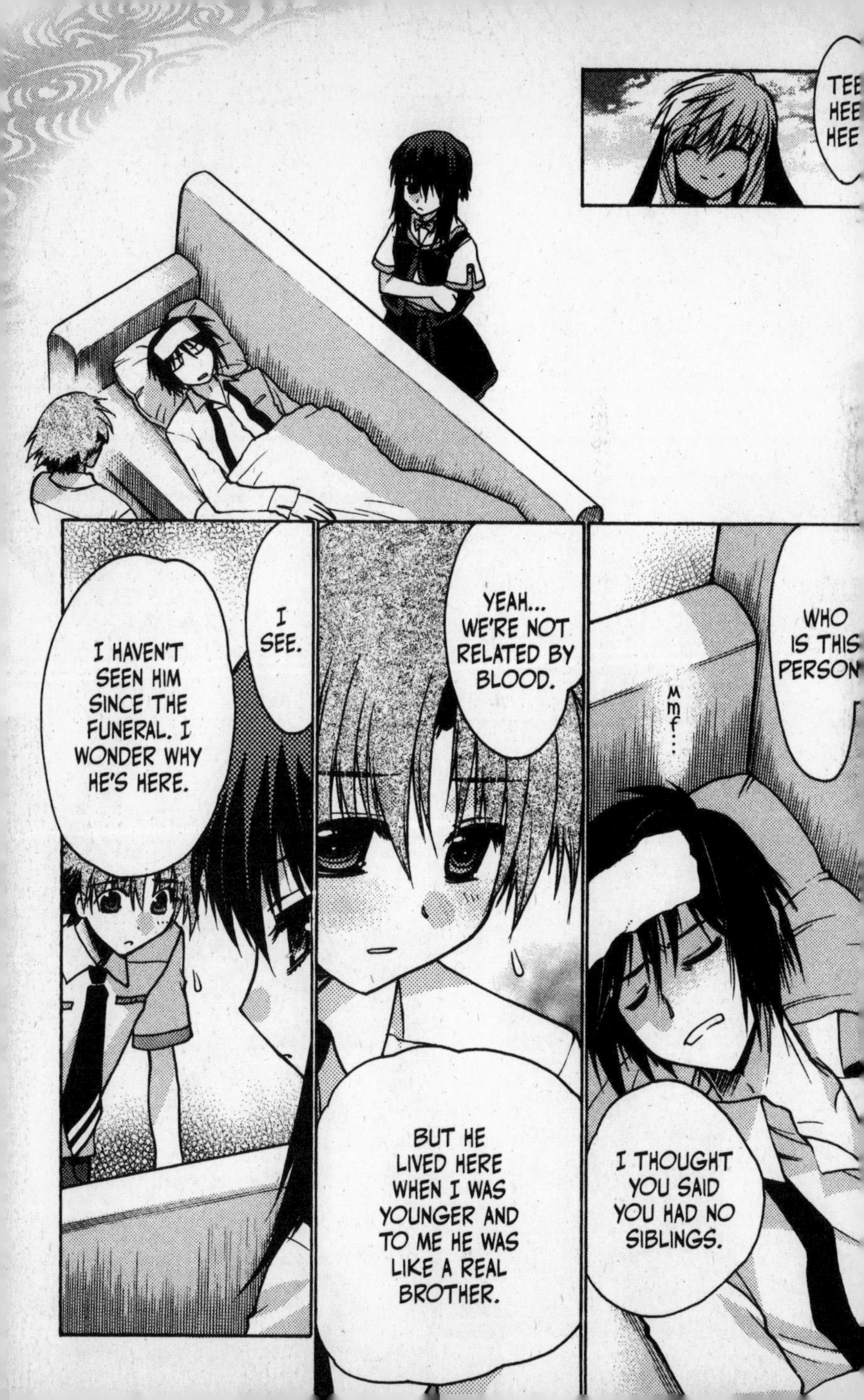
TEE HEE HEE
WHO IS THIS PERSON
mmf...
I THOUGHT YOU SAID YOU HAD NO SIBLINGS.
YEAH... WE'RE NOT RELATED BY BLOOD.
BUT HE LIVED HERE WHEN I WAS YOUNGER AND TO ME HE WAS LIKE A REAL BROTHER.
I SEE.
I HAVEN'T SEEN HIM SINCE THE FUNERAL. I WONDER WHY HE'S HERE.

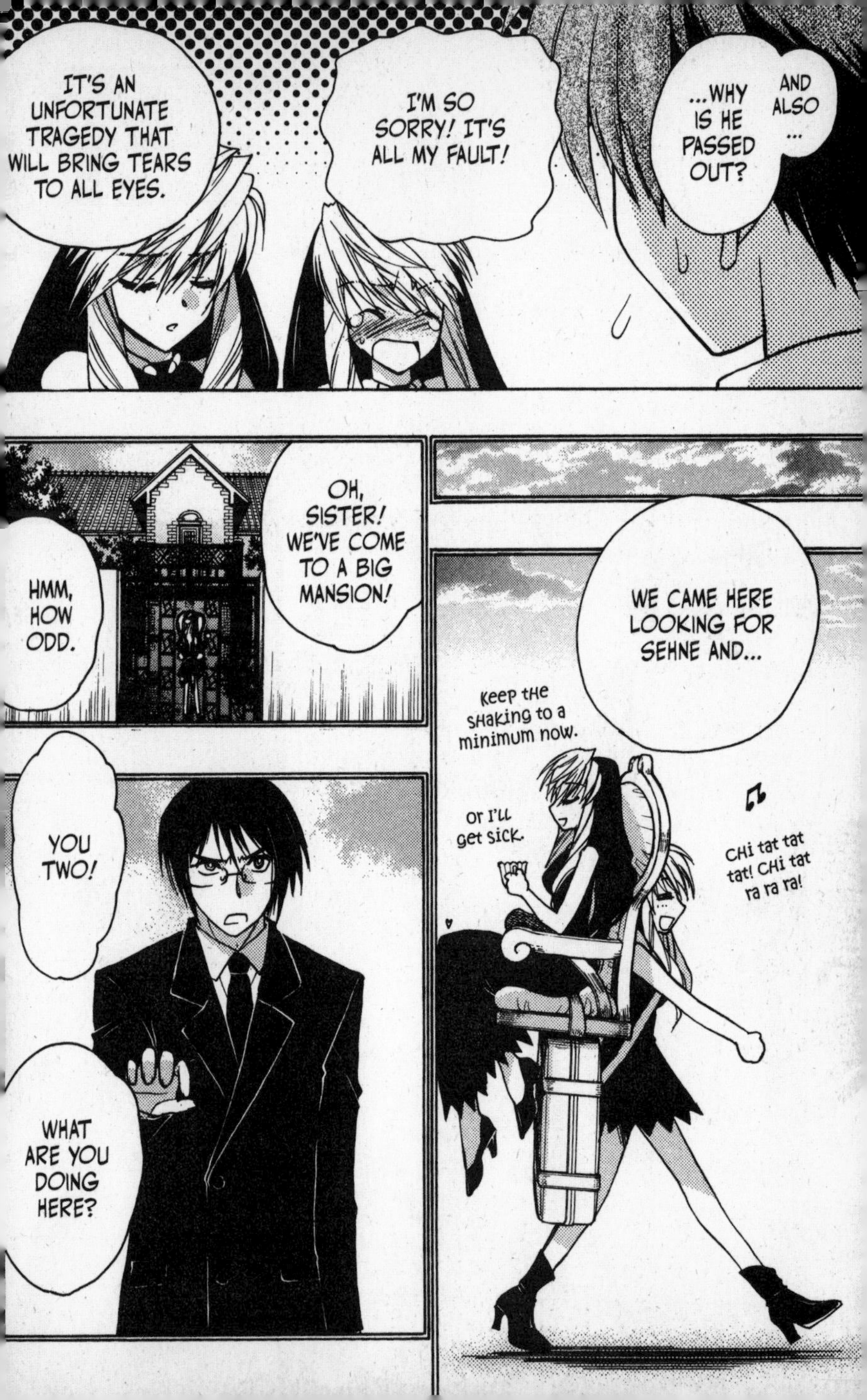
AND ALSO ...
...WHY IS HE PASSED OUT?
I'M SO SORRY! IT'S ALL MY FAULT!
IT'S AN UNFORTUNATE TRAGEDY THAT WILL BRING TEARS TO ALL EYES.
WE CAME HERE LOOKING FOR SEHNE AND...
CHi tat tat tat! CHi tat ra ra ra!
Keep tHe SHaking to a minimum now.
Or I'll get sick.
OH, SISTER! WE'VE COME TO A BIG MANSION!
HMM, HOW ODD.
YOU TWO!
WHAT ARE YOU DOING HERE?

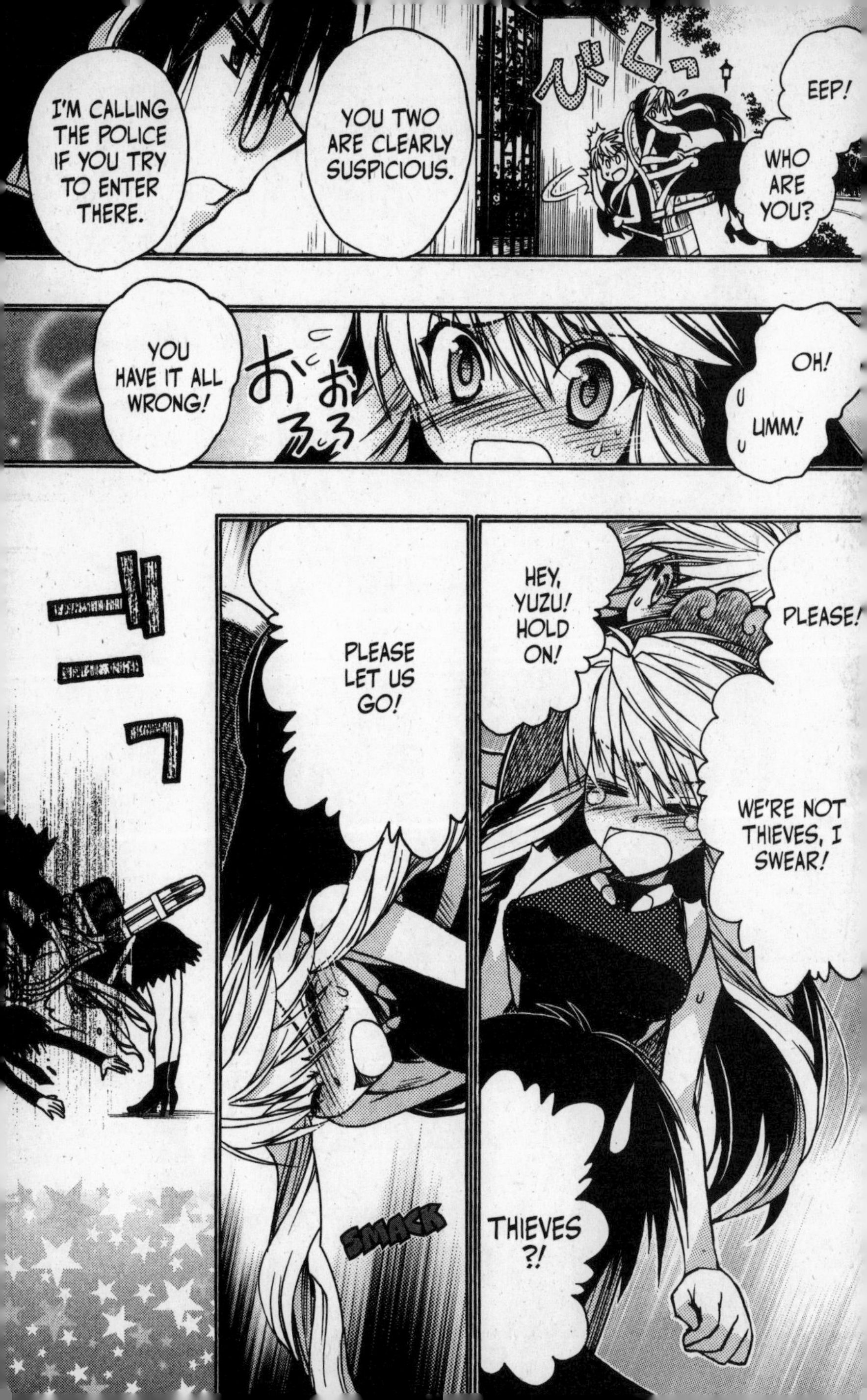
びくっ
EEP!
WHO ARE YOU?
YOU TWO ARE CLEARLY SUSPICIOUS.
I'M CALLING THE POLICE IF YOU TRY TO ENTER THERE.
OH!
UMM!
おろおろ
YOU HAVE IT ALL WRONG!
PLEASE!
HEY, YUZU! HOLD ON!
WE'RE NOT THIEVES, I SWEAR!
THIEVES?!
PLEASE LET US GO!
SMACK

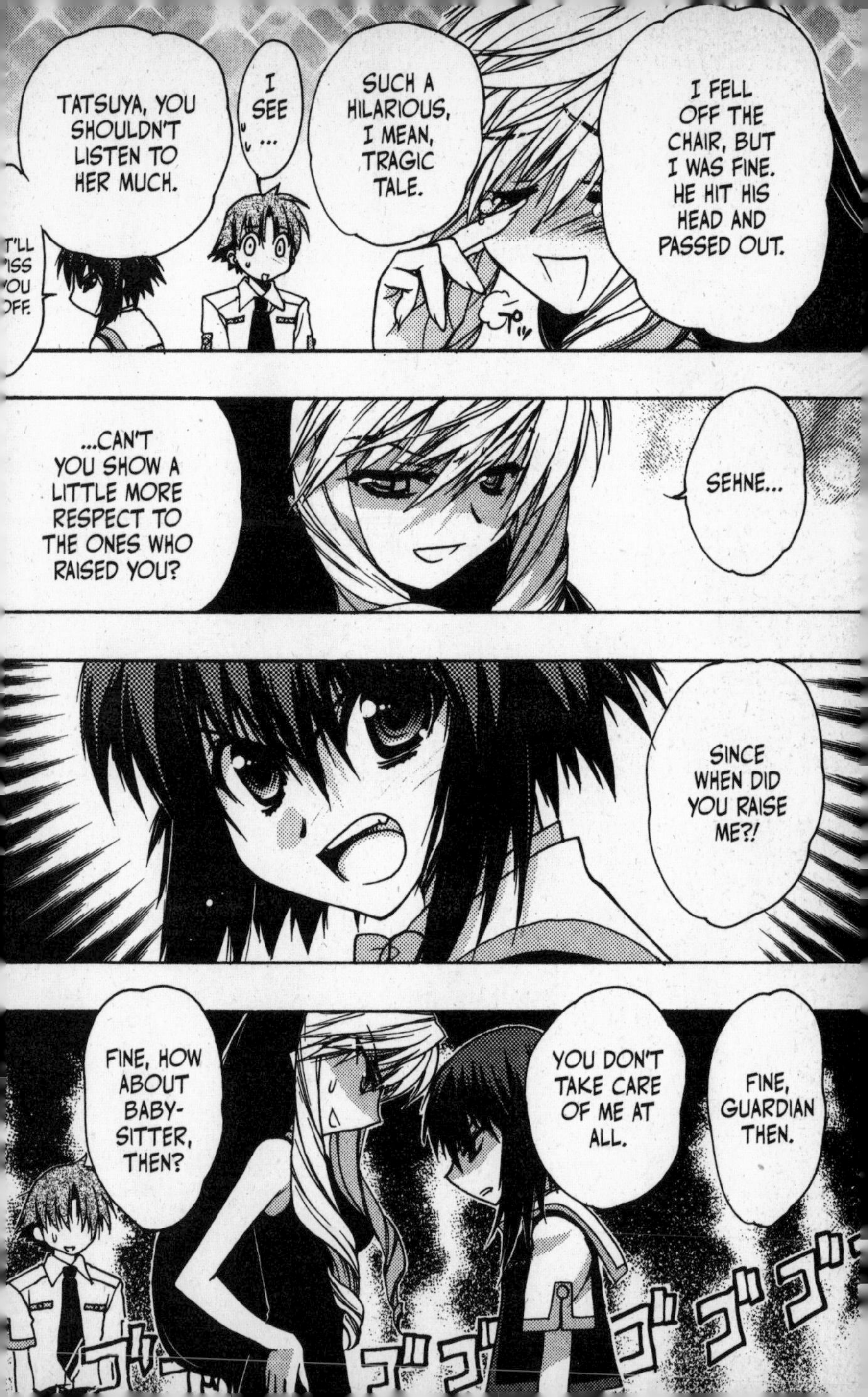
I FELL OFF THE CHAIR, BUT I WAS FINE. HE HIT HIS HEAD AND PASSED OUT.
SUCH A HILARIOUS, I MEAN, TRAGIC TALE.
I SEE...
TATSUYA, YOU SHOULDN'T LISTEN TO HER MUCH.
SEHNE...
...CAN'T YOU SHOW A LITTLE MORE RESPECT TO THE ONES WHO RAISED YOU?
SINCE WHEN DID YOU RAISE ME?!
FINE, GUARDIAN THEN.
YOU DON'T TAKE CARE OF ME AT ALL.
FINE, HOW ABOUT BABY-SITTER, THEN?

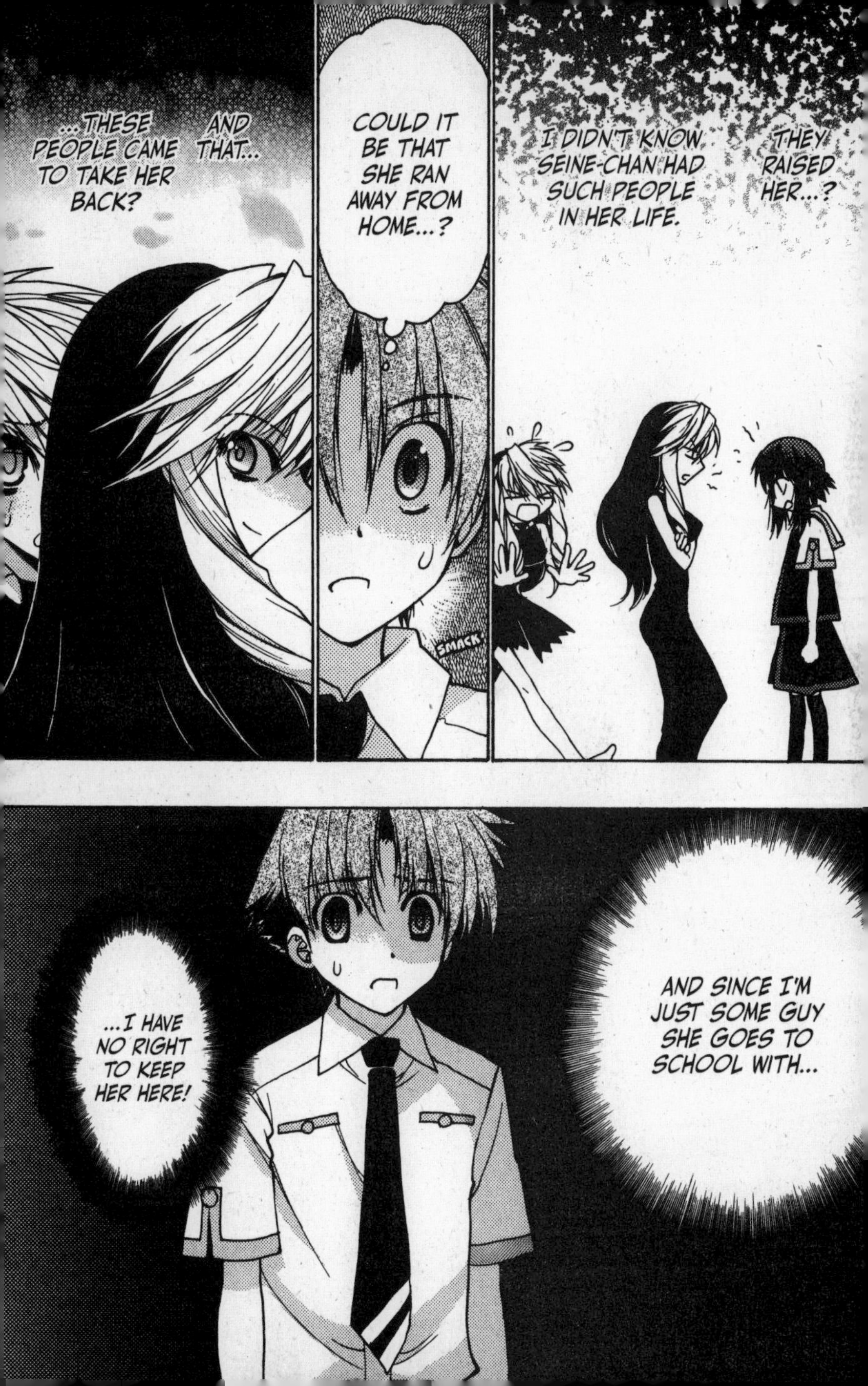
THEY RAISED HER...?
I DIDN'T KNOW SEINE-CHAN HAD SUCH PEOPLE IN HER LIFE.
COULD IT BE THAT SHE RAN AWAY FROM HOME...?
SMACK
AND THAT...
...THESE PEOPLE CAME TO TAKE HER BACK?
AND SINCE I'M JUST SOME GUY SHE GOES TO SCHOOL WITH...
...I HAVE NO RIGHT TO KEEP HER HERE!

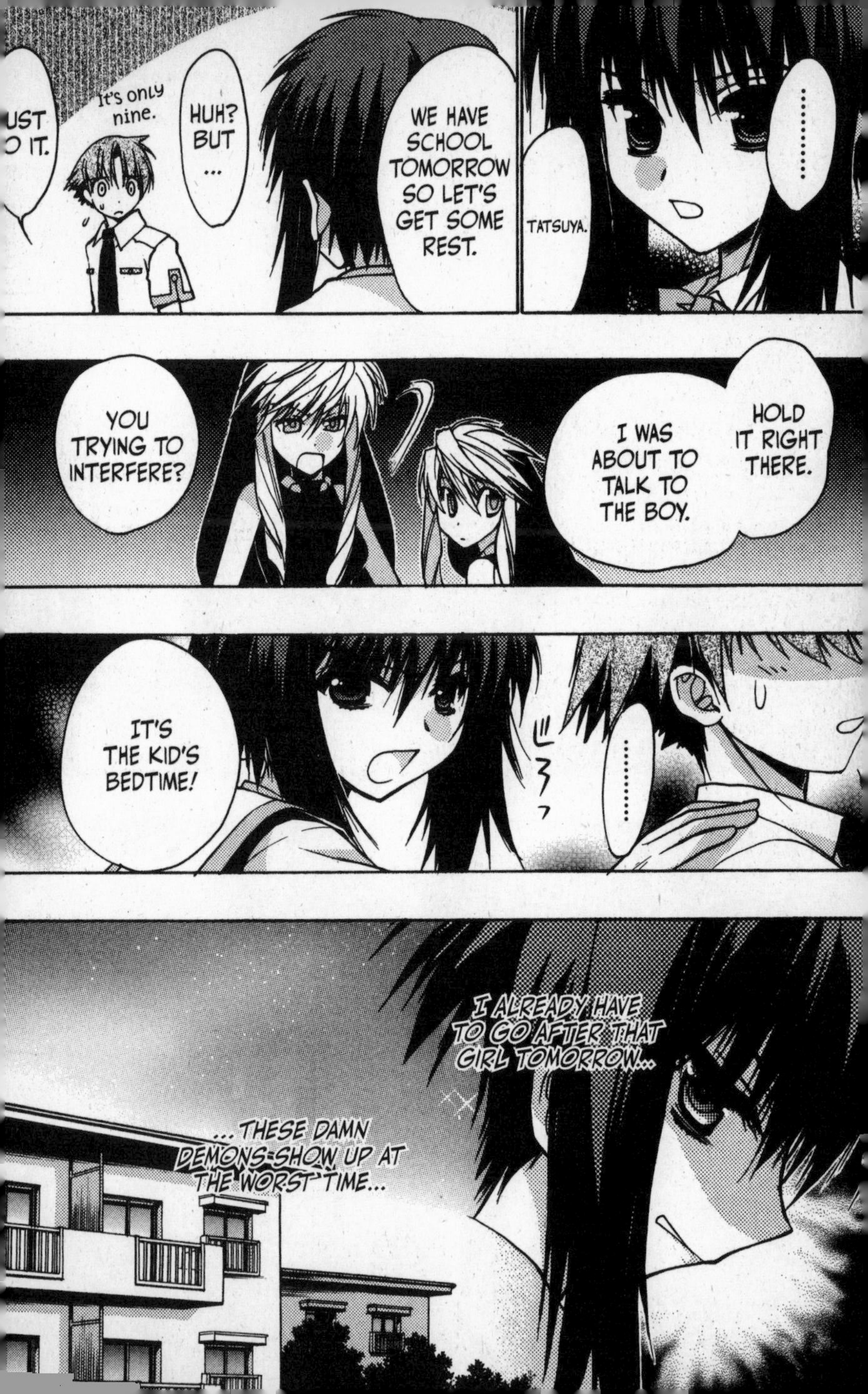

......
TATSUYA.
WE HAVE SCHOOL TOMORROW SO LET'S GET SOME REST.
HUH? BUT ...
It's only nine.
UST O IT.
HOLD IT RIGHT THERE.
I WAS ABOUT TO TALK TO THE BOY.
YOU TRYING TO INTERFERE?
......
ジロッ
IT'S THE KID'S BEDTIME!
I ALREADY HAVE TO GO AFTER THAT GIRL TOMORROW...
... THESE DAMN DEMONS SHOW UP AT THE WORST TIME...

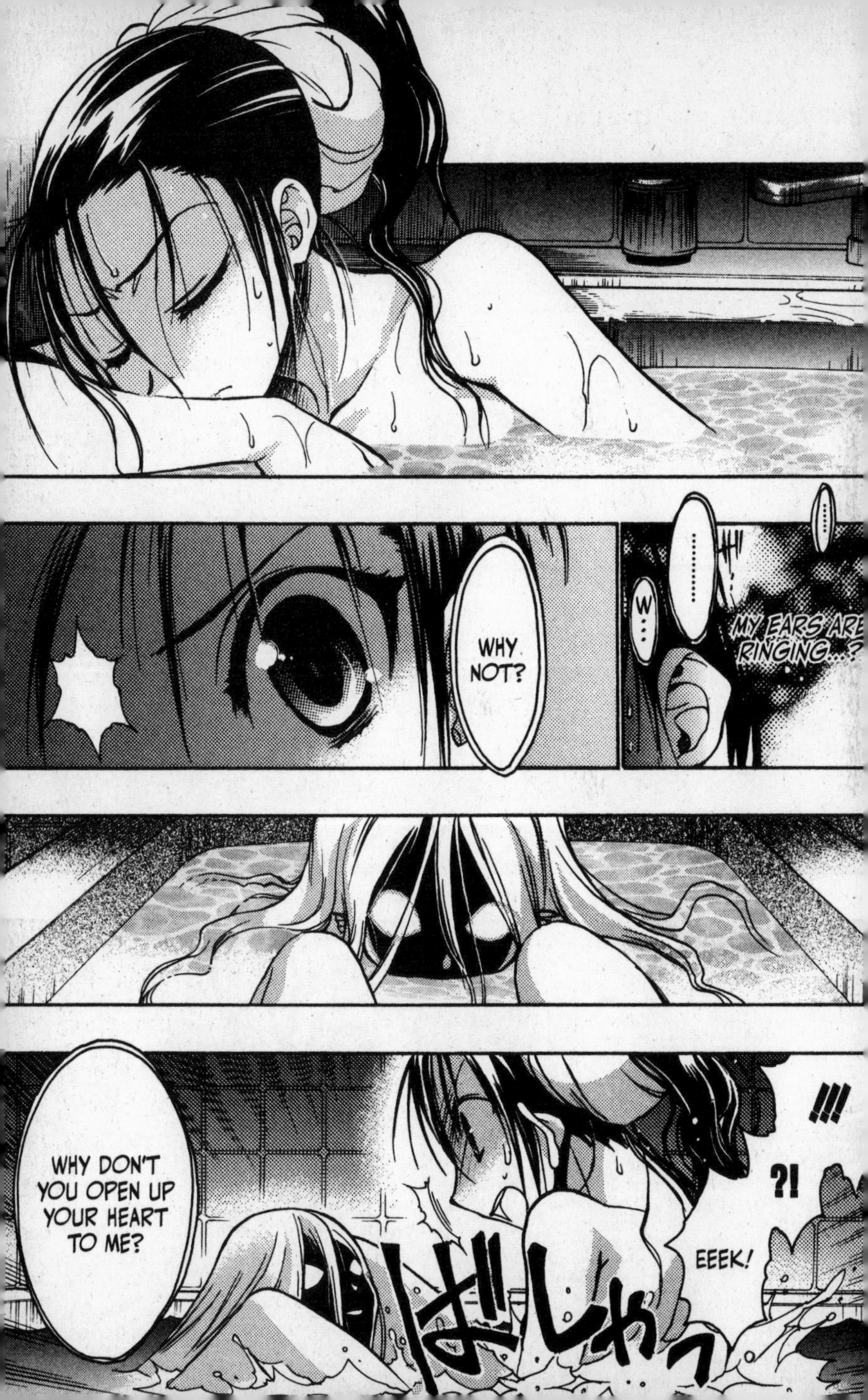

.....
....
MY EARS ARE RINGING...?
W...
WHY NOT?
!!!
?!
EEEK!
WHY DON'T YOU OPEN UP YOUR HEART TO ME?
ばしゃっ

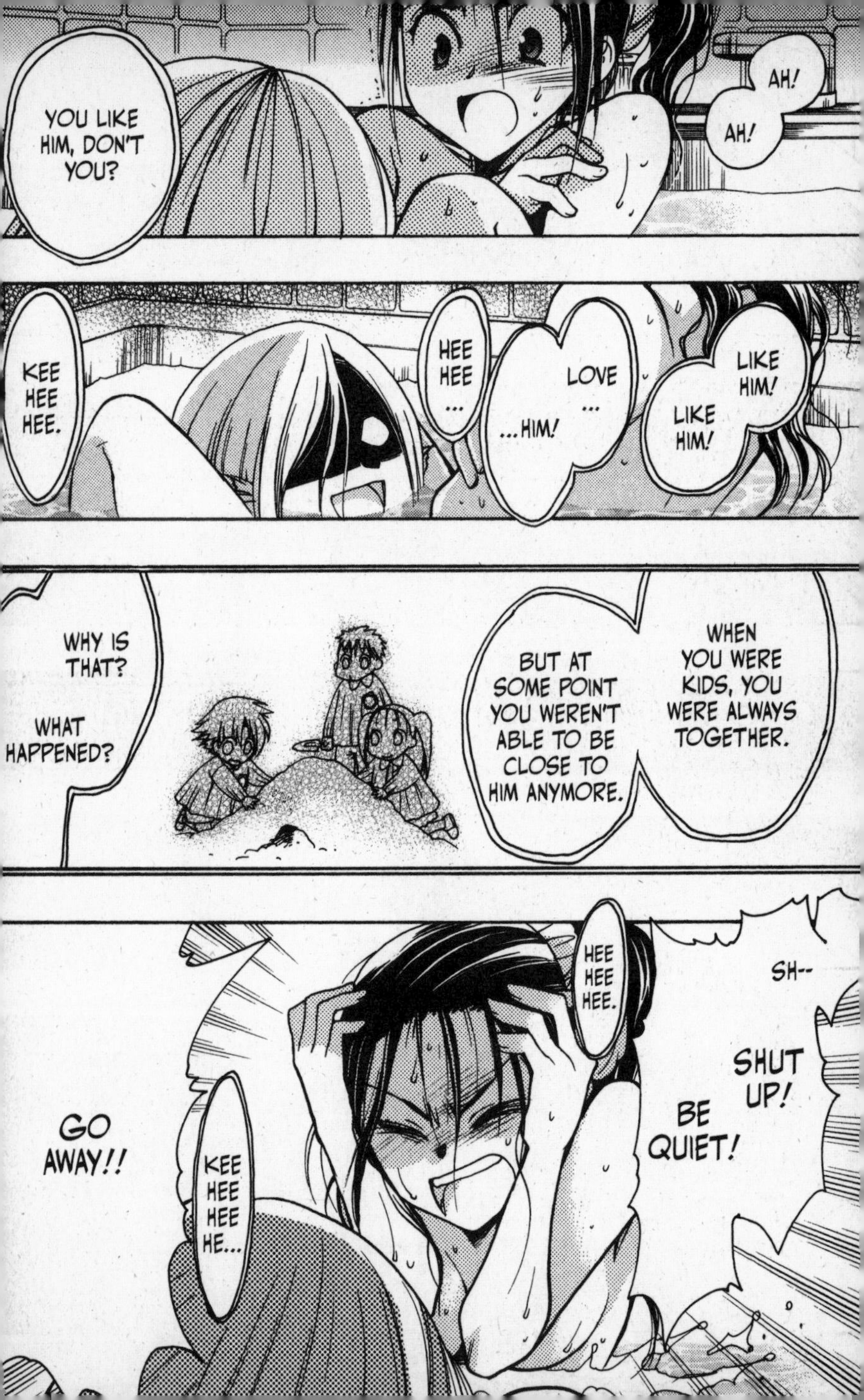
AH!
AH!
YOU LIKE HIM, DON'T YOU?
LIKE HIM! LIKE HIM!
LOVE ... ...HIM!
HEE HEE ...
KEE HEE HEE.
WHEN YOU WERE KIDS, YOU WERE ALWAYS TOGETHER.
BUT AT SOME POINT YOU WEREN'T ABLE TO BE CLOSE TO HIM ANYMORE.
WHY IS THAT?
WHAT HAPPENED?
SH--
SHUT UP!
BE QUIET!
HEE HEE HEE.
KEE HEE HEE HE...
GO AWAY!!

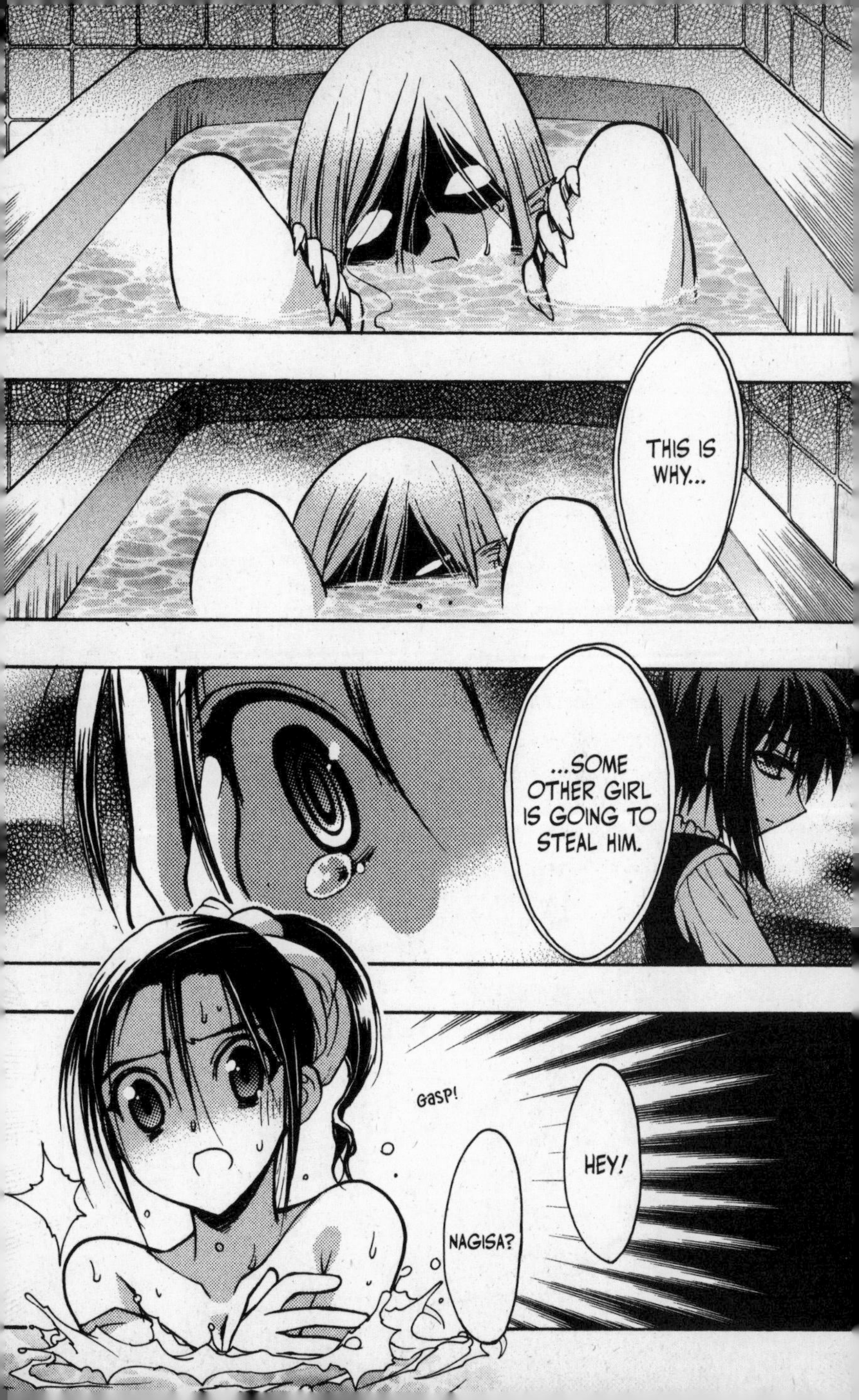
THIS IS WHY...
...SOME OTHER GIRL IS GOING TO STEAL HIM.
HEY!
NAGISA?
GASP!

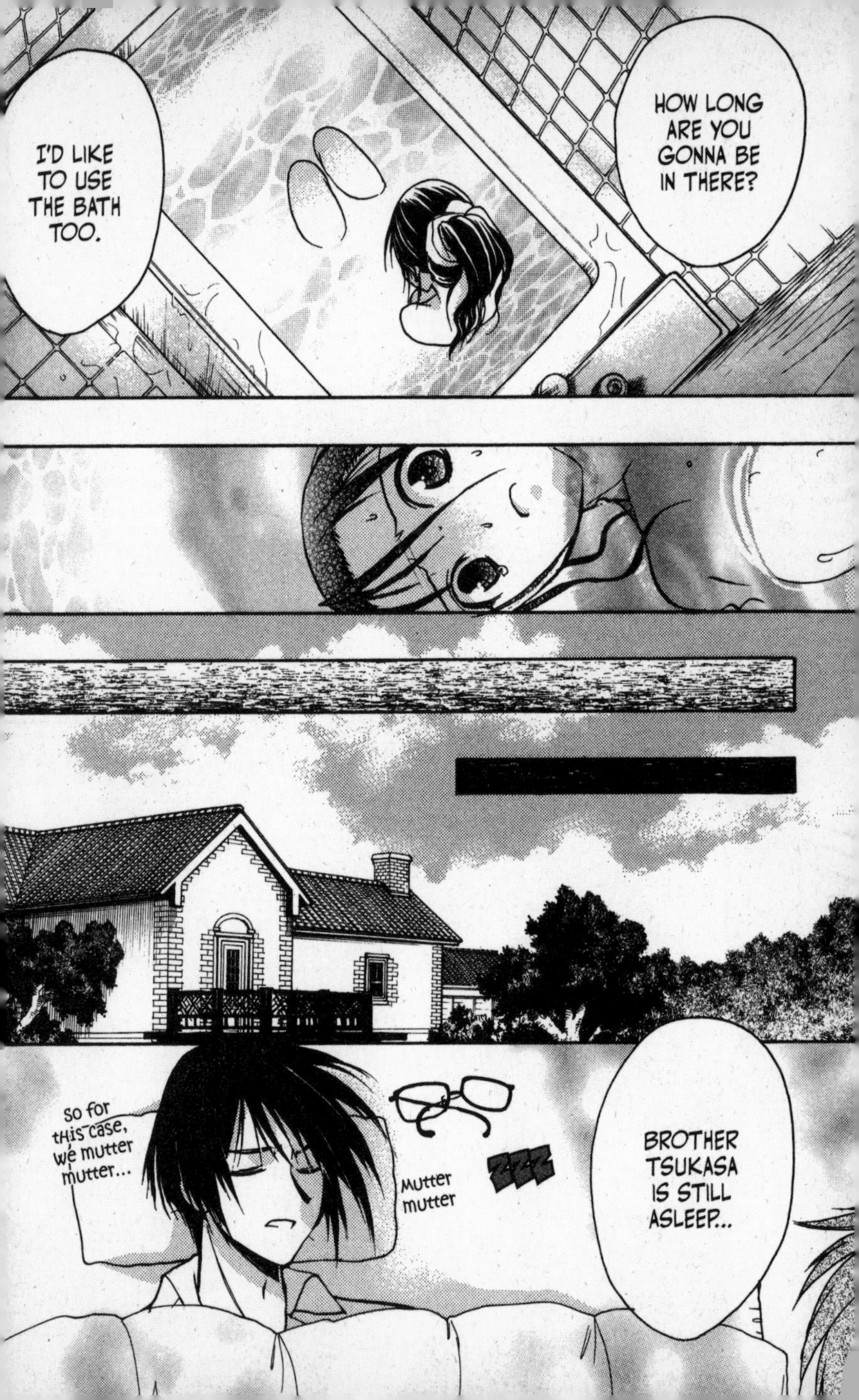
HOW LONG ARE YOU GONNA BE IN THERE?
I'D LIKE TO USE THE BATH TOO.
[redacted]
BROTHER TSUKASA IS STILL ASLEEP...
ZZZ
Mutter mutter
So for this case, we mutter mutter...

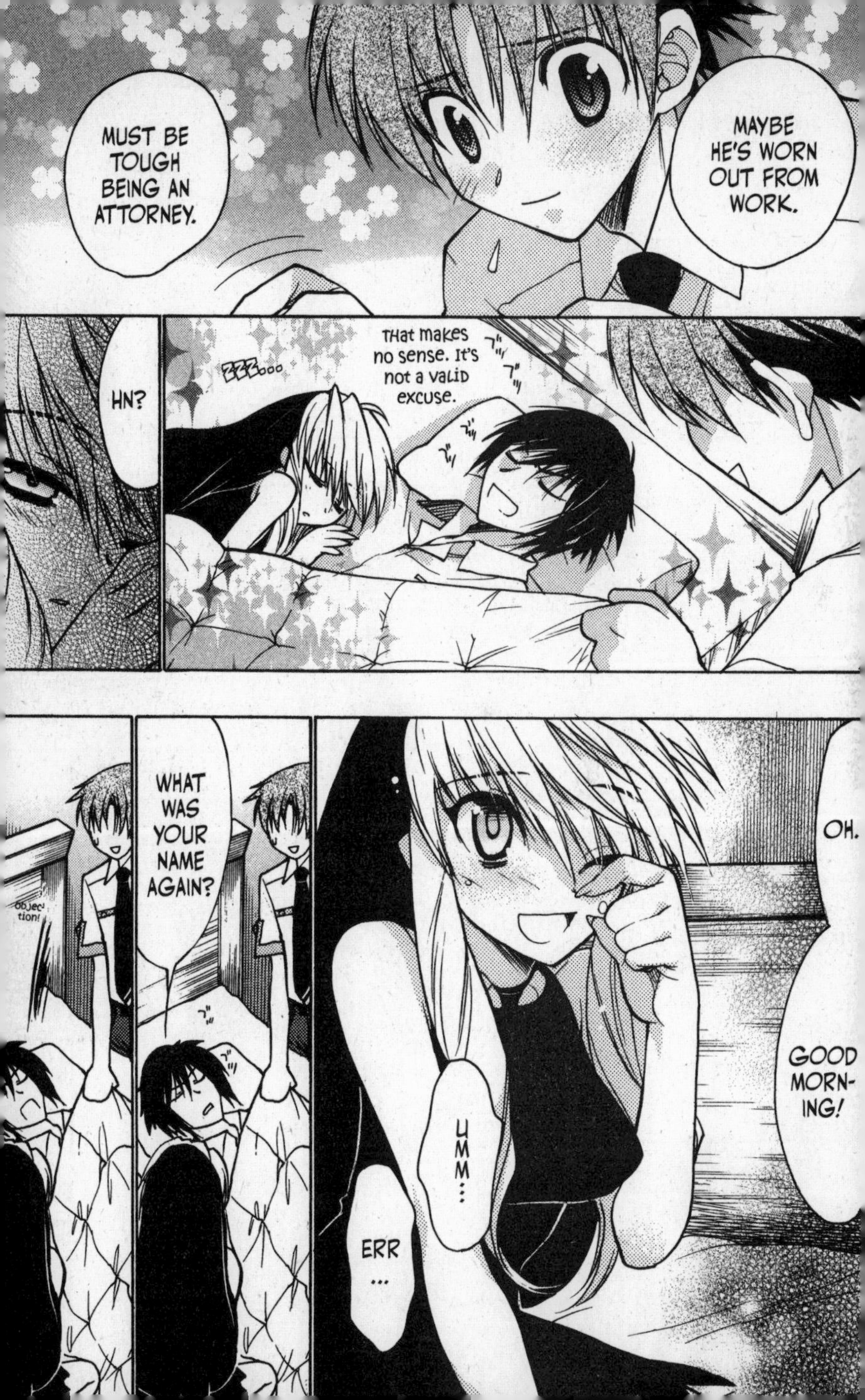
MAYBE HE'S WORN OUT FROM WORK.
MUST BE TOUGH BEING AN ATTORNEY.
That makes no sense. It's not a valid excuse.
ZZZ...
HN?
OH.
GOOD MORNING!
UMM...
ERR ...
WHAT WAS YOUR NAME AGAIN?
objection!

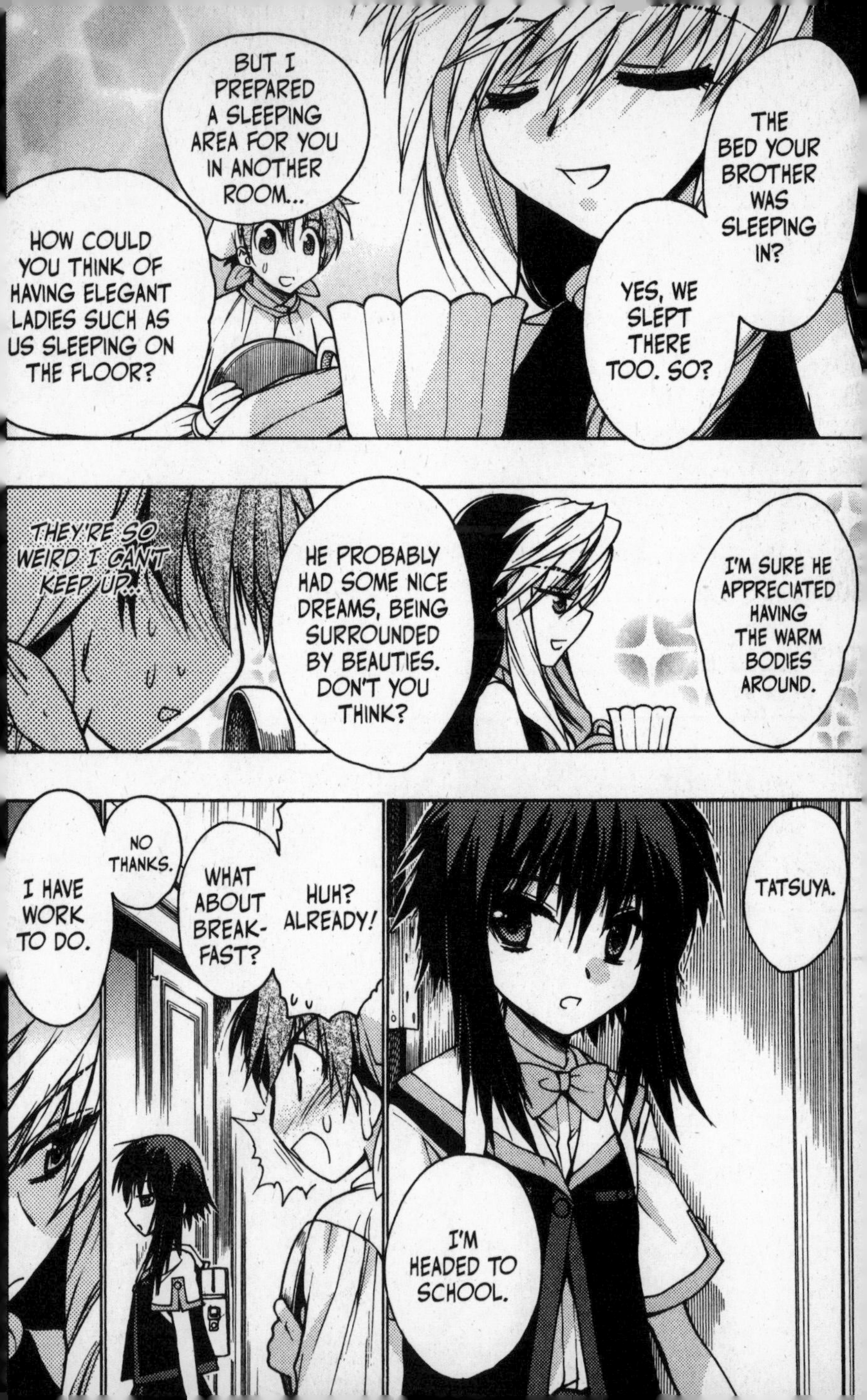
THE BED YOUR BROTHER WAS SLEEPING IN?
YES, WE SLEPT THERE TOO. SO?
BUT I PREPARED A SLEEPING AREA FOR YOU IN ANOTHER ROOM...
HOW COULD YOU THINK OF HAVING ELEGANT LADIES SUCH AS US SLEEPING ON THE FLOOR?
I'M SURE HE APPRECIATED HAVING THE WARM BODIES AROUND.
HE PROBABLY HAD SOME NICE DREAMS, BEING SURROUNDED BY BEAUTIES. DON'T YOU THINK?
THEY'RE SO WEIRD I CAN'T KEEP UP...
TATSUYA.
I'M HEADED TO SCHOOL.
HUH? ALREADY!
WHAT ABOUT BREAK-FAST?
NO THANKS.
I HAVE WORK TO DO.

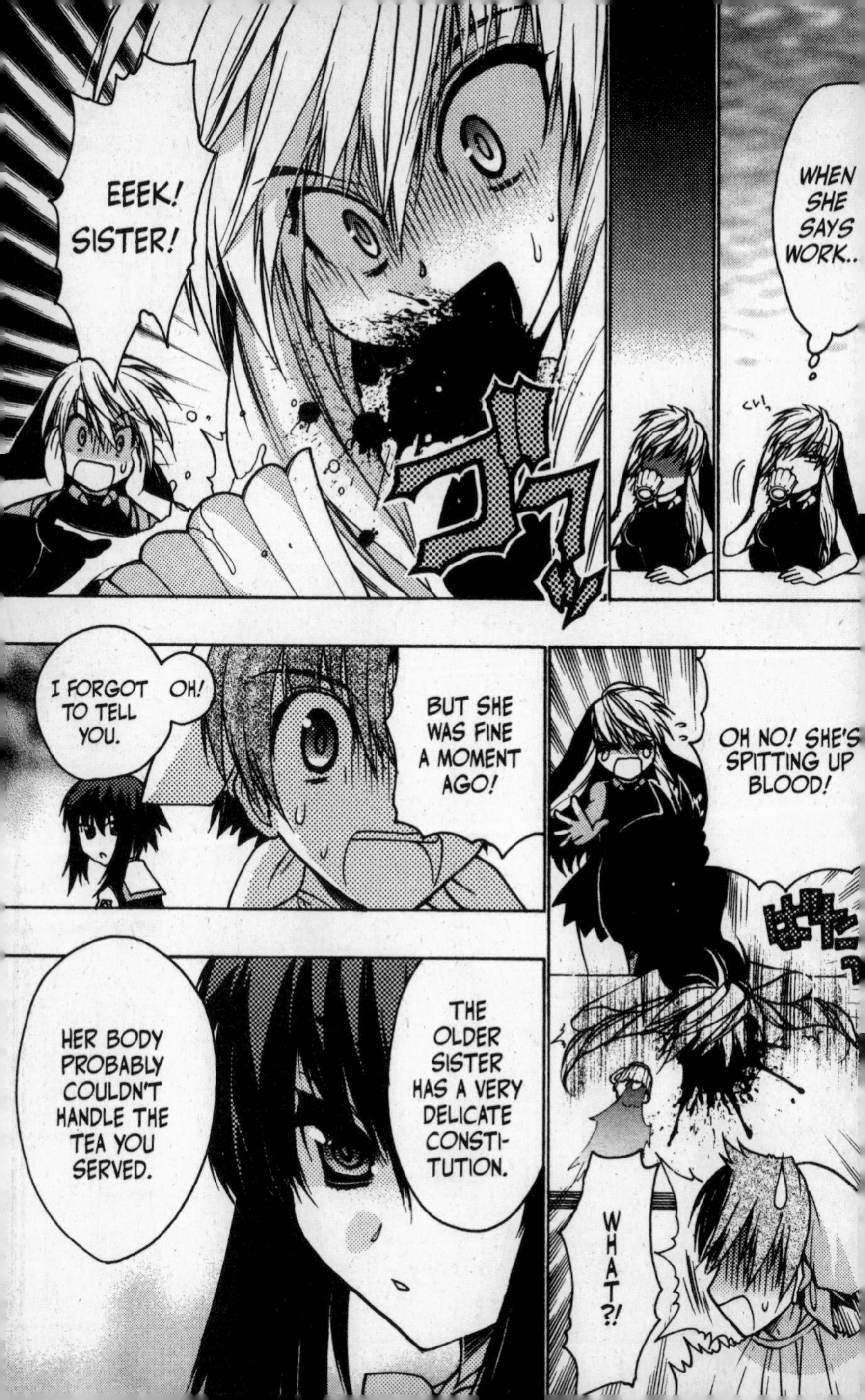
WHEN SHE SAYS WORK...
EEEK! SISTER!
OH NO! SHE'S SPITTING UP BLOOD!
WHAT?!
BUT SHE WAS FINE A MOMENT AGO!
OH! I FORGOT TO TELL YOU.
THE OLDER SISTER HAS A VERY DELICATE CONSTI-TUTION.
HER BODY PROBABLY COULDN'T HANDLE THE TEA YOU SERVED.

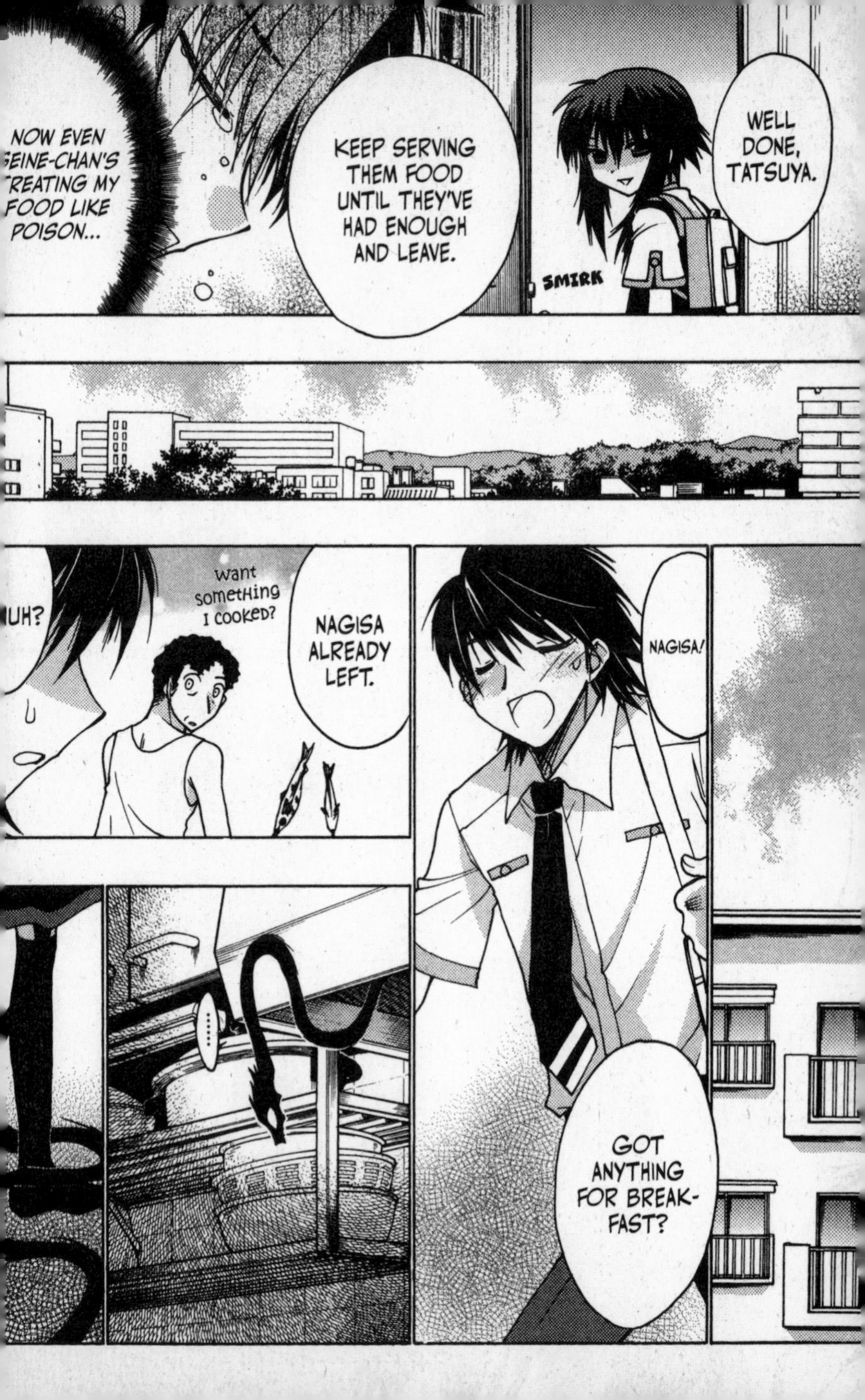
WELL DONE, TATSUYA.
SMIRK
KEEP SERVING THEM FOOD UNTIL THEY'VE HAD ENOUGH AND LEAVE.
NOW EVEN EINE-CHAN'S REATING MY FOOD LIKE POISON...
NAGISA!
GOT ANYTHING FOR BREAK-FAST?
NAGISA ALREADY LEFT.
Want something I cooked?
UH?

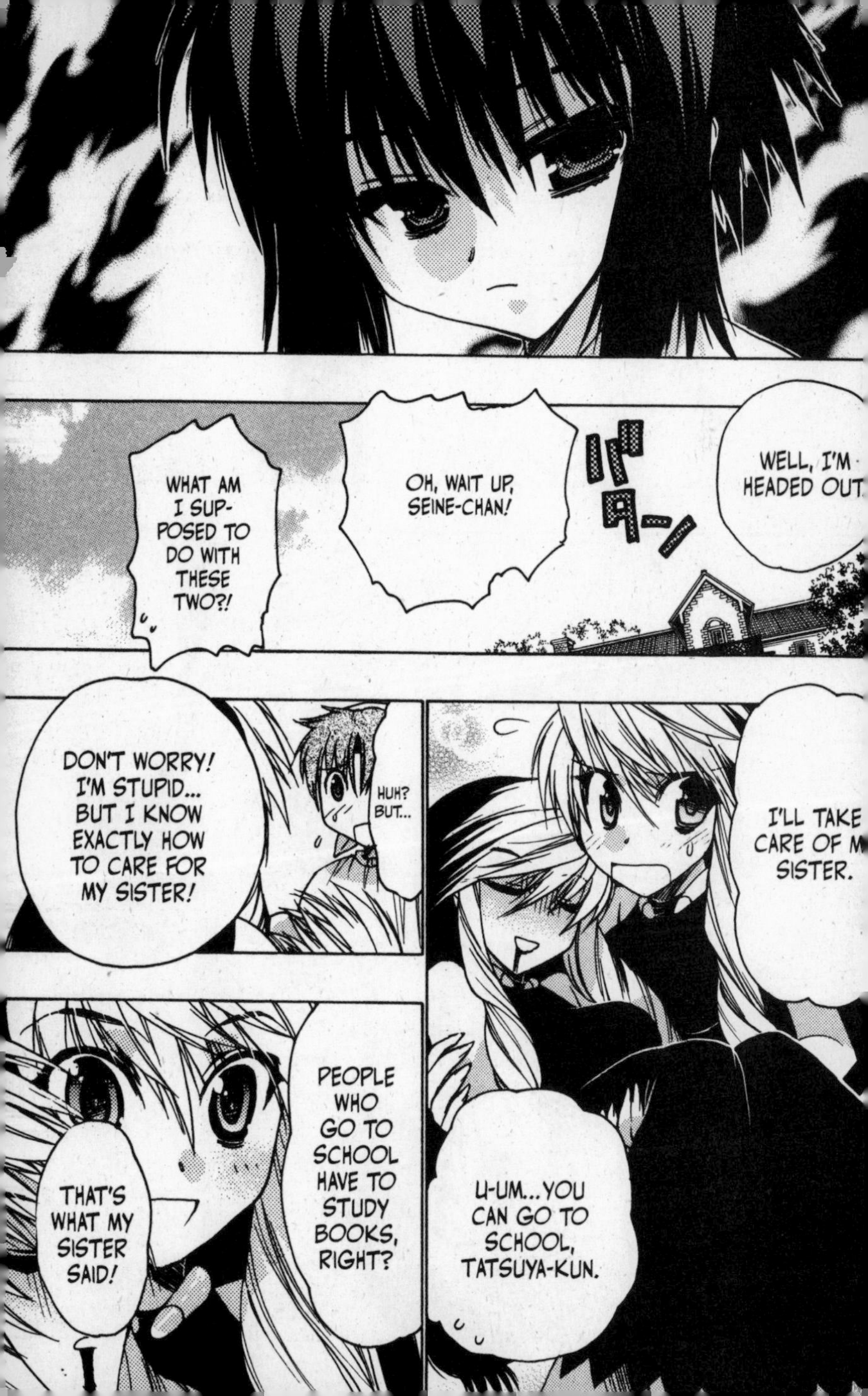
WELL, I'M HEADED OUT.
パターン
OH, WAIT UP, SEINE-CHAN!
WHAT AM I SUP-POSED TO DO WITH THESE TWO?!
I'LL TAKE CARE OF M SISTER.
U-UM...YOU CAN GO TO SCHOOL, TATSUYA-KUN.
HUH? BUT...
DON'T WORRY! I'M STUPID... BUT I KNOW EXACTLY HOW TO CARE FOR MY SISTER!
PEOPLE WHO GO TO SCHOOL HAVE TO STUDY BOOKS, RIGHT?
THAT'S WHAT MY SISTER SAID!

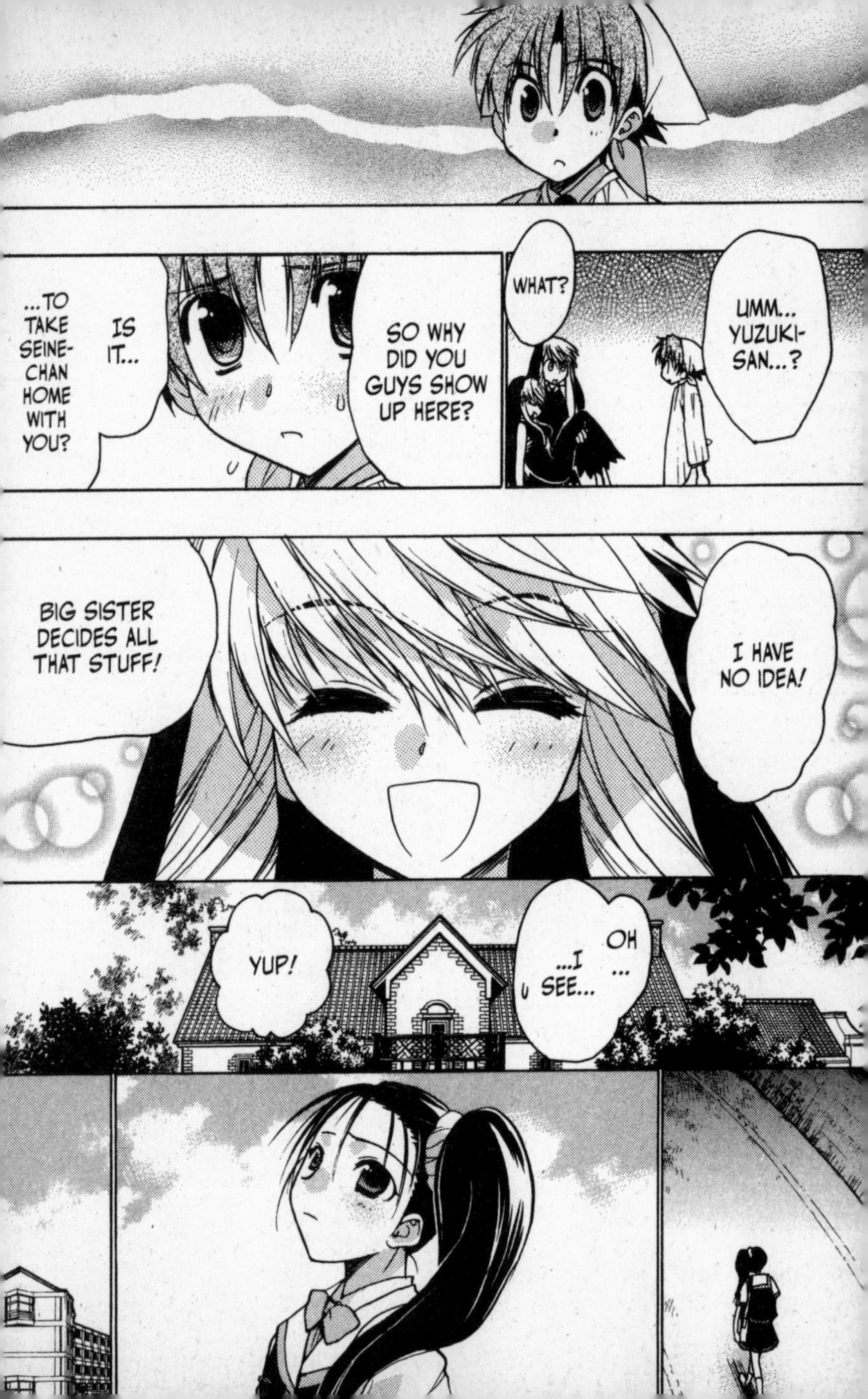
UMM... YUZUKI-SAN...?
WHAT?
SO WHY DID YOU GUYS SHOW UP HERE?
IS IT...
...TO TAKE SEINE-CHAN HOME WITH YOU?
I HAVE NO IDEA!
BIG SISTER DECIDES ALL THAT STUFF!
OH ... ...I SEE...
YUP!

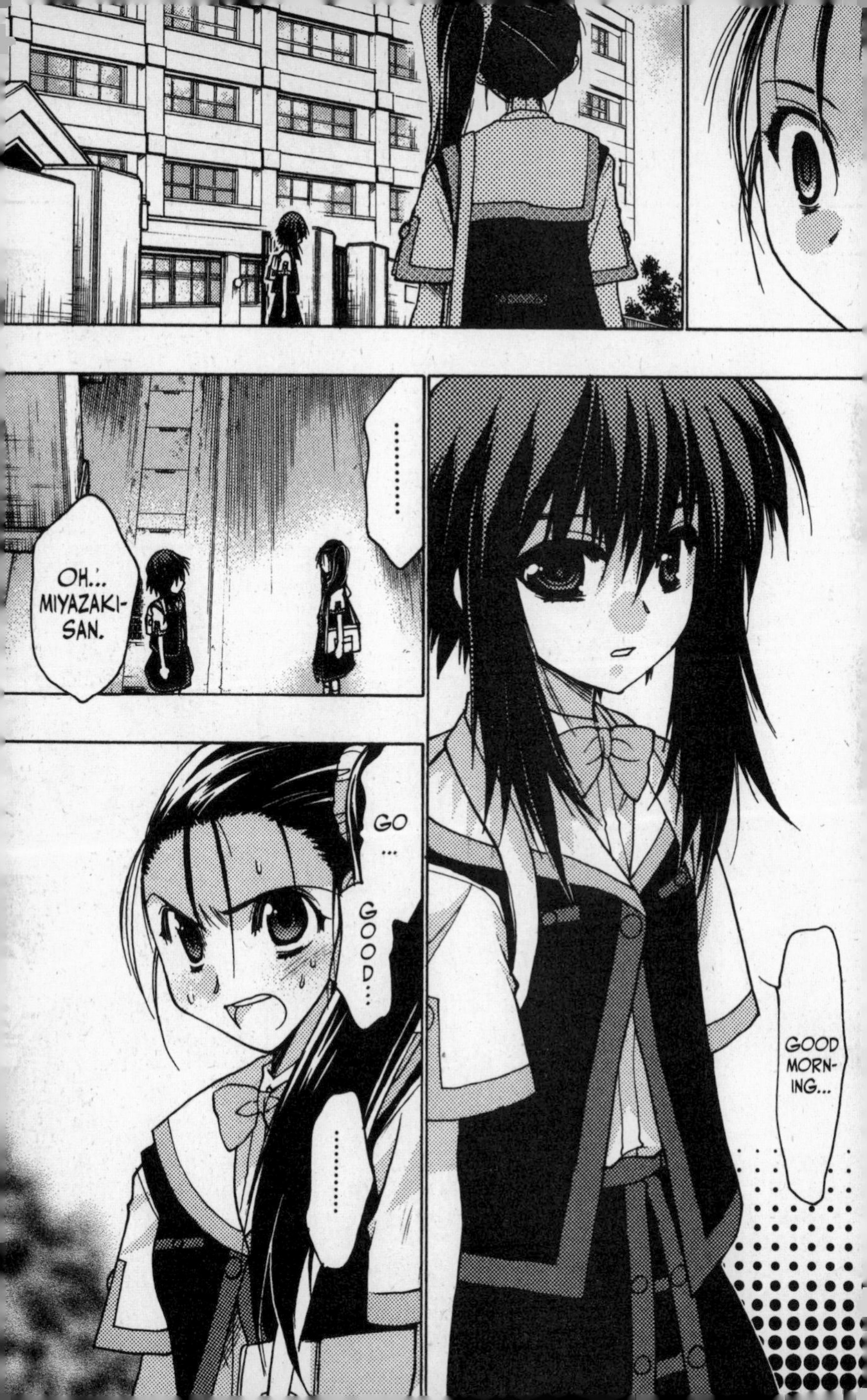
GOOD MORNING...
......
OH... MIYAZAKI-SAN.
GO ... GOOD...
......

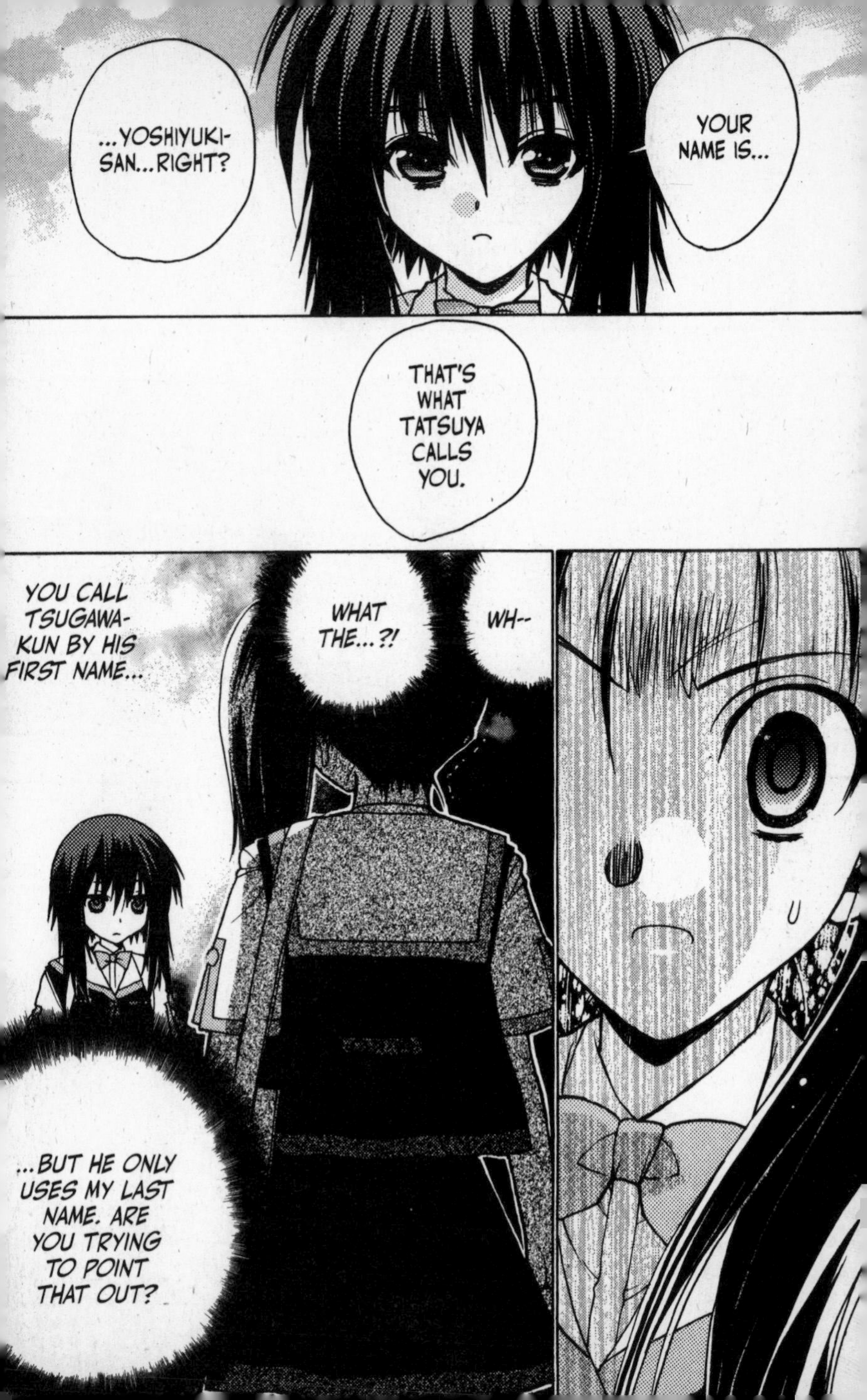
YOUR NAME IS...
...YOSHIYUKI-SAN...RIGHT?
THAT'S WHAT TATSUYA CALLS YOU.
WH--
WHAT THE...?!
YOU CALL TSUGAWA-KUN BY HIS FIRST NAME...
...BUT HE ONLY USES MY LAST NAME. ARE YOU TRYING TO POINT THAT OUT?

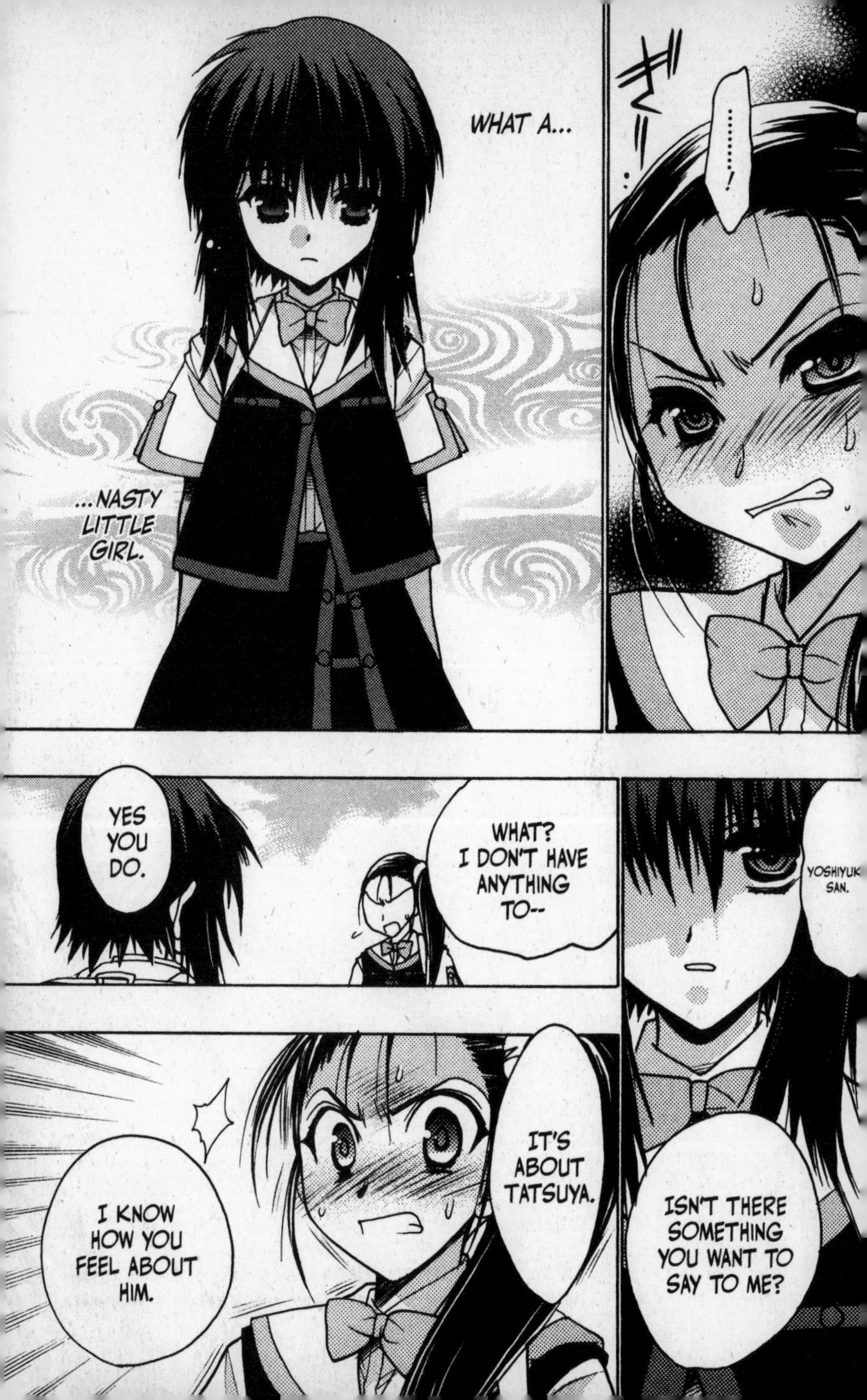
......!
WHAT A...
...NASTY LITTLE GIRL.
YOSHIYUK SAN.
ISN'T THERE SOMETHING YOU WANT TO SAY TO ME?
WHAT? I DON'T HAVE ANYTHING TO--
YES YOU DO.
IT'S ABOUT TATSUYA.
I KNOW HOW YOU FEEL ABOUT HIM.

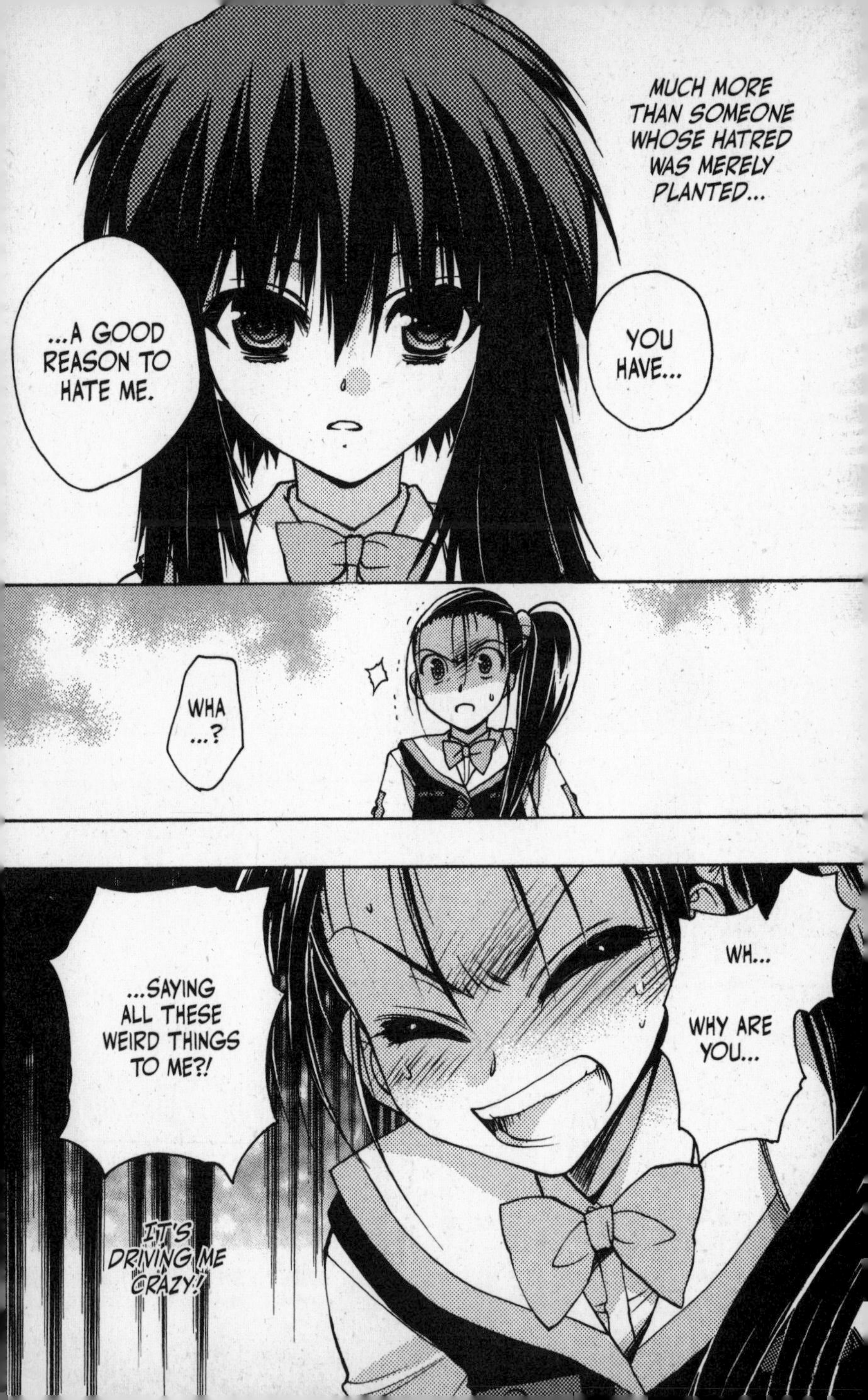
MUCH MORE THAN SOMEONE WHOSE HATRED WAS MERELY PLANTED...
YOU HAVE...
...A GOOD REASON TO HATE ME.
WHA ...?
WH...
WHY ARE YOU...
...SAYING ALL THESE WEIRD THINGS TO ME?!
IT'S DRIVING ME CRAZY!

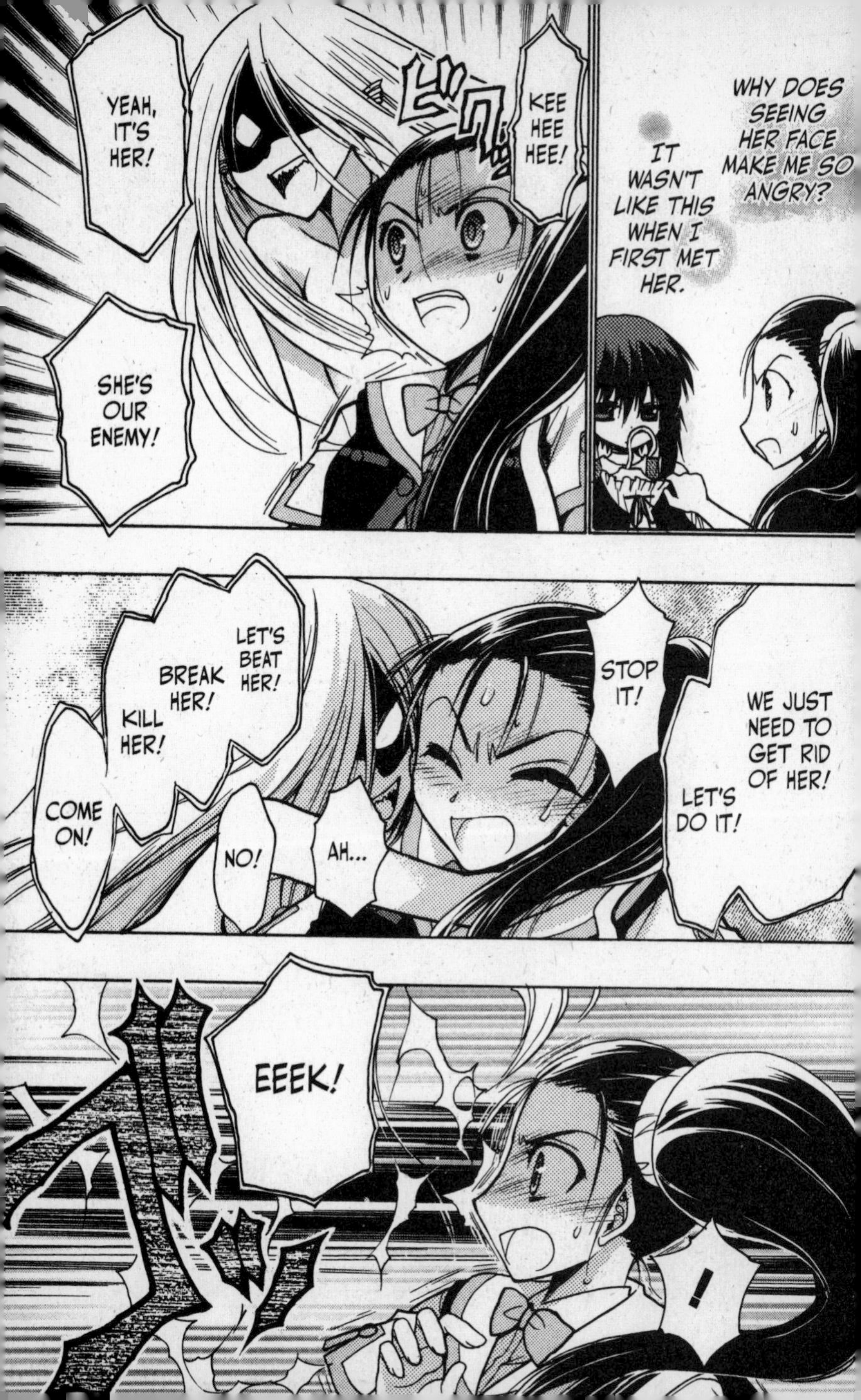
WHY DOES SEEING HER FACE MAKE ME SO ANGRY?
IT WASN'T LIKE THIS WHEN I FIRST MET HER.
KEE HEE HEE!
YEAH, IT'S HER!
SHE'S OUR ENEMY!
WE JUST NEED TO GET RID OF HER!
STOP IT!
LET'S DO IT!
LET'S BEAT HER!
BREAK HER!
KILL HER!
AH...
NO!
COME ON!
!
EEEK!

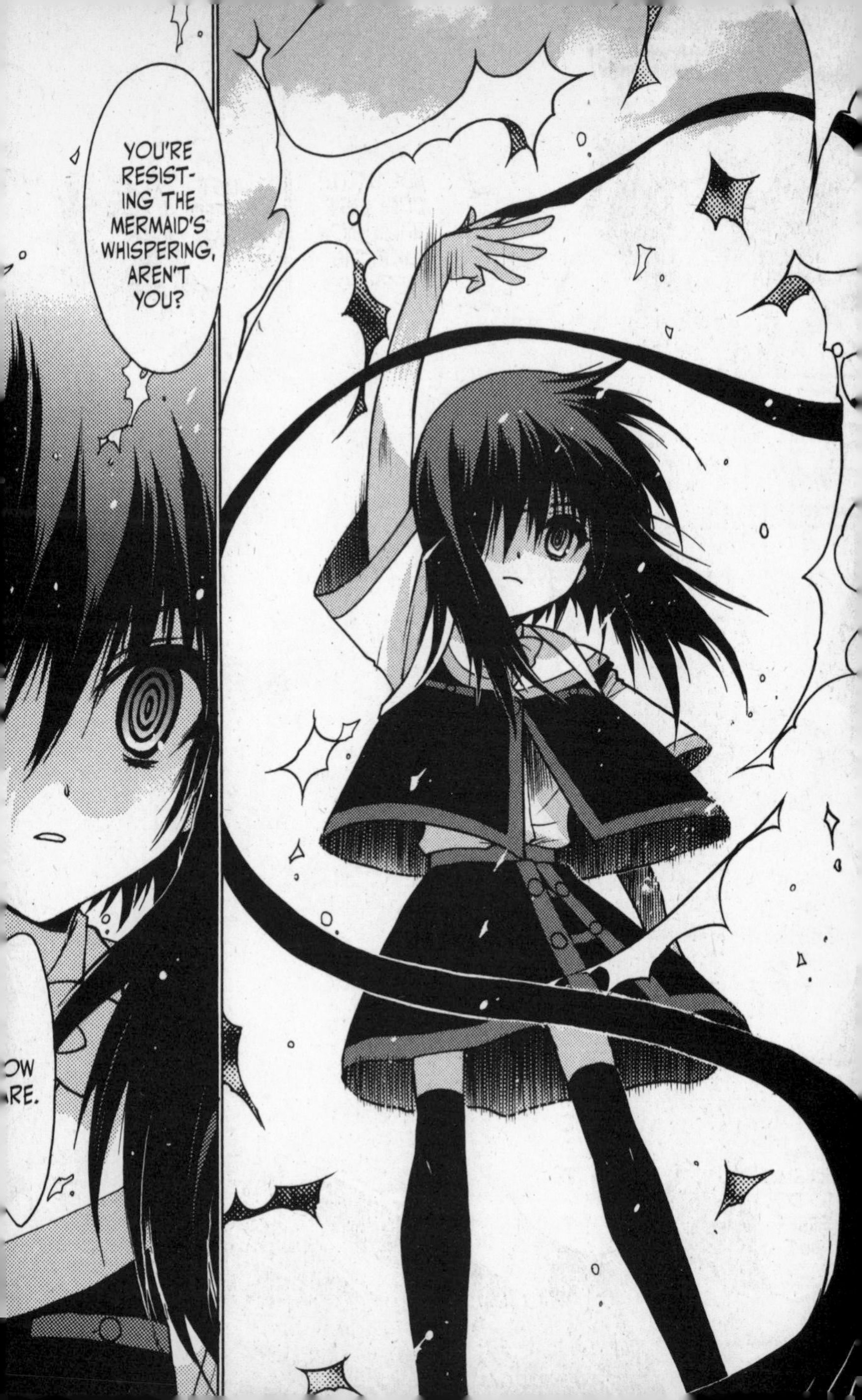
YOU'RE RESIST-ING THE MERMAID'S WHISPERING, AREN'T YOU?

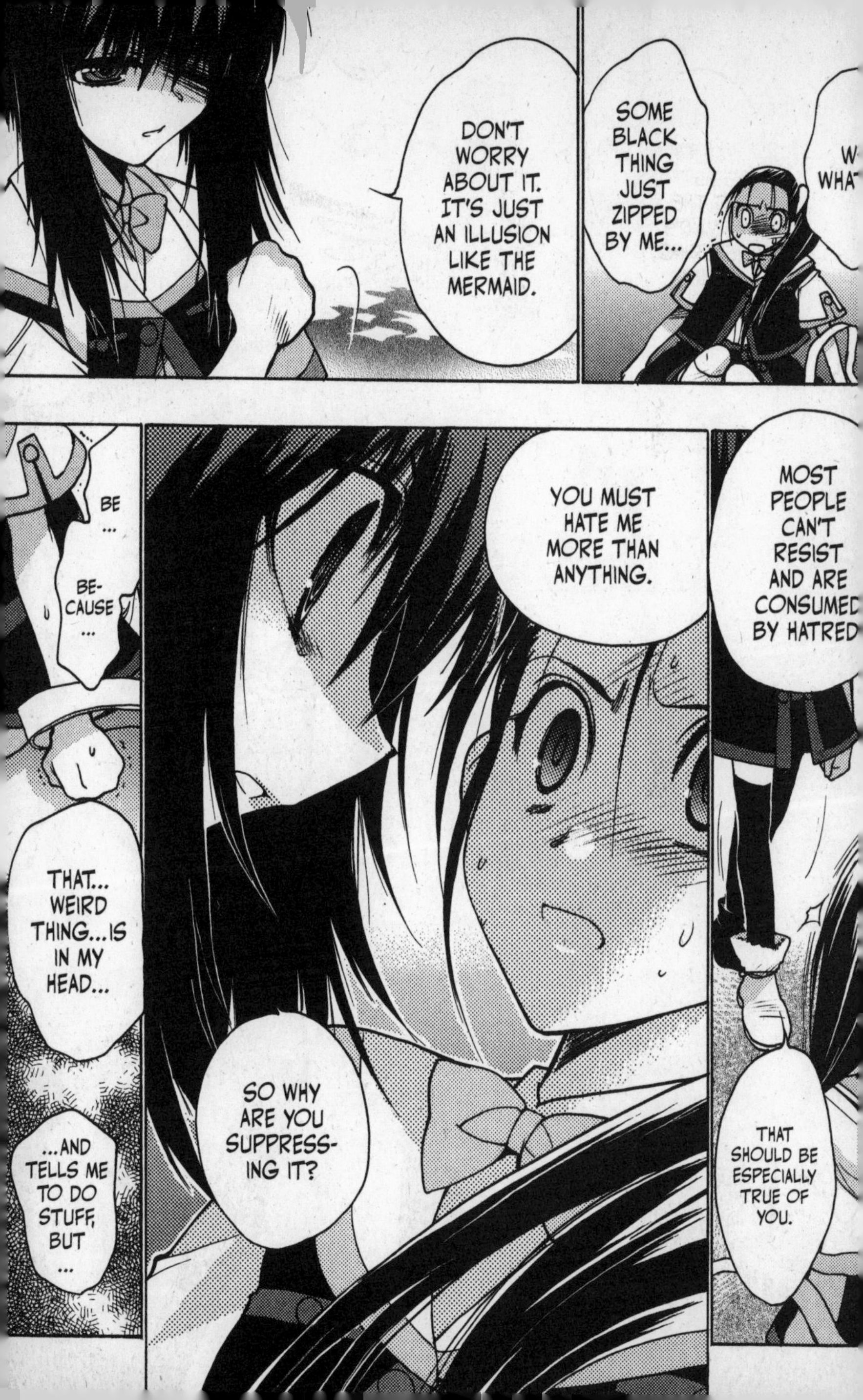
SOME BLACK THING JUST ZIPPED BY ME...
DON'T WORRY ABOUT IT. IT'S JUST AN ILLUSION LIKE THE MERMAID.
MOST PEOPLE CAN'T RESIST AND ARE CONSUMED BY HATRED
THAT SHOULD BE ESPECIALLY TRUE OF YOU.
YOU MUST HATE ME MORE THAN ANYTHING.
SO WHY ARE YOU SUPPRESSING IT?
BE...
BECAUSE...
THAT... WEIRD THING...IS IN MY HEAD...
...AND TELLS ME TO DO STUFF, BUT ...

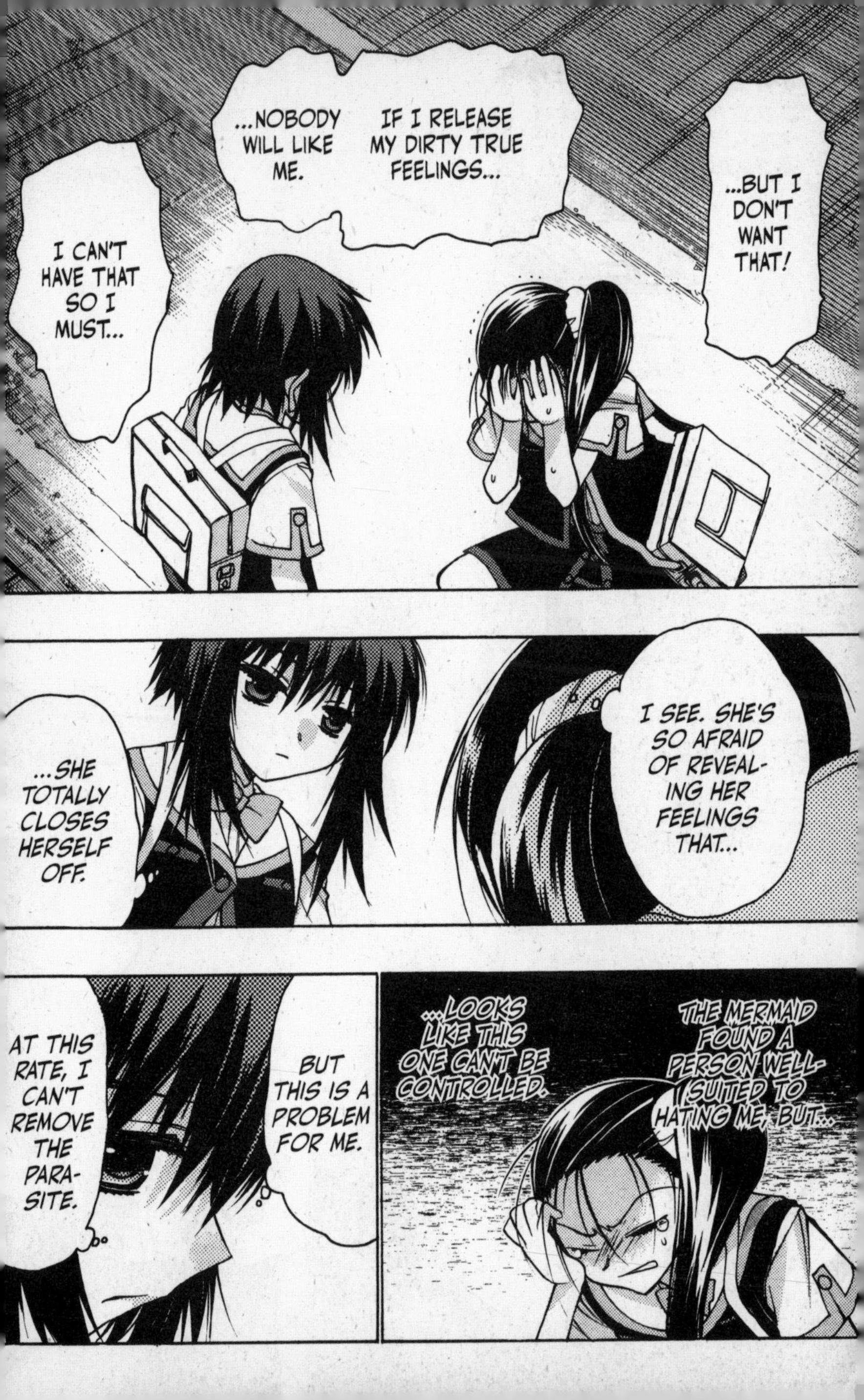
IF I RELEASE MY DIRTY TRUE FEELINGS...
...NOBODY WILL LIKE ME.
...BUT I DON'T WANT THAT!
I CAN'T HAVE THAT SO I MUST...
I SEE. SHE'S SO AFRAID OF REVEAL-ING HER FEELINGS THAT...
...SHE TOTALLY CLOSES HERSELF OFF.
THE MERMAID FOUND A PERSON WELL-SUITED TO HATING ME, BUT...
...LOOKS LIKE THIS ONE CAN'T BE CONTROLLED.
BUT THIS IS A PROBLEM FOR ME.
AT THIS RATE, I CAN'T REMOVE THE PARA-SITE.

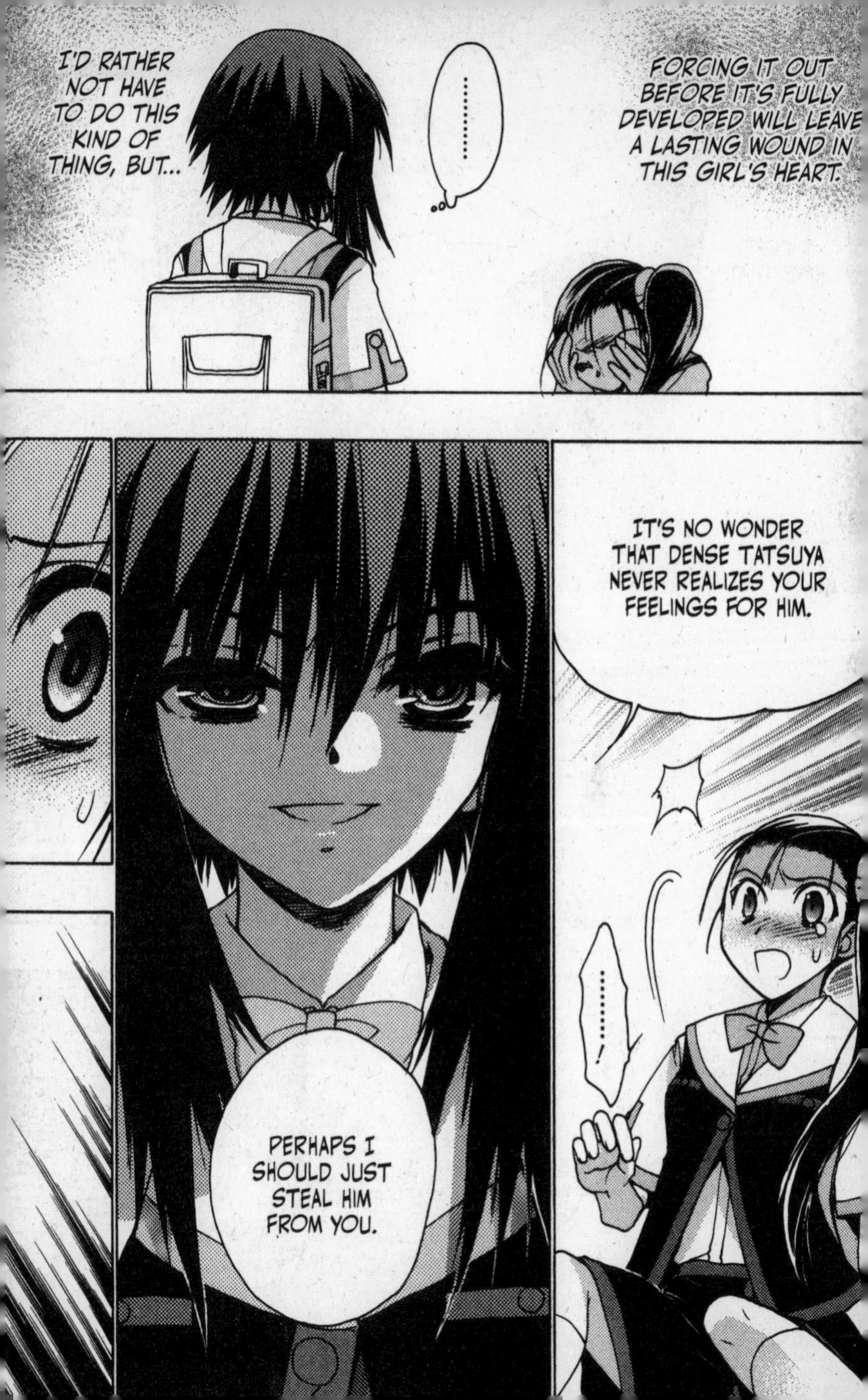
FORCING IT OUT BEFORE IT'S FULLY DEVELOPED WILL LEAVE A LASTING WOUND IN THIS GIRL'S HEART.
....
I'D RATHER NOT HAVE TO DO THIS KIND OF THING, BUT...
IT'S NO WONDER THAT DENSE TATSUYA NEVER REALIZES YOUR FEELINGS FOR HIM.
.........!
PERHAPS I SHOULD JUST STEAL HIM FROM YOU.

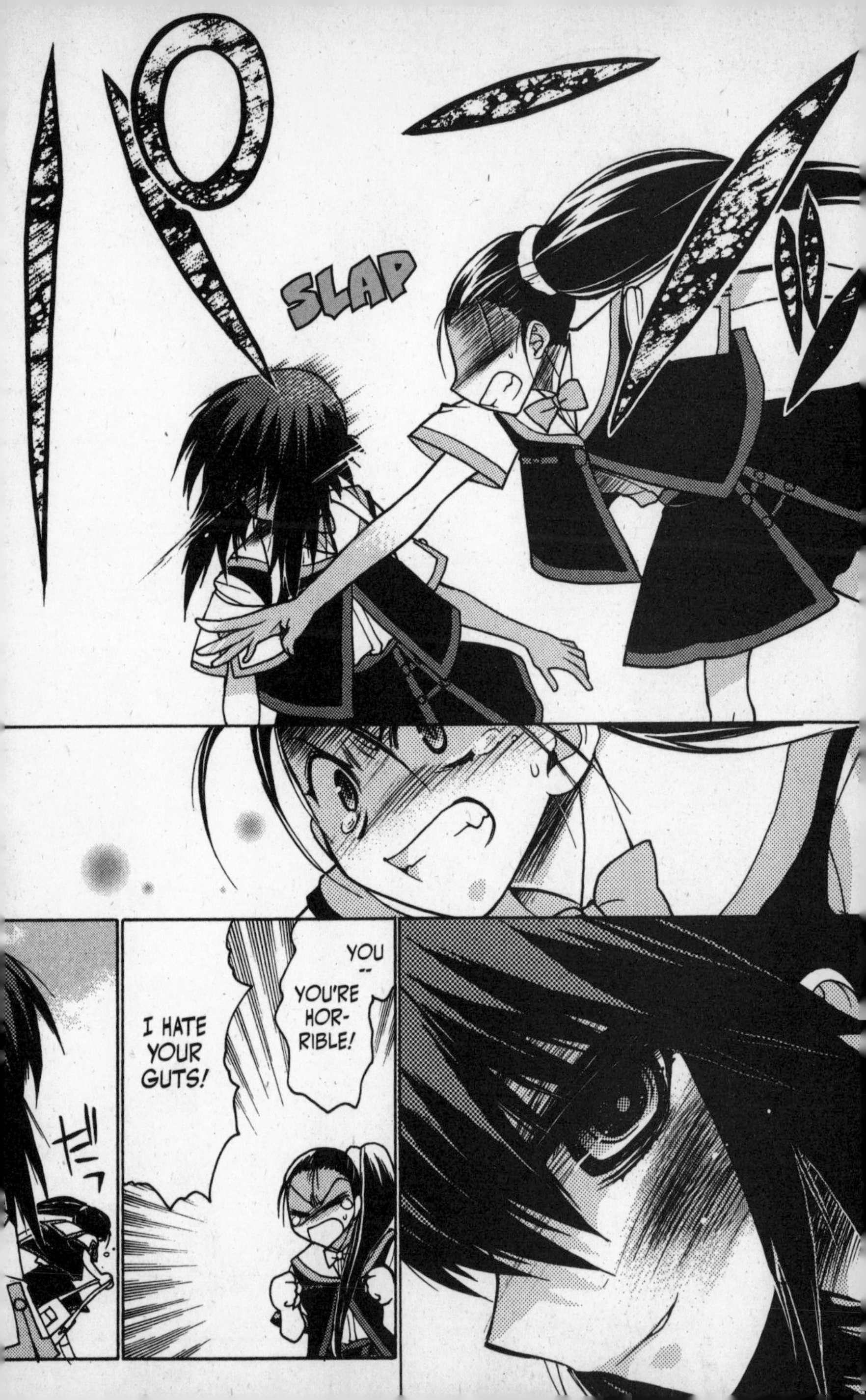
SLAP
YOU -- YOU'RE HOR-RIBLE!
I HATE YOUR GUTS!

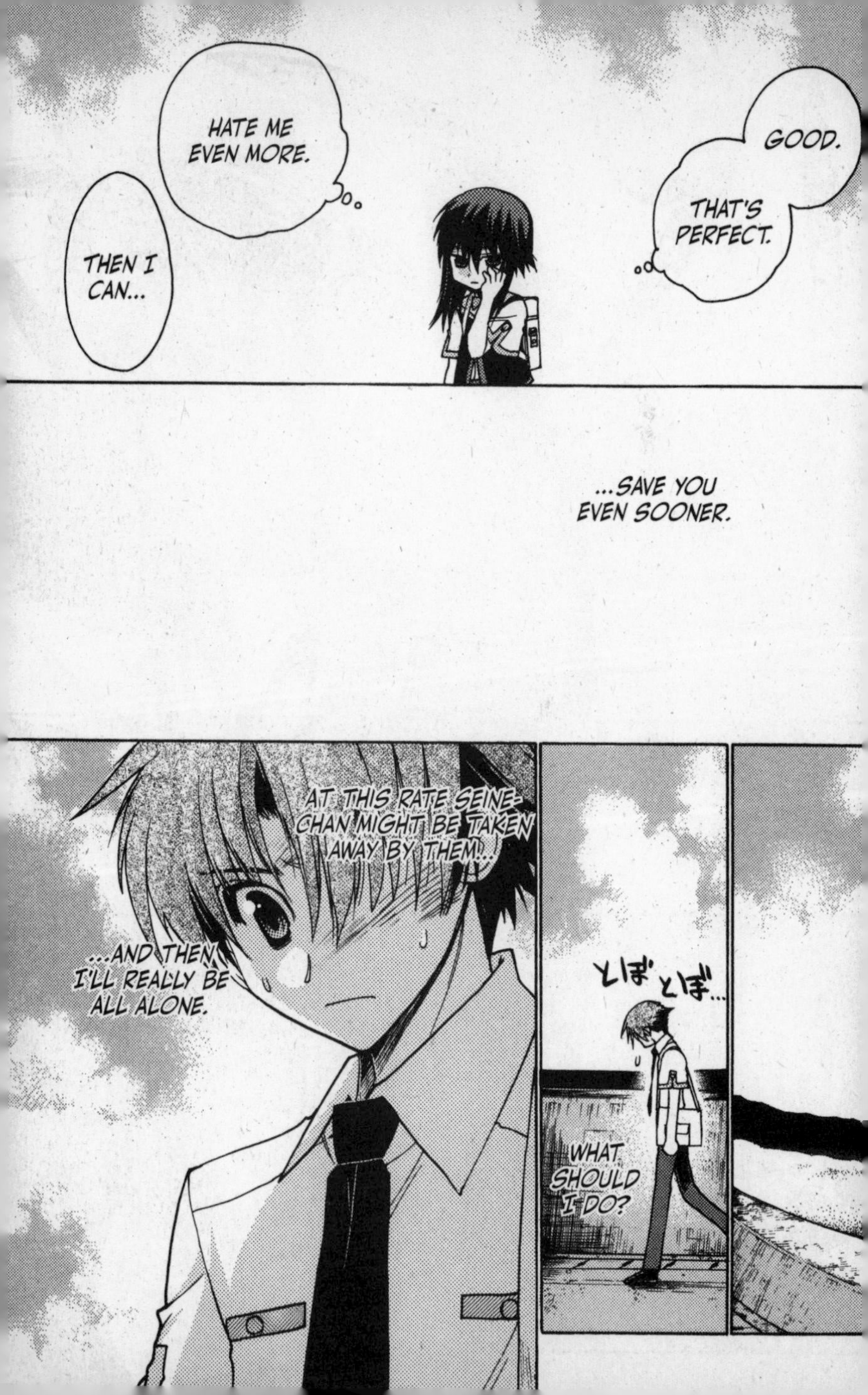
GOOD.
THAT'S PERFECT.
HATE ME EVEN MORE.
THEN I CAN...
...SAVE YOU EVEN SOONER.
WHAT SHOULD I DO?
とぼとぼ...
AT THIS RATE SEINE-CHAN MIGHT BE TAKEN AWAY BY THEM...
...AND THEN I'LL REALLY BE ALL ALONE.

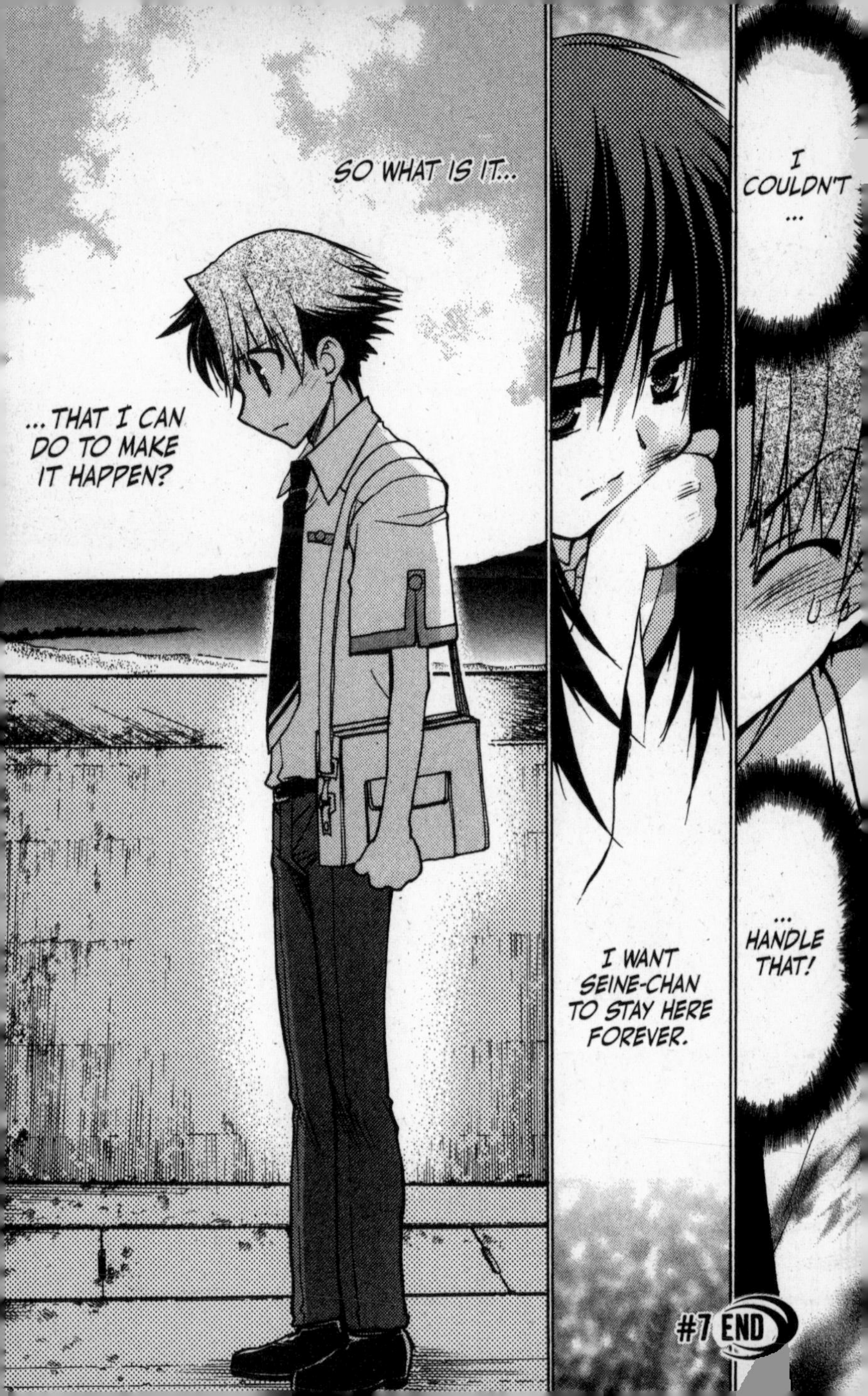
I COULDN'T ...
... HANDLE THAT!
I WANT SEINE-CHAN TO STAY HERE FOREVER.
SO WHAT IS IT...
...THAT I CAN DO TO MAKE IT HAPPEN?
#7 END

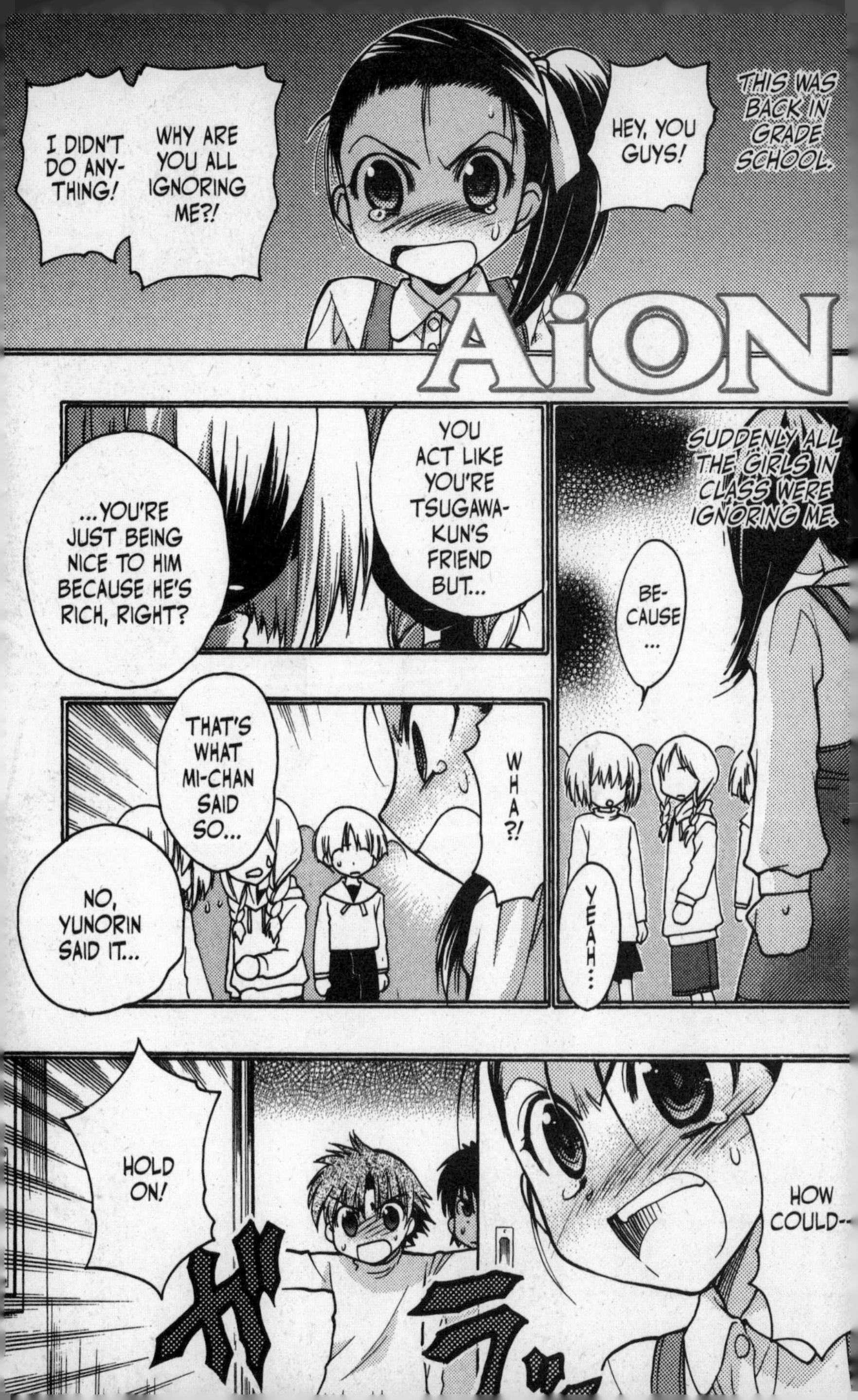

THIS WAS BACK IN GRADE SCHOOL.
HEY, YOU GUYS!
WHY ARE YOU ALL IGNORING ME?!
I DIDN'T DO ANY-THING!
AiON
SUDDENLY ALL THE GIRLS IN CLASS WERE IGNORING ME.
BE-CAUSE ...
YEAH...
YOU ACT LIKE YOU'RE TSUGAWA-KUN'S FRIEND BUT...
...YOU'RE JUST BEING NICE TO HIM BECAUSE HE'S RICH, RIGHT?
WHA?!
THAT'S WHAT MI-CHAN SAID SO...
NO, YUNORIN SAID IT...
HOW COULD--
HOLD ON!

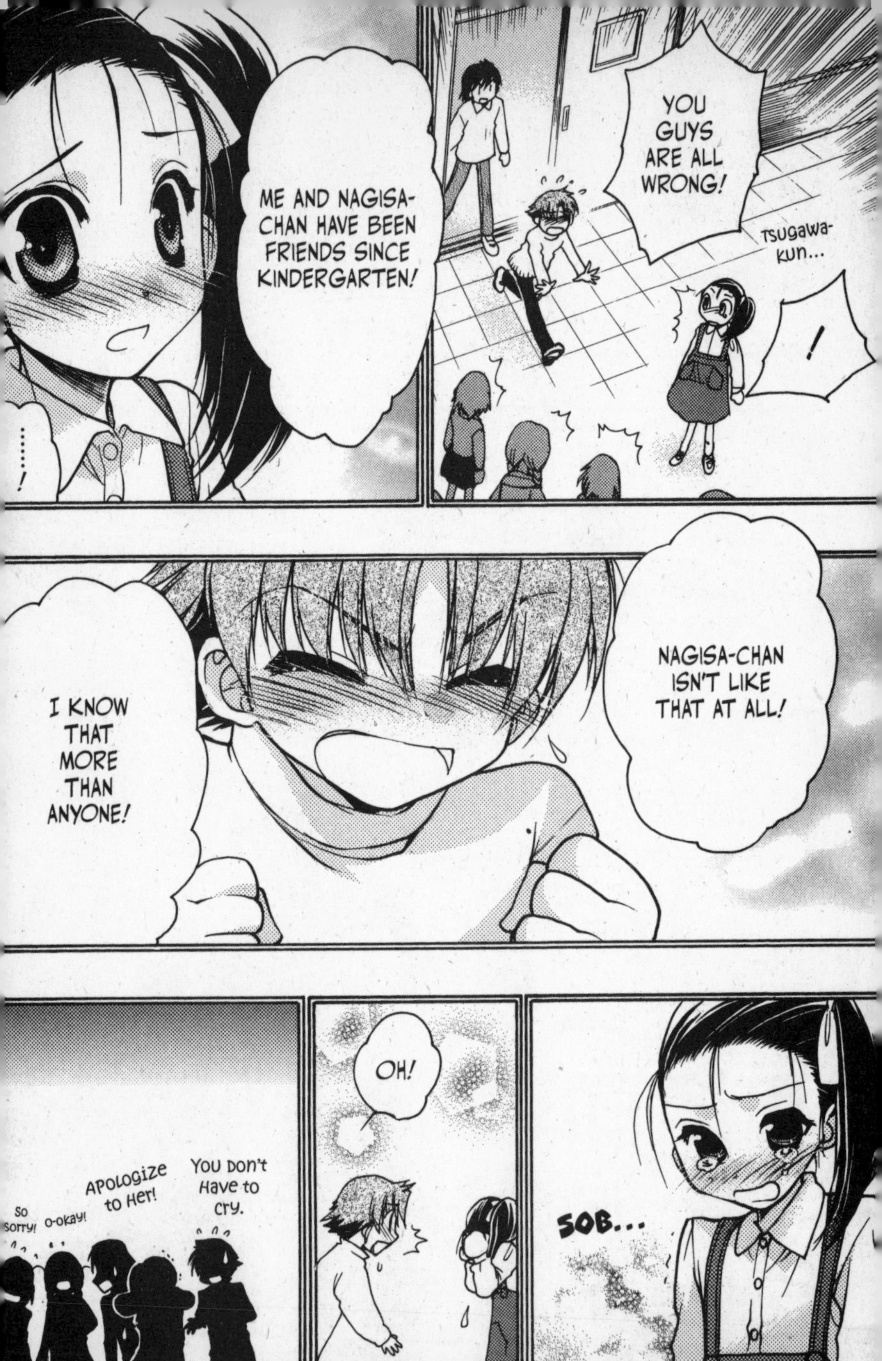

YOU GUYS ARE ALL WRONG!
TSUGAWA-KUN...
!
ME AND NAGISA-CHAN HAVE BEEN FRIENDS SINCE KINDERGARTEN!
......!
NAGISA-CHAN ISN'T LIKE THAT AT ALL!
I KNOW THAT MORE THAN ANYONE!
SOB...
OH!
You Don't Have to cry.
Apologize to Her!
O-okay!
So sorry!

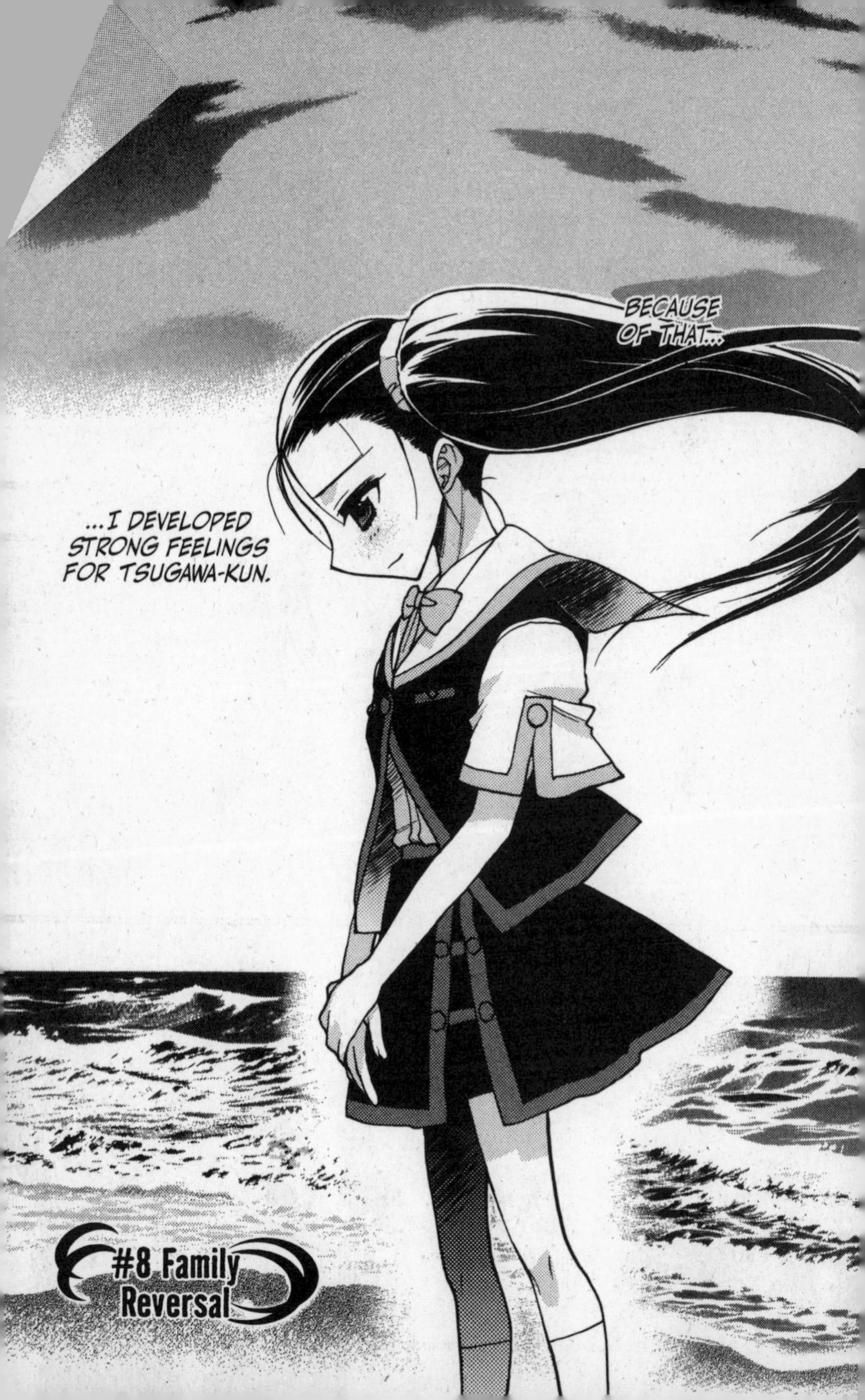
BECAUSE OF THAT...
...I DEVELOPED STRONG FEELINGS FOR TSUGAWA-KUN.
#8 Family Reversal

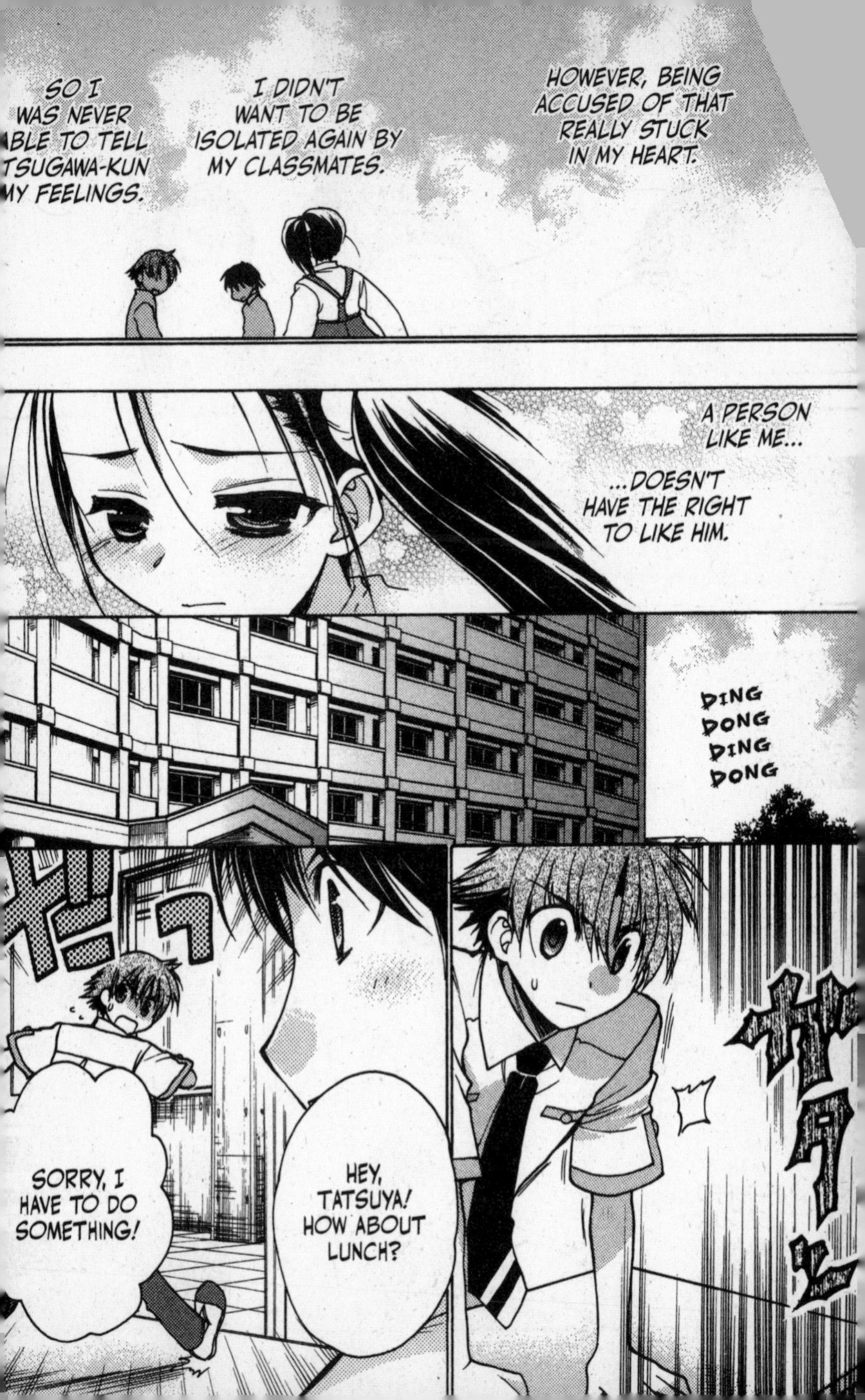
HOWEVER, BEING ACCUSED OF THAT REALLY STUCK IN MY HEART.
I DIDN'T WANT TO BE ISOLATED AGAIN BY MY CLASSMATES.
SO I WAS NEVER BLE TO TELL TSUGAWA-KUN MY FEELINGS.
A PERSON LIKE ME...
...DOESN'T HAVE THE RIGHT TO LIKE HIM.
DING DONG DING DONG
HEY, TATSUYA! HOW ABOUT LUNCH?
SORRY, I HAVE TO DO SOMETHING!

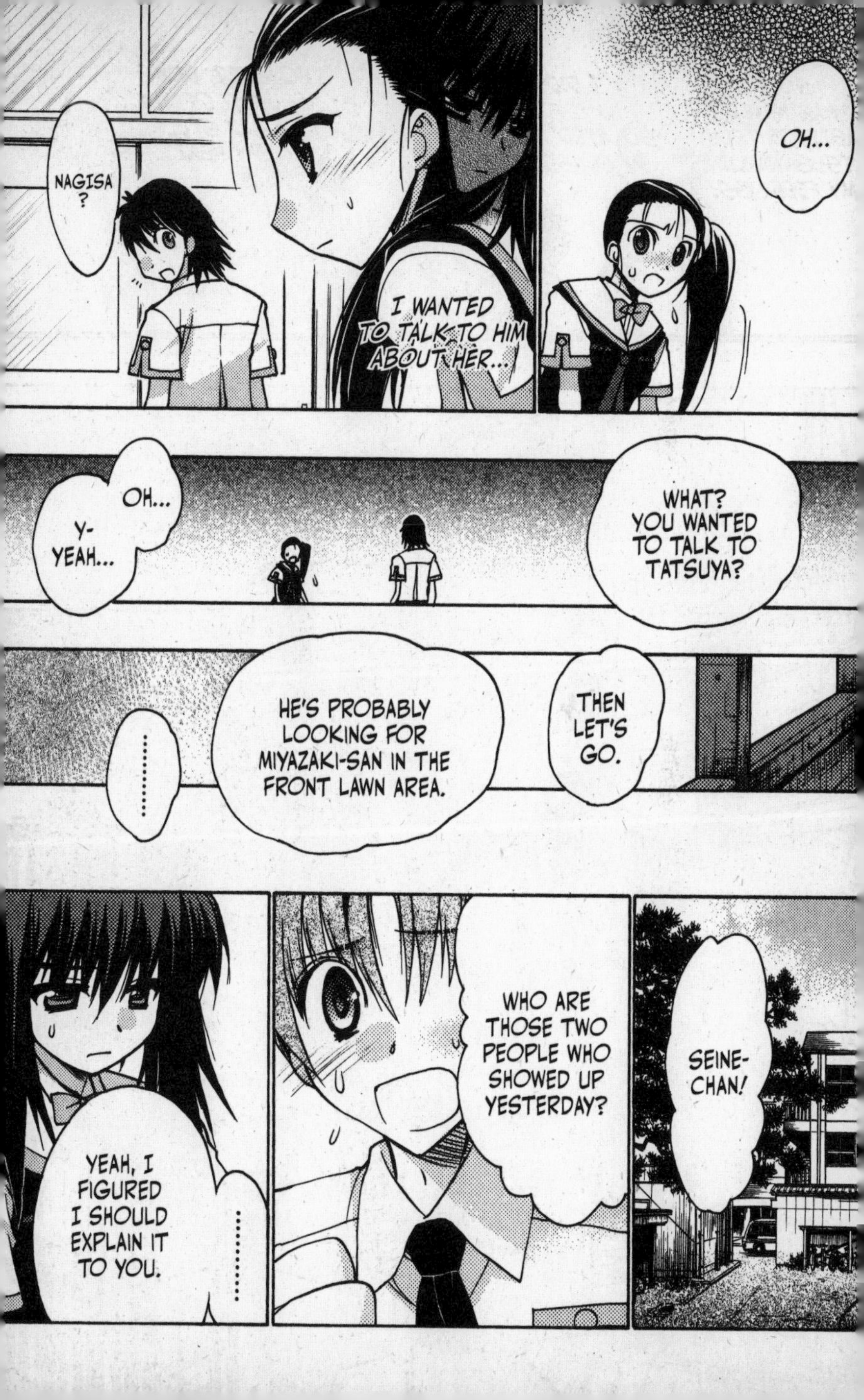
OH...
I WANTED TO TALK TO HIM ABOUT HER...
NAGISA?
WHAT? YOU WANTED TO TALK TO TATSUYA?
OH... Y-YEAH...
THEN LET'S GO.
HE'S PROBABLY LOOKING FOR MIYAZAKI-SAN IN THE FRONT LAWN AREA.
....
SEINE-CHAN!
WHO ARE THOSE TWO PEOPLE WHO SHOWED UP YESTERDAY?
....
YEAH, I FIGURED I SHOULD EXPLAIN IT TO YOU.

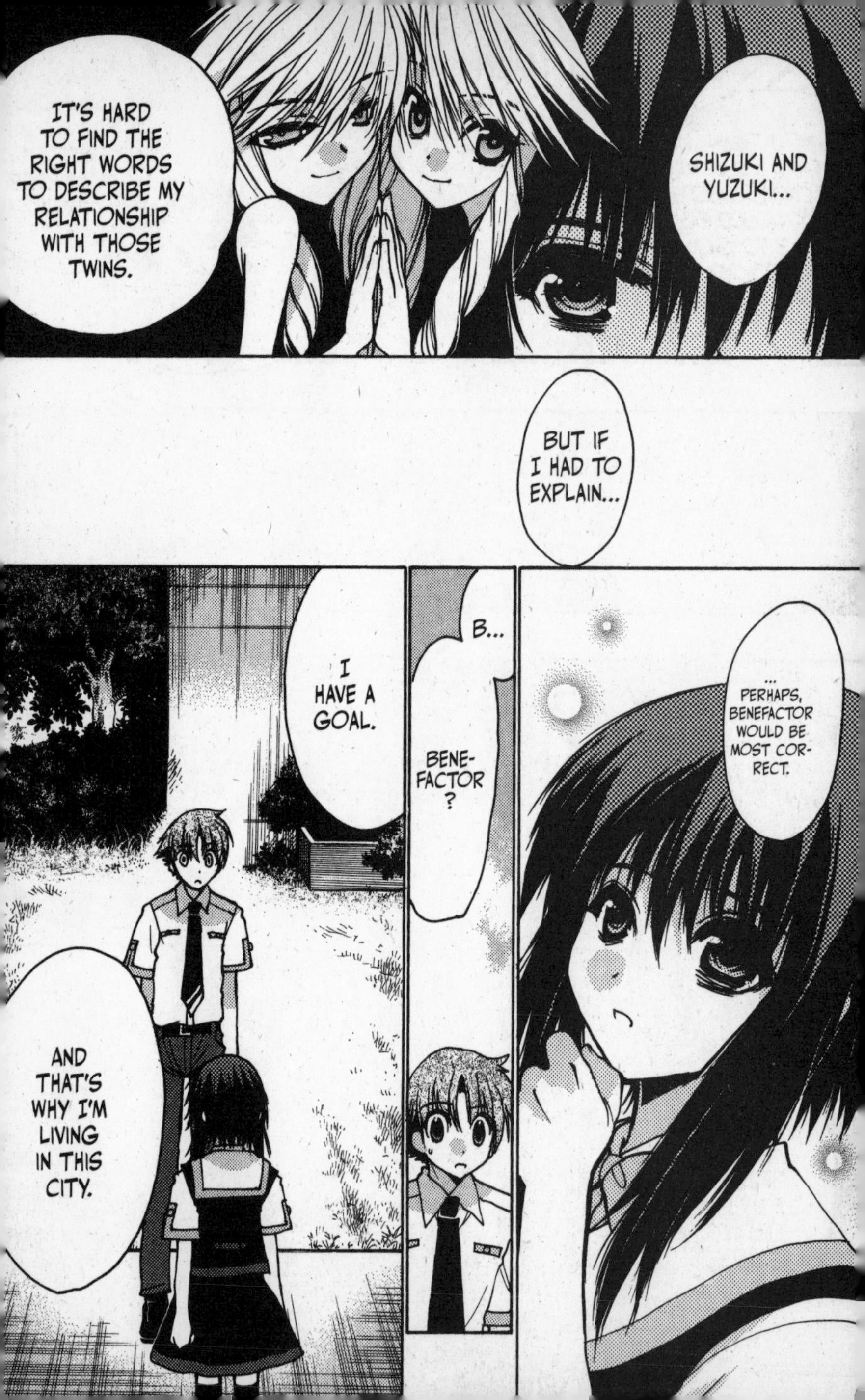
SHIZUKI AND YUZUKI...
IT'S HARD TO FIND THE RIGHT WORDS TO DESCRIBE MY RELATIONSHIP WITH THOSE TWINS.
BUT IF I HAD TO EXPLAIN...
... PERHAPS, BENEFACTOR WOULD BE MOST COR-RECT.
B...
BENE-FACTOR ?
I HAVE A GOAL.
AND THAT'S WHY I'M LIVING IN THIS CITY.

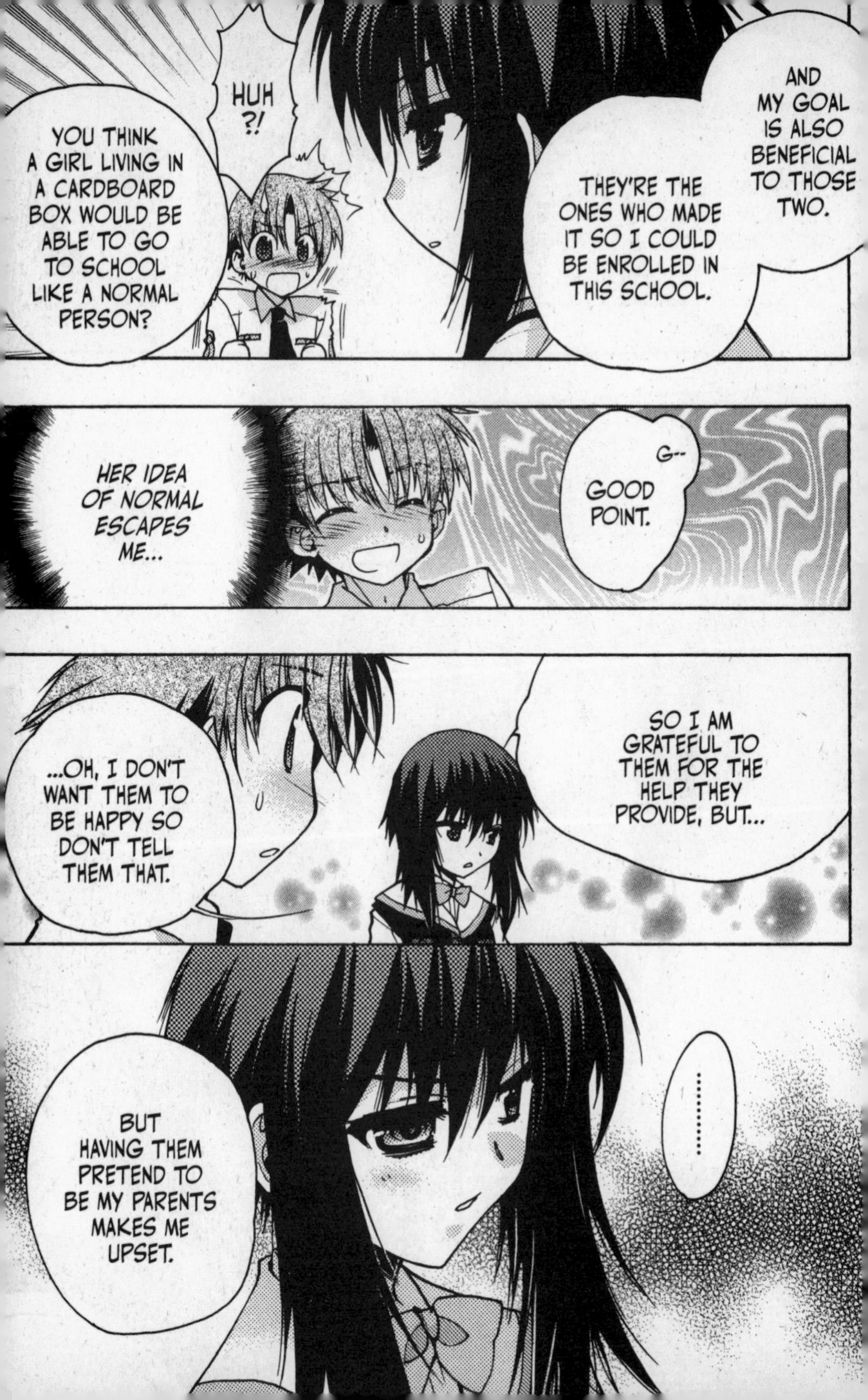
AND MY GOAL IS ALSO BENEFICIAL TO THOSE TWO.
THEY'RE THE ONES WHO MADE IT SO I COULD BE ENROLLED IN THIS SCHOOL.
HUH ?!
YOU THINK A GIRL LIVING IN A CARDBOARD BOX WOULD BE ABLE TO GO TO SCHOOL LIKE A NORMAL PERSON?
G-- GOOD POINT.
HER IDEA OF NORMAL ESCAPES ME...
SO I AM GRATEFUL TO THEM FOR THE HELP THEY PROVIDE, BUT...
...OH, I DON'T WANT THEM TO BE HAPPY SO DON'T TELL THEM THAT.
......
BUT HAVING THEM PRETEND TO BE MY PARENTS MAKES ME UPSET.

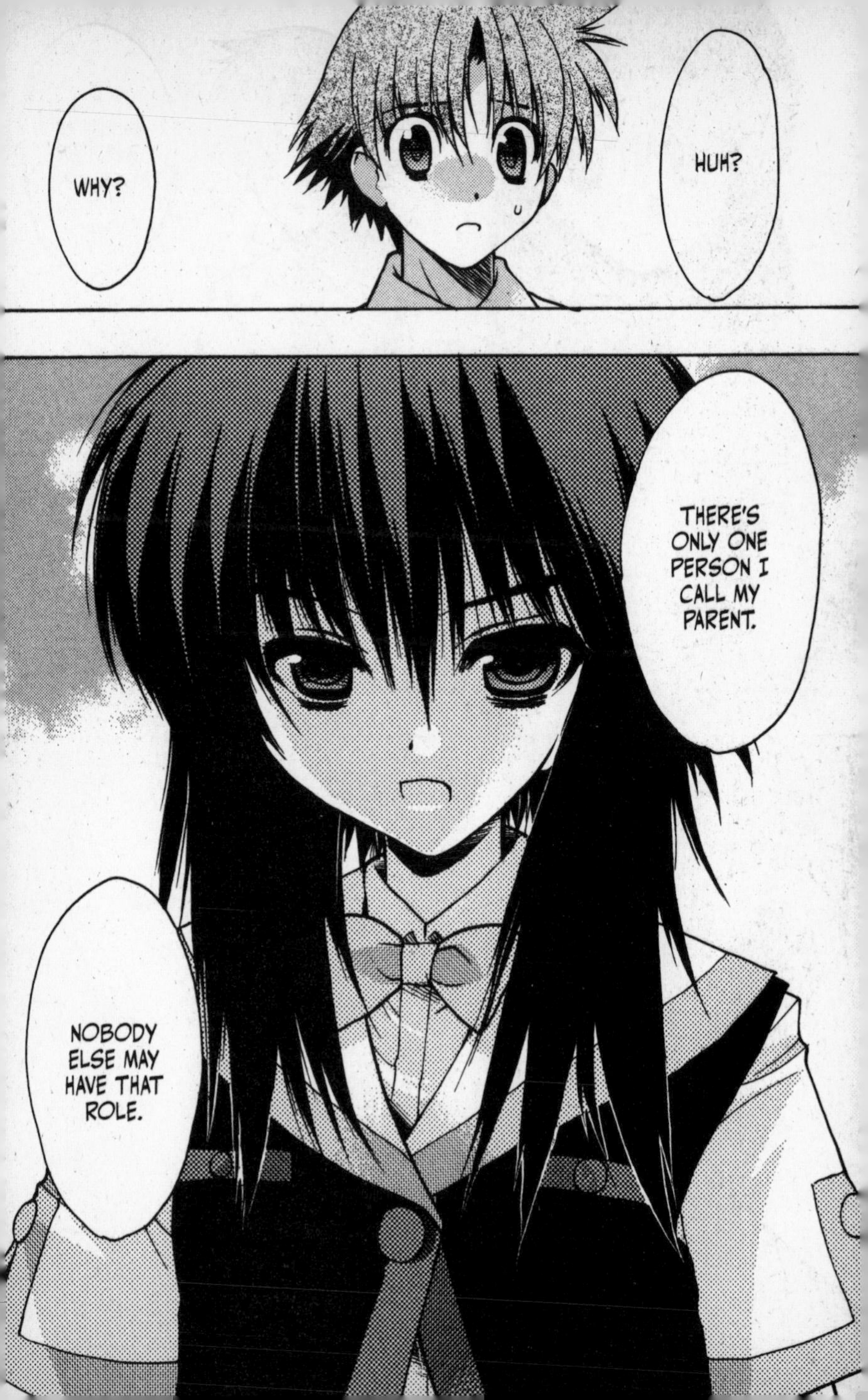
HUH?
WHY?
THERE'S ONLY ONE PERSON I CALL MY PARENT.
NOBODY ELSE MAY HAVE THAT ROLE.

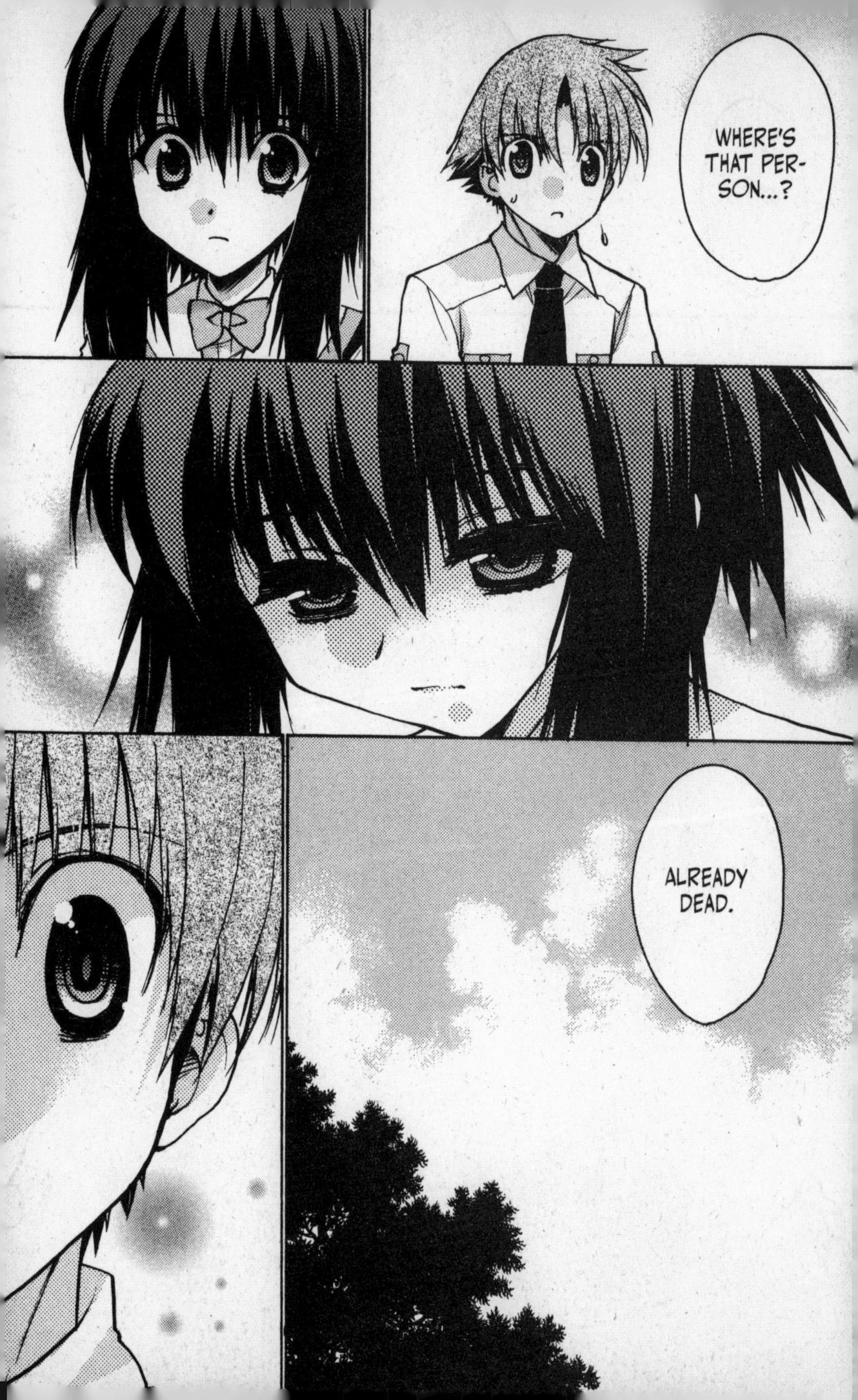
WHERE'S THAT PER-SON...?
ALREADY DEAD.

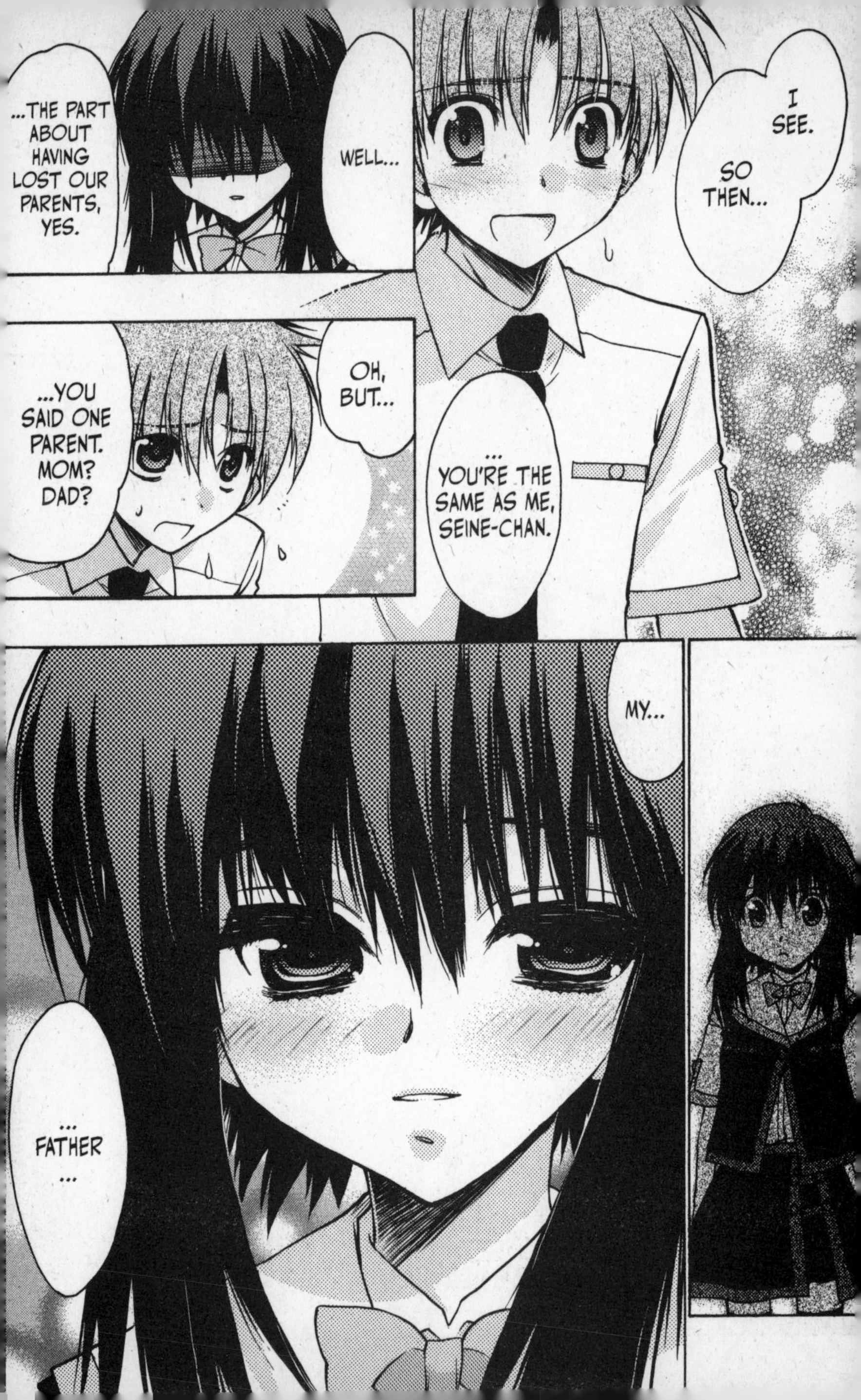
I SEE.
SO THEN...
...YOU'RE THE SAME AS ME, SEINE-CHAN.
WELL...
...THE PART ABOUT HAVING LOST OUR PARENTS, YES.
OH, BUT...
...YOU SAID ONE PARENT. MOM? DAD?
MY...
...FATHER...

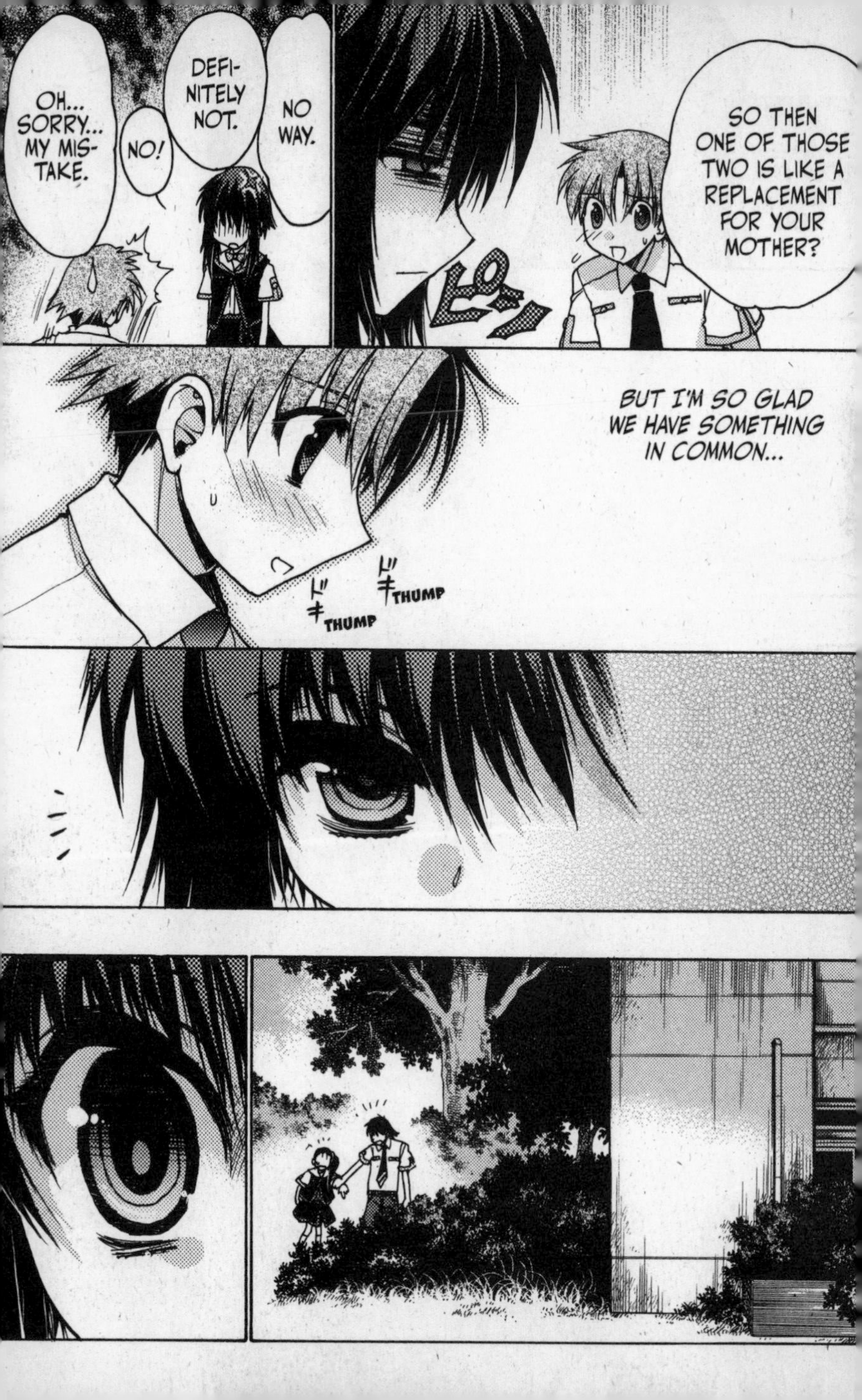
SO THEN ONE OF THOSE TWO IS LIKE A REPLACEMENT FOR YOUR MOTHER?
NO WAY.
DEFI-NITELY NOT.
NO!
OH... SORRY... MY MIS-TAKE.
BUT I'M SO GLAD WE HAVE SOMETHING IN COMMON...
ドキ THUMP
ドキ THUMP

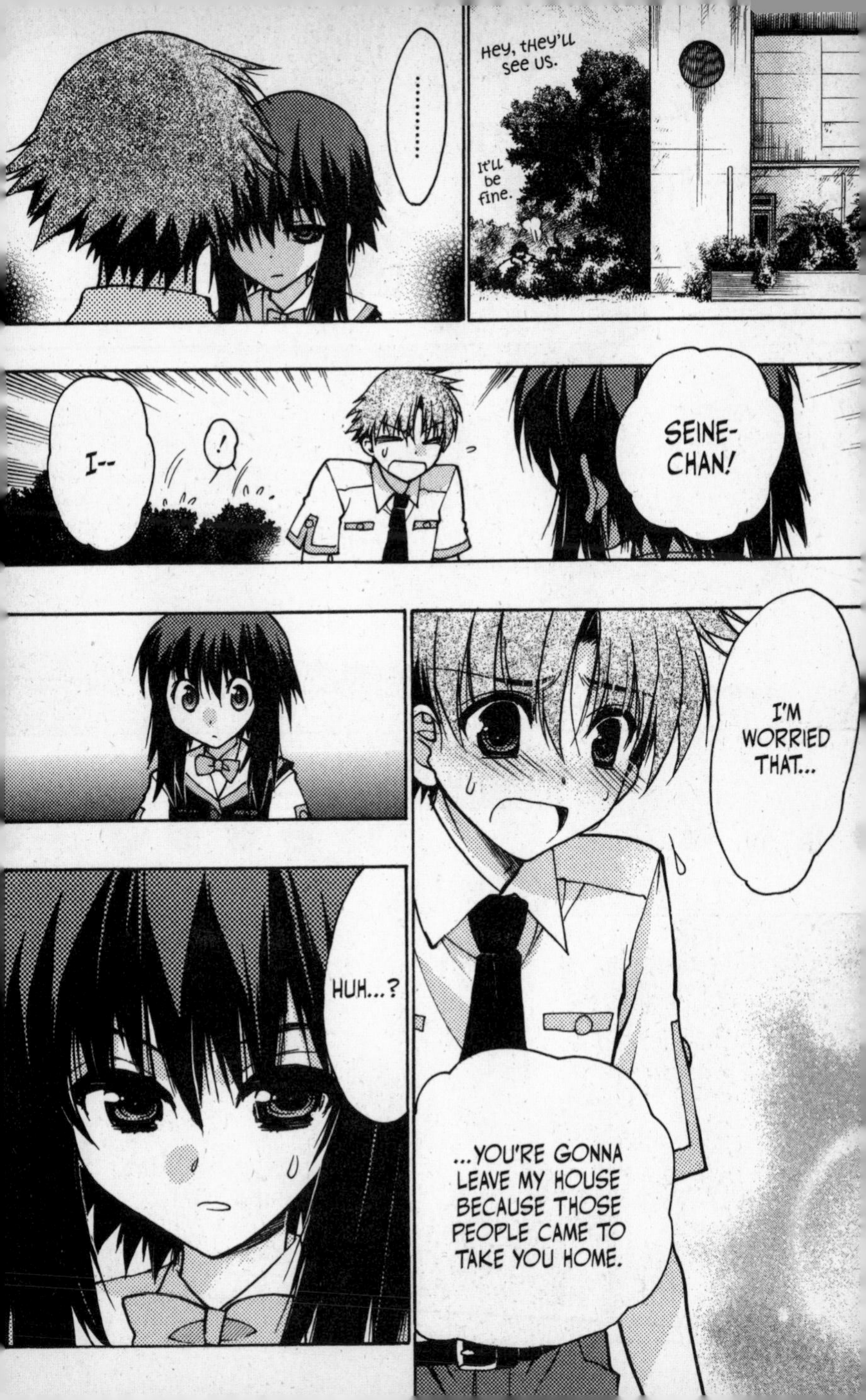
Hey, they'll see us.
It'll be fine.
......
SEINE-CHAN!
!
I--
I'M WORRIED THAT...
HUH...?
...YOU'RE GONNA LEAVE MY HOUSE BECAUSE THOSE PEOPLE CAME TO TAKE YOU HOME.

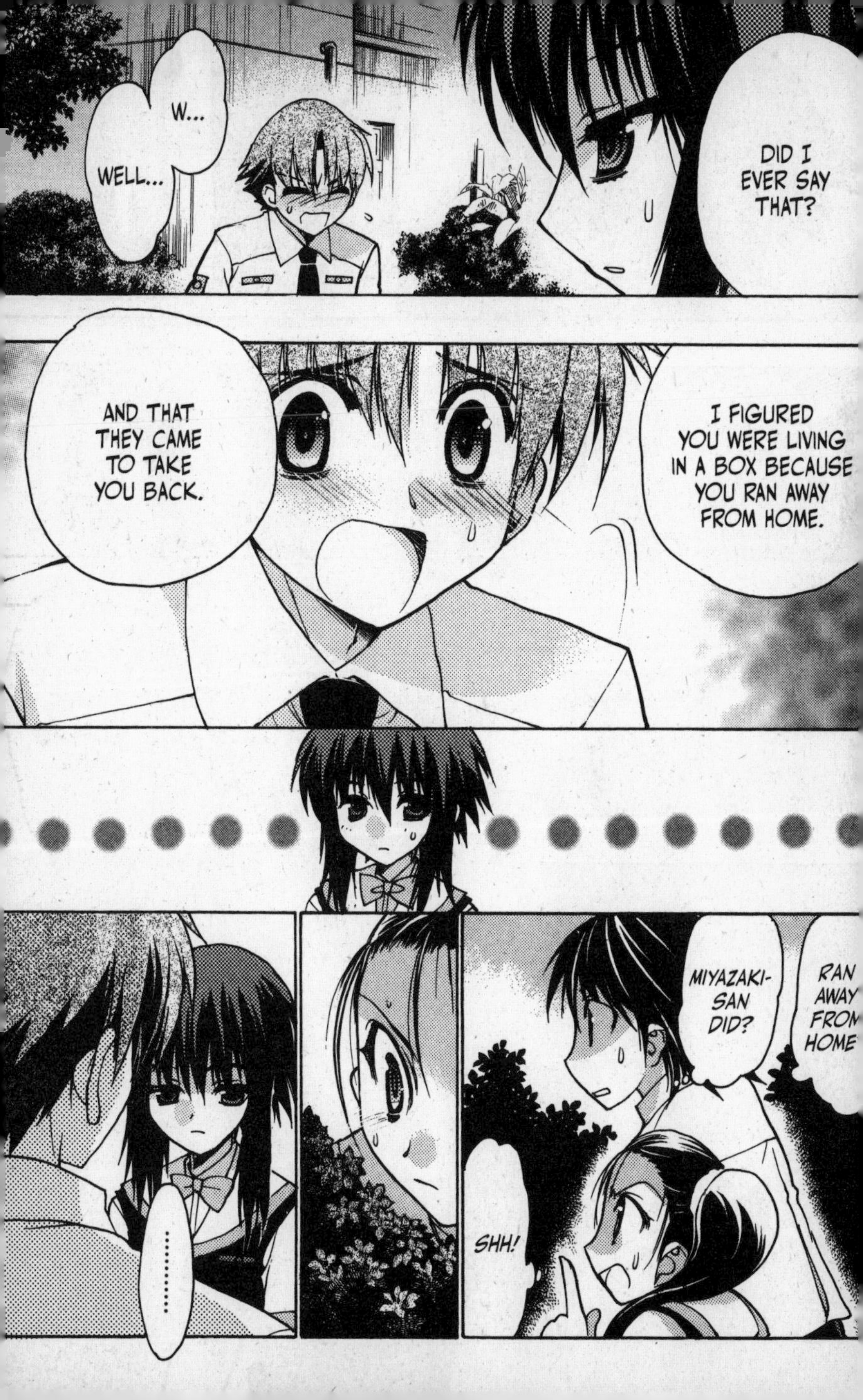
DID I EVER SAY THAT?
W... WELL...
I FIGURED YOU WERE LIVING IN A BOX BECAUSE YOU RAN AWAY FROM HOME.
AND THAT THEY CAME TO TAKE YOU BACK.
RAN AWAY FROM HOME
MIYAZAKI-SAN DID?
SHH!
......

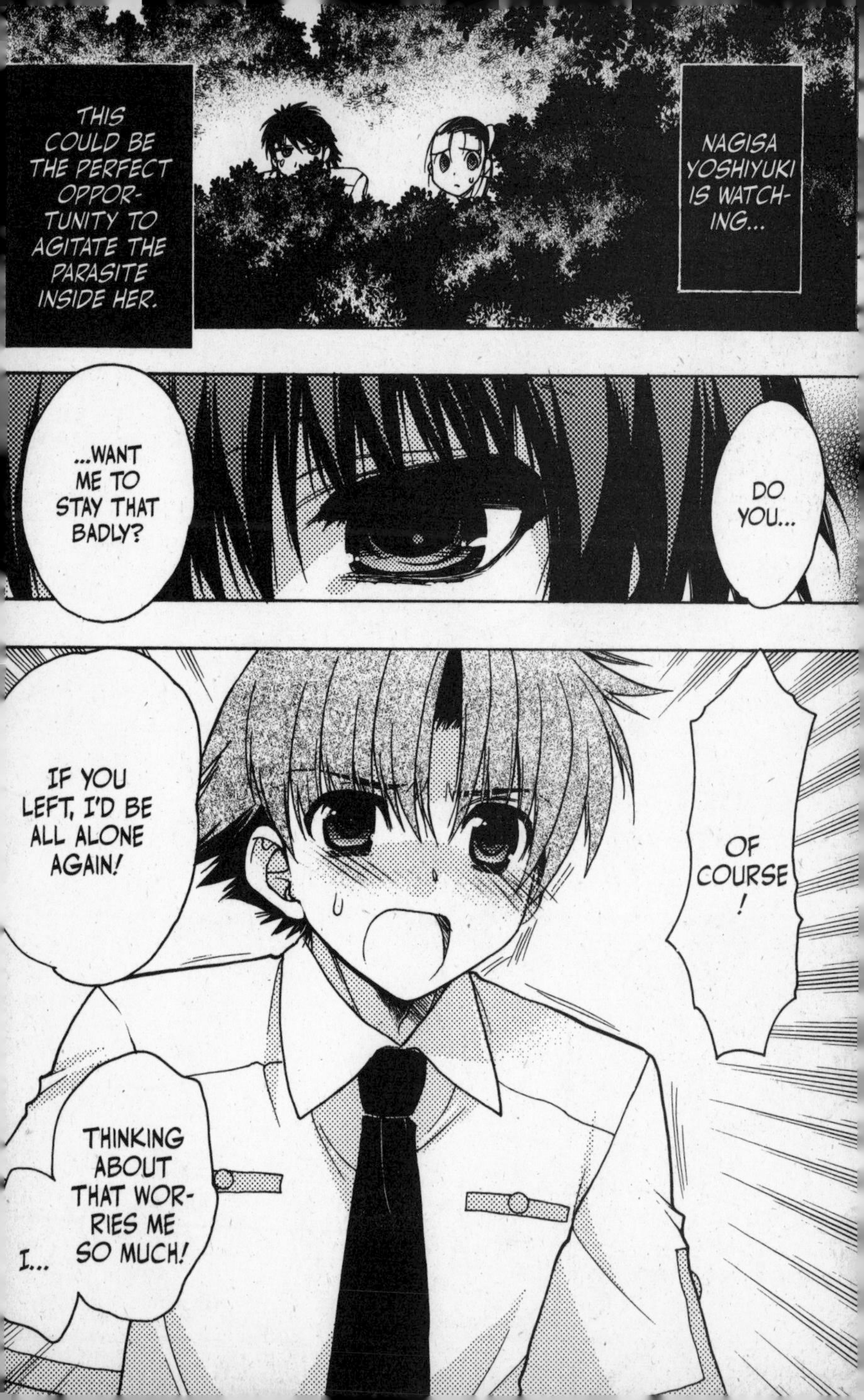
NAGISA YOSHIYUKI IS WATCHING...
THIS COULD BE THE PERFECT OPPORTUNITY TO AGITATE THE PARASITE INSIDE HER.
DO YOU...
...WANT ME TO STAY THAT BADLY?
OF COURSE!
IF YOU LEFT, I'D BE ALL ALONE AGAIN!
I...
THINKING ABOUT THAT WORRIES ME SO MUCH!

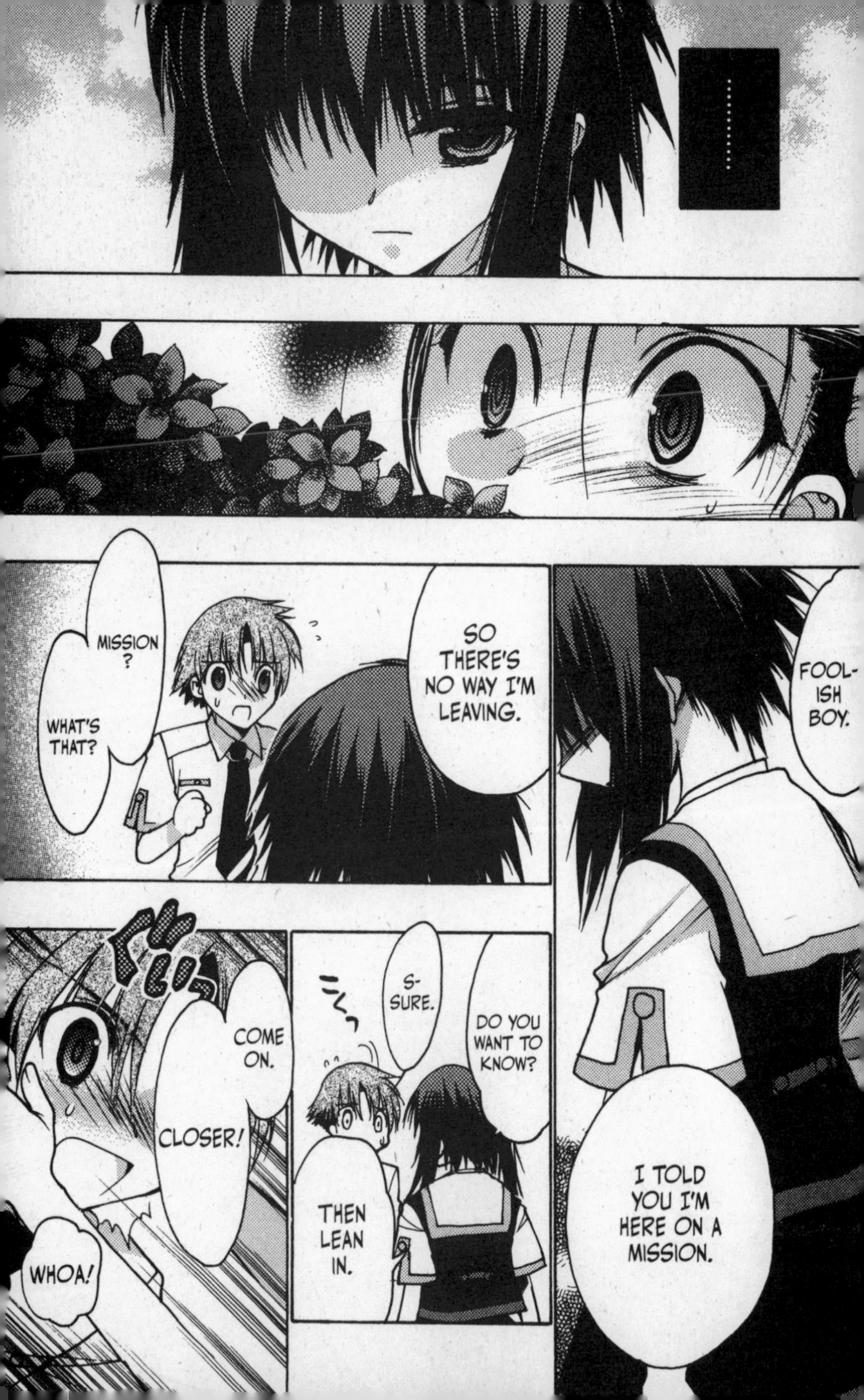
......
FOOLISH BOY.
I TOLD YOU I'M HERE ON A MISSION.
SO THERE'S NO WAY I'M LEAVING.
MISSION?
WHAT'S THAT?
DO YOU WANT TO KNOW?
S-SURE.
THEN LEAN IN.
COME ON.
CLOSER!
WHOA!

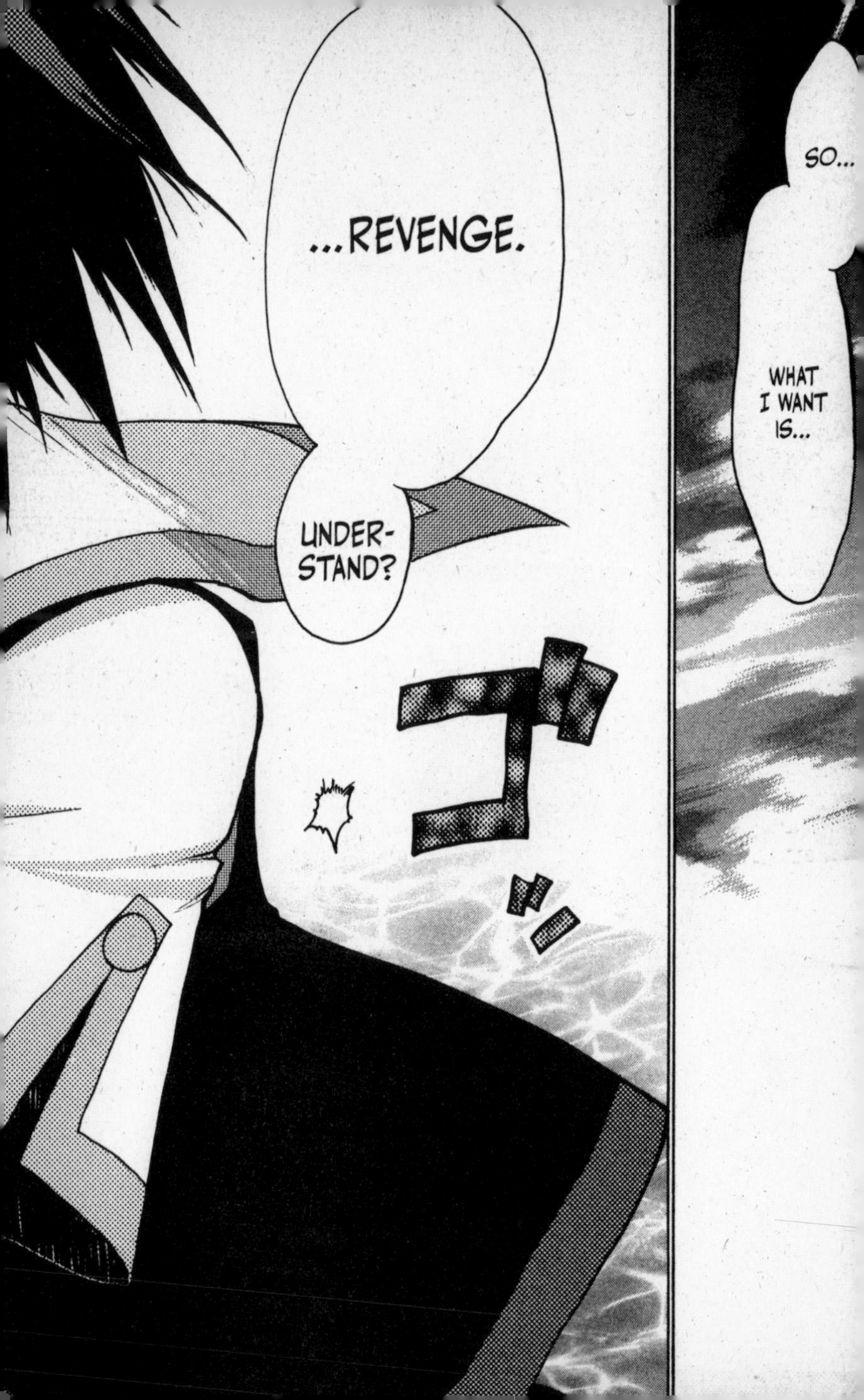
SO...
WHAT I WANT IS...
...REVENGE.
UNDER-STAND?

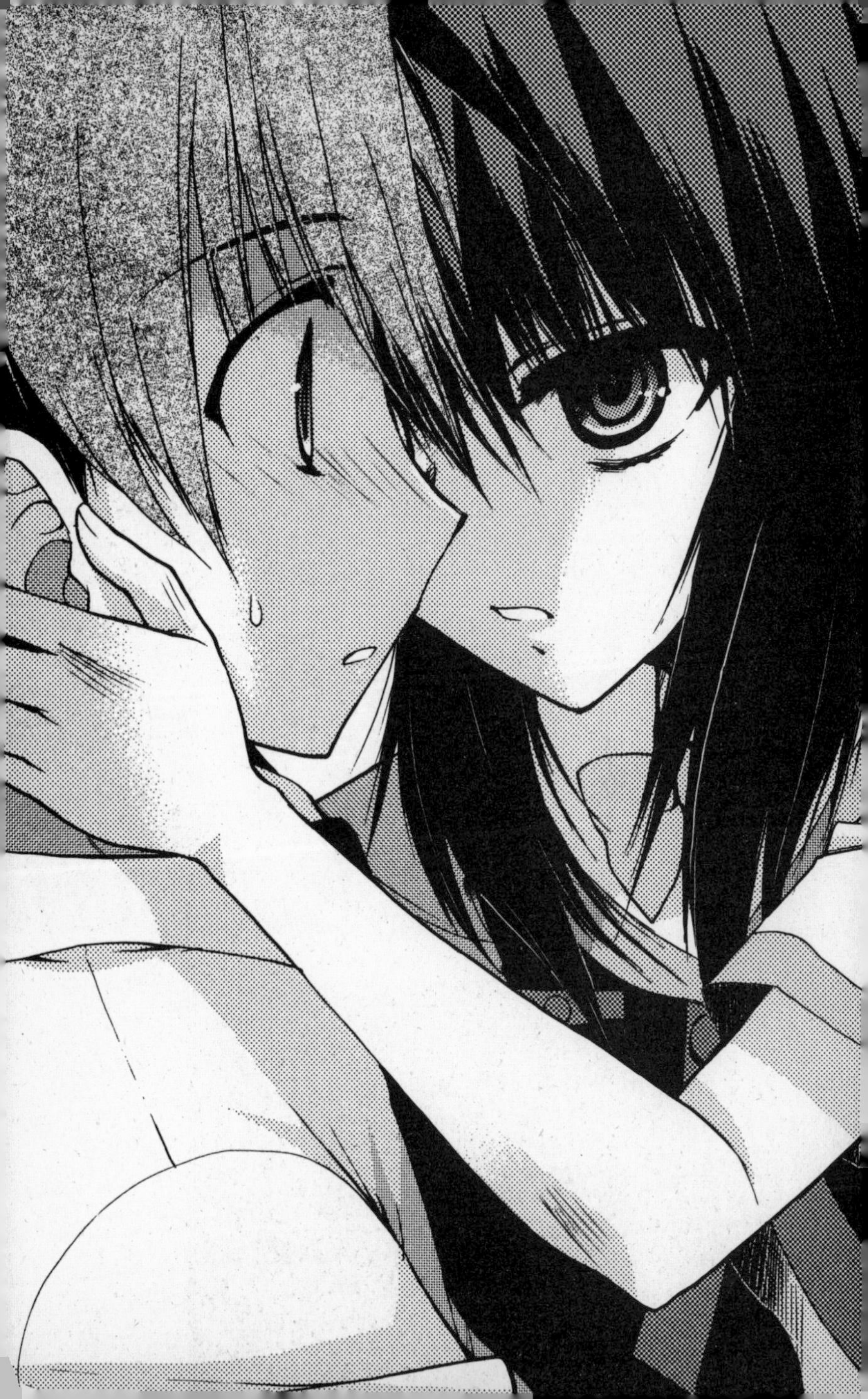

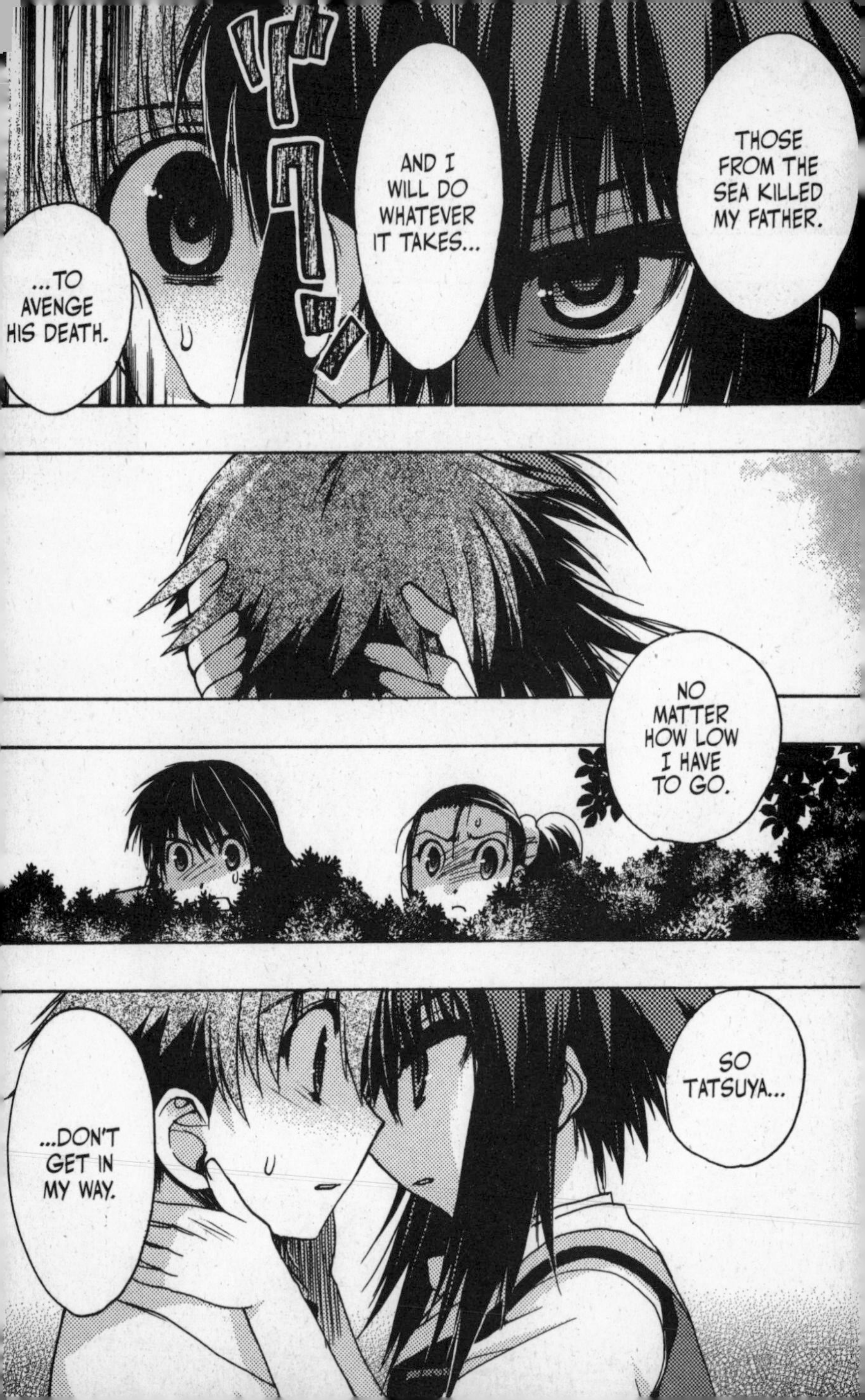
THOSE FROM THE SEA KILLED MY FATHER.
AND I WILL DO WHATEVER IT TAKES...
...TO AVENGE HIS DEATH.
NO MATTER HOW LOW I HAVE TO GO.
SO TATSUYA...
...DON'T GET IN MY WAY.

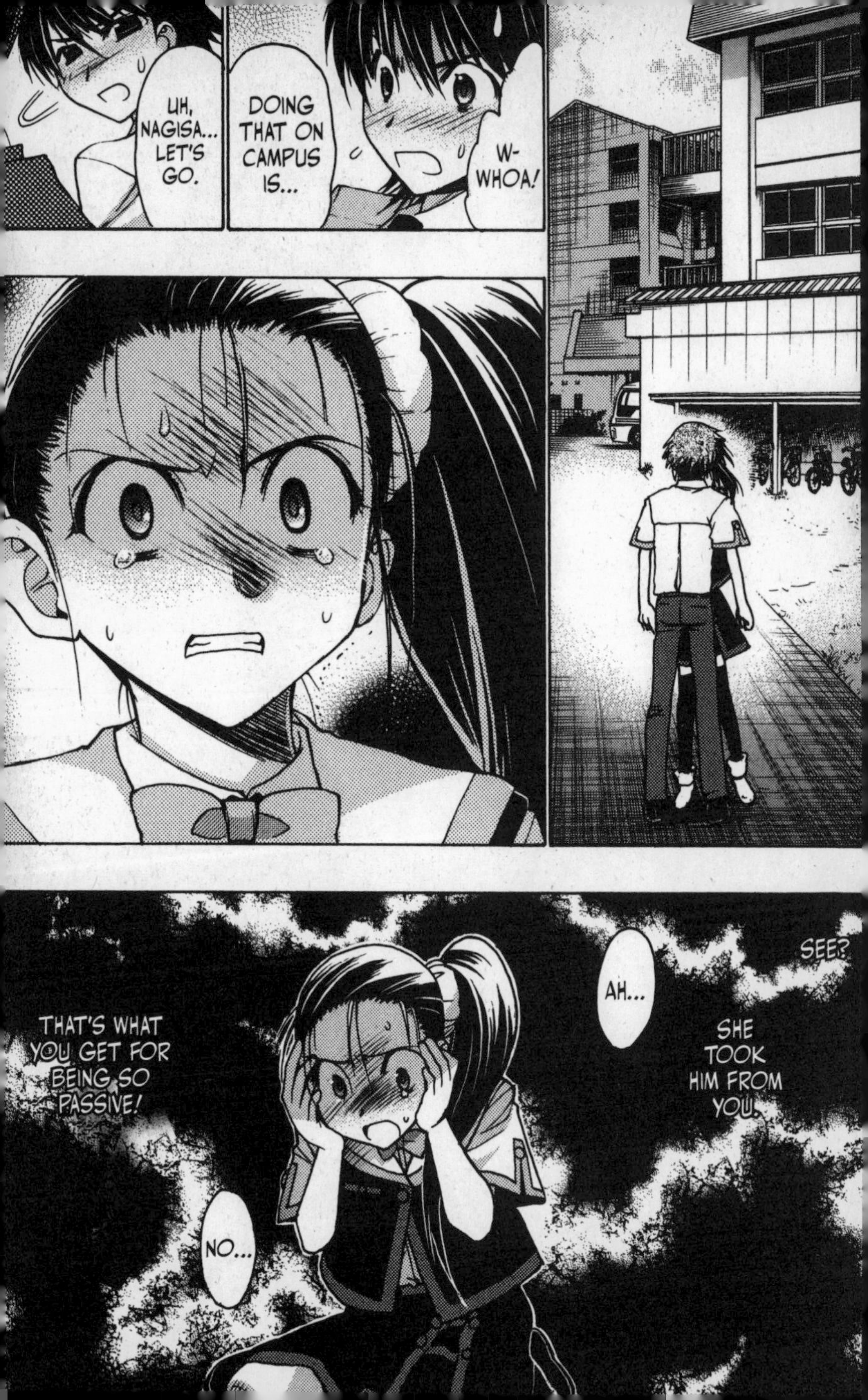
W-WHOA!
DOING THAT ON CAMPUS IS...
UH, NAGISA... LET'S GO.
SEE?
SHE TOOK HIM FROM YOU.
AH...
THAT'S WHAT YOU GET FOR BEING SO PASSIVE!
NO...

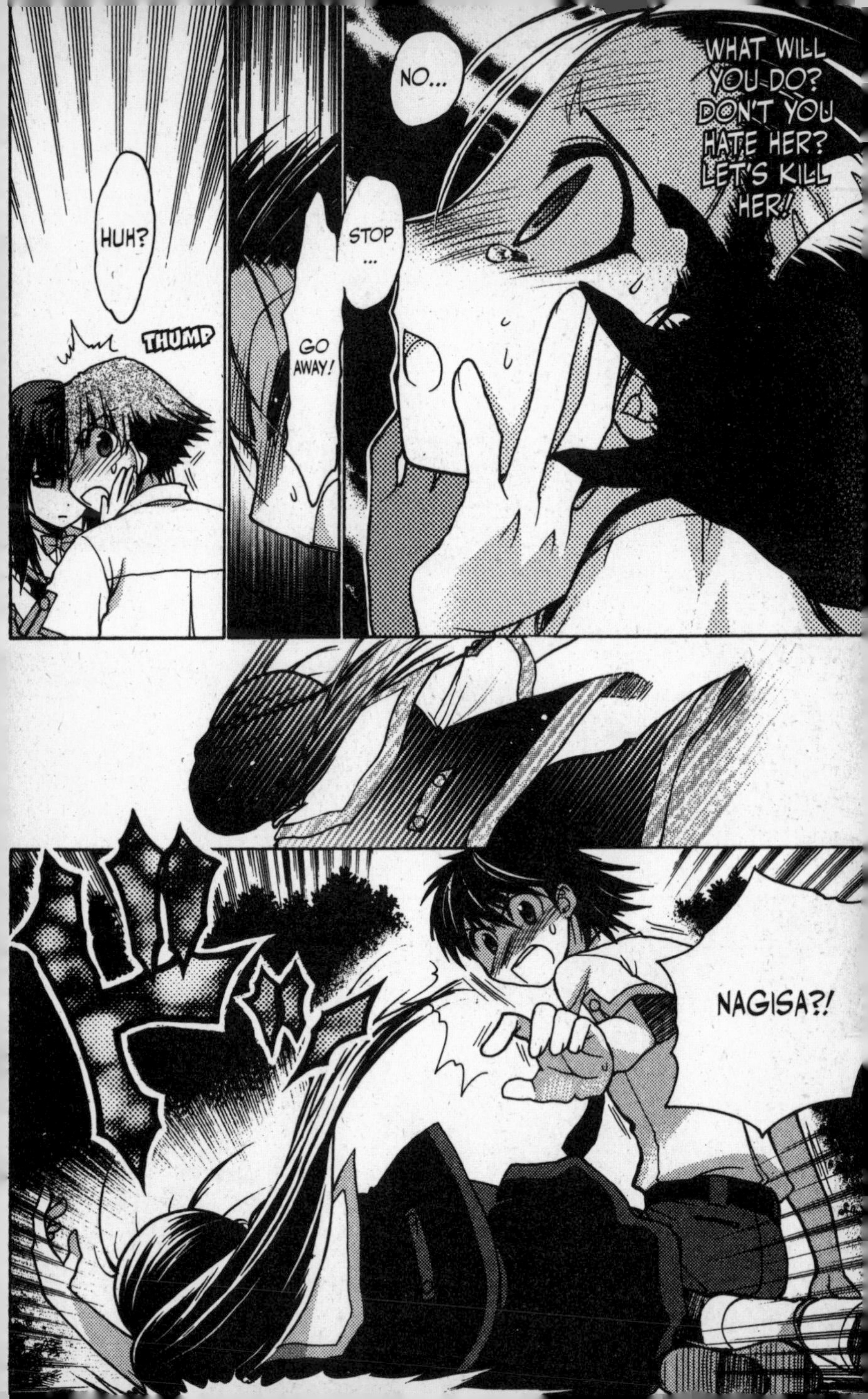
WHAT WILL YOU DO? DON'T YOU HATE HER? LET'S KILL HER!
NO...
STOP ...
GO AWAY!
HUH?
THUMP
NAGISA?!

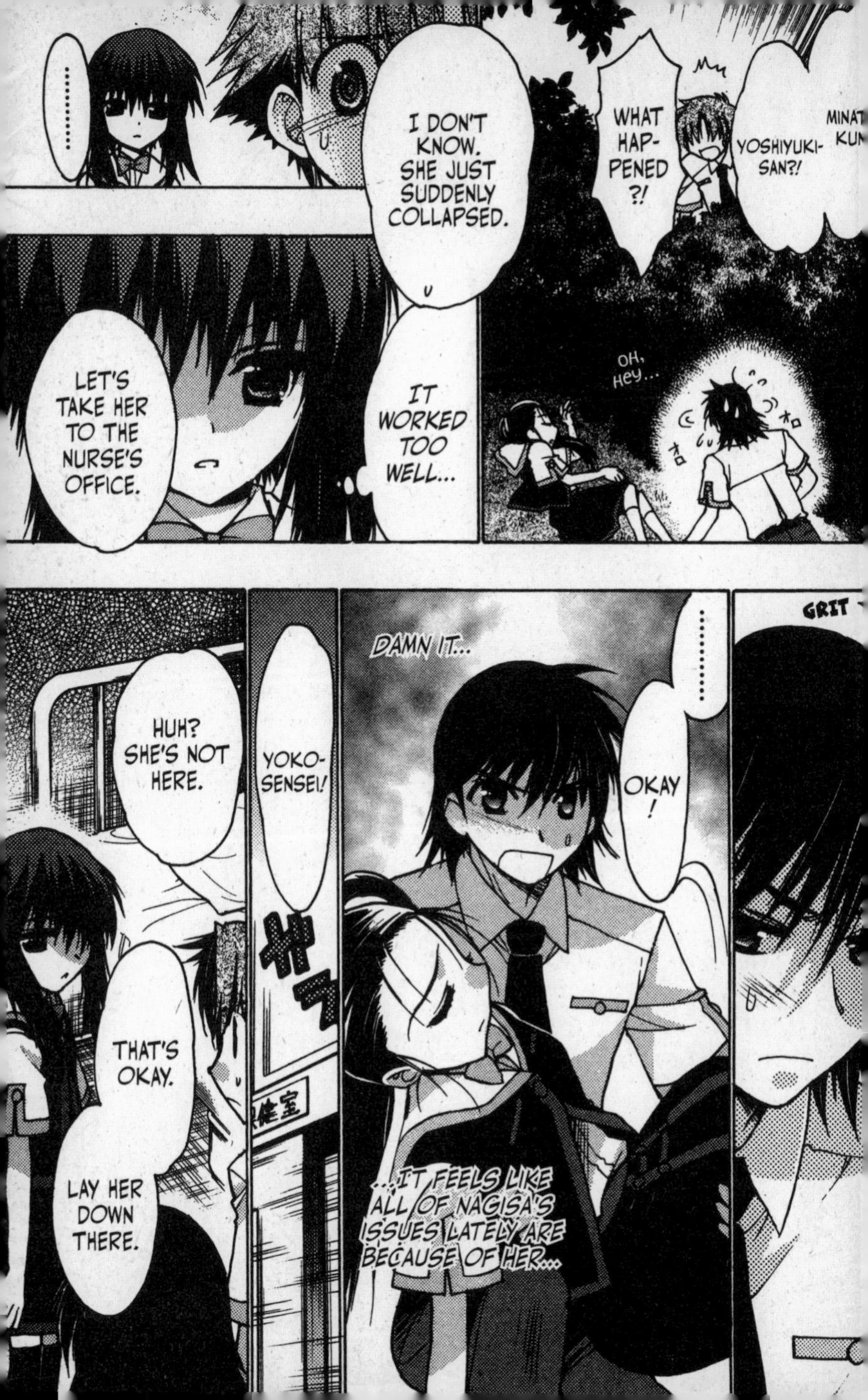
MINAT KUN
YOSHIYUKI-SAN?!
WHAT HAPPENED?!
OH, HEY...
I DON'T KNOW. SHE JUST SUDDENLY COLLAPSED.
......
IT WORKED TOO WELL...
LET'S TAKE HER TO THE NURSE'S OFFICE.
GRIT
......
OKAY!
DAMN IT...
...IT FEELS LIKE ALL OF NAGISA'S ISSUES LATELY ARE BECAUSE OF HER...
YOKO-SENSEI!
HUH? SHE'S NOT HERE.
THAT'S OKAY.
LAY HER DOWN THERE.

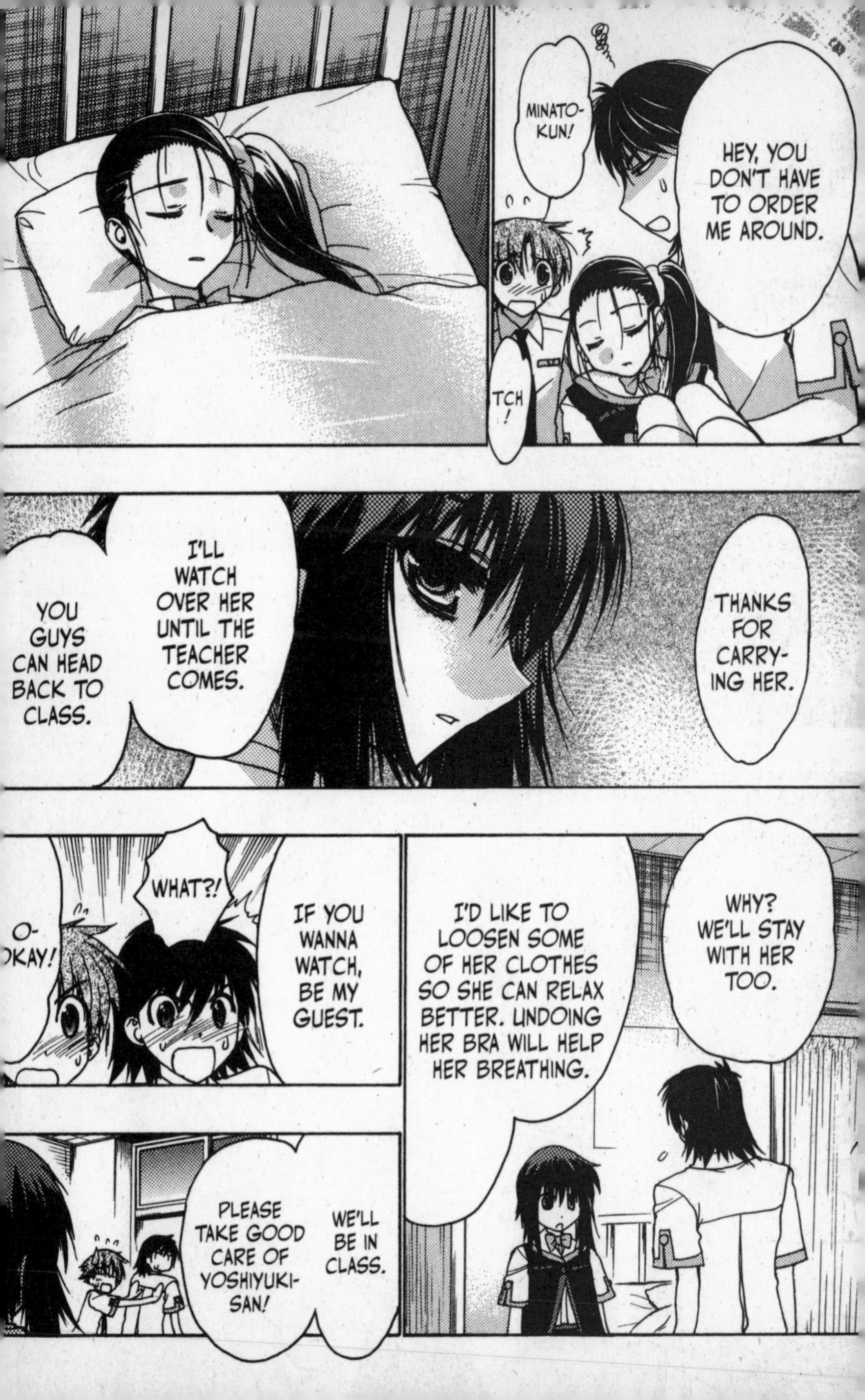
HEY, YOU DON'T HAVE TO ORDER ME AROUND.
MINATO-KUN!
TCH!
THANKS FOR CARRY-ING HER.
I'LL WATCH OVER HER UNTIL THE TEACHER COMES.
YOU GUYS CAN HEAD BACK TO CLASS.
WHY? WE'LL STAY WITH HER TOO.
I'D LIKE TO LOOSEN SOME OF HER CLOTHES SO SHE CAN RELAX BETTER. UNDOING HER BRA WILL HELP HER BREATHING.
IF YOU WANNA WATCH, BE MY GUEST.
WHAT?!
O-KAY!
WE'LL BE IN CLASS.
PLEASE TAKE GOOD CARE OF YOSHIYUKI-SAN!

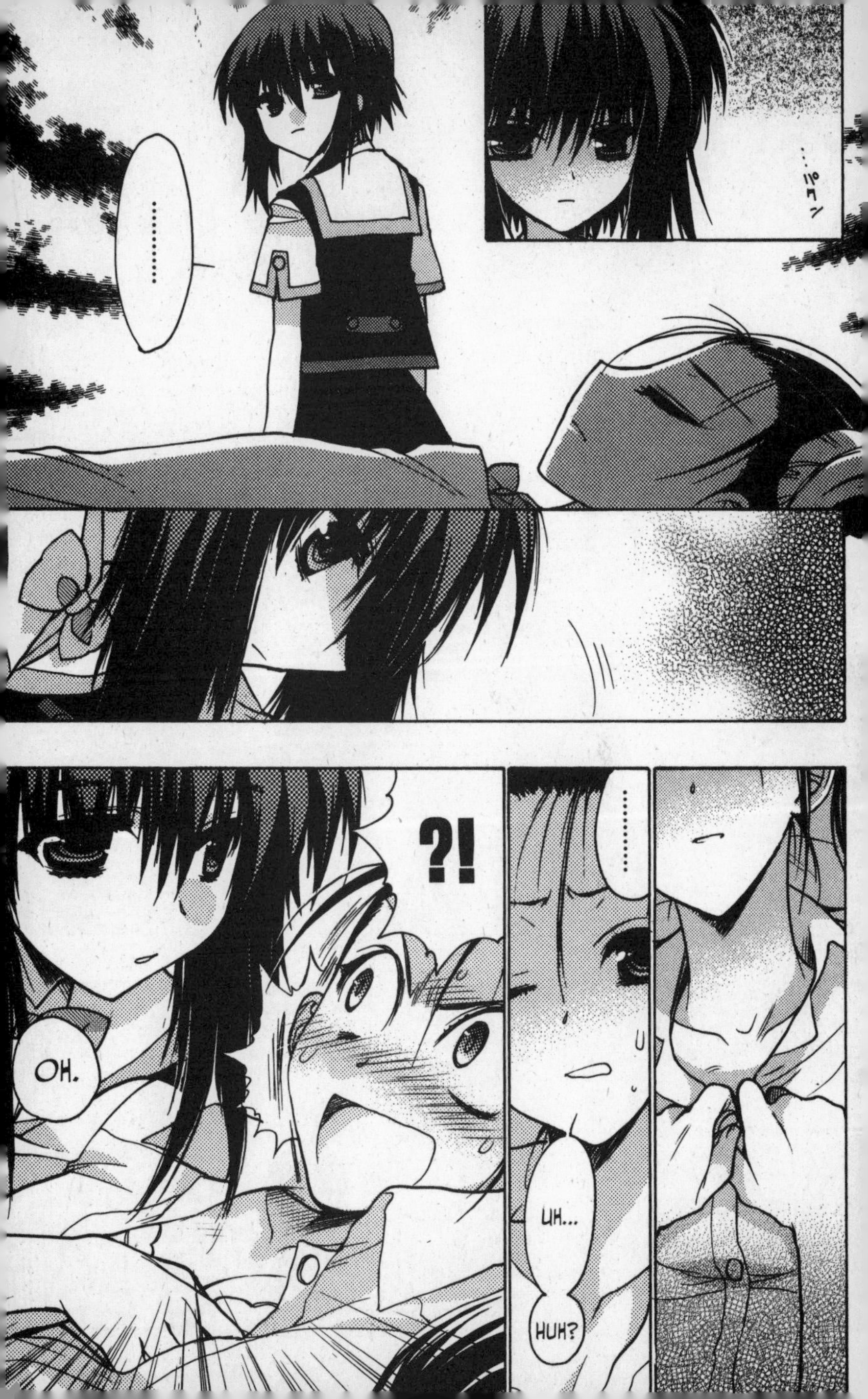
…ピクン
……
……
UH...
HUH?
?!
OH.

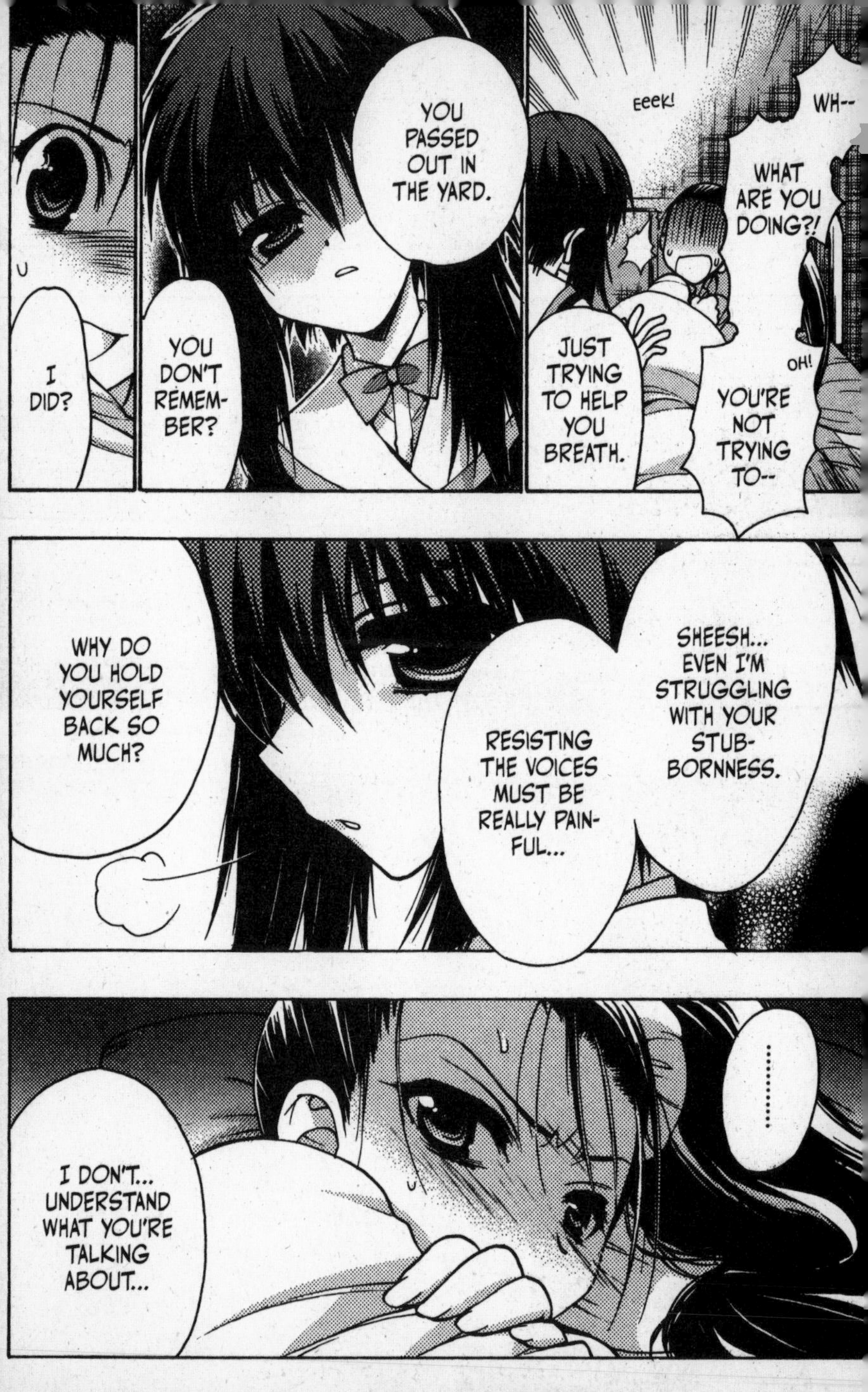
WH--
WHAT ARE YOU DOING?!
Eeek!
OH!
YOU'RE NOT TRYING TO--
JUST TRYING TO HELP YOU BREATH.
YOU PASSED OUT IN THE YARD.
YOU DON'T REMEMBER?
I DID?
SHEESH... EVEN I'M STRUGGLING WITH YOUR STUBBORNNESS.
RESISTING THE VOICES MUST BE REALLY PAINFUL...
WHY DO YOU HOLD YOURSELF BACK SO MUCH?
....
I DON'T... UNDERSTAND WHAT YOU'RE TALKING ABOUT...

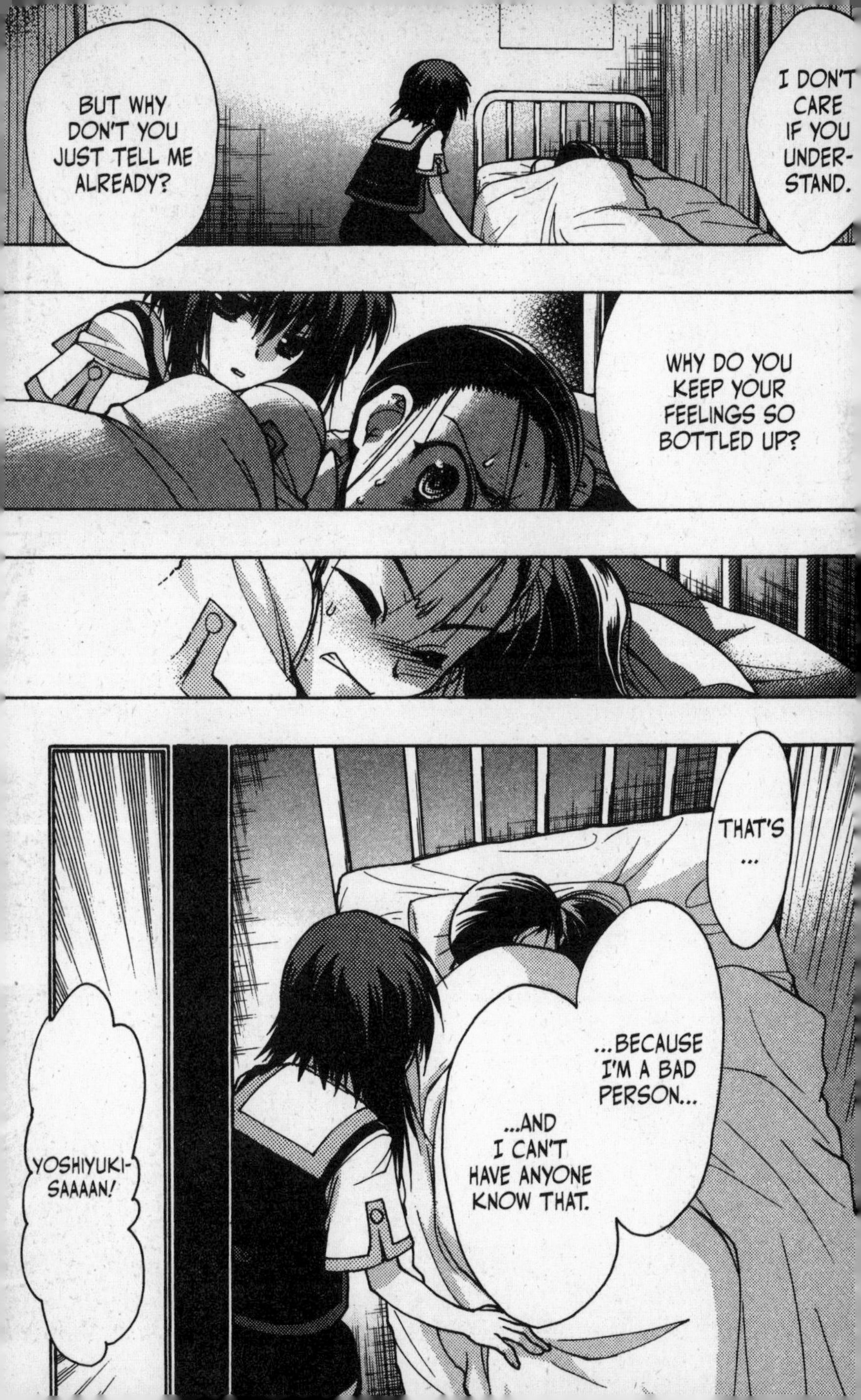
I DON'T CARE IF YOU UNDERSTAND.
BUT WHY DON'T YOU JUST TELL ME ALREADY?
WHY DO YOU KEEP YOUR FEELINGS SO BOTTLED UP?
THAT'S...
...BECAUSE I'M A BAD PERSON...
...AND I CAN'T HAVE ANYONE KNOW THAT.
YOSHIYUKI-SAAAAN!

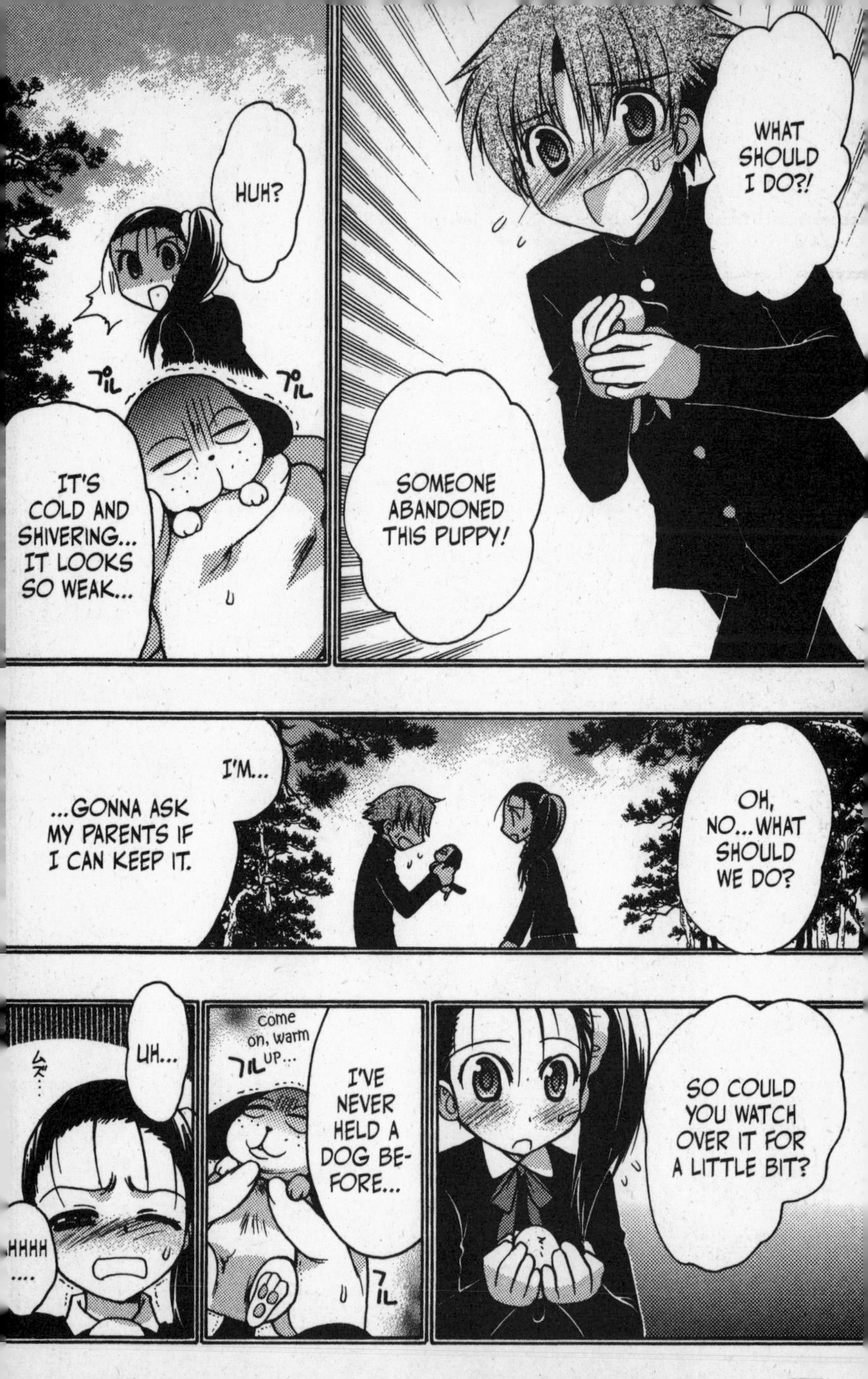
WHAT SHOULD I DO?!
SOMEONE ABANDONED THIS PUPPY!
HUH?
プル
プル
IT'S COLD AND SHIVERING... IT LOOKS SO WEAK...
OH, NO...WHAT SHOULD WE DO?
I'M...
...GONNA ASK MY PARENTS IF I CAN KEEP IT.
SO COULD YOU WATCH OVER IT FOR A LITTLE BIT?
I'VE NEVER HELD A DOG BE-FORE...
come on, warm up...
プル
プル
UH...
ムズ...
HHHH ....

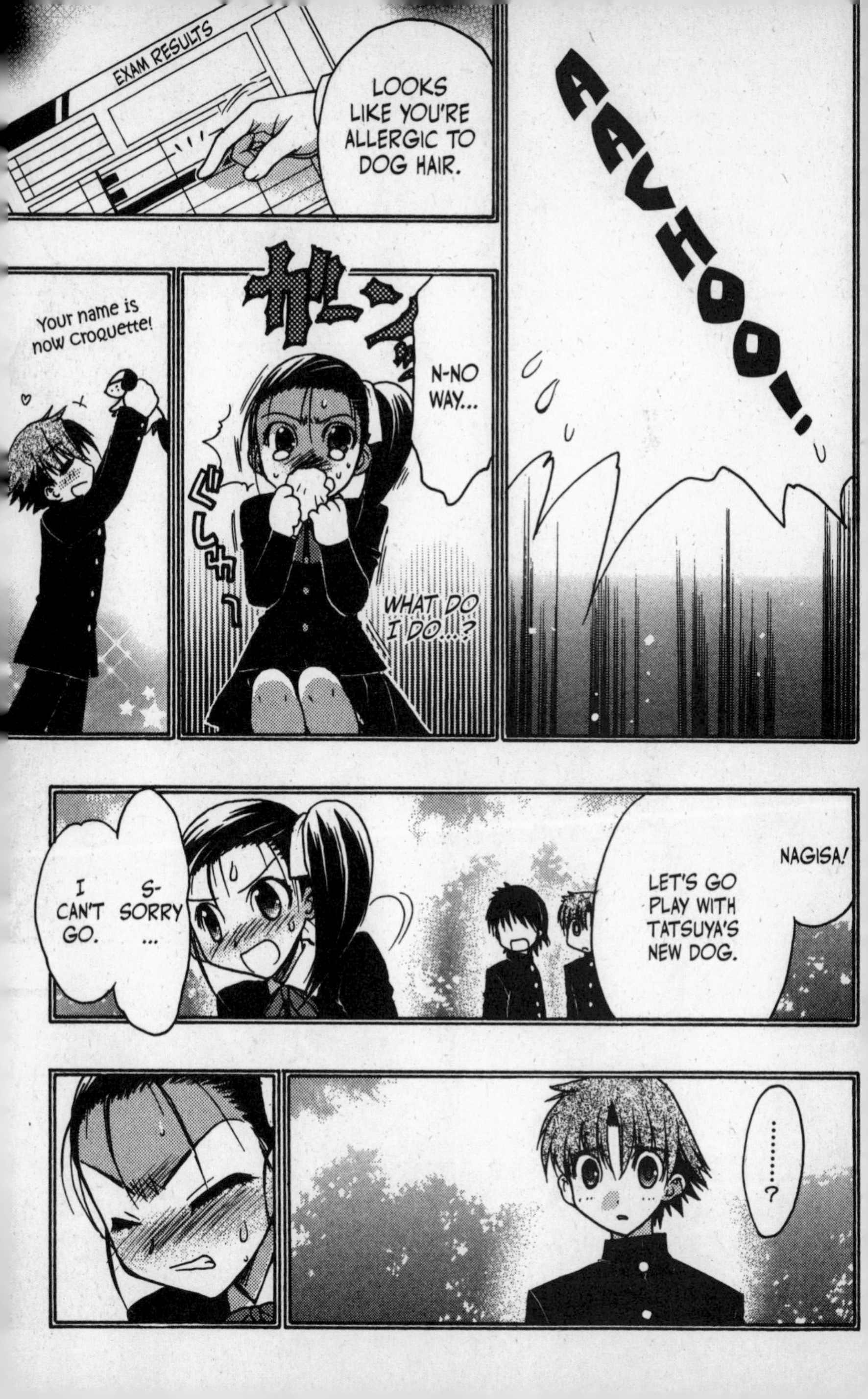
AAVHOO!!
EXAM RESULTS
LOOKS LIKE YOU'RE ALLERGIC TO DOG HAIR.
N-NO WAY...
WHAT DO I DO...?
Your name is now Croquette!
NAGISA!
LET'S GO PLAY WITH TATSUYA'S NEW DOG.
S-SORRY...
I CAN'T GO.
......?

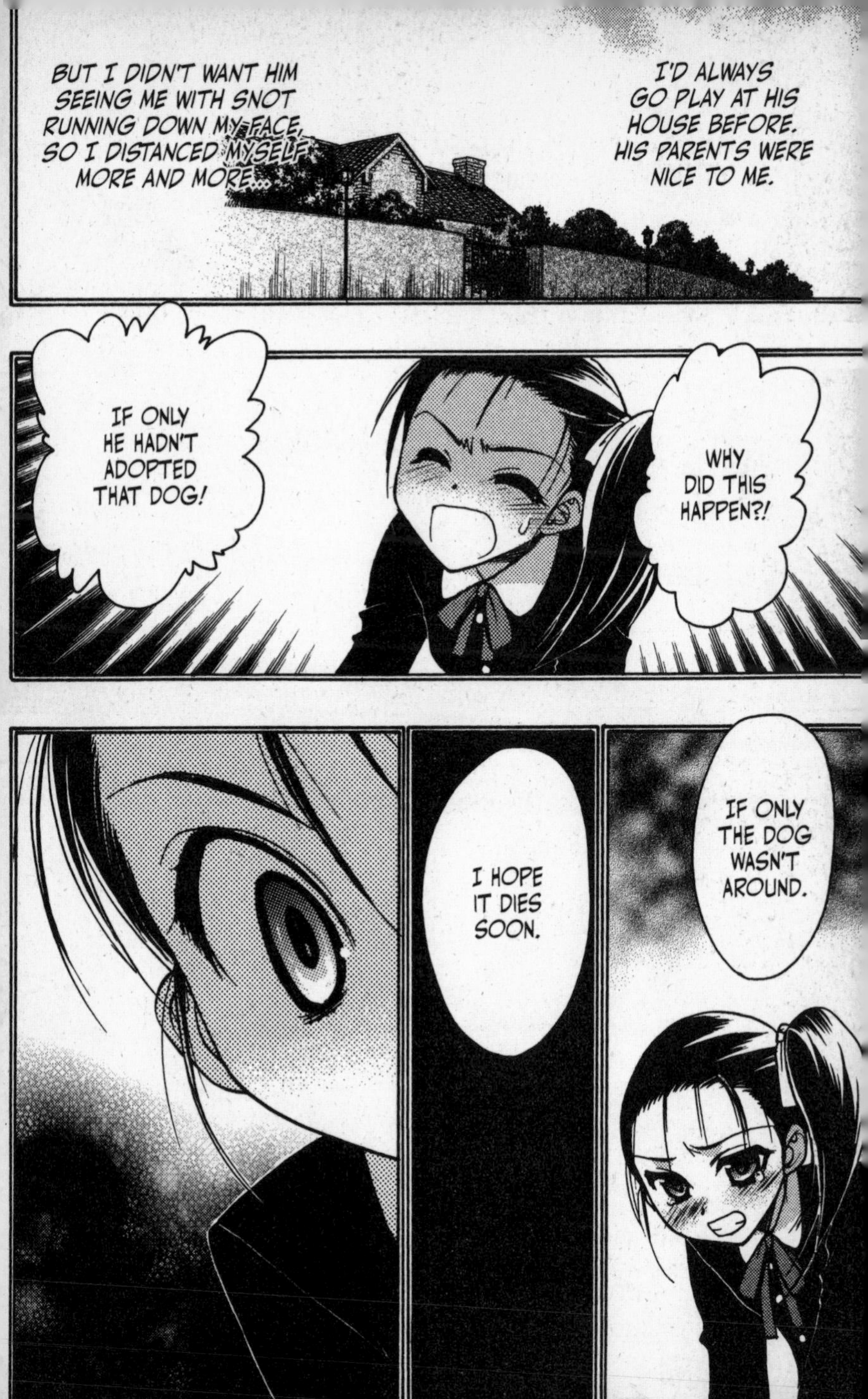
I'D ALWAYS GO PLAY AT HIS HOUSE BEFORE. HIS PARENTS WERE NICE TO ME.
BUT I DIDN'T WANT HIM SEEING ME WITH SNOT RUNNING DOWN MY FACE, SO I DISTANCED MYSELF MORE AND MORE...
WHY DID THIS HAPPEN?!
IF ONLY HE HADN'T ADOPTED THAT DOG!
IF ONLY THE DOG WASN'T AROUND.
I HOPE IT DIES SOON.

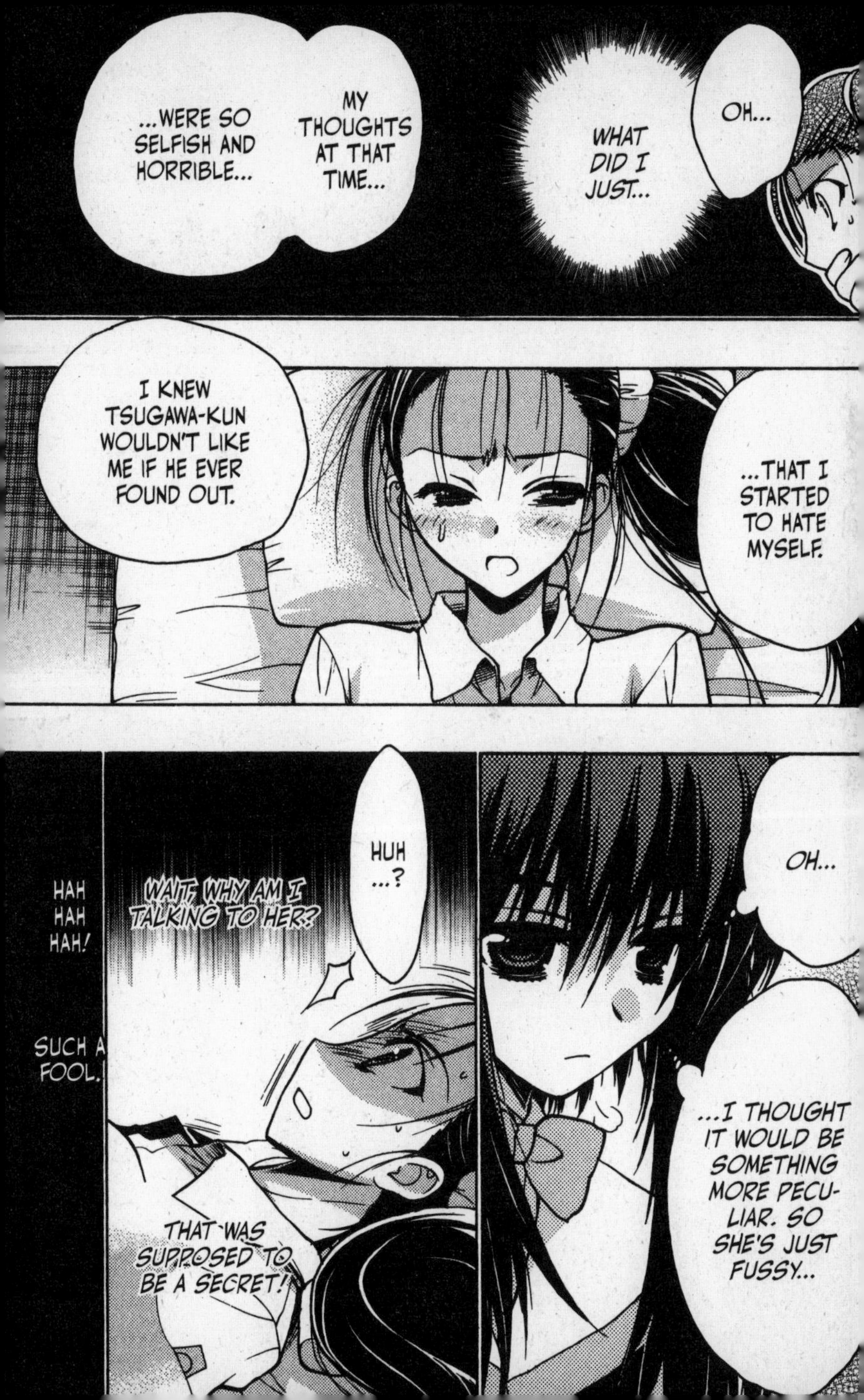
OH...
WHAT DID I JUST...
MY THOUGHTS AT THAT TIME...
...WERE SO SELFISH AND HORRIBLE...
...THAT I STARTED TO HATE MYSELF.
I KNEW TSUGAWA-KUN WOULDN'T LIKE ME IF HE EVER FOUND OUT.
OH...
...I THOUGHT IT WOULD BE SOMETHING MORE PECULIAR. SO SHE'S JUST FUSSY...
HUH ...?
WAIT, WHY AM I TALKING TO HER?
THAT WAS SUPPOSED TO BE A SECRET!
HAH HAH HAH!
SUCH A FOOL.

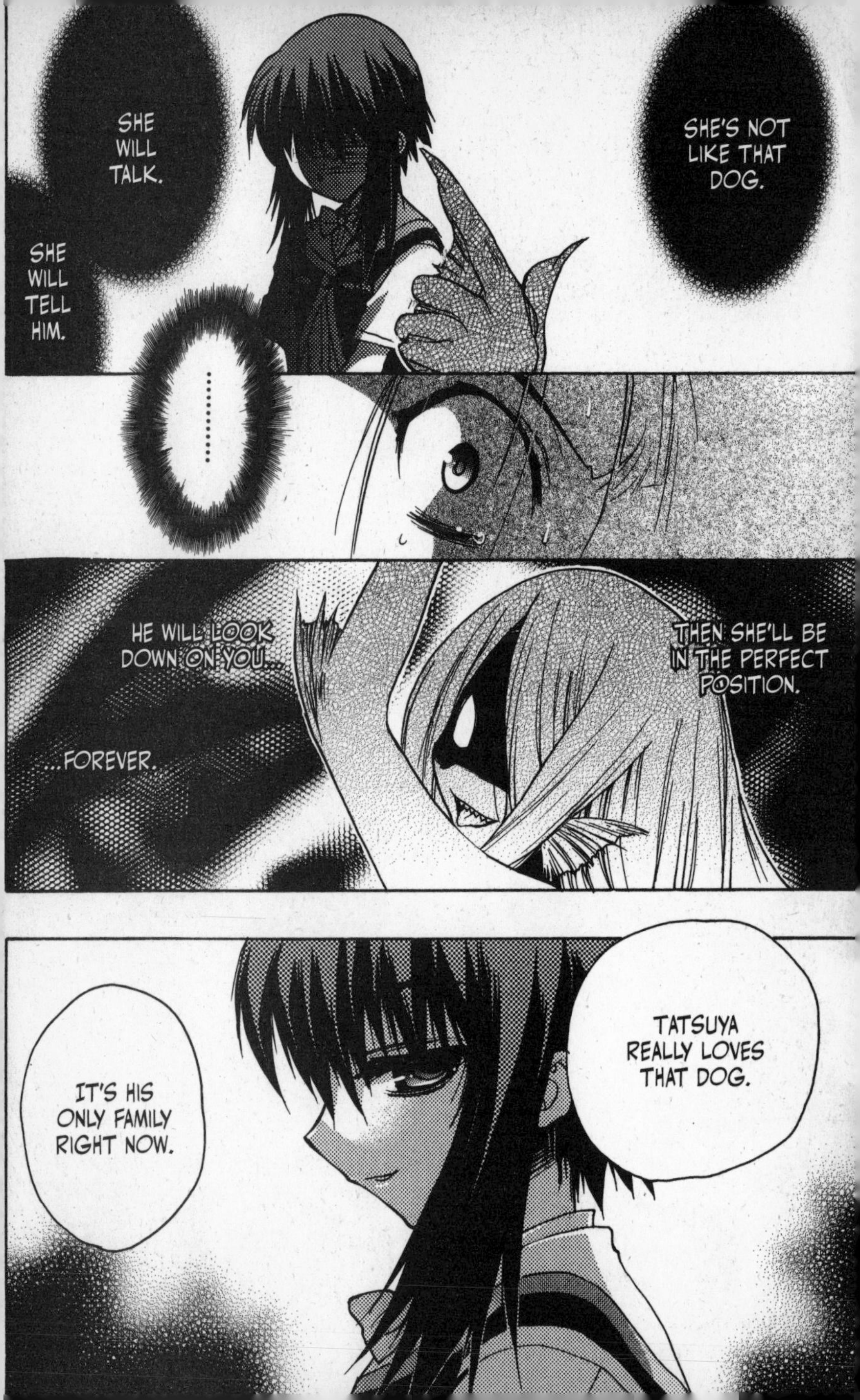
SHE'S NOT LIKE THAT DOG.
SHE WILL TALK.
SHE WILL TELL HIM.
......
THEN SHE'LL BE IN THE PERFECT POSITION.
HE WILL LOOK DOWN ON YOU...
...FOREVER.
TATSUYA REALLY LOVES THAT DOG.
IT'S HIS ONLY FAMILY RIGHT NOW.

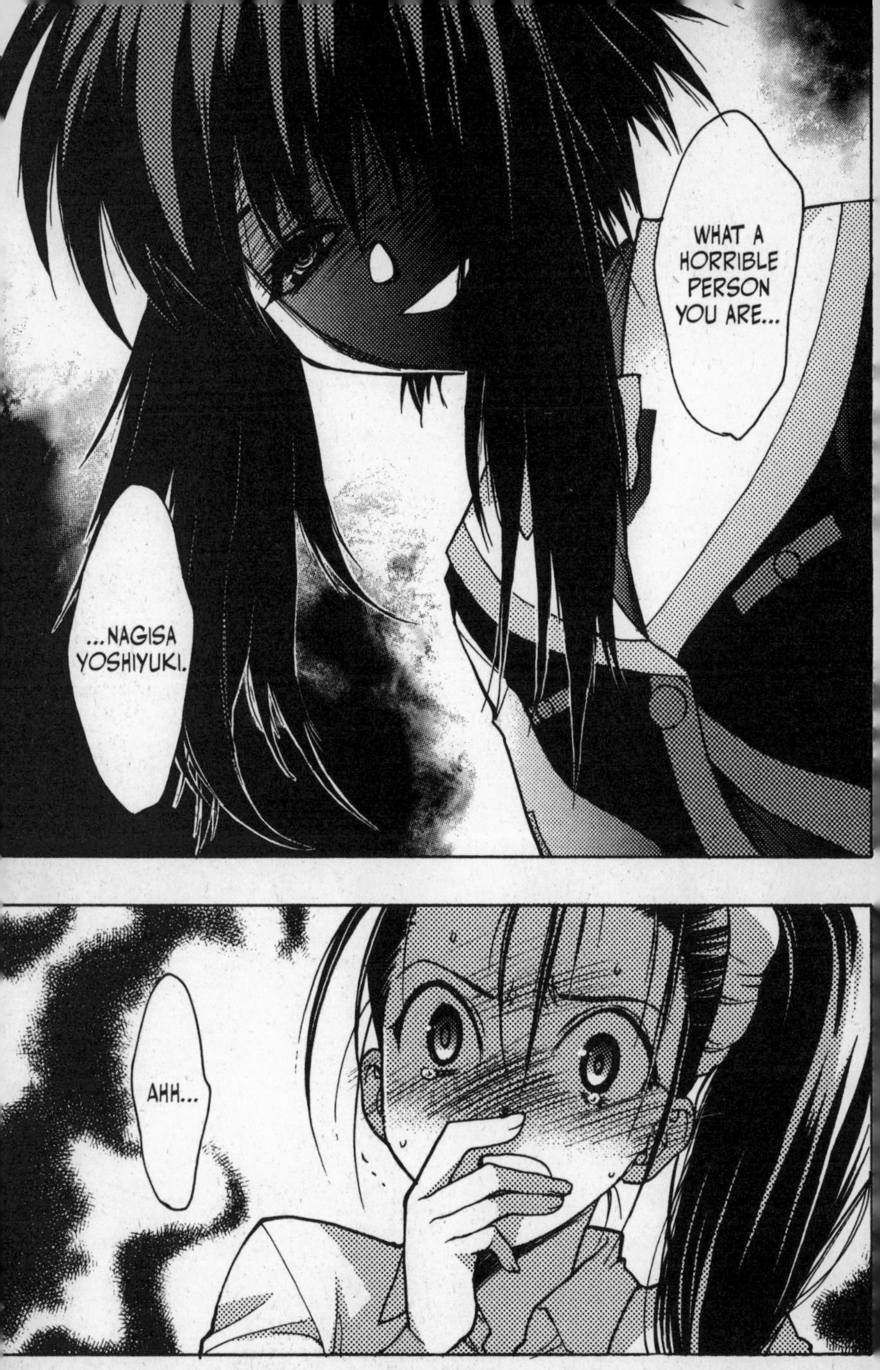
WHAT A HORRIBLE PERSON YOU ARE...
...NAGISA YOSHIYUKI.
AHH...

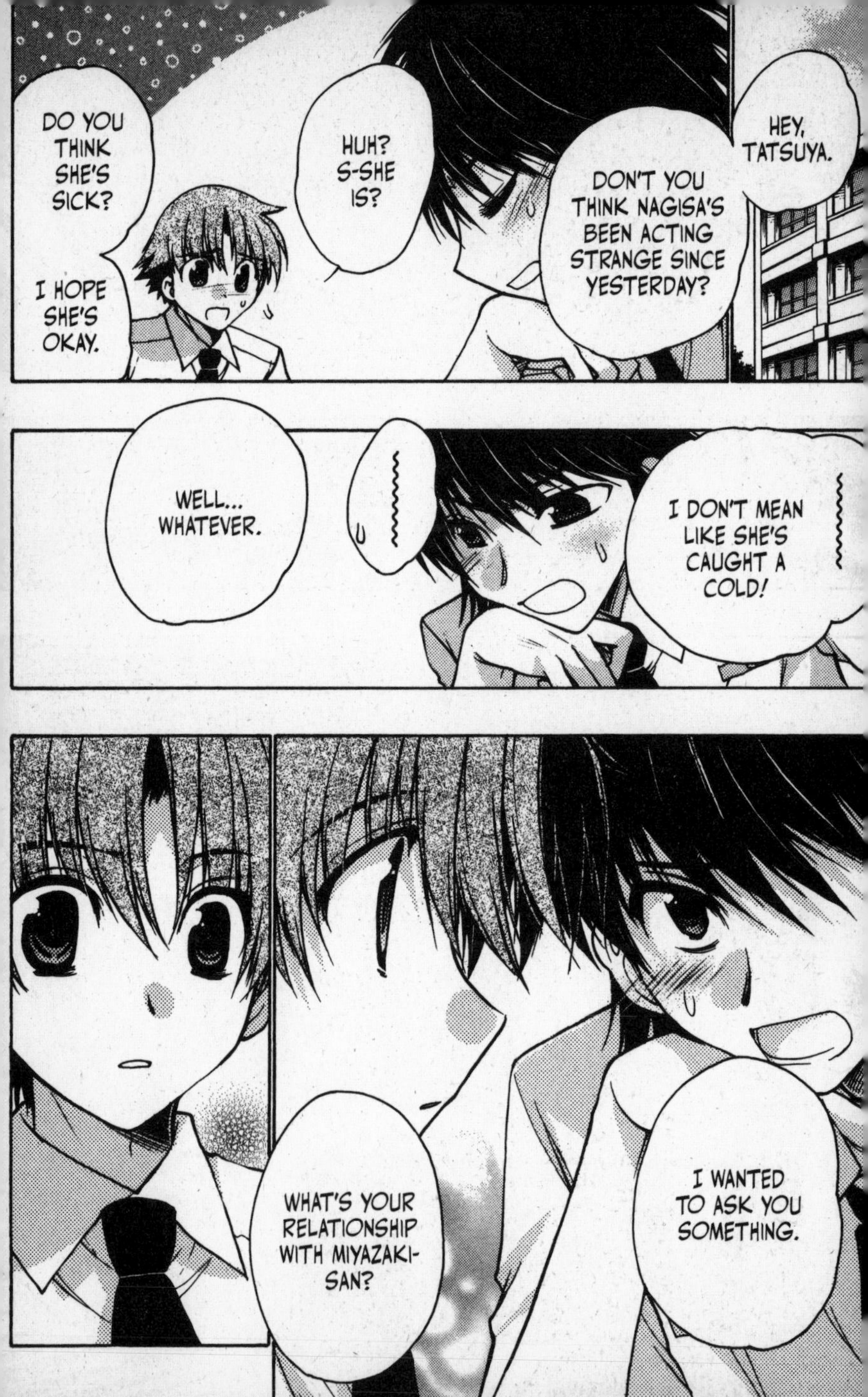
HEY, TATSUYA.
DON'T YOU THINK NAGISA'S BEEN ACTING STRANGE SINCE YESTERDAY?
HUH? S-SHE IS?
DO YOU THINK SHE'S SICK?
I HOPE SHE'S OKAY.
I DON'T MEAN LIKE SHE'S CAUGHT A COLD!
WELL... WHATEVER.
I WANTED TO ASK YOU SOMETHING.
WHAT'S YOUR RELATIONSHIP WITH MIYAZAKI-SAN?

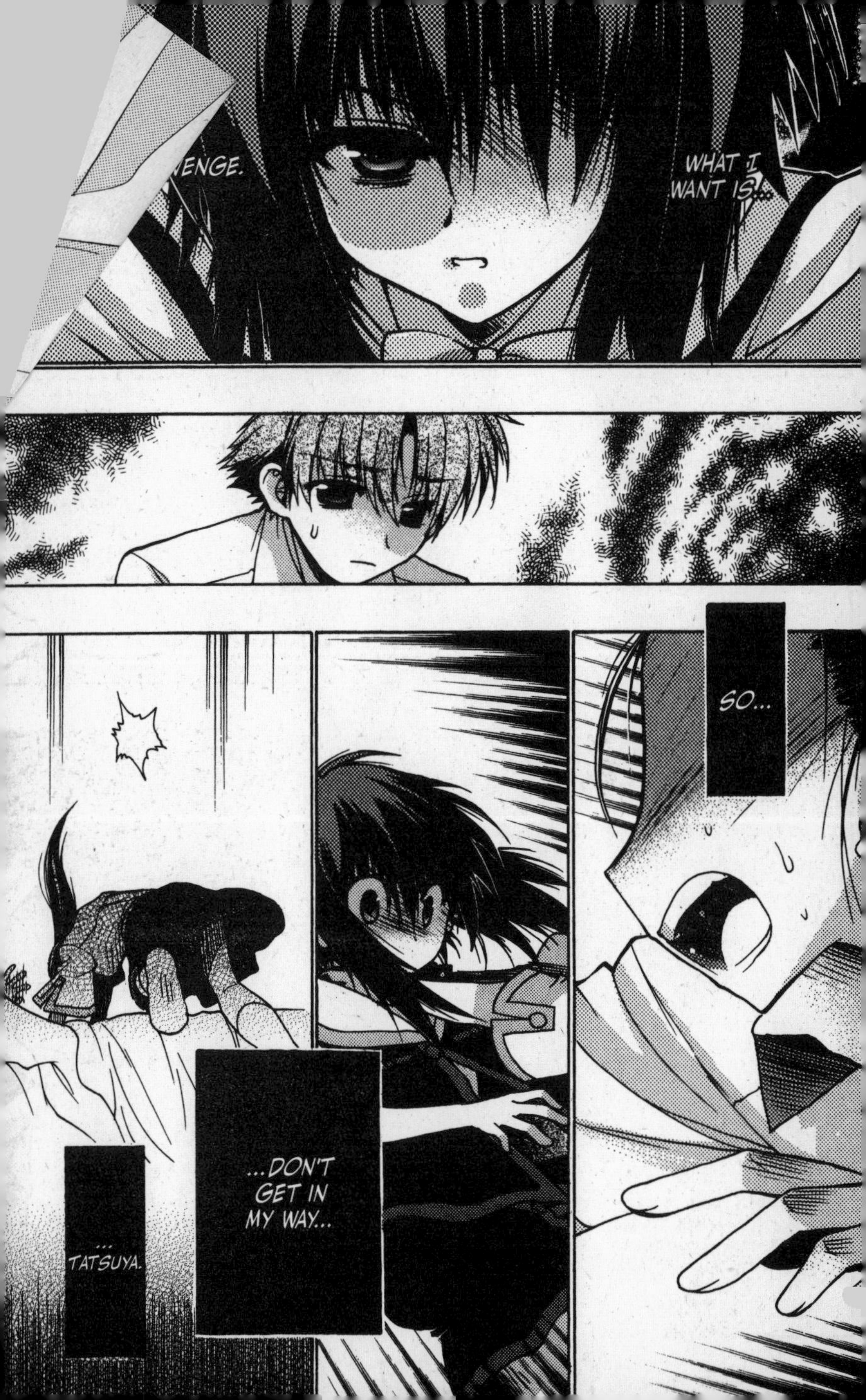
WHAT I WANT IS...
...ENGE.
SO...
...DON'T GET IN MY WAY...
... TATSUYA.

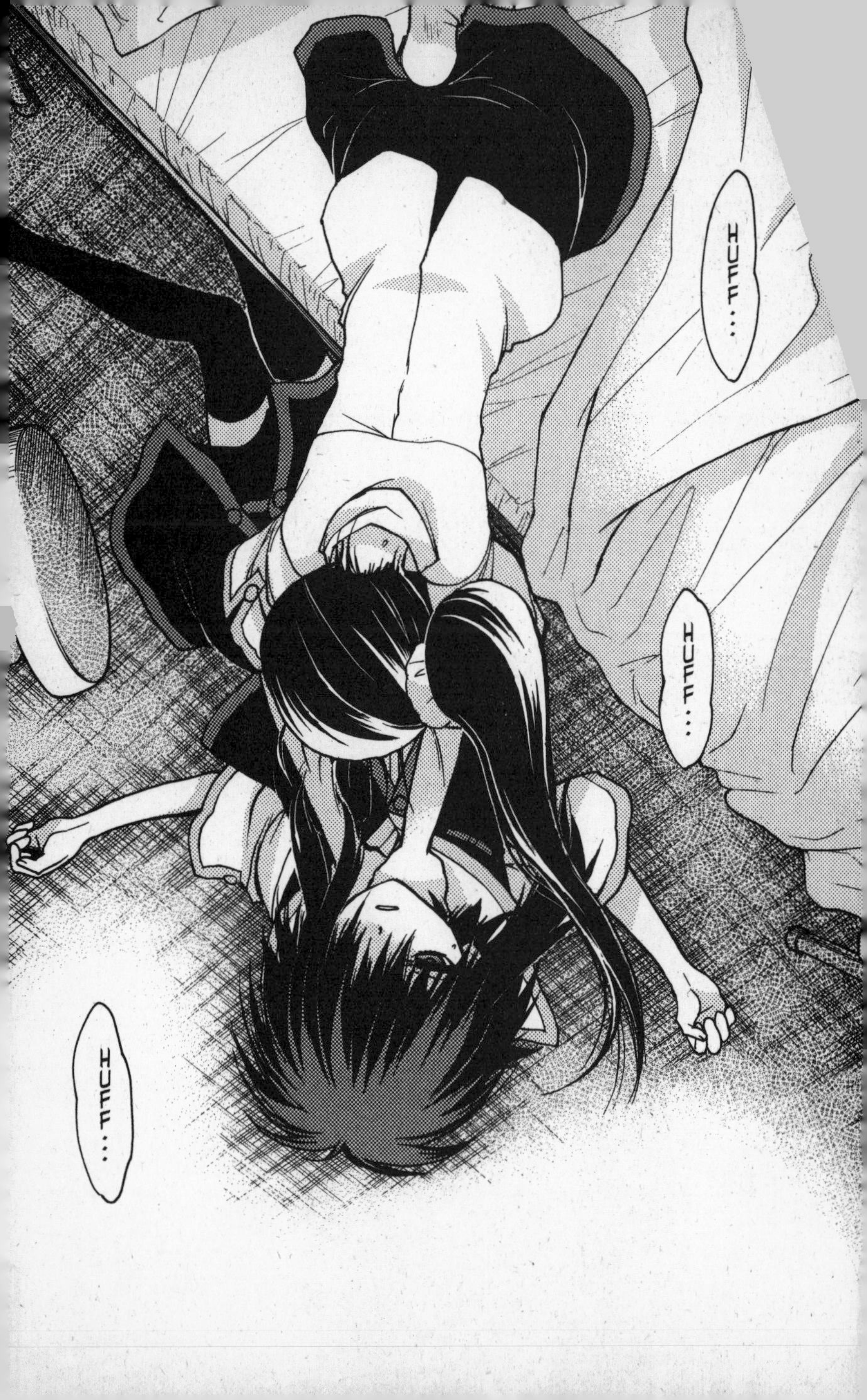
HUFF...
HUFF...
HUFF...

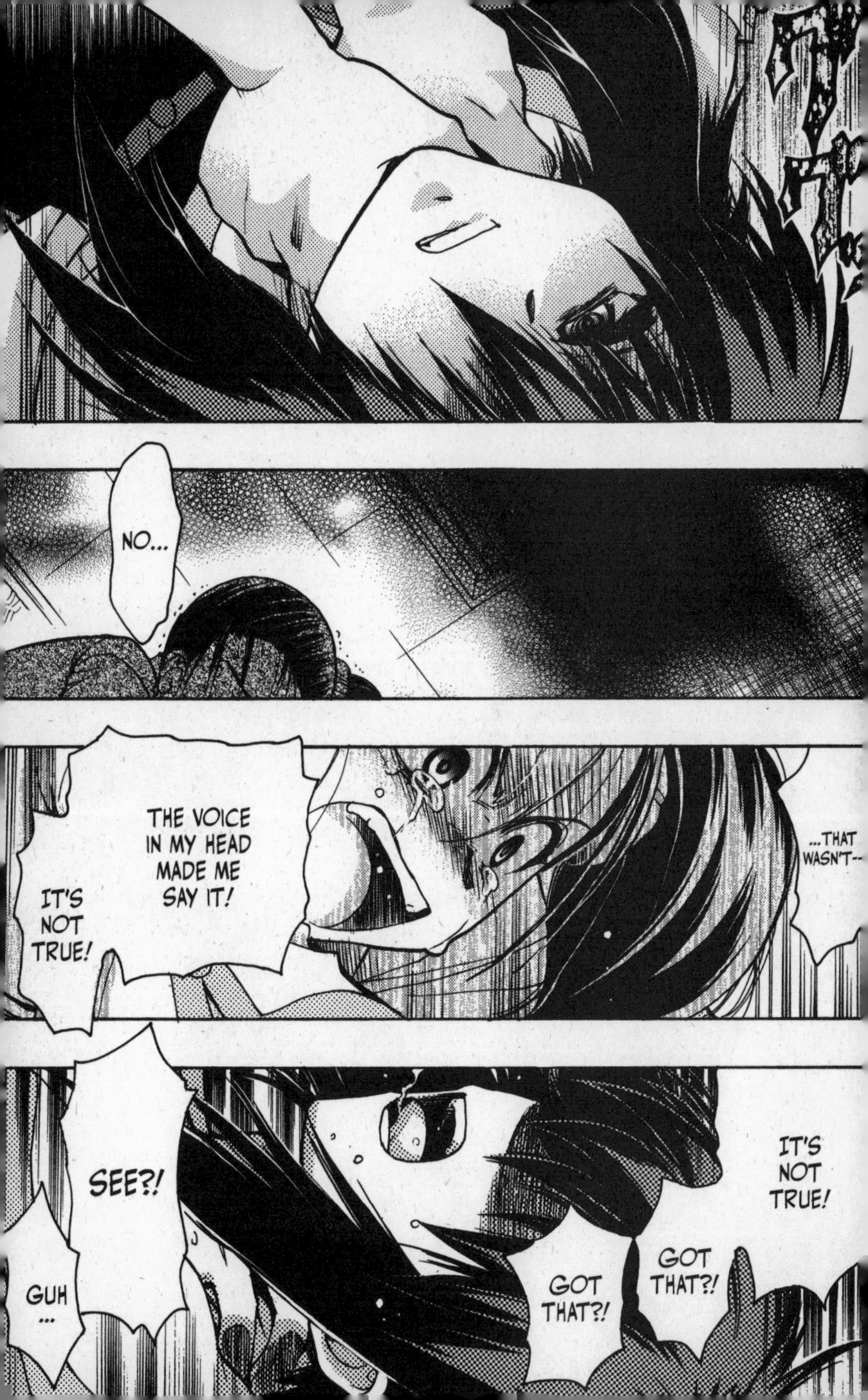
NO...
...THAT WASN'T--
THE VOICE IN MY HEAD MADE ME SAY IT!
IT'S NOT TRUE!
IT'S NOT TRUE!
GOT THAT?!
GOT THAT?!
SEE?!
GUH ...

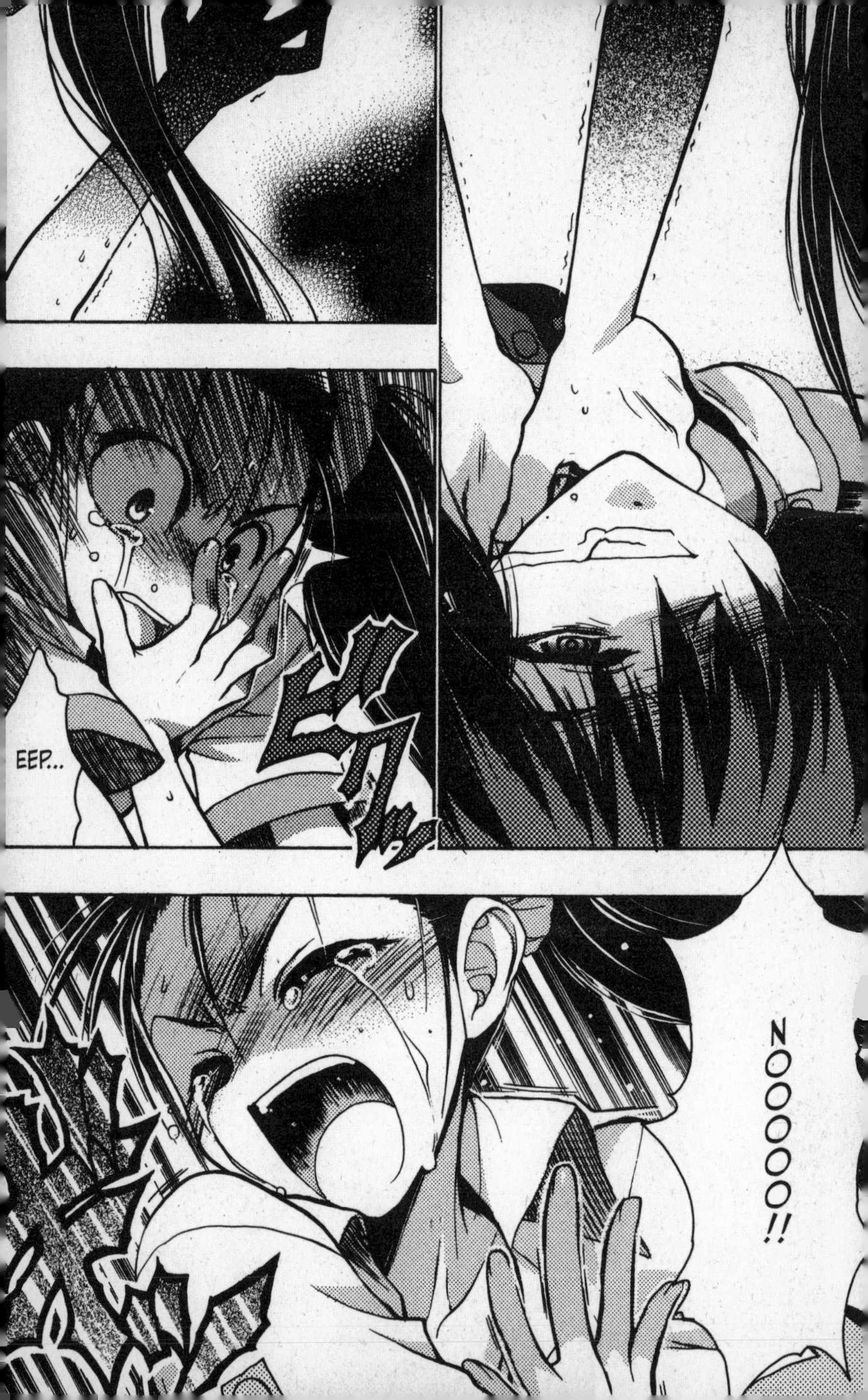
EEP...
NOOOOOO!!

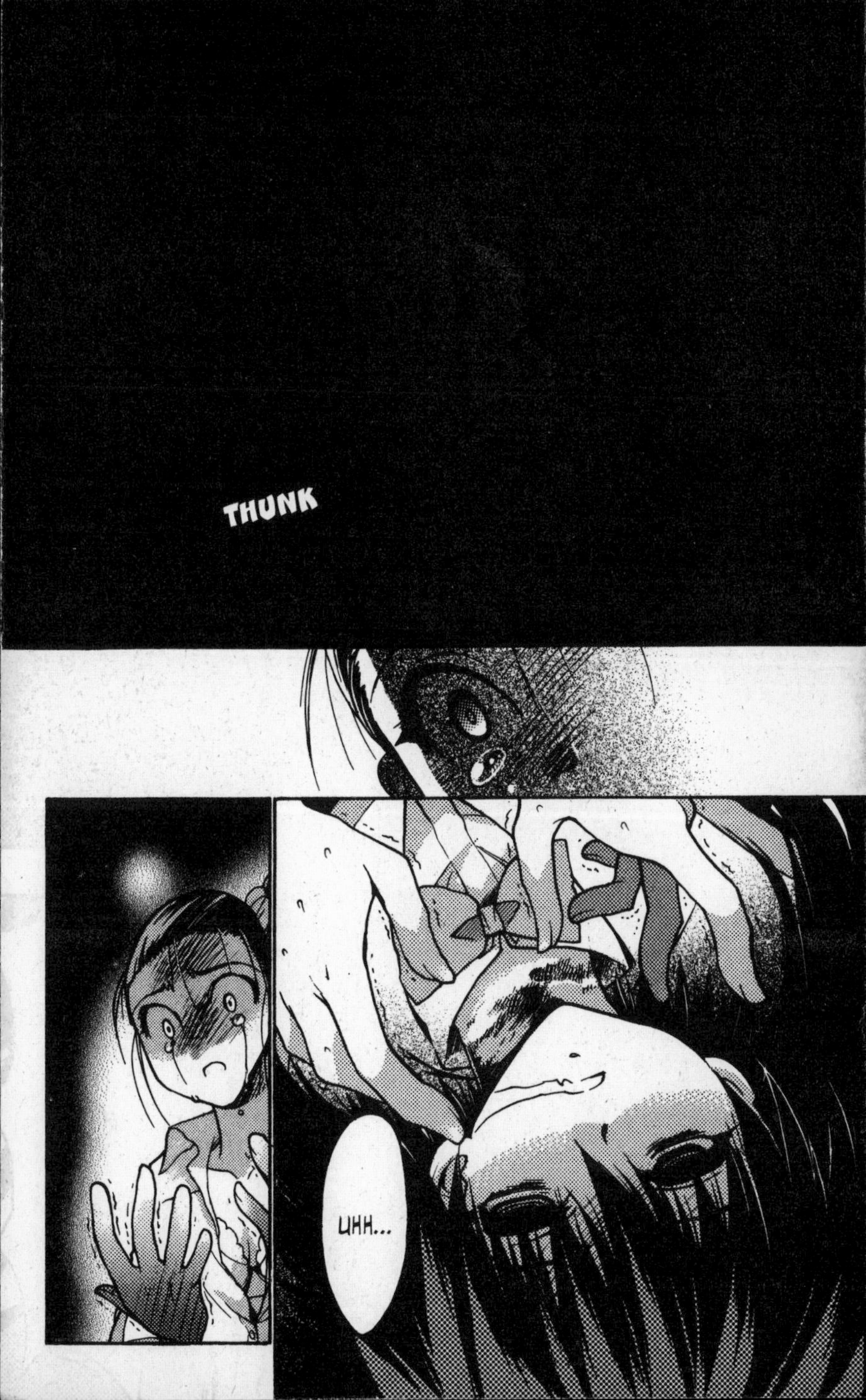
THUNK
UHH...

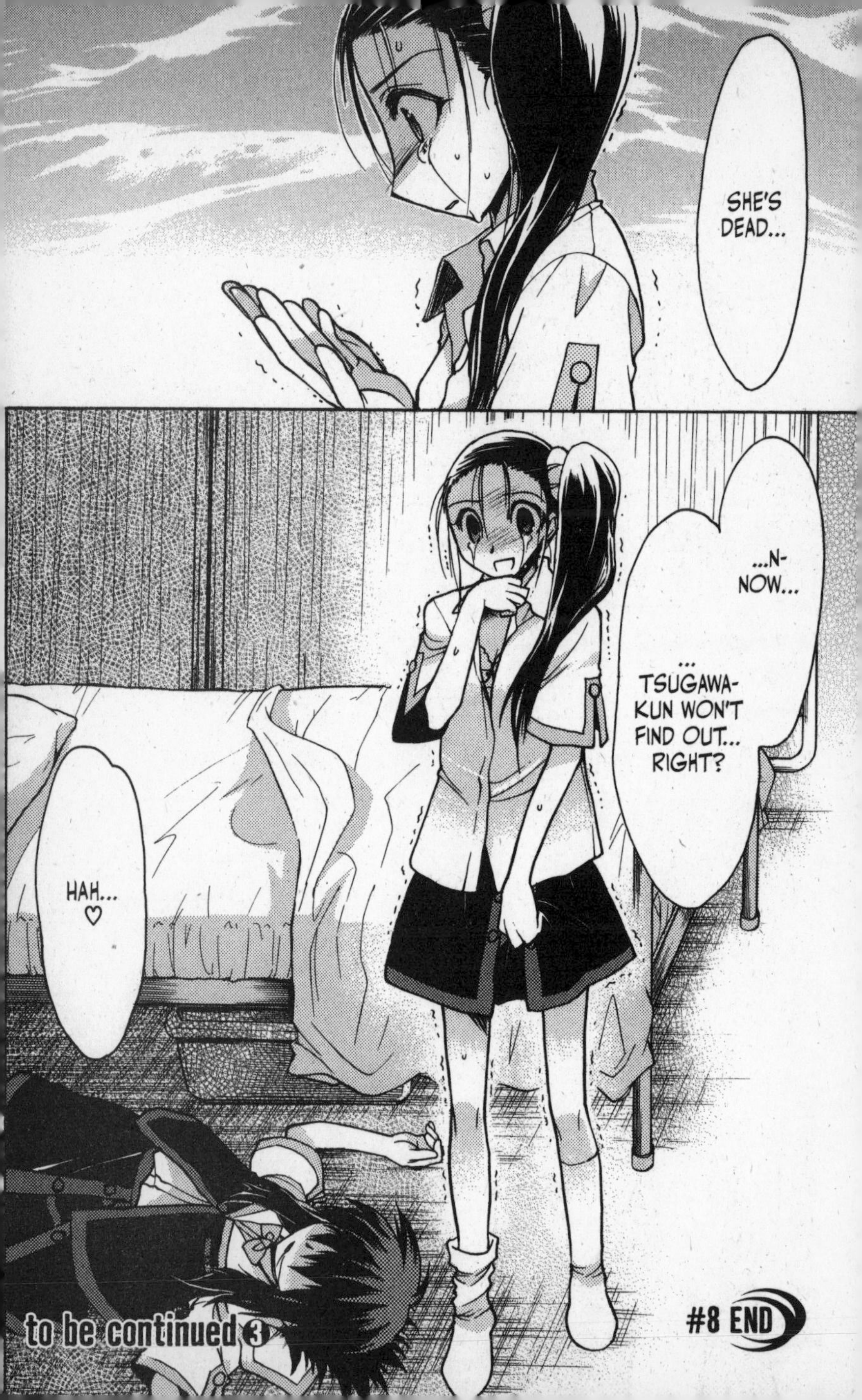
SHE'S DEAD...
...N- NOW...
... TSUGAWA-KUN WON'T FIND OUT... RIGHT?
HAH... ♡
#8 END
to be continued 3

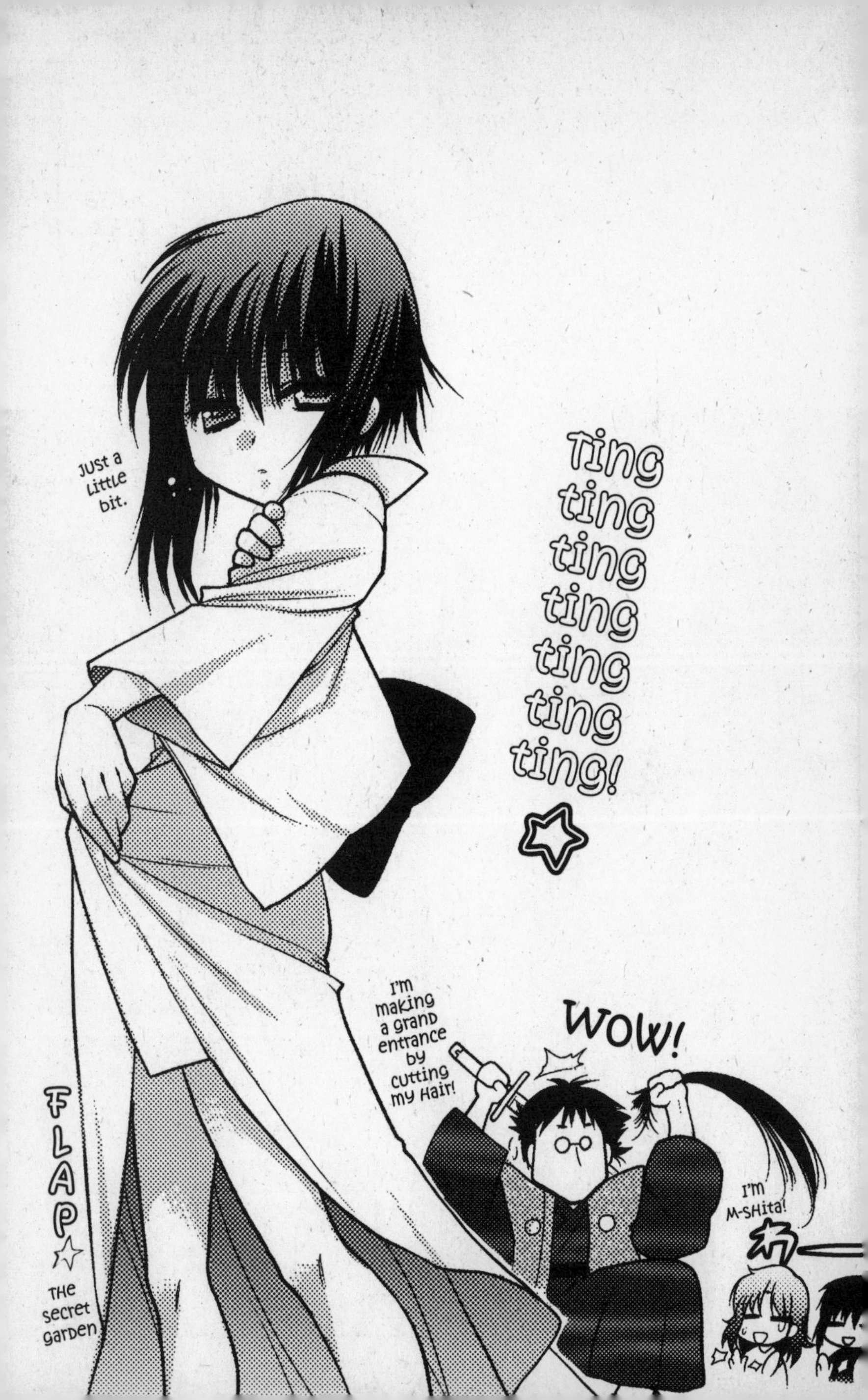

Ting ting ting ting ting ting ting!
Just a little bit.
WOW!
I'm making a grand entrance by cutting my hair!
I'm M-shita!
わー
FLAP
The secret garden

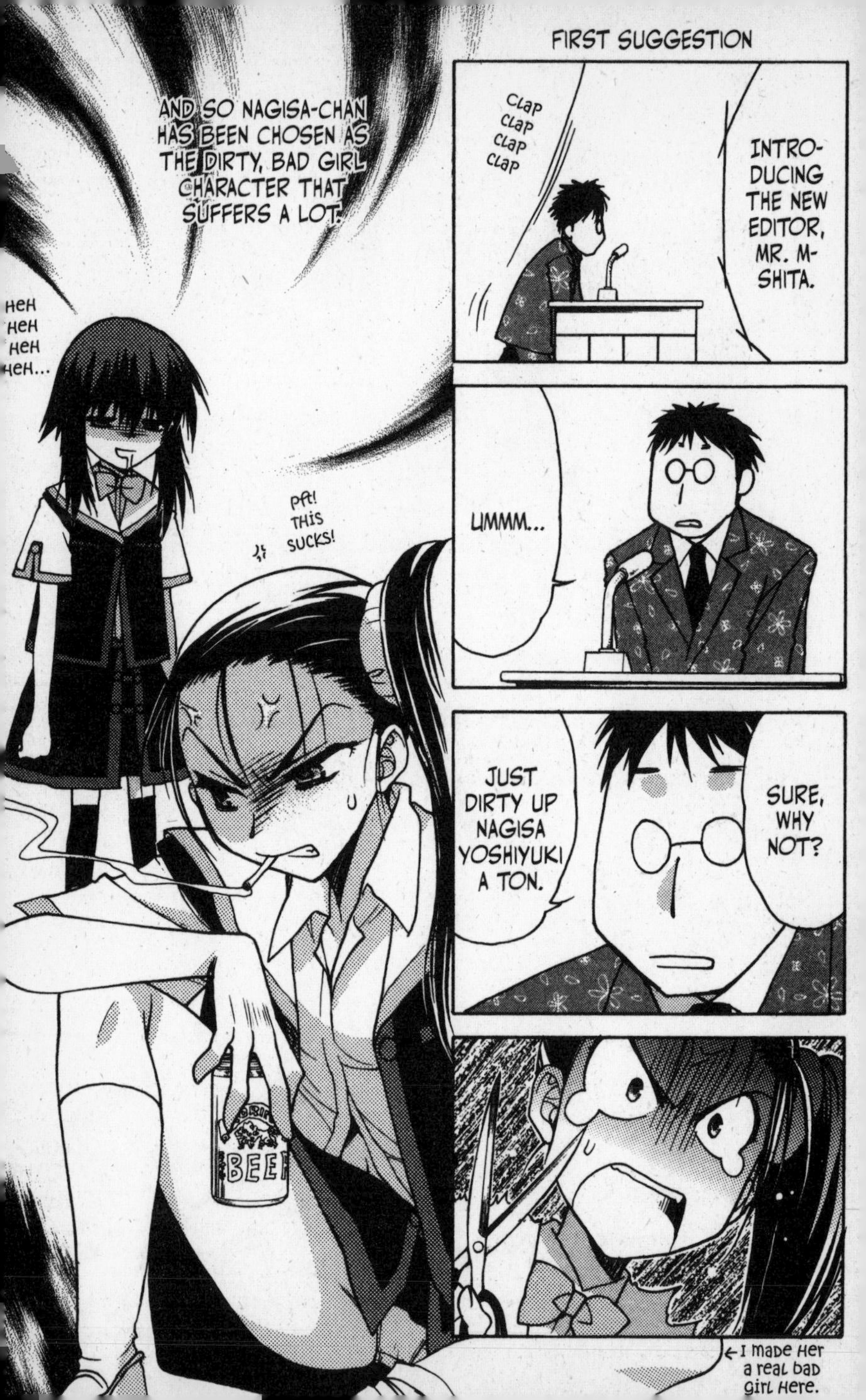
FIRST SUGGESTION
INTRODUCING THE NEW EDITOR, MR. M-SHITA.
Clap Clap Clap Clap
UMMM...
SURE, WHY NOT?
JUST DIRTY UP NAGISA YOSHIYUKI A TON.
← I made her a real bad girl here.
AND SO NAGISA-CHAN HAS BEEN CHOSEN AS THE DIRTY, BAD GIRL CHARACTER THAT SUFFERS A LOT.
Pft! THIS SUCKS!
HEH HEH HEH HEH...
BEER

Sick Mind

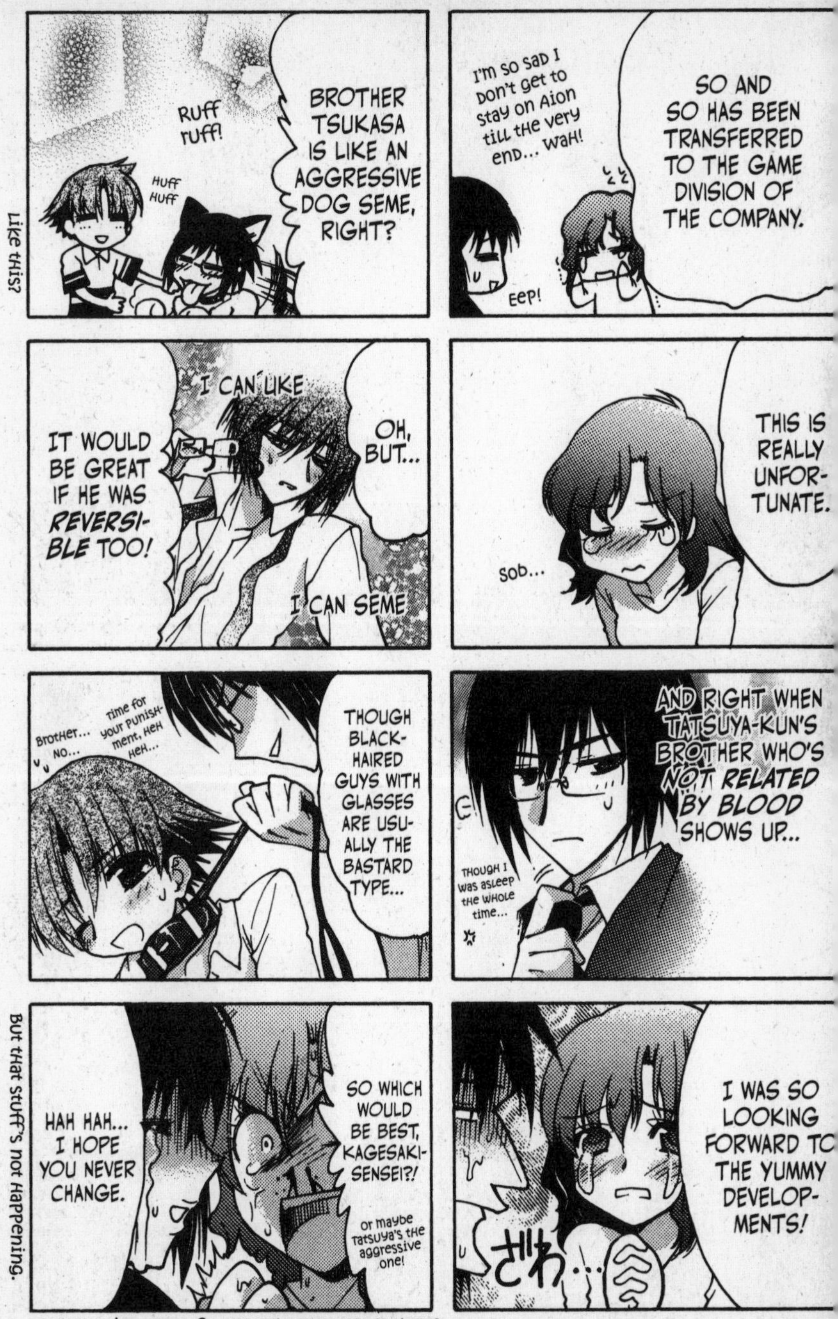

So and so has been transferred to the game division of the company.
I'm so sad I don't get to stay on Aion till the very end... Wah!
Eep!
This is really unfortunate.
Sob...
And right when Tatsuya-kun's brother who's not related by blood shows up...
Though I was asleep the whole time...
I was so looking forward to the yummy developments!
ざわ…
Brother Tsukasa is like an aggressive dog seme, right?
Ruff ruff!
Huff huff
Like this?
Oh, but...
I can uke
It would be great if he was reversible too!
I can seme
Though black-haired guys with glasses are usually the bastard type...
Time for your punishment, heh heh...
Brother... No...
So which would be best, Kagesaki-sensei?!
Or maybe Tatsuya's the aggressive one!
Hah hah... I hope you never change.
But that stuff's not happening.

So what lies ahead for the new character Tsukasa?

MY MOTHER'S DOG

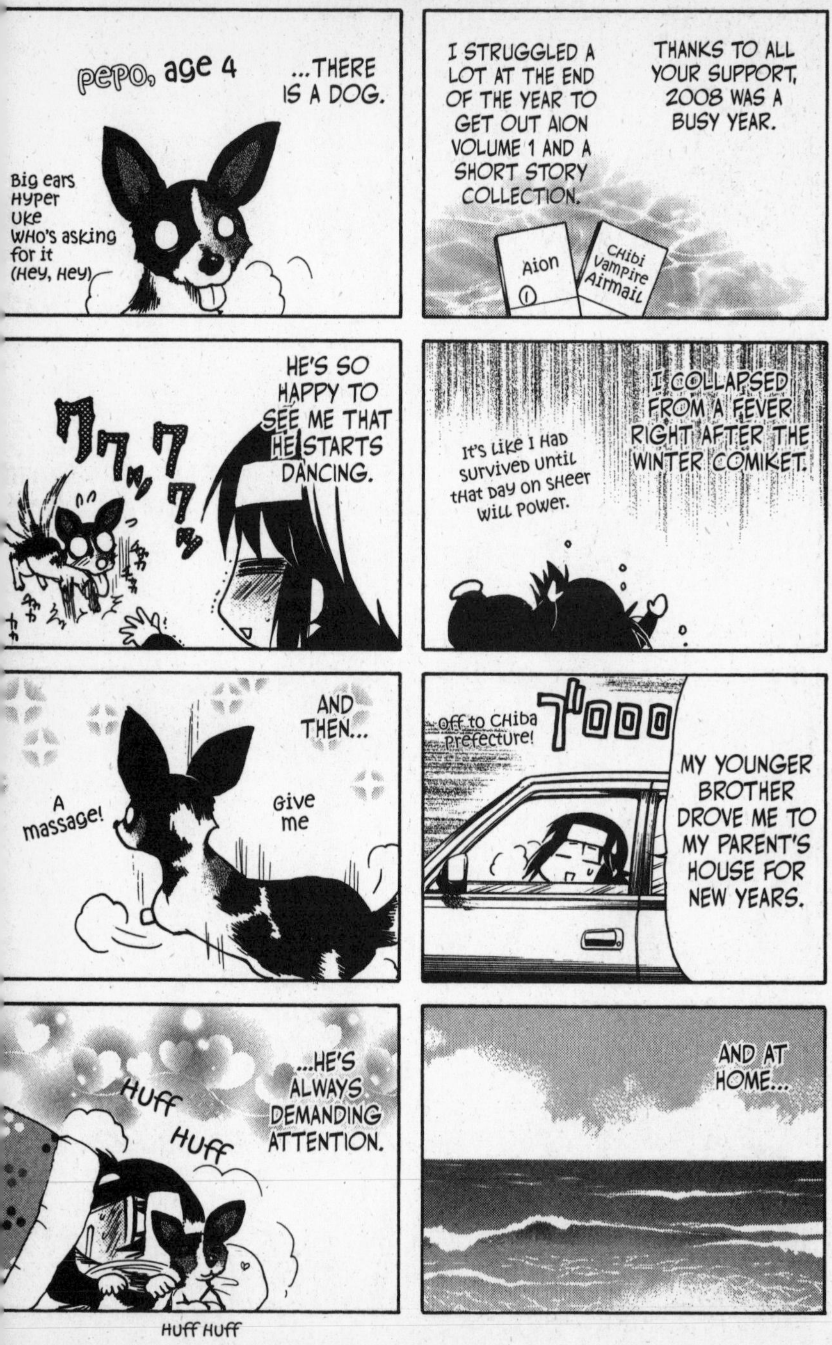

THANKS TO ALL YOUR SUPPORT, 2008 WAS A BUSY YEAR.
I STRUGGLED A LOT AT THE END OF THE YEAR TO GET OUT AION VOLUME 1 AND A SHORT STORY COLLECTION.
Aion 1
Chibi Vampire Airmail
I COLLAPSED FROM A FEVER RIGHT AFTER THE WINTER COMIKET.
It's like I had survived until that day on sheer will power.
MY YOUNGER BROTHER DROVE ME TO MY PARENT'S HOUSE FOR NEW YEARS.
Off to Chiba Prefecture!
AND AT HOME...
...THERE IS A DOG.
Pepo, age 4
Big ears
Hyper
Uke
Who's asking for it
(Hey, hey)
HE'S SO HAPPY TO SEE ME THAT HE STARTS DANCING.
AND THEN...
Give me
A massage!
...HE'S ALWAYS DEMANDING ATTENTION.
HUFF
HUFF
HUFF HUFF

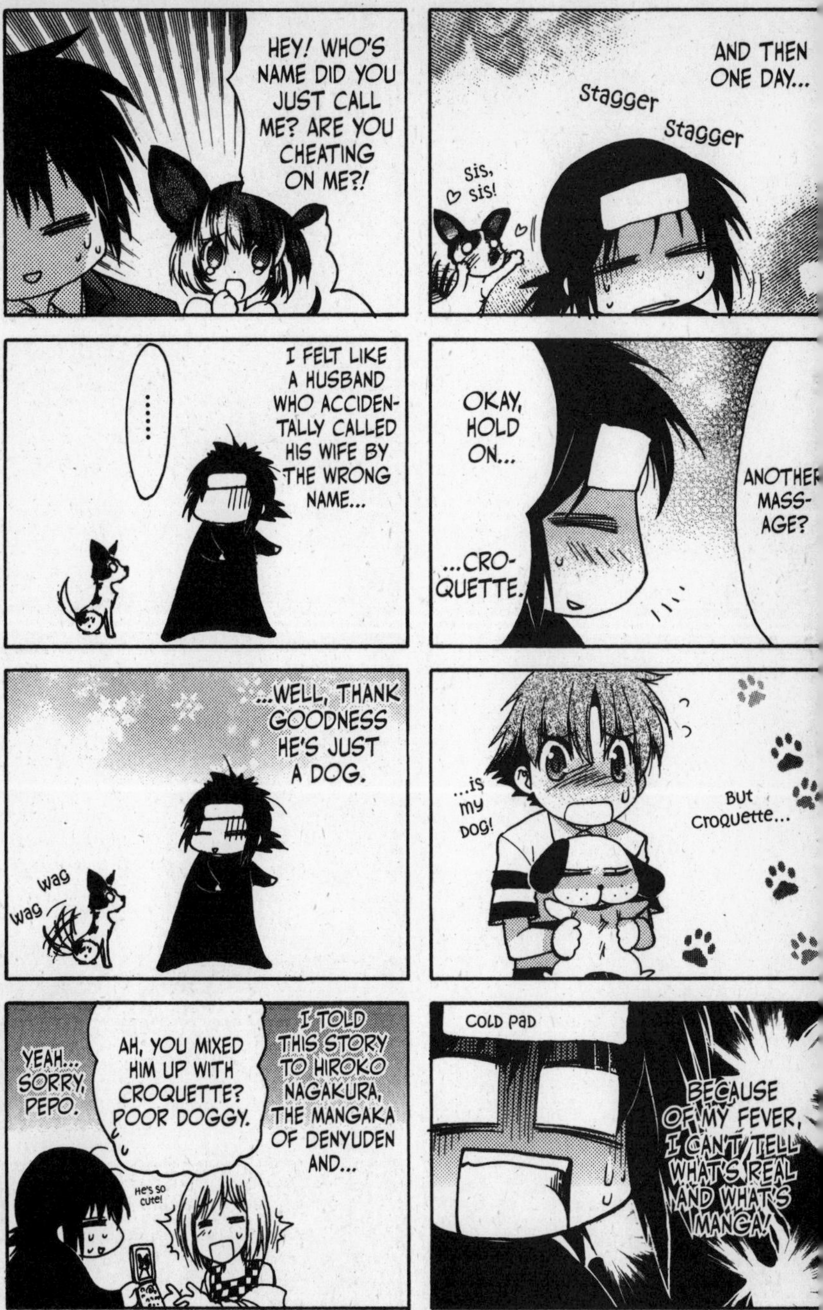
AND THEN ONE DAY...
Stagger
Stagger
Sis, ♡ sis!
ANOTHER MASSAGE?
OKAY, HOLD ON...
...CROQUETTE.
But Croquette...
...is my Dog!
COLD PAD
BECAUSE OF MY FEVER, I CAN'T TELL WHAT'S REAL AND WHAT'S MANGA!
HEY! WHO'S NAME DID YOU JUST CALL ME? ARE YOU CHEATING ON ME?!
I FELT LIKE A HUSBAND WHO ACCIDEN-TALLY CALLED HIS WIFE BY THE WRONG NAME...
......
...WELL, THANK GOODNESS HE'S JUST A DOG.
wag
wag
I TOLD THIS STORY TO HIROKO NAGAKURA, THE MANGAKA OF DENYUDEN AND...
AH, YOU MIXED HIM UP WITH CROQUETTE? POOR DOGGY.
YEAH... SORRY, PEPO.
He's so cute!

I'll bring you treats next time.

My cell phone screen is currently Pepo.

ペっ
FLIP
panties
ZZZZZZ
panties
Cardboard box

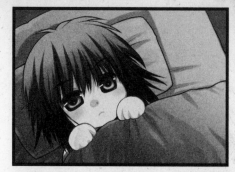

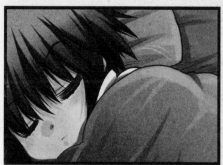

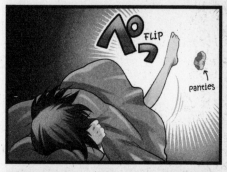

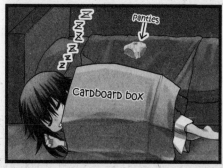

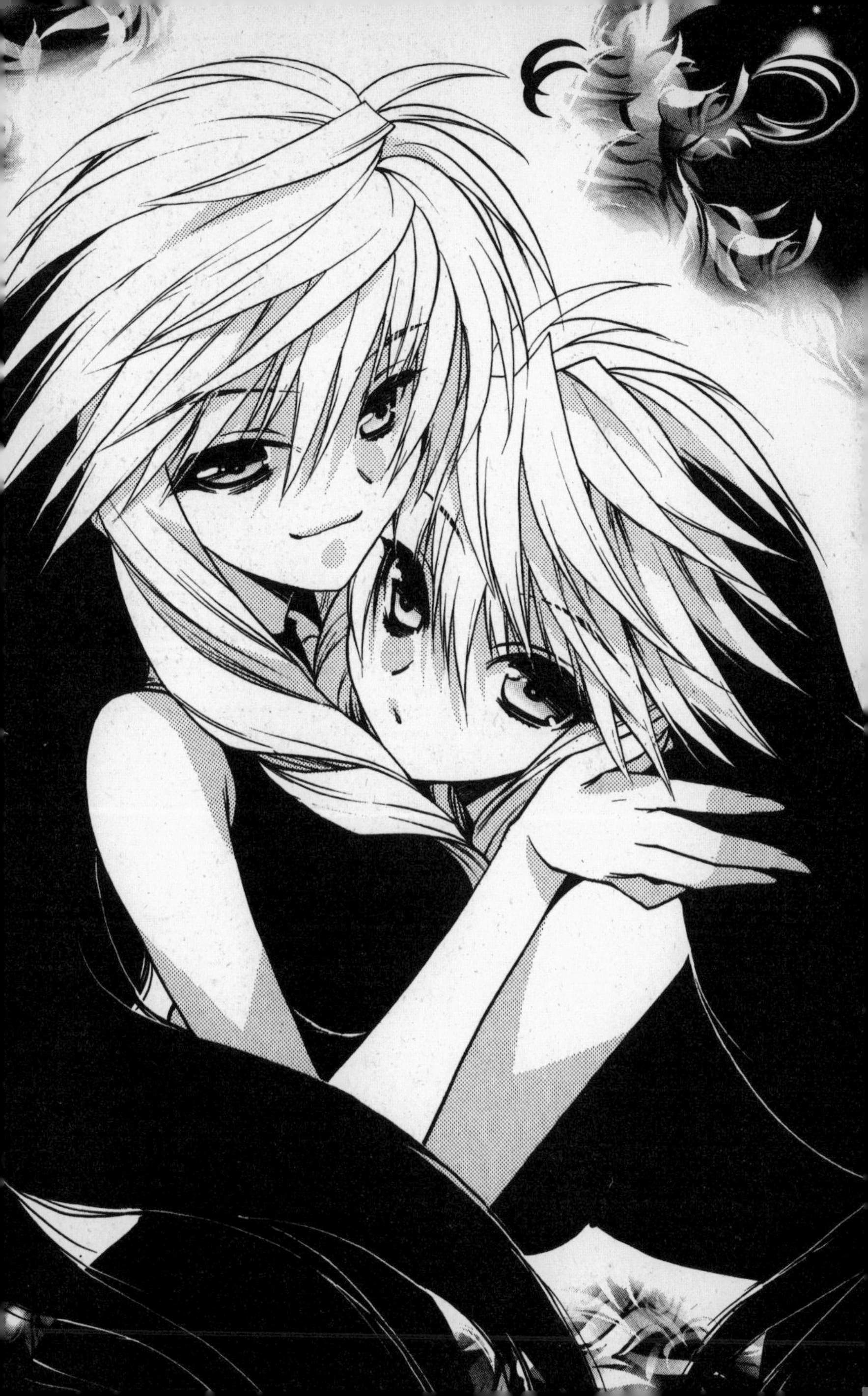

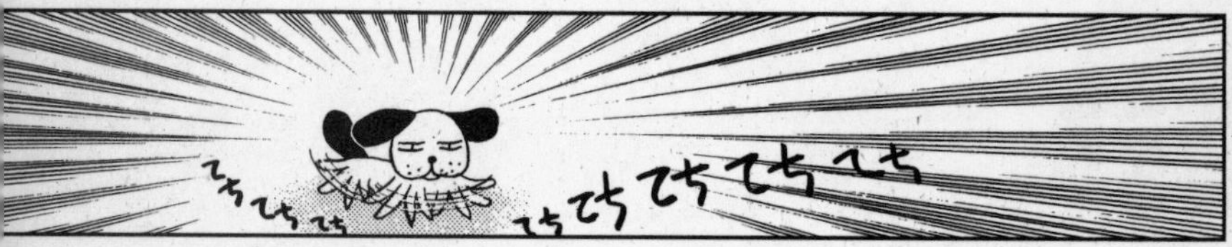
てちてちてちてちてち
てちてちてち

In the next volume of...

TATSUYA'S LIFE SEEMS TO BE MORE FUN
AND INTERESTING SINCE HIS MYSTERIOUS
SCHOOLMATE SEINE HAS ENTERED HIS LIFE.
HOWEVER, HIS CHILDHOOD FRIEND NAGISA
HAS BEEN INFECTED BY A PARASITE FROM
THE SEA AND IS COMPELLED TO GO AFTER
SEINE. TATSUYA WILL HAVE TO TEAM UP
WITH SEINE TO PROTECT HIS FRIEND, BUT
WHEN ONE OF THE EVIL MERMAIDS FROM THE
SEA SUDDENLY APPEARS AS A CUTE GIRL
IN TATSUYA'S SCHOOL, HE MAY BECOME
INVOLVED IN A WHOLE NEW LEVEL OF DANGER.

DOWNLOAD THE REVOLUTION.

Get the free TOKYOPOP app for manga, anytime, anywhere!

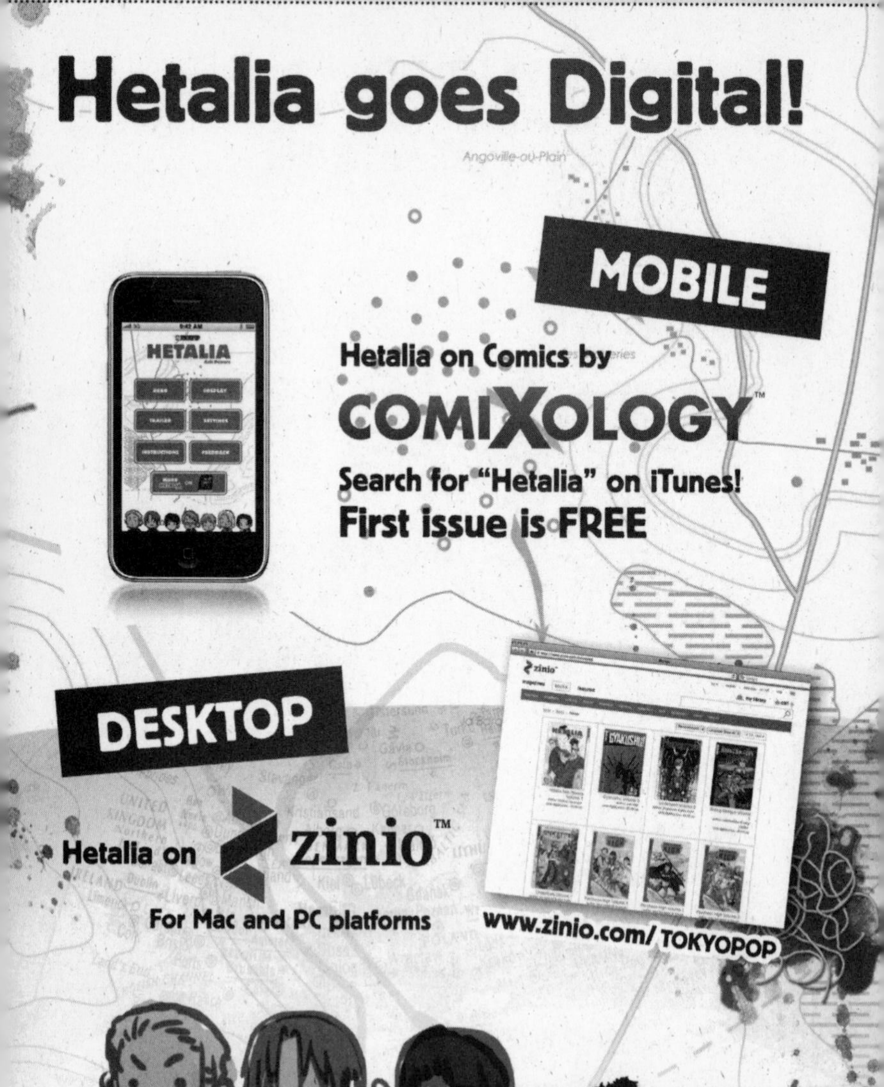
Hetalia goes Digital!
MOBILE
Hetalia on Comics by
COMIXOLOGY
Search for "Hetalia" on iTunes!
First issue is FREE
DESKTOP
Hetalia on zinio
For Mac and PC platforms
www.zinio.com/TOKYOPOP
HETALIA
Axis Powers

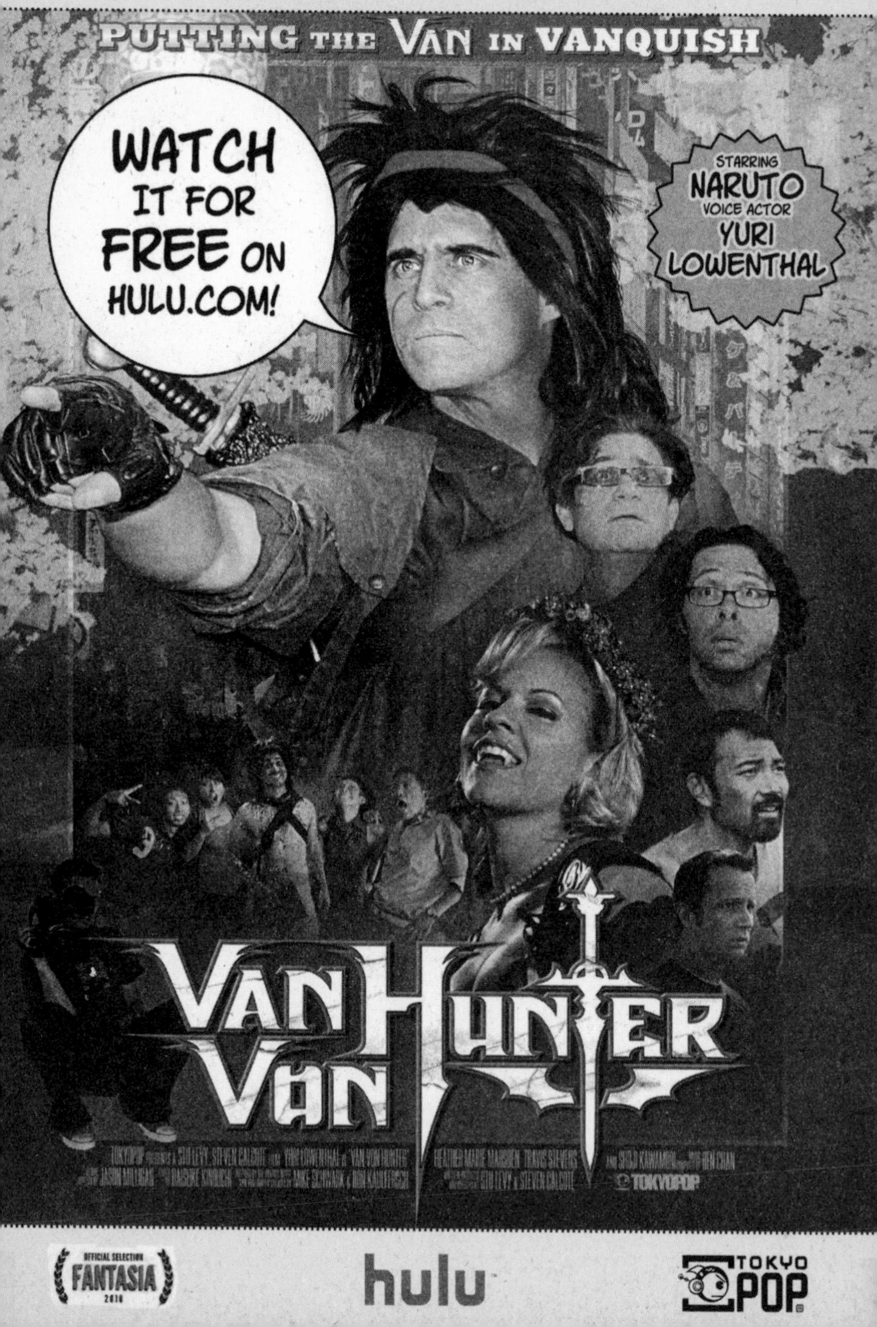
PUTTING THE VAN IN VANQUISH
WATCH IT FOR FREE ON HULU.COM!
STARRING NARUTO VOICE ACTOR YURI LOWENTHAL
VAN VON HUNTER
TOKYOPOP
OFFICIAL SELECTION FANTASIA 2010
hulu
TOKYO POP

STOP!

This is the back of the book.
You wouldn't want to spoil a great ending!

This book is printed "manga-style," in the authentic Japanese right-to-left format. Since none of the artwork has been flipped or altered, readers get to experience the story just as the creator intended. You've been asking for it, so TOKYOPOP® delivered: authentic, hot-off-the-press, and far more fun!

1
2
3
4
5
6
7
8
9
10

DIRECTIONS

If this is your first time reading manga-style, here's a quick guide to help you understand how it works.

It's easy... just start in the top right panel and follow the numbers. Have fun, and look for more 100% authentic manga from TOKYOPOP®!

THE MANGA REVOLUTION • LEADING THE MANGA REVOLUTION • LEADING

漫画革命